INTRODUCTOF CRIMINOLOGY

Introductory Criminology: The Study of Risky Situations takes a unique and intuitive approach to teaching and learning criminology. Avoiding the fragmentation of ideas commonly found in criminology textbooks, Marcus Felson and Mary A. Eckert develop a more practical, readable structure that engages the reader and enhances their understanding of the material. Their descriptive categories, simultaneously broad and realistic, serve better than the usual philosophical categories, such as "positivism" and "classicalism," to stimulate students' interest and critical thinking. Short chapters, each broken into 5–7 sections, describe situations in which crime is most likely to happen, and explain why they are risky and what society can and can't do about crime. They create a framework to organize ideas and facts, and then link these categories to the leading theories developed by criminologists over the last 100 years. With this narrative to guide them, students remember the material beyond the final exam.

This fresh new text was created by two professors to address the main points they encounter in teaching their own criminology courses. Problems solved include: reluctant readers, aversion to abstract thinking, fear of theory, and boredom with laundry lists of disconnected ideas. Felson, a leader in criminology theory with a global reputation for innovative thinking, and Eckert, an experienced criminal justice researcher, are uniquely qualified to reframe criminology in a unified arc. By design, they offer abstractions that are useful and not overbearing; their prose is readable, and their concepts are easy to comprehend and remember. This new textbook challenges instructors to re-engage with theory and present the essence of criminological thought for adult learners, coaching students to grasp the concept before any label is attached and allowing them to emerge with deeper understanding of what each theory means and offers. Lean, with no filler or fluff like stock photos, *Introductory Criminology* includes the authors' graphics to crystallize and expand concepts from the text.

Marcus Felson is the originator of the routine activity approach and author of *Crime and Everyday Life*. He has also authored *Crime and Nature*, and he serves as a professor at Texas State University in San Marcos, Texas. He has a B.A. from the University of Chicago and an M.A. and Ph.D. from the University of Michigan. He has received the 2014 Honoris Causa from the Universidad Miguel Hernandez in Spain, and he has been given the Ronald Clarke Award by the Environmental Criminology and Crime Analysis group and the Paul Tappan Award by the Western Society of Criminology. He has been a guest lecturer in Argentina, Australia, Belgium, Brazil, Canada, Chile, China, Denmark, El Salvador, England, Finland, France, Germany, Hong Kong, Hungary, Italy, Japan, Mexico, the Netherlands, New Zealand, Norway, Poland, Scotland, South Africa, Spain, Sweden, and Switzerland. He has applied routine activity thinking to many topics, including theft, violence, sexual abuse, white-collar crime, and corruption. Two books honoring Professor Felson's work have been published, one in English and another in Spanish.

Mary A. Eckert has devoted an active career to applied research in criminal justice and program evaluation. She has an M.A. and Ph.D. from New York University. Her B.A. is from the College of New Rochelle. Dr. Eckert served as Research Director of the New York City Criminal Justice Agency, Inc., where she authored many research reports and guided that agency's diverse research agenda, including work on pretrial risk assessment, court case processing, and evaluation of alternative-to-incarceration programs. She then served in the New Jersey Office of the Attorney General, with a special focus on statistical evaluation of vehicle stops to assist the New Jersey State Police in reducing the potential for racial profiling. Her work has been recognized by the New York Association of Pretrial Service Agencies and the State of New Jersey. She has also served as an adjunct professor at New York University, Montclair State University, and Texas State University. Marcus Felson's wife and life partner, this book is her second collaboration with her husband.

INTRODUCTORY CRIMINOLOGY

The Study of Risky Situations

MARCUS FELSON
and
MARY A. ECKERT

Routledge
Taylor & Francis Group

NEW YORK AND LONDON

First published 2018
by Routledge
711 Third Avenue, New York, NY 10017

and by Routledge
2 Park Square, Milton Park, Abingdon, Oxon, OX14 4RN

Routledge is an imprint of the Taylor & Francis Group, an informa business

© 2018 Taylor & Francis

Library of Congress Cataloging-in-Publication Data
Names: Felson, Marcus, 1947– author. | Eckert, Mary (Mary A.) author.
Title: Introductory criminology : the study of risky situations /
Marcus Felson and Mary Eckert.
Description: 1 Edition. | New York : Routledge, 2018. | Includes index.
Identifiers: LCCN 2017028284| ISBN 9781138668232 (hardback) |
ISBN 9781138668249 (pbk.) | ISBN 9781315618739 (ebook)
Subjects: LCSH: Criminology. | Criminal justice, Administration of.
Classification: LCC HV6025 .F397 2017 | DDC 364—dc23
LC record available at https://lccn.loc.gov/2017028284

ISBN: 978-1-138-66823-2 (hbk)
ISBN: 978-1-138-66824-9 (pbk)
ISBN: 978-1-315-61873-9 (ebk)

Typeset in Bembo
by Florence Production Ltd, Stoodleigh, Devon, UK

Visit the companion website: www.routledge.com/cw/felson

Dedicated to our parents, Ben and Ginny, and Bill and Mike, whose commitment to learning allowed us to grow and to meet one another.

"Ben and Ginny"

   Benjamin Felson (1913–1988)
   Virginia Raphaelson Felson (1914–2016)

"Bill and Mike"

   William M. Eckert (1916–1994)
   Margaret Cox Eckert (1918–1993)

CONTENTS

DETAILED CONTENTS

FIGURES

TABLES

BOXES

OUR TEACHING FRAMEWORK

For more than 180 years, criminologists have collected a wide range of interesting observations about crime. However, these observations are quite fragmented, making them hard to teach or to remember. The central purpose of our textbook is to make criminology less confusing to students by showing how each observation fits into a larger whole. Our textbook offers a single teaching framework. This framework is designed to help the student learn criminology and to remember what was learned after completing this book. Although our framework is new, it helps teach ideas from the past and the present. Our teaching framework is flexible enough to accommodate competing ideas, discussion, and critical thinking. It is also coherent enough to keep the student from getting lost. The framework is depicted in the summary figure.

The summary figure shows four boxes surrounding a diamond. The diamond depicts risky situations—any places or activities that generate relatively higher risk that a crime will occur. For example, a heavy-drinking barroom becomes a risky situation as the night progresses, potentially producing a criminal act. Several traditional crime

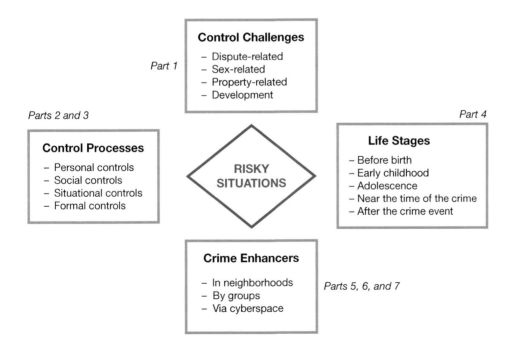

Summary of Our Teaching Framework

theories examine how risky situations develop and how they can be controlled. We organize relevant theories and research into four categories, each with its own box.

Control challenges (upper box): Part 1 of our book discusses four general challenges that face each society. Each society needs to contain disputes as well as sexual urges. Each society needs to protect property and to safeguard youths as they develop and grow up. When society fails to meet these challenges, crime and delinquency emerge. Disputes can escalate into fights; sexual urges can lead to sexual assaults or abuse; property can be stolen or vandalized; youths can be bullied or become dependent on alcohol or drugs.

Control processes (box on the left): Society tries to meet these challenges using four control processes depicted in the box to the left of the summary figure. These processes (discussed in Parts 2 and 3) include personal controls, social controls, situational controls, and formal controls. These efforts are highly imperfect, leading to risky situations and hence criminal acts that are dispute-related, sex-related, property-related, and development-related.

Life stages (box on the right): Crime and control of crime unfold over five life stages, introduced in Part 2 and elaborated in Part 4.

1. *Before birth* includes genetic and prenatal factors related to crime.

2. *Early childhood* is most relevant for self-control theories and early learning.

3. *Adolescence* is when peer influences and social control are central.

4. *Near the time of the crime* is when situational factors enter in.

5. *After a crime event* is when the justice system enters the scene.

Crime enhancers (lower box): Here we refer to processes that produce extra crime, enhancing other crime processes. This can happen in certain neighborhoods, through co-offending groups, or via cyberspace. Parts 5 through 7 explain how these processes generate *extra* crime in parts of society, making risky situations even riskier. Although youths in high-crime areas go through the same general processes as other youths, their special circumstances often worsen their crime participation levels. Part 5 emphasizes neighborhood processes that produce extra crime, disorder, and fear. Part 6 focuses on how these local processes create more insecurity for women. Part 7 examines group processes that multiply crime dangers. We also include in Part 7 a discussion of how crime is enhanced via cyberspace.

We include in our textbook some discussion of modern crime mapping techniques, which help reduce confusion about how, when, and where crime occurs. Criminologists have long known that crime is both a general problem and a problem of low-income urban areas. Is that a contradiction? Modern crime maps provide us with the information we need to address that question. In Part 5 you will learn that

- most blocks and addresses in a city have no crime;

- even within the "high-crime" side of town, most places are crime-free; yet

- low-income areas contain more than their share of bad blocks; which then

- tarnish their reputation further.

Much of criminology originated during the 1930s, emphasizing the urban side of crime. In today's world, however, a good deal of crime occurs in suburbs and in rural areas. We will present newer evidence that today's rural youths may exceed urban youths in drug and alcohol abuse. Although today's suburban youths are on par with central city youths in substance abuse, urban areas contain more *outdoor* drug sales, drawing more police attention. Nor does it make sense to teach that crime is simply a lower-class problem. Modern crime surveys and crime maps help us avoid committing *group attribution error*—blaming a whole group or neighborhood for what some of its members have done or what occurs on some of its blocks.

We have tested our teaching framework in several classes. Our students tell us that this framework is coherent and helps them learn, understand, assemble, and remember criminological ideas. Each part of the textbook is divided into several units that can be assigned alone or in combination to fit your teaching schedule and approach. Each unit includes discussion questions aimed at helping students integrate the information and a list of important terms and names to help students focus on important points. The end of each part provides both a summary and perspective on the material. We include many hundreds of notes at the end of units to help students get into the literature. Most importantly, we have sought to synthesize and integrate many facts and ideas to tell a coherent story about crime and criminology.

Marcus Felson and Mary A. Eckert
June 6, 2017

ACKNOWLEDGMENTS

We thank Kim Rossmo and Lucia Summers for their support as we wrote this book, and all our colleagues at Texas State University. Steve Rutter recommended us to Routledge as potential authors. While writing this textbook, we sent emails requesting papers and asking questions of many colleagues, including Martin Andresen, Wim Bernasco, Gisela Bichler, Remi Boivin, Kate Bowers, Vania Ceccato, Ronald V. Clarke, John Eck, Adam Graycar, Shane Johnson, Johannes Knutsson, Tamara Madensen, Carlo Morselli, Ken Pease, Jerry Ratcliffe, George Rengert, Wes Skogan, Frank Weerman, Pamela Wilcox, and Richard Wortley. We also got helpful legal suggestions from Steve Felson and Ed Felson. Rich Felson offered social psychological references and suggestions. We appreciate the entire membership of our informal society, ECCA, all of whom have been helpful over a period of many years. We also thank the Routledge team, including Pam Chester, who has been so helpful to us from the beginning, Helen Strain, and Maggie Reid.

We know we have missed some people who helped us, and hope they forgive us.

Getting Started

This textbook focuses on crime and the **risky situations** in which crime emerges. We also review many ideas in criminology that help organize information about how crime happens, what motivates offenders, and how crime can be reduced. In writing this textbook, we quickly realized that the information and ideas in criminology are so diverse that they are difficult to unify. We worked very hard to assemble this information within a coherent framework to help you learn, remember, and put criminology to use in reducing crime.

We have broken the text into seven parts, each containing several manageable units. We start each part by asking some questions and end with a perspective, including matters for further discussion. Within each part, several units provide you with ideas and information on each topic along with numerous charts to help clarify the points made. A few major themes and concepts serve to organize the entire textbook.

Criminality, Crime, and Criminology

First, we distinguish **criminality** from **crime**. *Criminality* refers to a general tendency to commit crime. In contrast to this general tendency, a *crime* refers to a *specific* event. An individual with a high criminal tendency might not have the opportunity to put that tendency into action. Somebody without a high criminal tendency might still be drawn into crime by easy crime opportunities or by peer influences. Our textbook considers both criminality and opportunity factors.

Just what behavior is a crime and what is not? Some behaviors, such as murder, are bad in and of themselves: These crimes are called **mala in se**, and they are treated as criminal acts under almost all justice systems. But there is more to defining crime, and criminologists have used several different approaches to testing whether something is a crime or not.

- We can use a ***literal test***. This means looking at the current justice system in one place. Ideally, its written laws should help us decide whether a given behavior is a crime or not within that jurisdiction.

- We can use a ***normative test***. In any given society, we can inquire whether a behavior violates the widespread norms (social expectations) of that society, as understood by most of its people.

- We can apply the ***common law test***. How did judges in the past handle the situation when someone used force or fraud against another person? Previous decisions and judicial experience accumulate over a long period of time, helping judges decide what is a crime. We can ask ourselves whether common law has been violated.

As we look at different points in history or different parts of the world, we get *different answers* about what is a crime. That's why we suggest a larger definition of crime that looks beyond any one society or any single period of history.

To understand what we mean, imagine that we have a list of all the animals that ever existed throughout natural history. Some animals that presently live on one continent do not live on another. Some are extinct. Yet all can be classified in the same animal kingdom. We also have a "natural kingdom" of criminal laws. These laws vary from one nation to another and from one period of history to another. Some laws are extinct. Some laws were never enforced. Some are old and some are new. If we put all these together, we have a grand list of enforced criminal laws through human history. That list leads to a ***historical test*** of what is or has been a crime: In broad historical terms, crime is any identifiable behavior that an appreciable number of governments has specifically prohibited and formally punished, across the entirety of human history.

Thus, some crimes are extinct, while some crimes are present on one continent but not another. Some crimes are called ***mala prohibita***, since the banned behavior is not intrinsically immoral. For example, some states have legalized the medicinal use of marijuana, others have legalized some recreational use and purchase, while still others consider all marijuana use a crime. Even behaviors that are intrinsically wrong are not uniformly banned by law. We might agree that rudeness is intrinsically wrong while disagreeing about whether such behavior should be considered illegal. Encouraging good human behavior is a general problem in society through history, and law is only one factor in working towards that goal. That's why we recognize variations among and within societies in how law is defined and applied across the world and over history.

Our textbook treats ***criminology as a broad field of study***, looking beyond the particular features of any one justice system or society. We consider how crimes, criminals, and justice officials fit into a larger society and economy. We take the broader approach because it helps explain how, why, and when crimes occur and how fear and insecurity affect people. That's why we look beyond crime to consider more general *disorder*, including unpleasant problems on neighborhood streets or in entertainment districts. Citizens can be very upset about dilapidated and abandoned buildings, garbage dumped on streets, people hanging around drunk, or insecurity in the local park. Criminologists have learned that citizens complain more about annoyances in their neighborhood than about crime as officially defined. Disorder is important because it *reminds* people of crime, creating extra fear and harming neighborhood cooperation. Citizens are especially upset by **overt crimes** that occur in public places. By looking at crime within a larger perspective, we gain a better understanding of all the pieces and how they fit into a coherent whole. Our textbook works very hard to provide that coherence and to help you learn criminology, remember it, and put it to work to reduce crime.

Why We Have Theory

People cannot handle too many facts and ideas all at once. That's the reason to develop theories. A good **theory** can summarize a vast amount of information that would otherwise be fragmented. Included are

- very general theories;

- middle-range theories; and

- specific theories that deal with one problem at a time.

Very general theories are often difficult to prove or disprove. Criminologists have many general theories about offenders, often linked to even more general theories about human nature. We will touch upon several of these theories and show where they fit into our framework. Yet we prefer more modest theoretical ideas that are easier to use, understand, and remember. By setting more modest theoretical goals, we sometimes achieve more success. Thus, we can explain how and when *specific criminal events* occur better than we can explain *very general social forces*. We can better explain how *some types* of crimes occur without trying to explain *all crimes* all the time or all human aspects of criminality. As you proceed through our textbook, you will notice that we try to break down theoretical ideas into more modest ideas that are better understood.

As noted above, criminologists sometimes use more specific theories. The age–crime curve is based on a specific theoretical idea that summarizes how crime participation grows during adolescence and then trails off as youths get older. It is a very useful specific theory, so long as we apply it modestly. Our textbook includes quite a few theoretical ideas helping to organize information on specific topics.

Some students have an allergic reaction to the word "theory," perhaps because theories seem to be too abstract to understand. We overcome that problem by offering many concrete examples. In Part 2, we explain self-control theory in terms of children resisting marshmallows or college students studying for exams. In Part 4, we explain peer theories with teenagers evading parents. We explain neutralization theory by offering examples of how people find alibis for their own rule-breaking. Our general theme, "risky situations," is explained in terms of barrooms and dark alleys. In other words, we make sure you understand the general categories by offering tangible illustrations from real life.

We also unify diverse frameworks by offering a single teaching framework. Our framework starts by asking: What are the basic problems that society must address every day? The general idea can be traced back to 1651 when Thomas Hobbes stated the "problem of order."[1] We suggest that society, including its justice system, faces four ongoing challenges:

- to control disputes;

- to contain sexual temptations;

- to protect property; and

- to safeguard youths.

All four of these general problems can generate crime risk.

We selected our list of four challenges after examining calls for police service (discussed further in Part 3). The public complain about disputes, annoyances, sexually offensive behaviors, property incursions, misbehaving teenagers, and neglected younger children. They complain not only about crimes but also about behaviors that fall short of lawbreaking. Their multitude of small, medium, and large complaints can be summed up in the four general problems listed above. Part 1 will spell these problems out in greater detail.

Zeroing In on Risky Situations

Exposure to risk is a central concept for our entire book.[2] A good example of dangerous exposure is driving a car too fast. We start with a simple paradox:

- On the one hand, fast driving exposes people to more risk of accident, including a lethal accident.

- On the other hand, most fast driving results in no accident at all. Even when an accident occurs, it is usually not fatal.

Exposure to risk does not mean that the worst happens *every* time. It merely tells us that there is higher *average* risk that something bad will happen.

Most everyday situations are safe. But some situations are risky, including speeding or driving while drunk. Criminology's great challenge is to explain when, where, and how crime risk is highest. That's a difficult task since crime usually does *not* occur as people go about their daily lives in ordinary ways. Even when problems emerge, normally no crime takes place. For example, one neighbor is annoyed with another for some reason. Usually they work it out quietly, but sometimes an argument breaks out. Usually the argument dies down, but sometimes it escalates into an illegal attack.[3] You can readily see that the give-and-take of everyday social life sometimes leads to criminal outcomes.

Such risks are certainly not randomly distributed. In the course of this book, you will learn which ages bring more risk as well as which places and times concentrate crime. You will learn how crime maps across a metropolis. You will learn that some popular images of crime risk are false or only partly true. In other words, you will learn a great deal about risky situations that expose people to crime participation, whether as offenders or as victims. A situation can be risky in two senses, ***objective risk*** and ***subjective risk***. We decide that a situation is objectively risky because crime statistics tell us so. Thus a place that has a lot of crime in a short period of time is especially risky. Second, a situation can be risky in a subjective sense, because it scares people. In the first four Parts of the textbook, we focus on objective risk. In Parts 5 and 6, we pay greater attention to subjectively risky situations, where people are afraid of crime even when it is not happening. Both objective and subjective risk are important, and it is a challenge to society to help its citizens to *be* safe and to *feel* safe.

Risky places include barrooms and other nightlife locations.[4] However, not all bars are risky. As we study the statistical details of crime, we find that *some* bars are especially risky, while other bars have moderate or low risk of crime. In fact, we keep learning more and more information showing us that crime is highly concentrated in particular slices of daily life. These details are not only important for learning criminology, but are also important for directing crime reduction policy to where it will have the most impact.

As our crime statistics have gotten better over the decades, we also learn that risky times are concentrated—midday burglary in residential areas, afternoon crime on the way home from school, nighttime crime in entertainment districts. Even over the life cycle, crime concentrates in certain ages and certain periods.

Figure A makes this point with a bar representing the ***life course***, ranging from preadolescence through adolescence to adulthood. Risk of crime participation is relatively low in the white sections of the life course; namely, before and after adolescence. Adolescence is the risky period. Within adolescence, the middle of period often has the greatest risk. Within middle adolescence, some months may have the greatest risk of crime participation, such as at the beginning or end of the school term, or the spring months when adult control wanes.

FIGURE A
Risky, Riskier, and Riskiest Periods

We can draw even sharper pictures of where and when crime risk concentrates. Figure B presents the risk of violent victimization for youths aged 15 to 19 in various situations.[5] Going to and from school creates by far the greatest risk at young ages. Hour for hour, going to and from school is at least 20 times riskier than being home and four times as risky as ordinary leisure. Part 4 goes into quite a bit of detail about risky situations during adolescence, linking these situations to various criminological theories.

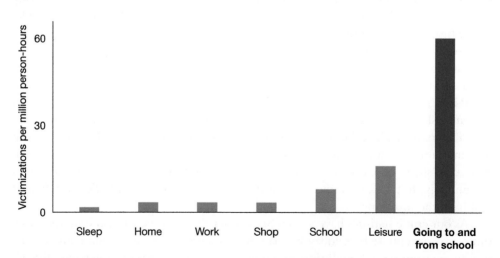

FIGURE B
Hour-for-Hour Risks of Violent Crime Victimization, Ages 15–19

Source: Adapted from A. M. Lemieux (2011). *Risks of violence in major daily activities, United States, 2003–2005*. Doctoral dissertation, Rutgers University Graduate School.

The concentration of crime risk applies to many circumstances. American college women are most subject to risk of sexual attack during the first year at the university[6] and during "spring break,"[7]—periods also involving intense use of alcohol. Most students survive these periods uninjured, but the general pattern of activities enhances the risk that something bad will happen. Similar patterns are found in European vacation destinations where youths around age 20 engage in heavy use of risky drugs.[8] In studying risky situations, we have to pay attention to risky ages, risky times, and risky places. Interestingly, risky situations often mix positive experiences with negative outcomes.

Mixing the Good and the Bad

To illustrate the mixing of good and bad, consider casual sexual encounters, known colloquially as "hooking up."[9] In a survey in the United States, 50–75 percent of undergraduate students reported hooking up on some occasion in the previous year.[10] Results can be very positive, including sexual release, companionship, and satisfaction. A study of 250 male and female undergraduates concluded that the emotional reactions to hooking up are more positive than negative, especially when a follow-up sexual encounter occurs.[11] On the other hand, meeting strangers or casual acquaintances can lead to unwanted sex or forcible rape,[12] and casual sex is associated with the spread of disease. The great irony is that so many bad and good outcomes are linked together. The very same behavior includes a notable risk of something bad happening alongside a substantial chance of a positive result.

This is true more generally of time spent at parties and in bars, which usually provides positive social experiences. People may make new friends while also keeping old friendships alive. They enjoy a meal and drinks together. Unattached males and females meet. Casual acquaintances become less casual. On the other hand, new encounters can lead to forcible rape, spread of disease, or simple sexual harassment. Again, the bad and good are intertwined.

The mixing of good and bad can occur within the course of a single evening. Imagine several young men just over 21 years old are having an informal party. They begin to drink casually, and everything is fine for the first hour or so. In time, some of them become very intoxicated, but still do nothing illegal. Yet this situation creates an elevated risk that a conflict might arise, usually with someone outside of the group, and then escalate into a crime. That's why much of the crime risk occurs later in the night.[13] As we've noted, most risky situations do not result in crime, but sometimes an illegal act bursts forth. That's why we study crime within a wider perspective.

Crime theorists have different interpretations of the example just given. Some theorists emphasize self-control or social control that prevents problems from escalating into crime. Other theorists pay closer attention to learning processes that enhance or inhibit misbehavior. Part 2 presents these conflicting theories. Despite their differences, criminologists in the end have to face a common reality: Certain situations produce an elevated risk that a criminal act will occur.

"Deviance" and Risky Situations

When society's rules are broken without crossing the line into illegal behavior, we call that "*deviance*." It includes drinking too much. It includes being rude and foul-mouthed against another person, even though that behavior is *not* usually against the law. It includes being a bad parent or husband, or a poor employee.

Even with these behaviors, a line may be crossed. Drinking too much in public, drinking underage, drinking while driving—these behaviors cross the line into illegality, even though all three are also tolerated by society. Much deviant behavior starts out as legal until it moves across that line, and much initially acceptable behavior reaches beyond the point of public tolerance. Inside a bar, someone may be drinking legally, then go to the parking lot and start the car. Someone may begin the evening drinking within bounds but end up beyond those bounds. Someone may start out being mildly disagreeable, then end up in a fight. Thus, bad behavior creates risky situations that *might* lead to a criminal event.

Figure C presents a scale helping to clarify how crime, deviant, and nondeviant behaviors are related. Category 1 refers to behaviors that are legal and approved by society—neither illegal nor deviant. These include work, school, family life, and minor levels of alcohol consumption. At the other end of the scale, Category 4 refers to behaviors that are both illegal and deviant, not tolerated by society. These include fights, assaults, and burglaries.

In the middle of the scale, note the **marginal activities** that society disapproves of but in some sense tolerates. Category 2 includes disapproved activities that remain legal,

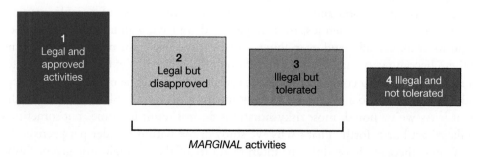

MARGINAL activities

FIGURE C
Four Steps Relating Crime to Deviance

including excess drinking in private settings. Category 3 includes disapproved and illegal acts that society generally tolerates, such as public urination on the side of the road. In large cities, illegal prostitution is often tolerated, fitting Category 3. Many illegal behaviors are largely tolerated by society, including public drunkenness in entertainment districts and drunk driving in late hours. These marginal activities find a place in society because they are either legal or legally tolerated. You can see that the written laws do not tell us the whole story about crime or deviance.

Some people begin the evening drinking mildly (Category 1), become increasingly annoying (Category 2), reach a point of illegal public drunkenness that society tolerates (Category 3), then commit an illegal act that society can no longer brush aside (Category 4). Thus we see that illegal activity can emerge from deviant behavior and that both illegal and deviant behavior can emerge from acceptable human activity.

People sometimes become involved in crime while doing what they are supposed to—going to school or earning a living. Indeed, exposure to crime risk can occur during work, school, or other conventional activities, such as having late-night jobs or jobs involving deliveries.[14] Consider a restaurant employee who works very hard to earn a living and support her family. Yet she risks being robbed while leaving the job very late at night. We can see that crime can occur while engaging in behaviors that society discourages as well as those that it encourages.

Risky Public Places

Risky situations often emerge in public places, as Professors Cohen and Felson noted in the 1979 paper that developed the "routine activity approach,"[15] which will be discussed in Part 2. They discovered how crime risk varies by time spent in different activities (see Note 5.)

Cohen and Felson found dramatic shifts in crime risks among different daily activities, with street risks the greatest, as charted in Figure D. (Part 6 will focus on street risk.)

As you see in the chart, home is the safest place to be on an hour-for-hour basis. Risk of victimization increases for both robbery and assault when people spend time away from home. The riskiest time is spent on streets—more than 50 times riskier for both robbery and assault relative to time spent there. However, if you forget to divide by time spent in each setting, home *seems* riskier because people spend so much time there compared to time on the street. Of course, some people do spend more time on the streets. In Parts 5 and 6, we will see that streets have a major impact on crime and that society needs to improve how it manages public places so they will be safer.

As we proceed, we will also consider barrooms and other places where the public goes for recreation. Often crime risks are enhanced during informal activities—with

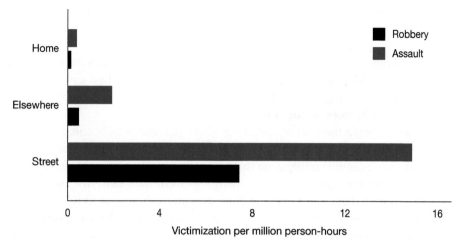

FIGURE D

Crime Victimization by Strangers per Million Person-Hours at Risk, United States, Early Routine Activity Study

Source: Data drawn from L. E. Cohen & M. Felson (1979). Social change and crime rate trends: A routine activity approach. *American Sociological Review, 44*(4), 588–608; Table 3, Panel D.

people socializing together or hanging out with others. How much free time do people have? Working mothers find almost all their time booked, especially if their children are young.[16] American teenagers are usually not so booked up. They may have as many as 68 informal hours a week. As they age, they spend less time with or near parents, as documented in Part 4. In general, this book pays great attention to *informal* life, including recreation and leisure, trips to and from school, and any settings where youths hang out away from adults (see Part 4). As you shall see, these are risky situations that give rise to minor substance abuse, property crime, and sometimes worse. As this book progresses, you will see how these risky settings relate to several crime theories and processes, including social control, self-control, learning, strains, and neighborhood effects.

Moving Forward

We do not want you to get lost among the many theories of crime. That's why our textbook has an organizing framework. Here, we

- defined crime in a broad manner, across times and societies;

- explained that criminology fits into the larger study of social life;

- made three distinctions that help clarify several topics in criminology –
  o criminality from crime,
  o crime from disorder, and
  o overt crime from covert crime;
- saw how theories summarize information;
- introduced some very general problems that challenge all societies, in various eras and parts of the world;
- defined risky situations and why they are important to studying crime and deviance;
- distinguished between objective and subjective risk; and
- saw how legal and illegal activities can occur together.

The same problems that challenge societies also challenge crime theorists, as we shall see in Part 1. After that, Part 2 explains the alternative ways that society seeks to contain these problems. Part 3 concentrates on formal controls in society—the police, courts and punishment—and demonstrates their limitations in addressing these problems. Part 4 shows how risky situations vary over the life course, making some ages riskier than others.

While these first four Parts concentrate on objective risks, the next two focus more on subjective risk. Our distinctions between crime and disorder and between overt and covert crime are also especially important in Part 5, examining crime risk at the street and neighborhood level, and in Part 6, detailing settings that are especially risky for women. In Part 7, we explain how crime is enhanced by group offending and by cyber technology. We end with a wrap up of the whole textbook. We hope the criminology you learn from this textbook will serve you well and that you will use it to reduce crime as you proceed through life.

FLASHCARD LIST FOR GETTING STARTED

- Crime (definition), literal test, normative test, common law test, historical test
- Criminality
- Criminology as a broad field of study

- Deviance
- Disorder
- Exposure to risk
- Life course
- *Mala in se*
- *Mala prohibita*
- Marginal activities

- Objective risk
- Overt crimes
- Risky situations
- Subjective risk
- Theory

DISCUSSION QUESTIONS

1. In the past week, did you find yourself in any risky situations? What made them risky?

2. Can you give several examples of deviant behavior that are not criminal?

Notes

1　Hobbes, T. (2006 [1651]). *Leviathan*. London: A&C Black.

2　For more on exposure to risk in criminology, see Stafford, M. C., & Galle, O. R. (1984). Victimization rates, exposure to risk, and fear of crime. *Criminology, 22*(2), 173–185. Maxfield, M. G. (1987). Lifestyle and routine activity theories of crime: Empirical studies of victimization, delinquency, and offender decision-making. *Journal of Quantitative Criminology, 3*(4), 275–282.

3　Tedeschi, J. T., & Felson, R. B. (1994). *Violence, aggression, and coercive actions*. Washington, DC: American Psychological Association.

4　Hobbs, D., Hadfield, P., Lister, S., & Winlow, S. (2005). Violence and control in the night-time economy. *European Journal of Crime, Criminal Law and Criminal Justice, 13*(1), 89–102.

5　The calculations were made by dividing the number of victimizations in each activity by the time spent in each. See Part 4 for a description of how this is done.

6　Carey, K. B., Durney, S. E., Shepardson, R. L., & Carey, M. P. (2015). Precollege predictors of incapacitated rape among female students in their first year of college. *Journal of Studies on Alcohol and Drugs, 76*(6), 829–837.

7　Josiam, B. M., Hobson, J. P., Dietrich, U. C., & Smeaton, G. (1998). An analysis of the sexual, alcohol and drug related behavioural patterns of students on spring break. *Tourism Management, 19*(6), 501–513.

8　Bellis, M. A., Hughes, K., Bennett, A., & Thomson, R. (2003). The role of an international nightlife resort in the proliferation of recreational drugs. *Addiction, 98*(12), 1713–1721.

9　Littleton, H., Tabernik, H., Canales, E. J., & Backstrom, T. (2009). Risky situation or harmless fun? A qualitative examination of college women's bad hook-up and rape scripts. *Sex Roles, 60*(11–12), 793–804.

10　Stinson, R. D. (2010). Hooking up in young adulthood: A review of factors influencing the sexual behavior of college students. *Journal of College Student Psychotherapy, 24*(2), 98–115.

11　Snapp, S., Ryu, E., & Kerr, J. (2015). The upside to hooking up: College students' positive hookup experiences. *International Journal of Sexual Health, 27*(1), 43–56.

12　Flack, W. F., Daubman, K. A., Caron, M. L., Asadorian, J. A., D'Aureli, N. R., . . . & Stine, E. R. (2007). Risk factors and consequences of unwanted sex among university students: Hooking up, alcohol, and stress response. *Journal of Interpersonal Violence, 22*(2), 139–157.

13　Rowe, S., Wiggers, J., Kingsland, M., Nicholas, C., & Wolfenden, L. (2012). Alcohol consumption and intoxication among people involved in police-recorded incidents of violence and disorder in non-metropolitan New South Wales. *Australian and New Zealand Journal of Public Health, 36*(1), 33–40.

14 Block, R., Felson, M., & Block, C. (1985). Crime victimization rates for incumbents of 246 occupations. *Sociology and Social Research, 69*(3), 442–451. Lynch, J. P. (1987). Routine activity and victimization at work. *Journal of Quantitative Criminology, 3*(4), 283–300. Mayhew, C. (2002). Occupational violence in industrialized countries: Types, incidence patterns and "at risk" groups of workers. In M. Gill, B. Fisher, & V. Bowie (Eds.), *Occupational violence in industrialized countries*, pp. 21–40. London: Willan Press.

15 Cohen, L. E., & Felson, M. (1979). Social change and crime rate trends: A routine activity approach. *American Sociological Review, 44*(4), 588–608.

16 For more on time use, read about the American Community Survey at www.census.gov/programs-surveys/acs/. For information about time use surveys around the world, see www.unece.org/file admin/DAM/stats/gender/timeuse/Downloads/MTUS%20in%20short.pdf.

PART 1

The Crime Challenge

In 1651, Thomas Hobbes[1] asked a very general question: How does society maintain order and avoid falling into chaos?

Hobbes thus raised "the problem of order" that all societies must confront. Order depends on minimizing any behaviors that can threaten the health and safety of citizens or the whole society. Order means that people are following basic rules of good behavior and are not fighting and stealing from each other. Society's many institutions—families, neighborhoods, private organizations, and governments—play a role in maintaining order. Social life also includes tolerance—allowing people to drive a bit over the speed limit and to make some noise on Friday nights. Every society makes decisions about what it will tolerate and what it considers beyond the limits.

The ***Hobbesian problem of order***[2] spans a wide range of social and criminological ideas. It also raises several very serious issues, since the very institutions we need to keep society orderly can also do a great deal of harm:

1. These institutions can create dictatorship or oppression, killing the fun of life and stamping out the human spirit.

2. These institutions can produce extra crime and disorder through corruption and abuse of power, harming the very people they are supposed to serve or assist.

Society has not "solved" the problem of order, how to deliver it, and how to avoid harmful side effects. The problem is ongoing, posing an endless challenge.

Maintaining order depends on more than law. Order depends on all of society's institutions. It depends on containing ordinary rudeness, alcohol consumption, and minor problems, which could spill over and produce something worse. Human imperfections apply at all levels—individuals, families and households, communities, and public agencies—often challenging everyday life. Society faces *four ongoing challenges*, to

- *control disputes*;

- *contain sexual temptations*;

- *protect property*; and

- *safeguard youths*.

As we stated in our introduction to you (Getting Started), we arrived at these four challenges after examining the daily calls that citizens make to police and emergency services. Most of these calls are about disputes and nuisances, sexually offensive behaviors, property issues, misbehaving teenagers, barking dogs, or noisy parties. Fewer callers report assaults or other criminal acts in progress. Rather, citizens report on *pre-criminal situations*—problems that have *not yet escalated* into a crime event. Sometimes, crime bursts forth from what began as a relatively minor misbehavior; for example, some youths have been drinking too much for a considerable time, after which two of them get into a fight.

When its institutions are working well, society minimizes disputes and contains sexual temptations while also safeguarding property and helping youths grow up. A successful society minimizes risky situations and, when they occur, does a good job of containing these situations so that criminal acts usually do not result. Throughout our book, we consider how daily life generates these *risky situations*, and how criminal acts sometimes emerge.

Figure 1a sums up what we have said so far, depicting the general problem of order and the four challenges to society that emerge from it. These challenges show up every day as risky situations emerge. In Part 2 you will learn how society tries to contain these problems. As our textbook proceeds, we fill in many specific examples of how society tries to avoid creating risky situations and to manage these situations when they occur.

Our textbook organizes numerous and diverse criminological theories and ideas about how crime emerges and how society tries to contain it. We discuss the various institutions that seek to contain crime and maintain order, and we allow room for substantial discussion. As you shall see, society's institutions, from families to governments, are highly imperfect.

Criminology studies how crime emerges and how society seeks to contain or prevent it. The justice system is just one of the major tools used by society for

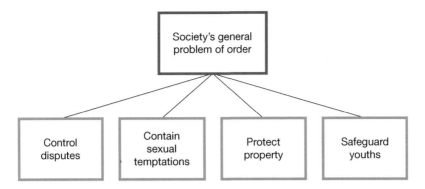

FIGURE 1A
Ongoing Challenges for Every Society

maintaining order and delivering justice. Our textbook views social order as a trial-and-error process, an ongoing part of everyday life. We begin in Unit 1.1 with ordinary disputes, discussing how these can escalate into a criminal event. Unit 1.2 describes the necessity to control sexual temptations so they do not result in criminal behavior. Unit 1.3 then shows that society seeks to manage the ownership and protection of property. Finally, in Unit 1.4, we discuss the need to minimize risky situations for youth, keeping them safe and away from crime. Part 1 ends with a Perspective section that sums up our main points in Units 1.1 through 1.4.

FLASHCARD LIST FOR PART 1: THE CRIME CHALLENGE

- Contain sexual temptations
- Control disputes
- Four ongoing challenges
- Hobbesian problem of order
- Pre-criminal situations
- Protect property
- Safeguard youths
- Theory

QUESTIONS ADDRESSED IN PART 1

1. Why does society need to control disputes?

2. Why does society need to contain sexual temptations?

3. Why must society protect property and manage property issues?

4. Why and how does society safeguard youths and help them grow up?

Notes

1   Hobbes, T. (2006 [1651]). *Leviathan*. London: A&C Black.

2   Ellis, D. P. (1971). The Hobbesian problem of order: A critical appraisal of the normative solution. *American Sociological Review, 36*(4), 692–703.

UNIT 1.1 The Need to Control Disputes

When police are called, that often means that a dispute has escalated too far. To understand the process, keep in mind that

- disputes are quite common; and

- most disputes do not escalate, never resulting in crime; yet

- most violent assaults occur after a dispute has emerged and escalated.[1]

Social psychologists have studied how this can happen. More often than not, disputes fizzle out or settle down.[2] Others climb the pyramid to become a more serious problem.[3]

The importance of ordinary disputes cannot be overstated. Many experimental studies show us how some disputes can escalate. If a dispute occurs in front of an audience, one party may be especially embarrassed and angered, thus more likely to retaliate. When a younger male has a disagreement with an older female, he is more likely to back away from further conflict, while a dispute with another young male is more likely to escalate. A peacemaker can help defuse a situation, while a troublemaker can enhance the dispute and contribute to its escalation. You can see that dispute escalation is highly situational.[4]

The volume of "minor" disputes in society is very important since some of these minor disputes can escalate into something major. Consider that most homicides begin as simple grievances over matters that seem trivial at first. Minor disputes create risky situations that can help us comprehend crime. That's why society's institutions face a challenge to contain grievances and minimize **rude encounters** that violate the norms of everyday polite interaction. Even those encounters that seem trivial from the outside are not always trivial to those involved.[5] These are also called **incivilities** since they typically occur in public and run counter to the idea that citizens have common obligations.

Dispute Escalation

A simple theoretical sequence outlines a *dispute escalation process* that helps us understand why containing plain rudeness is important for society and for criminological theory:

1. Everyday life sometimes produces a rude encounter;[6]

2. which sometimes is countered, producing a dispute;

3. which sometimes escalates verbally;[7]

4. which sometimes leads to a threat;[8]

5. which sometimes escalates to shoves;

6. which sometimes lead to blows;

7. which sometimes produce injuries;

8. which occasionally are serious.

The last three items on the list tell us why 75 percent of violent victimizations of college students result in no injury at all. Minor injuries make up 20 percent, with the remaining 5 percent including serious injuries as well as rape victims. Only about 3 percent go for emergency treatment.[9]

The eight-step progression above fits our point that crime is embedded within a larger reality. That reality includes disputes and incivilities, most of which do not escalate, though some progress further. Our theoretical challenge is to explain how this progression is inhibited or enhanced. Each step is increasingly unlikely—for example, most verbal responses do not escalate further, and most escalations stop short of physical attacks. Yet this sequence helps us understand why society needs to contain minor disputes. Figure 1b shows that rude encounters appear in everyday life. Most of these are rude statements that are ignored or verbal disagreements that go no further. Even when a dispute emerges, it is likely to be resolved without escalation. However, sometimes escalation occurs, and a fight or assault can take place.

Disputes can generate criminal responses on the spot. They can also generate criminal revenge later. Thus, disputes can lead not only to *violent crimes* but also to *property crimes*, including vandalism, arson, and theft.[10] Some people angry about a dispute then vandalize the property of their adversary, even when the initial dispute had nothing to do with that property. A study in Finland found that roughly one-half of interpersonal assaults were motivated by revenge, as were a significant portion of vandalism and robbery incidents.[11] Each society faces a control challenge—to minimize

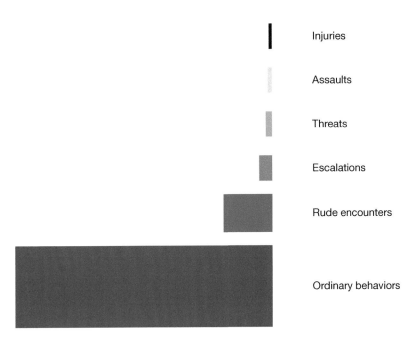

Injuries

Assaults

Threats

Escalations

Rude encounters

Ordinary behaviors

FIGURE 1B
How Rude Encounters Can Escalate, But Not Most of the Time

rude encounters and keep them from escalating into criminal acts or unpleasant community relations.[12]

Disputes can harm people emotionally, even without leading to a criminal act. As we will see in Part 5, many unpleasant events can undermine a neighborhood and *indirectly* foster more crime. In a large city, thousands of daily calls to police report ordinary disputes, including those that quiet down before anything serious happens. In a large society, millions of rude encounters and potential disputes require containment. In this book we present various crime theories that can help us understand this containment process. Rude encounters can occur in several domains of daily life. We begin by discussing public settings.

Strangers, Streets, and Disputes

Crime experts find that a good share of dispute-related crime occurs in public places, including entertainment venues as well as streets and sidewalks on the way to and from work, school, and recreation. This fits with what we know about the location of rude encounters, including some that escalate into crime. ***Aggression in public places*** often involves encounters with strangers. A statistical study of rude everyday encounters with strangers showed that they occur most often while people are driving in cars, walking on sidewalks, or using public transit.[13] The most common rude encounters included:

- pushing in front of me;

- bodily gestures, swearing;

- blocking my way;

- bumping into me, screaming or shouting;

- invading personal space; or

- loudness.[14]

Most rudeness was carried out by apparently respectable and rather well-dressed people in transit to or from work. This fits research on drivers admitting that they cut in front of other drivers. Many people also admit to driving at faster speeds than they favor for speed limits. Moreover, as income rises, speeding increases.[15]

Rude behaviors are diverse and often seem trivial to an outsider. Most incidents are simply selfish and insensitive, not deliberately aggressive. Yet we need to take these encounters seriously to understand crime. Some 35 percent of victims of rudeness responded by saying or doing something negative in return. The initial offender responded after being chided in 15 percent of all cases, and the victim answered back again 4 percent of the time. That fits with Figure 1b in the previous section, which showed that rudeness sometimes leads to an escalation.

Of course, rude encounters among strangers are not the same in every local area. In some big cities, people ride public transit to and from work and are rather likely to bump into one another.[16] The older transit systems of New York and London generate more problems with crime and uncivil behavior than newer systems with more room and better design.[17] In areas where people drive to and from work, rudeness is most likely to emerge with inconsiderate driving and "road rage."[18]

The Pew survey on "rudeness in America" found that rude experiences were widespread.[19] Some 79 percent of the sample agreed with the statement: "A lack of respect and courtesy is a serious problem for our society, and we should try to address it." Surprisingly, 41 percent of the public confessed to having been rude and disrespectful themselves. Fully 88 percent said they sometimes come across people who are rude and disrespectful. Most rude encounters occurred at work, at malls, or on the road, but not in respondents' own neighborhoods. Respondents reported bad language in public, and loud cell phone use in public places. The road rage problem came up once more, with two-thirds of respondents reporting seeing aggressive and reckless driving on the road.

The Pew report also confirms the danger of escalation from random acts of rudeness. More than two-thirds of respondents stated, "I am less likely to be nice when I have to deal with someone who is very rude and impolite." As we noted earlier, a rude encounter can escalate into an argument, and an argument can escalate still further to produce a criminal act.

Swear words are widely used in daily discourse and need not result in any conflict. Swearing

- is widespread in American society;

- can have positive, negative, or inconsequential results;

- communicates emotions, like the horn on your car does;

- can be used carefully or carelessly; and

- might cause significant problems in homes, schools, or workplaces.[20]

Taboo words are often innocuous, but that is not always the case. In some settings, rude words have consequences. An employee often knows that talking back to a customer, even if the customer deserves it, can lead to dismissal. An employee also has strong incentives not to answer an insult from the boss. Rude persons encountered on the way to and from work are usually gone quickly, leaving no time for an argument to explode. On the other hand, those drinking in a barroom setting have time for rude encounters to escalate.

Police officers may be called upon to contain rude encounters in public places. That in turn can generate conflicts between police and the communities they work in. Unfortunately, containing public rudeness is a difficult task for policing, and other public institutions are not always able to assist. Rudeness can feed conflicts between racial or ethnic groups, fear of crime, fear of using public transit, and even outmigration to avoid metropolitan problems.

Rudeness and Crime on the Job

For many occupations, ***workplace aggression*** is a matter of concern.[21] Those who work at night in the entertainment industry have extra risks of rude encounters, sometimes leading to crime victimization. Risks are also greater for those in public service contact with customers and those who make deliveries outside their workplace. Rude behaviors on the job include personal and role-related rudeness, such as:

- gestures (e.g., eye-rolling, sighing) to express impatience;

- inappropriate manner of addressing you (e.g., "hey you");

- rude gestures to get your attention (e.g., snapping fingers); or

- nasty comments about your appearance.

Employees also complain about customers

- creating an unnecessary mess for you to deal with;

- expecting you to stop what you were doing to help the complainer;

- expecting better service because of their perceived status; or

- continuing to complain despite your efforts to help.

Still other rudeness interferes with the employee's relationship to the boss or larger organization; for instance, when the customer

- blamed you for a problem you did not cause;

- did not appreciate your going out of your way to help them;

- pestered you to make exceptions to company policy; or

- went above your head when you were doing the right thing.[22]

You can see why the workplace often demands a great deal of self-control to avoid further conflict—an important part of criminological theory and a topic taken up in Part 2. You can see that some occupations put people into risky situations involving customers or the public. For example, police officers have a considerable number of rude encounters and minor violent incidents—taken up in Part 3. Other officials also experience rudeness and aggression, including traffic enforcement officers and court officials.[23]

A good illustration of occupational risk of rudeness comes from interviews with 665 bus drivers along Australia's beautiful Sunshine Coast. More than half the drivers had bad experiences. These included 79 violent incidents, 298 instances of verbal abuse by customers, 337 incivilities, 151 cases of property damage, and 286 road rage events, including threats, name-calling, and nasty gestures. Public transport staff are much more likely to face threats of violence at work than other workers. Australian research found that bus drivers experience disproportionate assaults, especially if they are located too close to passengers and if few people are around.[24]

Articles on rude customers have appeared in a wide-ranging occupational literature, extending from bank tellers to service personnel. Medical personnel have to deal with rude and difficult patients. Undergraduate students often report rude encounters as part of their work obligations. They tend to hold frontline jobs as waiters, store clerks, delivery persons, or other service occupations. They are thus exposed to substantial public contact and greater risk of unpleasant encounters. Indeed, those lower on the hierarchy often have more unpleasant dealings at the frontlines. Bartenders have perhaps the highest risk of falling victim to workplace violence, higher than law enforcement officers. Rudeness involves not only customers and clients but also fellow workers, usually not leading to crime but creating that possibility.

Sometimes disputes on the job arise because a co-worker fails to do a necessary task that others depend on. This could be done out of rudeness or neglect. An experimental study set up a work task with undergraduate students, building in noncompliance with a necessary "work task" upon which others depended. The researchers found that others began by making additional requests, but then went through a process of escalation. They made demands, then complaints, then angry statements, then threats, then harassment, then abuse of the person who they considered noncompliant.[25] Again you can see that conflict has a pattern and anger has a structure.

Rudeness and Neighborhood Crime

Most disputes are handled informally without calling police. However, most calls for police service are about minor matters: quarrels, noisemaking, barking dogs, etc. Once police or other officials are summoned, they probably have to do something. Usually they try to handle these matters without arresting people.

Police may end up mediating heated disagreements between dog owners and other citizens. Dog owners want to walk their dogs in the park, while others dislike dogs and don't want to walk where dogs have defecated. Towns enact a variety of planning rules to minimize these land-use conflicts. Some communities provide special dog parks. Other communities allow residents to walk their dogs around the perimeter of city parks, but not to enter the center. Cleanup rules are enacted, and civil fines for noncompliance are stipulated. All of these exemplify the attempt to dampen disputes and to avoid as much as possible involving the criminal justice system. Each community goes through a trial-and-error process as it seeks to contain disputes and prevent them from escalating into crime.

Conflicts between households are more common than meets the eye. Police receive far more calls about noisy parties than they receive about felonies. In university areas, college students are often involved in noise complaints from residents. College students often keep later hours, while neighboring families need to get up early in the morning to go to work or to send children to school. Roommates also have disputes over sleeping and personal matters. On a campus, such disputes are seldom reported to police, but they are disputes nonetheless. Most of these disputes are handled privately or by university personnel on university property, and they seem to fade away. However, such disputes are risky situations that could escalate.

Residential conflicts within households include disputes between partners, between parents and children, or among children. Almost all families quarrel at least on occasion.[26] Minor family quarreling can be frequent without escalation. However, *intrafamilial violence* is often concealed from public view and therefore does not necessarily enter police statistical systems.

Is family violence high or low? The answer depends on how you think about it. Even though some homes have violent flare-ups, the vast amount of time families spend together is peaceful. The hour-for-hour risk of violence within families and at home is very low.[27] It is much riskier to spend time among strangers or in public places, as indicated in Figure D of the Getting Started section, presented earlier.

Preventing grievances from emerging and then escalating is an especially serious challenge for a modern society, with many strangers interacting in public highways, parking lots, transit facilities, and entertainment districts. A large system creates millions of daily encounters among family, friends, and acquaintances as well as millions of additional encounters among strangers. Part 2 explains the alternative ways that society seeks to contain these problems, while introducing you to relevant crime theories that can help understand such containment efforts.

We have reviewed several risky situations and showed how low-level disputes can sometimes escalate into something much more. Society addresses disputes in many ways. These variations are especially evident with sexual rules and efforts to enforce them, as we will see in the next unit.

FLASHCARD LIST FOR UNIT 1.1

- Aggression in public places
- Dispute escalation process
- Incivilities
- Intrafamilial violence
- Property crimes
- Rude encounters
- Violent crimes
- Workplace aggression

DISCUSSION QUESTIONS

1. Review the sorts of rudeness that occur in job situations, and discuss how escalations are prevented.

2. Consider conflict situations in drinking settings, how they can escalate or not.

Notes

1   Felson, R. B., & Steadman, H. J. (1983). Situational factors in disputes leading to criminal violence. *Criminology*, *21*(1), 59–74.

2   Felstiner, W. L. (1975). Avoidance as dispute processing: An elaboration. *Law and Society Review*, *9*(4), 695–706.

3   Calavita, K., & Jenness, V. (2013). Inside the pyramid of disputes: Naming problems and filing grievances in California prisons. *Social Problems*, *60*(1), 50–80. Albiston, C. R., Edelman, L. B., & Milligan, J. (2014). The dispute tree and the legal forest. *Annual Review of Law and Social Science*, *10*, 105–131.

4   Tedeschi, J. T., & Felson, R. B. (1994). *Violence, aggression, and coercive actions*. Washington, DC: American Psychological Association. Felson, M., & Eckert, M. A. (2016). *Crime and everyday life*. Thousand Oaks, CA: Sage.

5   Felson, R. B. (1982). Impression management and the escalation of aggression and violence. *Social Psychology Quarterly*, *45*(4), 245–254.

6   Kienpointner, M. (1997). Varieties of rudeness: Types and functions of impolite utterances. *Functions of Language*, *4*(2), 251–287. Bousfield, D., & Locher, M. A. (Eds.). (2008). *Impoliteness in language: Studies on its interplay with power in theory and practice*. Berlin: de Gruyter.

7   Luckenbill, D. F. (1977). Criminal homicide as a situated transaction. *Social Problems*, *25*(2), 176–186.

8   Andersson, L. M., & Pearson, C. M. (1999). Tit for tat? The spiraling effect of incivility in the workplace. *Academy of Management Review*, *24*(3), 452–471.

9   Baum, K., & Klaus, P. (2005). *Violent victimization of college students, 1995–2002*. Washington, DC: Bureau of Justice Statistics.

10   Icove, D. J., & Estepp, M. H. (1987). Motive-based offender profiles of arson and fire-related crimes. *FBI Law Enforcement Bulletin*, *56*(4), 17–23.

11   Kivivuori, J., Savolainen, J., & Aaltonen, M. (2016). The revenge motive in delinquency: Prevalence and predictors. *Acta Sociologica*, *59*(1), 69–84.

12   Taylor, R. B. (1999). The incivilities thesis: Theory, measurement, and policy. In R. H. Langworthy (Ed.), *Measuring what matters: Proceedings from the Policing Research Institute Meetings*, pp. 65–88. Washington, DC: National Institute of Justice.

13   Phillips, T., & Smith, P. (2003). Everyday incivility: Towards a benchmark. *The Sociological Review*, *51*(1), 85–108.

14   Smith, P., Phillips, T. L., & King, R. D. (2010). *Incivility: The rude stranger in everyday life*. Cambridge, U.K.: Cambridge University Press.

15   Schroeder, P., Kostyniuk, L., & Mack, M. (2013). *2011 National Survey of Speeding Attitudes and Behaviors*. Report No. DOT HS 811 865. Washington DC: National Highway Traffic Safety Administration. See also: Lennon, A., & King, M. (2015). Sharing social space with strangers: Setting, signalling and policing informal rules *of* driving etiquette. In *Proceedings of the 2015 Australasian Road Safety Conference*. 14–16 October, Gold Coast, Australia.

16   Marteache, N., Bichler, G., & Enriquez, J. (2015). Mind the gap: Perceptions of passenger aggression and train car supervision in a commuter rail system. *Journal of Public Transportation*, *18*(2), 61–73.

17   La Vigne, N. G. (1997). *Visibility and vigilance: Metro's situational approach to preventing subway crime*. Washington, DC: National Institute of Justice. Smith, M. J., & Cornish, D. B. (2006). *Secure and*

tranquil travel: Preventing crime and disorder on public transport. London: Routledge. Ceccato, V. (2013). *Moving safely: Crime and perceived safety in Stockholm's subway stations.* Lanham, MD: Lexington Books. Newton, A. D. (2004). Crime on public transport: "Static" and "non-static" (moving) crime events. *Western Criminology Review, 5*(3), 25–42. Newton, A. D., Johnson, S. D., & Bowers, K. J. (2004). Crime on bus routes: An evaluation of a safer travel initiative. *Policing: An International Journal of Police Strategies & Management, 27*(3), 302–319.

18 Harding, R. W., Morgan, F. H., Indermaur, D., Ferrante, A. M., & Blagg, H. (1998). Road rage and the epidemiology of violence: Something old, something new. *Studies on Crime and Crime Prevention, 7*(2): 221–238.

19 Farkas, S., Johnson, J., Duffet, A., & Collins, K. (2002). *Aggravating circumstances: A status report on rudeness in America.* New York: Pew Charitable Trust.

20 Jay, T. (2009). The utility and ubiquity of taboo words. *Perspectives on Psychological Science, 4*(2), 153–161.

21 Johnson, P. R., & Indvik, J. (2001). Rudeness at work: Impulse over restraint. *Public Personnel Management, 30*(4), 457–465.

22 Wilson, N. L., & Holmvall, C. M. (2013). The development and validation of the Incivility from Customers Scale. *Journal of Occupational Health Psychology, 18*(3), 310–326.

23 Culpeper, J., Bousfield, D., & Wichmann, A. (2003). Impoliteness revisited: With special reference to dynamic and prosodic aspects. *Journal of Pragmatics, 35*(10), 1545–1579.

24 Lincoln, R., & Gregory, A. (2014). *Violence against urban bus drivers: Short report to industry partners for the Researchers in Business pilot project.* Bond University, Gold Coast, Australia. Lincoln, R., & Gregory, A. (2015). Moving violations: A study of incivility and violence against urban bus drivers in Australia. *International Journal of Education and Social Science, 2*(1), 118–127.

25 Mikolic, J. M., Parker, J. C., & Pruitt, D. G. (1997). Escalation in response to persistent annoyance: Groups versus individuals and gender effects. *Journal of Personality and Social Psychology, 72*(1), 151–163.

26 Montemayor, R. (1983). Parents and adolescents in conflict: All families some of the time and some families most of the time. *Journal of Early Adolescence, 3*(1–2), 83–103.

27 See: Lemieux, A. M., & Felson, M. (2012). Risk of violent crime victimization during major daily activities. *Violence and Victims, 27*(5), 635–655.

UNIT 1.2 Containing Sexual Temptations

The urge for a sexual orgasm powerfully affects individuals in all societies. Orgasms can be accomplished by following or by violating society's sexual rules. Violations may include forcing, cajoling, or tricking somebody else. They can also include disapproved consensual sex. Sexual violations put individuals in conflict with their own society.

Sexual misbehavior is very closely tied to risky situations, as you shall see in the course of our book. Large chunks of a normal day involve no sexual misbehavior and little immediate sexual risk. For example, when men and women are working together in larger numbers, their behavior usually conforms to conventional rules, even if temptations present themselves. Inappropriate behavior is most likely to occur when an offender can avoid scrutiny. After other workers have gone home; in a hidden corner of the building; in a bar after work; in a private email message—these are risky situations for sexual misbehavior.

On the positive side, the sexual urge helps cement romantic relationships, replenish the population, and keep parents near children for an extended period. The sexual urge can encourage couples to stay together because the pleasure it provides can offset some of the natural strains that couples experience.

But it can all go terribly wrong. The same powerful urge that helps cement relationships can also tempt people to leave their partners and families in search of more sex. The same urge that leads to acceptable mating can lead to risky situations that turn temptations into rape, incest, trickery, infidelity, and abuse. The same urge that helps reinforce relationships can also destroy them, leading to broken hearts and deflated spirits. Society tries to cope with this challenge by defining sexual rules.

Sexual Taboos

Taboos are forbidden behaviors. Every society has *sexual taboos*—strong rules that seek to contain the sexual urges of the population. These taboos draw a line, telling people what sexual behaviors and sex partners are off limits. Is anal sex forbidden or permitted? Is oral sex taboo? Is masturbation condoned or discouraged? Is homosexuality accepted, tolerated, or banned? At what age is sexual intercourse allowed? What age gap between sex partners is permitted?[1] The answers are offered by culture and often by law.

Anthropologists report that every society has some type of *incest taboo*—rules stating that certain relatives are off limits for sexual intercourse.[2] Although the incest taboo is universal,[3] its details can vary from culture to culture. One society bans sex between first cousins, while another society does not apply the incest taboo to them. Certain historic periods allow sex between people of vastly different ages, but other periods forbid it. These variations do not contradict the underlying general point—that every society draws sexual lines and forbids sexual access on some basis as it seeks to contain and channel the sexual urge.

Even though the legal system does not formally deal with every incursion against sexual rules, legal intervention can occur. For example, legal systems may consider the consent of the partner and designate an age of consent—the age a partner is deemed mature enough to understand the consequences of sexual intercourse.

- If sexual intercourse is forced upon an unwilling partner, this is called *forcible rape*.

- If someone over the age of consent finds a willing partner under the age of consent, this is considered *statutory rape*.

Some sexual acts between consenting adults have been criminalized in some eras. The notable case is homosexuality. At times oral and anal sex have been criminalized even if the partners are consenting adults. In the past 50 years, most modern societies have decriminalized sexual intercourse between consenting adults, including those of the same sex. In some places the old laws remain on the books but have faded into oblivion, unenforced. However, homosexuality often remains a taboo, especially in rural areas of modern nations[4] and in some nations more than others.

It is a mistake to think that homosexuality only emerged in the modern world. Homosexual behaviors were tolerated and even accepted in ancient Greece and Rome. In North and South America, homosexuality was common among several tribes, including Aztecs and Mayans, as well as the Tupinambá of Brazil. Cross-dressing and stereotypically gay behavior long have been tolerated in Filipino culture despite its Christian identity. We see that *sexual standards* vary greatly among and even within societies.

Although modern society is generally more sexually tolerant than in the past, do not think for a minute that all sexual taboos have vanished. Modern societies strongly condemn adults having sex with underage youths, especially when teachers, coaches, or clergy abuse their access to young people. An example is the well-publicized scandal involving Jerry Sandusky, an assistant coach for the Penn State University football team, who developed an extensive youth group to provide himself sexual access to numerous teenage boys.

History contains a wide variety of sexual taboos. Some periods reflected strong intolerance of homosexuality, and other periods were quite tolerant. Sometimes a false image of the past is broadcast. The past was less punitive than we may think. Some periods were sexually repressive and others sexually open. Many centuries experienced great epidemics of sexually transmitted disease. It is also a mistake to think that norms against forcible rape are a modern invention. In 1955, at least 18 American states permitted capital punishment in rape cases.[5]

Although some sexual behaviors and taboos shift, three important facts seem to hold over time:

- the recurrent and assertive sexual urge;

- society's efforts to contain that urge; and

- society's spotty record at containment.

Even when there is substantial consensus about sexual rules, modern society faces quite a challenge in enforcing them. Perhaps the main explanation is that sex acts (including those that break the rules) occur in private settings. It is more difficult for society and its legal system to enforce and protect victims when it comes to covert rule-breaking.[6] We should think of the legal system as a *backup* that tries to remind citizens that they *might* be subject to punishment if they cross certain lines. That's why society depends on other control mechanisms in its efforts to contain the sexual urge. What about situations in which consensus about sexual rules is absent?

Conflict between Rules and Realities

Émile Durkheim was a social theorist who used the word ***anomie*** to describe a condition in which society provides little moral guidance.[7] In a modern society, sexual rules are often inconsistent, unclear, and lacking in consensus. It is very difficult for the criminal justice system or other institutions of society to enforce muddled rules.

As an example of society's inconsistency, consider that sexual intercourse prior to marriage is normal in a modern society. This conflicts with religious norms that have not disappeared. Parents differ in the ages at which they can accept the onset of sexual intercourse for their daughters and sometimes their sons. As we just mentioned, homosexuality is increasingly accepted in modern societies, but not universally so— another example of inconsistency. Laws prohibiting oral sex, always difficult to enforce, are almost entirely unenforceable in a modern society. Indeed, oral sex is a widespread modern sexual experience. The National Health Statistics Reports note that 65 percent of those aged 18–19 in the United States have engaged in oral sex, with the number increasing to 85 percent at ages 20–24.[8] Unlike the past, youthful experience with oral sex in modern society often comes at a younger age than vaginal sex.

A modern society also departs from traditional patterns of sexual union and early fertility. Late marriage becomes common.[9] At the same time, with better nutrition, youths mature sexually at an earlier age. Figure 1c depicts the historical change. In the past puberty occurred at ages 14 or 15. Through most of human history, most young men had to do farm work or other physical labor and formed sexual unions as teenagers, soon after puberty arrived. They did not need to go to college or even finish high school, and many received little or no elementary education.

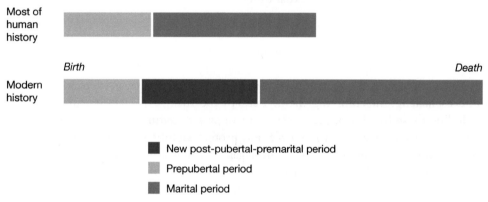

FIGURE 1C
Modern Life Creates a New and Long Period between Puberty and Marriage

Society has always faced some problems with misbehavior by youths. In the Biblical era such misbehavior was recognized.

> If any man has a stubborn and rebellious son who will not obey his father or his mother, and when they chastise him, he will not even listen to them, then his father and mother shall seize him, and bring him out to the elders of his city at the gateway of his home town. And they shall say to the elders of his city, "This son of ours is stubborn and rebellious, he will not obey us, he is a glutton and a drunkard." Then all the men of his city shall stone him to death; so you shall remove the evil from your midst, and all Israel shall hear of it and fear.[10]

On November 6, 1636, the Puritans in Massachusetts enacted this in law and subjected rebellious children to the death penalty.[11]

Youth independence from parents is enhanced in the modern world in two ways: by accelerated sexual maturity and by delayed onset of adult roles. Today puberty is more likely to arrive at age 12 or earlier, adding a couple years of sexual exposure.[12] Modern parents are not ready to accept fully the early sexual capacities of their 12-year-old son or daughter, and modern society provides no legitimate outlet for sexual intercourse at these ages. Figure 1c also sums up the life cycle from birth (on the left) to death (on the right). Note that people live much longer in the modern world, but their lives are configured very differently.

In today's world, people live longer but arrive at puberty early. Yet they do not begin a marital period until a dozen or more years later. They spend many years in school. That creates a *postpubertal-premarital period* (shown in dark blue in Figure 1c), but does not prevent the sexual urge from asserting itself; we should not be surprised that people do something about it.

Social scientists use the term *cultural lag* to describe how cultural rules from the past linger on well after they are no longer viable in terms of modern reality.[13] Traditional sexual taboos conflict with modern work and school realities. Indeed, society faces many gaps between rules and its capacity to enforce them.

Sexual License and Tolerance

Every society seems to have grey areas where behaviors are officially disapproved but privately tolerated. Consider the officially segregated history of many American states, where interracial marriages were illegal and interracial sex was taboo. Nonetheless, white males were allowed sexual leeway by fellow whites, and hence could have sex with Afro-American women—both during the slavery period and after emancipation.[14] However, Afro-American men were not allowed to have sex with Caucasian women, and any hint of their doing so could result in whites killing them.[15]

Those with *puritan values* today do not necessarily follow their own rules in real life. American society, like most societies, has a grey area. For example, many Americans have long accepted sexual relationships among those engaged to be married or during college years or away from home.[16] The Korean and American governments cooperated in sponsoring prostitutes for American servicemen serving in Korea.[17] Even within the United States, cities have created unofficial prostitution zones where law violations were tolerated—attempting to channel temptations into specialized areas. Storyville in New Orleans, roughly where the French Quarter is located today, was an official zone of prostitution and entertainment.[18] A similar history is found for the 42nd Street area of Manhattan.[19]

TABLE 1A **Sexual Fantasies Reported by a Sample of Normal Adults**

	"I have fantasized about"	Females %	Males %
Type of sexual act	Being masturbated by my partner	71.4	71.7
	Masturbating my partner	68.1	76.4
	Being masturbated by an acquaintance	36.8	64.7
	Being masturbated by an unknown person	33.4	62.5
	Having anal sex	32.5	64.2
Domination	Being dominated sexually	64.6	53.3
	Dominating someone sexually	46.7	59.6
	Being spanked or whipped for sexual pleasure	36.3	28.5
	Spanking, whipping someone for sexual pleasure	23.8	43 5
	Being forced to have sex	28.9	30.7
Type of sex partner	Having sex with someone I know, not my spouse	66.3	83.4
	Having sex with a star or well-known person	51.7	61.9
	Having sex with an unknown person	48.9	72.5
	Having homosexual or gay sex	36.9	20.6
	Having sex with someone much older than me	34.2	48.0
	Having sex with someone much younger than me	18.1	57.0
Number of sex partners	Having sex with two men	56.5	15.8
	Having sex with two women	36.9	84.5
	Having sex with over three people, men and women	30.9	45.2
	Having sex with over three people, all men	28.3	13.1
	Having sex with over three people, all women	24.7	75.3
	Sexual swinging with a couple I do not know	26.9	39.6
	Sexual swinging with a couple that I know	17.5	42.3
Exhibitionism & voyeurism	Making love openly in a public place	57.3	66.1
	Watching two women make love	42.4	82.1
	Being photographed or filmed during sex	31.9	43.9
	Watching two men make love	19.3	16.2
	Showing myself in public naked, partially naked	16.6	23.2

Adapted from C. C. Joval, A. Cossette, & V. Lapierre (2015). What exactly is an unusual sexual fantasy? *The Journal of Sexual Medicine*, *12*(2), 328–340.

It is a mistake to think that most members of society would never think of violating its sexual rules. Studies of the ***sexual fantasies*** of college students show that both males and female minds wander in many sexual directions, some of these going beyond the social norms.[20] It is striking that females have many of the same fantasies as males. Other researchers drew similar conclusions from a non-collegiate sample[21] as indicated in Table 1a.

Note in Table 1a the percentages of females and males that have fantasies of group sex, including with strangers. Also included are some acts that are patently illegal, such as having sex with someone underage. It is a matter for discussion which of these behaviors is innocuous and which is harmful to society. Several of the domination desires could well become forcible rape. Sex with groups and with strangers is likely to spread sexual diseases. You can see why society has reasons to contain the sexual urge and limit temptations to act on it.

By 1950 the United States had already reached a level where its own sexual rules were often broken. ***Alfred Kinsey*** and subsequent researchers discovered that a substantial share of the public has at some time experimented with one or more major violations of sexual rules. We should not be surprised that ministers and congressmen end up in sex scandals or that those who profess purity are so often caught in hypocrisy.

These contradictions are very important. They remind us that the rules of larger society conflict harshly with the urges and temptations faced by real people. Many parental rules conflict with natural growth processes and even with the parents' own behavior when they were young. Sexual rule-breaking usually occurs covertly. Those child abusers who use internet media for anonymity may also lure underage partners to relatively safe and unsupervised locations. Even those conducting sexual affairs, though not an illegal activity, seek times and places that allow secrecy.

Yet society cannot fully accept unbridled sexuality, unwanted pregnancies, abandonment of wives and children. Nor can society allow sexual jealousies, aggression, and trickery to rule. Where prostitution is legal or tolerated, society still has to try to minimize ancillary violence and sexually transmitted diseases. No matter how liberal or conservative a society, it needs to worry about where the sexual urge will lead. For example, sex workers are exposed to high rates of disease, assaults, and robberies.[22] Informal sexual encounters with many different partners also expose people to risks, a problem enhanced among those using the Internet to find sex partners.[23]

This point applies as well to university students. Student involvement in the sex industry is noted in Australia,[24] Germany,[25] Canada,[26] Britain,[27] and the United States.[28] In a rather large British sample, 1 in 20 students had participated in the sex industry. Their roles included prostitution, stripping, phone sex jobs, naked modeling, and porn acting. Even more interesting is the fact that one in five respondents indicated they had *considered* involvement in the sex industry, with females having a slightly higher rate (24 percent).[29] Again we see evidence why the sexual urge is a topic for regulatory discussion.

Sexual Harassment

We like to think that society can protect women from sexual pestering and children from sexual exploitation. Yet many of these sexual infractions occur under the radar screen, creating quite a challenge for society. Researchers have documented dozens of types of sexual aggression by men against women, showing that such aggression is found in numerous countries.[30] Included are multiple unwanted phone calls, asking her friends and associates about her behind her back, asking repeatedly for unwanted dates, sending unsolicited emails or texts, visiting uninvited, making inappropriate sexual comments, following her or going to her home uninvited. These issues are not limited to the expected settings. Three out of four female attorneys reported some form of gender-related rudeness or unwanted sexual attention, not only from fellow attorneys but also from judges, court personnel, marshals, and court security officers.[31] Others have observed and counted instances of sexual harassment in barrooms.[32] Criminologists have also provided evidence that women in big cities are frequently harassed while riding public transit settings,[33] another example in which protections are difficult to deliver. We take up aggression against women at length in Part 6.

You can see that the challenges to society are diverse. We have covered the need to control disputes and to contain sexual urges. We now turn to issues of property.

FLASHCARD LIST FOR UNIT 1.2

- Anomie
- Conflicts between rules and realities
- Cultural lag
- Forcible rape
- Incest taboo

- Kinsey, Alfred
- Postpubertal-premarital period
- Puritan values
- Sexual fantasies
- Sexual harassment

- Sexual license
- Sexual standards
- Sexual taboos
- Statutory rape

DISCUSSION QUESTIONS

1. Do you think sexual taboos vary from one layer of society to another?

2. Is it ever impractical for society to try to contain the sexual urge?

Notes

1   Bullough, V. L. (1976). *Sexual variance in society and history.* Chicago: University of Chicago Press.

2   Twitchell, J. B. (1987). *Forbidden partners: The incest taboo in modern culture.* New York: Columbia University Press.

3   Slater, M. K. (1959). Ecological factors in the origin of incest. *American Anthropologist, 61*(6), 1042–1059.

4   van den Akker, H., van der Ploeg, R., & Scheepers, P. (2013). Disapproval of homosexuality: Comparative research on individual and national determinants of disapproval of homosexuality in 20 European countries. *International Journal of Public Opinion Research, 25*(1), 64–86.

5   Reifsnyder, R. (1955). Capital crimes in the States. *The Journal of Criminal Law, Criminology, and Police Science, 45*(6), 690–693.

6   For background, see Bryden, D. P., & Lengnick, S. (1997). Rape in the criminal justice system. *The Journal of Criminal Law and Criminology, 87*(4), 1194–1384.

7   Jones, R. A. (1986). *Emile Durkheim: An introduction to four major works.* Thousand Oaks, CA: Sage.

8   Copen, C. E., Chandra, A., & Martinez, G. (2012). *Prevalence and timing of oral sex with opposite-sex partners among females and males aged 15–24 years: United States, 2007–2010.* National Health Statistics Reports, No. 56. Hyattsville, MD: National Center for Health Statistics.

9   Hymowitz, K. S., Carroll, J. S., Wilcox, W. B., & Kaye, K. (2013). *Knot yet: The benefits and costs of delayed marriage in America.* Charlottesville, VA: National Marriage Project, University of Virginia.

10   Deuteronomy 21:18–21.

11   Sutton, J. R. (1981). Stubborn children: Law and the socialization of deviance in the Puritan colonies. *Family Law Quarterly, 15*(1), 31–64.

12   Daw, S. F. (1970). Age of boys' puberty in Leipzig, 1727–49, as indicated by voice breaking in J. S. Bach's choir members. *Human Biology, 42*(1), 87–89. Juul, A., Magnusdottir, S., Scheike, T., Prytz, S., & Skakkebæk, N. E. (2007). Age at voice break in Danish boys: Effects of pre-pubertal body mass index and secular trend. *International Journal of Andrology, 30*(6), 537–542.

13   Ogburn, W. F. (1957). Cultural lag as theory. *Sociology and Social Research, 41*(3), 167–174.

14   Jennings, T. (1990). "Us colored women had to go through a plenty": Sexual exploitation of African-American slave women. *Journal of Women's History, 1*(3), 45–74.

15   Allen, J., Als, H., Lewis, J., & Litwack, L. F. (2000). *Without sanctuary: Lynching photography in America.* Santa Fe, NM: Twin Palms Publisher.

16   Kinsey, A., Pomeroy, W., Martin, C., & Gebhard, P. (1953). *Sexual behavior in the human female.* Philadelphia: Saunders.

17   Moon, K. H. (1997). *Sex among allies: Military prostitution in U.S.–Korea relations.* New York: Columbia University Press.

18   Foster, C. L. (1990). Tarnished angels: Prostitution in Storyville, New Orleans, 1900–1910. *Louisiana History: The Journal of the Louisiana Historical Association, 31*(4), 387–397.

19   Bianco, Anthony (2004). *Ghosts of 42nd Street: A history of America's most infamous block.* New York: Harper-Collins Books.

20   Leitenberg, H., & Henning, K. (1995). Sexual fantasy. *Psychological Bulletin, 117*(3), 469–496.

21 Joyal, C. C., Cossette, A., & Lapierre, V. (2015). What exactly is an unusual sexual fantasy? *The Journal of Sexual Medicine, 12*(2), 328–340.

22 Barnard, M. (1993). Violence and vulnerability: Conditions of work for streetworking prostitutes. *Sociology of Health and Illness, 15*(1), 5–14. Church, S., Henderson, M., Barnard, M., & Hart, G. (2001). Violence by clients towards female prostitutes in different work settings: Questionnaire survey. *British Medical Journal, 322*(7285), 524–525.

23 McFarlane, M., Bull, S. S., & Rietmeijer, C. A. (2000). The internet as a newly emerging risk environment for sexually transmitted diseases. *JAMA, 284*(4), 443–446.

24 Reilly, T. (2008). Students turn to sex work to help pay for university. *The Age* (Australia). March 2. Lantz, S. (2005). Students working in the Melbourne sex industry: Education, human capital and the changing patterns of the youth labor market. *Journal of Youth Studies, 8*(4), 385–401.

25 Blumenschein, E. (2017). Third of Berlin university students consider sex work. Unpublished manuscript reported by *Reuters*, May 11.

26 Sinacore, A. L., Jaghori, B., & Rezazadeh, S. M. (2014). Female university students working in the sex trade: A narrative analysis. *Canadian Journal of Counselling and Psychotherapy, 48*(4), 40–56.

27 Sagar, T., Jones, D., Symons, K., & Bowring, J. (2015). Student participation in the sex industry: Higher education responses and staff experiences and perceptions. *Journal of Higher Education Policy and Management, 37*(4), 400–412. Roberts, R., Bergström, S., & La Rooy, D. (2007). UK students and sex work: Current knowledge and research issues. *Journal of Community & Applied Social Psychology, 17*(2), 141–146. Sanders, T., & Hardy, K. (2015). Students selling sex: Marketisation, higher education and consumption. *British Journal of Sociology of Education, 36*(5), 747–765.

28 Haeger, H., & Deil-Amen, R. (2010). Female college students working in the sex industry: A hidden population. *NASPA Journal About Women in Higher Education, 3*(1), 4–27.

29 Sagar, T., Jones, D., Symons, K., Tyrie, J., & Roberts, R. (2016). Student involvement in the UK sex industry: Motivations and experiences. *The British Journal of Sociology, 67*(4), 697–718.

30 Luthar, V. K., & Luthar, H. K. (2002). Using Hofstede's cultural dimensions to explain sexually harassing behaviours in an international context. *International Journal of Human Resource Management, 13*(2), 268–284.

31 Cortina, L. M., Lonsway, K. A., Magley, V. J., Freeman, L. V., Collinsworth, . . . & Fitzgerald, L. F. (2002). What's gender got to do with it? Incivility in the federal courts. *Law & Social Inquiry, 27*(2), 235–270. Cortina, L. M. (2008). Unseen injustice: Incivility as modern discrimination in organizations. *Academy of Management Review, 33*(1), 55–75.

32 Graham, K., Bernards, S., Osgood, D. W., Abbey, A., Parks, M., . . . & Wells, S. (2014). "Blurred lines?" Sexual aggression and barroom culture. *Alcoholism: Clinical and Experimental Research, 38*(5), 1416–1424.

33 Natarajan, M. (2016). Rapid assessment of "eve teasing" (sexual harassment) of young women during the commute to college in India. *Crime Science, 5*(6). https://doi.org/10.1186/s40163-016-0054-9.

Unit 1.3 Protecting Property

Society faces a challenge in defining property and then protecting its ownership. Property issues are quite relevant to crime and the justice process. Consider these four examples:

Example 1—A police officer stops you and asks to see your driver's license, then checks your license plate registration. The officer discovers that your driver's license is valid but that the car belongs to your uncle, and he starts to ask more questions. This encounter is actually about property ownership. Did your uncle give you permission to drive his car?[1]

Example 2—A woman calls police claiming her ex-live-in boyfriend stole her television set. The ex-boyfriend says the television is his and that he took it with him when he moved out. This conflict is as much about property ownership as it is about crime. Who really owns that television set?

Example 3—An illegal prostitute and her customer get into a fight over how much she is paid for her services. An officer notices them quarreling and intervenes, but they stop talking. Their monetary agreement is not a legal contract that the state can reinforce. What should the officer do now?[2]

Example 4—A burglar breaks into your house, stealing your jewelry. The thief then sells the jewelry to someone who thinks it is a legitimate sale. Must the buyer give the jewelry back to you?

All four examples show that a good deal of justice system activity is generated by property issues. Society tries to resolve as many of these property issues as possible outside the criminal justice system. This is accomplished using:

- informal processes;

- contracts;

- registration or licenses;

- insurance;[3] and

- private policing.[4]

This list tells an important story: Society has a vast array of organizations designed to assign, handle, and protect **property rights** and resolve **property disputes**. We always need to keep the criminal justice system in perspective, remembering that it is just one of society's organs for dealing with property conflicts.

Informal Processes to Resolve Property Issues

The justice system cannot handle most of everyday property disputes. One child grabs his sibling's toy. The wronged child cries out to parents for assistance. This requires that parents define which toy belongs to which child and then enforce ownership. For toys assigned for joint use, a family needs rules to prioritize which child has access when. With teenagers, disagreements emerge over borrowing a parent's car in the evening or other property usage. These property disputes are normally handled by *informal processes* within the family, and we hope such disputes do not spill into the justice system.

Informal processes also resolve property issues outside of family settings. Despite our images of the Wild West from cowboy movies, in fact, cattle ranchers in the Western United States today tend to settle disputes informally and peacefully among themselves. The informal rule is that the owner of livestock is responsible for what the animals do. If wandering cattle damage the property of a neighboring rancher, the cattle owner pays for the damage voluntarily.[5] Similarly, suburban neighbors do not usually wait until the city gives them a ticket for grass that has grown too high. People usually cut the grass sooner to keep the neighbors happy. The vast majority of property rules and disputes are avoided or informally handled without legal intervention.

Contracts and Conflicts

When the law intervenes, *criminal law is usually not involved at all!* Most attorneys are non-criminal lawyers working in various branches of *civil law*. That is, they work on contracts, disputes, divorces, and many forms of negotiation occurring out of court, involving issues between two people or organizations. The job of these attorneys is to use civil law, not criminal law, to resolve disputes before they become criminal issues. Most civil cases never go to court. When a case does go to civil court, there is no prosecutor; both sides in the dispute present their case to a judge and jury, who adjudicate the case. Even cases that might have involved criminal wrongdoing are often handled as civil matters. Criminal courts have a higher level of proof—somebody must be proven *guilty beyond a **reasonable doubt***. In civil court, a lower level of proof is required—the ***preponderance of evidence*** must support one side over the other. Nobody is to be locked up, so constitutional requirements are lower.

Contracts are especially important because they assign property ownership. Contracts quietly govern much of our lives—every time we sign a credit card bill and every time a store sells us a pack of gum. College roommates often don't realize that their verbal agreements that *seem* to be informal are really contracts protected by law. Roommates may well discover themselves fully liable when another roommate fails to pay her share. The Maryland Attorney General's Office warns university students:

> Problems with landlords are common for students living off-campus. Unaware of their rights as a tenant, and the laws regarding landlord tenant issues, college students often get into sticky situations involving leases in Maryland. Renting requires some sort of rental agreement between the landlord and tenant. . . . Oral agreements are legal in Maryland for lease terms that are less than one year. . . . Make sure when you apply to rent, you are signing an application, not a lease.[6]

Civil law includes ***contract law***, by which the government enforces property agreements between private parties. Contract law tells you that you really must meet your car payments. You really must pay your rent. A property dispute might become a ***tort***—a civil case to resolve the specific issues of any given dispute. A divorce can easily lead to a property dispute, perhaps resolved in family court. Laws cannot cover every possible issue of every dispute, which is why society depends on negotiation.

Despite the formality of contract law, most property disputes are handled informally. You politely ask your landlord to shorten the lease you signed. You ask the university official to allow an extra month to pay tuition. You ask an attorney or even a friend to help mediate a problem. These many methods keep property issues from spilling into the court process. The criminal justice system is part of a much larger set of institutions serving to protect property. These alternative institutions help society to *avoid* the criminal justice system, seeking to resolve property disputes without violence, vandalism, or vindictiveness.

Registrations and Licenses Assign Criminal Responsibility

After Karl Benz invented the modern automobile, he irritated his neighbors so much with its noise and smell that in 1888 he had to obtain written permission to drive it. The *registering* and licensing of vehicles and drivers clearly assigns property responsibility as a matter of public record. This minimizes property issues because official documents make absolutely clear who owns a vehicle and who has a right to drive. *Licensing* agencies can also act as gatekeepers, denying a license to those moving into a state with a license revoked in another state. Thus, even outside the criminal justice system itself, government administrative agencies help discourage lawbreaking. Licensing also applies to attorneys, physicians, nurses, hairdressers, and other occupations—an idea going back to the guilds in the Middle Ages.[7]

Licenses are supposed to provide a means of group regulation. Thus, attorneys have a Bar Association that is supposed to make sure that they act responsibly, not cheating their clients or failing to provide services. Medical boards are supposed to discipline physicians who break the rules. Real estate boards are expected to control or expel irresponsible agents. Some critics argue that professional licensing boards may fail to discipline unethical or incompetent practitioners.[8] However, society depends on these non-criminal processes to hold people accountable and to take the burden off the back of the criminal justice system.

Insurance Takes Some Pressure Off the Police

Insurance is designed to spread risk. Buying insurance allows each of us to avoid paying fully for bad luck. When one person smashes another's vehicle, insurance companies pay a good part of the costs and, in effect, assign fines to those deemed responsible by increasing their insurance costs or revoking their insurance coverage.[9] This avoids both civil and criminal law, except when damages or injuries are severe and the criminal justice system has to get into the act.

Many property disputes are settled by insurance companies or other intermediaries *outside the official legal system.*[10] They adjudicate who is at fault and put it on record. Insurance adjusters make far more decisions than police. They decide who is responsible for an accident and allocate damages. By revoking coverage or raising rates, the insurance process is perhaps the most important method used by society to protect property and to control individuals. This process minimizes the use of police, courts, and prisons.

The Justice System as a Backup

Informal and contractual processes, licensing and registration, insurance—all of these techniques are used by society to protect property and resolve property disputes. All help avoid the justice system. But we still need that system because people sometimes cannot resolve their disputes or will not comply with authorities. Some people keep trespassing after they are asked not to do so. Some people violate their contracts or do not respond to a civil court order. Some people drive without a license or take a car without authorization. Some people drive without car insurance, in defiance of the law. Somebody has to stop them—which falls to the justice system.

Yet the criminal system depends on these other processes. You cannot charge someone with auto theft without having a clear idea of who owns the vehicle. You cannot convict someone of residential burglary without establishing that the offender had no right to be there. Even in socialist societies, places and things are assigned and thefts are defined and punished. In most modern societies, intricate laws define ownership and property rights, with the criminal justice establishment backing this up.

As an illustration, you will note that law officers are often stationed at departments of motor vehicles and in civil courts, and that law officers back up civil court orders. Even when officers are not visible, the criminal justice system is standing behind the curtain in case it is needed.

The Shadow of the Law

The law does not *really* work as you see it on television. Criminal cases seldom result in trials. Most cases are weeded out long before a trial might occur, but those that remain are usually settled by plea bargaining between prosecutor and defense attorney. In Part 3 we go into the plea-bargaining process in detail. To some extent, plea bargains reflect what goes on in real trials. This is called "the *shadow of the law*," because the formal trial punishment levels provide a standard for attorneys to follow.[11]

Our detailed legal system tries to guide society. We need that system, but we must also recognize its limits and know how much we depend on other institutions. The great irony is that a modern society depends on the many laws on the books, and yet government cannot directly enforce these laws. The formal systems *cannot handle* the great variety of disputes and potential disputes over property and other issues. That's why we hope that the tax attorney and taxpayer will observe tax law and court rulings. We hope that insurance companies will deal properly with accidents. We hope that citizens will pay their bills and that debtors and creditors will work things out, not requiring police action. We hope that landlords will not take advantage of student ignorance about contracts, and that students will read before they sign.

FLASHCARD LIST FOR UNIT 1.3

- Civil law
- Contract law
- Informal processes
- Insurance
- Licensing

- Preponderance of evidence
- Property disputes
- Property rights
- Reasonable doubt

- Registering
- Shadow of the law
- Tort

DISCUSSION QUESTIONS

1. How does society try to minimize property disputes?

2. When property disputes start to escalate, how does society try to keep them from entering the civil courts? The criminal courts?

Notes

1   Quinton, P., Bland, N., & Miller, J. (2000). *Police stops, decision-making and practice.* London: Home Office.

2   Silbert, M. H., & Pines, A. M. (1981). Occupational hazards of street prostitutes. *Criminal Justice and Behavior, 8*(4), 395–399.

3   Roach Anleu, S., Green Mazerolle, A., & Presser, L. (2000). Third-party policing and insurance: The case of market-based crime prevention. *Law & Policy, 22*(1), 67–87. Hutter, B. M., & Jones, C. J. (2007). From government to governance: External influences on business risk management. *Regulation & Governance, 1*(1), 27–45.

4   Rigakos, G. S., & Greener, D. R. (2000). Bubbles of governance: Private policing and the law in Canada. *Canadian Journal of Law and Society, 15*(1), 145–185.

5   Ellickson, R. C. (2009). *Order without law: How neighbors settle disputes.* Cambridge, MA: Harvard University Press.

6   Ericson, R. V., Doyle, A., & Barry, D. (2003). *Insurance as governance.* Toronto: University of Toronto Press.

7   Gustafsson, B. (1991). The rise and economic behaviour of medieval craft guilds. In B. Gustafsson (Ed.), *Power and economic institutions: Reinterpretations in economic history*, pp. 69–106. Aldershot, U.K.: Edward Elgar.

8   Hogan, D. B. (1983). The effectiveness of licensing: History, evidence, and recommendations. *Law and Human Behavior, 7*(2–3), 117–138.

9   Jacobs, J. B. (2013). *Drunk driving: An American dilemma.* Chicago: University of Chicago Press.

10 Ross, H. L. (1970). *Settled out of court: The social process of insurance claims adjustment.* New York: Aldine.

11 Cooter, R., Marks, S., & Mnookin, R. (1982). Bargaining in the shadow of the law: A testable model of strategic behavior. *The Journal of Legal Studies, 11*(2), 225–251.

Unit 1.4 Safeguarding Children

Safeguarding and supervising young people is another fundamental problem that societies face. This problem becomes more complex in a modern society. Compare rural North Carolina of the past to the same parts of this state today, having strong commitment to modern education. In the past many children were poor, walking barefoot in areas where rattlesnakes and copperheads were abundant. Protecting youths from harm in the woods was important for survival.

Rural North Carolina is very different today. Young children are similar to those in the rest of the metropolitan United States. Their parents worry about them getting hit by a car, not a rattlesnake. They are usually bused to a large and consolidated school. Their parents likely want them to go to college, delay marriage, and prepare for a good job. These goals depend on protecting children from mistreatment by other youths, abuse by adults, and a variety of criminal and delinquent behaviors.

Mistreatment by Other Youths

The greatest dangers to young people are other young people. **Bullying** is commonplace in most societies, including nations known to have low crime rates. Bullying often begins in elementary school, but can also be a problem at junior high and high school levels. Bullying can have serious consequences beyond physical injury. It produces emotional injuries while also interfering with education and school attendance.[1]

Sexual abuse is another worry for young ages. It is a widespread misconception that sexual abuse of youths is carried out exclusively by adults. In fact, youths face risk of sexual abuse by other youths. For example, 15- and 16-year-olds may victimize 12-year-olds, and so on.[2] Teenagers do so by arranging to be alone with younger youths. Adolescent sex offenders are better able than adult offenders to use games and joint activities as a prelude to sexual abuse, quite easily creating a risky situation.[3]

Abuse by Adults

Child neglect means that some parents have neglected their own children, leaving them unfed and unclothed even to the point where their lives are endangered. Approximately 1 in 30 children are neglected in some way.

> Neglect can have substantial and long-term effects on children's physical and mental health and cognitive development. Examples include fatalities, impaired brain development, and adult problems such as liver and ischemic heart disease. Neglect also has been associated with inferior academic performance, emotional, and behavioral problems, as well as depression and suicidality decades later.[4]

Although child neglect is a serious issue, *sexual abuse of children* has received more attention. Underage victims of sexual abuse are most often 15 years old—regardless of whether victims *or* offenders are males or females, and regardless of the age of the offender. There is little difference between heterosexual and homosexual abuse patterns or rates. It seems that 15 is the prime age because it combines sexual attractiveness with vulnerability. Despite all the media attention, most sexual abuse victims are *not small children*. Rather, they are past puberty and thus capable of sexual activity.[5]

In about a third of cases, the underage victim is a willing participant or even the initiator of a sexual liaison with someone older. As we discussed in Unit 1.2, that does not exempt the older person from criminal liability, but it does tell us that society has a difficult problem enforcing its own laws. In an era of internet contact, it is very easy for sex partners to discover one another and to ignore a variety of laws in so doing— including the laws against adult sex with underage youths.

Youths Mistreating the Rest of Society

The *mid-teenage years* are very important because they are ages of both victimization and offending. The peak age of burglary and common thefts in modern societies is 16 or 17 years old.[6] These are also prime ages of shoplifting, fights, minor assaults, and sometimes more serious behaviors. Although many of the victims of youths are other youths, this is not always the case. You can see why society pays a good deal of attention to juvenile offending and worries about whether youths will grow safely to adulthood.

A substantial amount of juvenile offending occurs from 3:00 pm to 4:00 pm on school days, when youths are no longer under adult supervision. Thefts and other problems occur on the route home from school or near youth hangouts. In addition, afternoons bring clashes between youths and merchants, bus drivers, and other adults. Problems include noise and unruliness, some of which is entirely unintentional. Many teenagers are unaware how much they irritate adults and are not actually trying to hurt anybody. So we should not interpret all damage as intentional. Indeed, alcohol and drugs are usually not abused with any intent to harm.

Adolescent Substance Abuse

Adolescent substance abuse is taken seriously by society because it can interfere with growing up and becoming productive. The simplest illustration is the discovery by researchers that students who habitually drink too much alcohol have very low rates of completion. Substance use is consistently associated with dropping out of high school.[7] Substance use also decreases the odds of going on to attend college; and at college, students who drink too much are considerably less likely to complete their degrees.[8] Although some people are functioning alcoholics or find ways to combine social drinking with work and school, others are not so versatile.

Society wants young people to finish school, get a job, have successful sexual partnerships, and become good parents. Substance abuse can interfere with all of these, so society has a reason to contain it. Controlling substance abuse is part of society's effort to protect children, including those who have reached adolescence. Controlling substance abuse also serves to protect adulthood, since substance addictions usually begin during adolescence. We have noted that society's control efforts are full of trial and error. This is surely true for preventing substance abuse or helping people to escape compulsive habits they have formed.

Truancy

A *truant* is someone who skips school without permission. In a modern society truancy diminishes the chances of gaining an education and proceeding to college and a successful career. Some youths disappear from school for days and weeks at a time. School districts usually have a rule for designating a youth as a "*habitual truant,*" notifying parents, and perhaps bringing the juvenile court into the act.[9]

However, habitual truancy is not the whole story. A very large majority of secondary school students skip school for a day here or there. An even larger number skip out for an hour or two, then return to school to keep their absence from being noticed.[10] Youths tend to know which teachers take careful attendance, which classes have substitute teachers, and other chinks in the school system that give them room to skip for a while. While away from school, youths are more likely to smoke or drink, and more likely to commit property crimes, trespass, or break other laws. Moreover, they are missing classes and thus preparing less adequately for their future.

Youths find a wide range of evasive behaviors. Some drop out of school entirely, legally or not. Some are chronic truants, but return to school after a week or two. Some occasionally skip for an hour or two. Some are at school every hour of every day. These patterns relate to society's success in educating youths, preparing them for the future, helping them avoid substance abuse, and minimizing crime events. At some point chronic truancy can become an issue for the justice system. Even those who skip school for a few hours might be caught in the midst of a crime.

Other Status Offenses

Police in some jurisdictions have authority to take truant youths into custody, or at least to take them back to school. Truancy is part of a larger category known as **status offenses**. These are so called because they do not apply to everybody—only those who fit a given status, such as a specific age group.[11] Another common example of a status offense is drinking alcohol underage. Drinking alcohol is legal in general, but that does not apply to those below the age cutoff. Such laws draw lines crudely, not considering that some are more mature at 17 years old than others are at 24. Law is a blunt instrument, missing many nuances about real people.

Legal systems can be very messy in drawing lines by age. In the United States, one can vote at age 18, but cannot legally drink for another three years. You can enter a porn shop at 18 but view porn online at any age with impunity. The age of sexual consent varies by state, as does the age of marriage and school-leaving age. The ages for driving and for smoking are usually lower, but also vary. Each of these represents the disorganized attempt by the legal system to regulate and protect youths.

An excellent example of the contradiction among status offenses is found in Texas strip clubs, where exotic dancers 18 through 20 years old can legally perform sexual dances, with further sexual contact often tolerated by police, but are strictly forbidden from drinking a beer. These strippers are required to wear bracelets designating their age. While banned from drinking beer, they can dance naked and take a customer to the back room with nobody supervising.

Nations vary in their **age of majority**; that is, the age at which somebody is considered an adult. Even within the United States, we find a great deal of inconsistency. It is OK to vote and enter the military at 18, but the drinking age is 21. States differ on when to treat a criminal offender as an adult or a juvenile. The age of sexual consent varies, and this becomes important for deciding whether somebody has taken sexual liberties with a child. These "age of majority" rules are subject to normative variations.

Historical change is also noteworthy. When automobiles first came out, a driver's license was not even required, and it was some years before minimal ages were set in place. Even then it was recognized that farm boys were old enough to run tractors and other motor vehicles by age 12 or 13. As society modernized and the numbers of cars multiplied a hundredfold, the need to regulate young drivers became more compelling.

Societies find different answers, but they all face the same problem—how to protect and supervise youths. That includes minimizing the harm youths do to one another, to themselves, and to the larger society, seeking to nurture them for a successful future.

The 80–20 Rule

The **80–20 rule** states that crime is highly concentrated. For example, 20 percent of the youths commit 80 percent of the crimes. When we study neighborhoods in Part 5, we will also learn that crime is concentrated in rather few city blocks. The point right now is that a minority of offenders do far more than their share of crimes. Authorities are forever seeking to control the minority of frequent offenders in hope of reducing greatly the overall crime rate. Unfortunately, these policy wishes are often disappointing.

To understand that disappointment, suppose that a society is home to a million youths. By the 80–20 rule, some 200,000 youths commit 80 percent of the society's crime. That number is far too large to punish or rehabilitate efficiently. Imagine that only *1 percent* of youths commit 99 percent of the crime—this is only imaginary. In that case, society could focus on "only" 10,000 youths, since it could count on the other 990,000 to avoid crime on their own. You can see why formal crime control creates such burdens for the justice system.

Moreover, it is very difficult to predict early who will commit more crime during adolescence. It is not legal to arrest people because you *think* they may well commit crimes in the future. With most youths committing a few crimes each, society has great difficulty reducing crime by identifying and focusing on a small number of delinquent youths.

Public authorities usually cannot figure out a working policy. By the time youths have completed adolescence, they have already done most of the damage they are going to do. The most active offenders create more trouble per person, but the rest of the adolescent population creates plenty of problems because they are numerous. You can readily understand why the justice system can easily become overwhelmed.

FLASHCARD LIST FOR UNIT 1.4

- 80–20 rule
- Adolescent substance abuse
- Age of majority
- Bullying
- Child neglect
- Habitual truant
- Mid-teenage years
- Sexual abuse of children
- Status offenses
- Truant

DISCUSSION QUESTIONS

1. Why are the mid-teenage years important to understanding crime and victimization?

2. How harshly would you punish status offenses?

Notes

1   Olweus, D. (2003). A profile of bullying at school. *Educational Leadership*, *60*(6), 12–17.

2   Barbaree, H. E., & Marshall, W. L. (Eds.). (2008). *The juvenile sex offender.* New York: Guilford Press.

3   Leclerc, B., & Tremblay, P. (2007). Strategic behavior in adolescent sexual offenses against children: Linking modus operandi to sexual behaviors. *Sexual Abuse: A Journal of Research and Treatment*, *19*(1), 23–41. Leclerc, B., & Felson, M. (2016). Routine activities preceding adolescent sexual abuse of younger children. *Sexual Abuse*, *28*(2), 116–131.

4   Dubowitz, H. (2013). Neglect in children. *Psychiatric Annals*, *43*(3), 106–111; p. 106.

5   For more on the age pattern, see Finkelhor, D., Shattuck, A., Turner, H. A., & Hamby, S. L. (2014). The lifetime prevalence of child sexual abuse and sexual assault assessed in late adolescence. *Journal of Adolescent Health*, *55*(3), 329–333.

6   Jennings, W. G., & Reingle, J. M. (2012). On the number and shape of developmental/life-course violence, aggression, and delinquency trajectories: A state-of-the-art review. *Journal of Criminal Justice*, *40*(6), 472–489.

7   Townsend, L., Flisher, A. J., & King, G. (2007). A systematic review of the relationship between high school dropout and substance use. *Clinical Child and Family Psychology Review*, *10*(4), 295–317.

8   King, K. M., Meehan, B. T., Trim, R. S., & Chassin, L. (2006). Marker or mediator? The effects of adolescent substance use on young adult educational attainment. *Addiction*, *101*(12), 1730–1740.

9   Rocque, M., Jennings, W. G., Piquero, A. R., Ozkan, T., & Farrington, D. P. (2016). The importance of school attendance findings from the Cambridge study in delinquent development on the life-course effects of truancy. *Crime & Delinquency*. Published online July 26. https://doi.org/10.1177/0011128716660520.

10   Dahl, P. (2016). Factors associated with truancy: Emerging adults' recollections of skipping school. *Journal of Adolescent Research, 31*(1), 119–138.

11   Blum, L. N. (2013). Criminals without crime: The dilemma of the status offender. *Pepperdine* Law *Review, 5*(3), Article 4. http://digitalcommons.pepperdine.edu/plr/vol5/iss3/4. (retrieved August 1, 2017).

PERSPECTIVE ON PART 1

Society has a very complicated job to perform. That job not only carries on over the months and years, but occurs every single day. The challenge to society is to maintain order so as not to face an array of problems that could escalate into something worse. Many institutions in society must work to contain these problems. We are struck by how small a role the criminal justice system plays compared to the many other institutions of society—family, school, voluntary and religious associations, informal contacts among people, neighborhoods, and civil authorities. Most of life is lived informally. Even at work and at school, people engage in small group activity and small-scale interactions. Leisure activities almost always occur in group situations and at a small scale. Even in a large bar or restaurant, people sit with those they know. When they try to meet new people, they do so one or two at a time. Some of these are risky situations where disputes and temptations are more likely to arise and get out of hand. This requires society to regulate or at least contain conflicts and sexual urges. It also challenges society to protect property and make sure children can grow up with a reasonable degree of safety.

One of the great ironies of society is that so many good and bad outcomes are intertwined. Sexual temptation helps produce family life, yet can also destroy families. Prosperity allows people to purchase good food, but they might also purchase and use dangerous substances. Sports competition yields good health and team spirit, but also generates fights. These ironies were articulated by Judge Noah S. "Soggy" Sweat, Jr. in 1952 at an evening banquet:

I want you to know that I do not shun controversy. On the contrary, I will take a stand on any issue at any time, regardless of how fraught with controversy it might be. You have asked me how I feel about whiskey. All right, this is how I feel about whiskey.

If when you say "whiskey" you mean the devil's brew, the poison scourge, the bloody monster that defiles innocence, dethrones reason, destroys the home, creates misery and poverty, yea, literally takes the bread from the mouths of little children; if you mean the evil drink that topples the Christian man and woman from the pinnacle of righteous, gracious living into the bottomless pit of degradation, and despair, and shame, and helplessness, and hopelessness—then certainly I am against it.

But, if when you say "whiskey" you mean the oil of conversation, the philosophic wine, the ale that is consumed when good fellows get together, that puts a song in their hearts and laughter on their lips, and the warm glow of contentment in their eyes; if you mean Christmas cheer; if you mean the stimulating drink that puts the spring in the old gentleman's step on a frosty, crispy morning; if you mean the drink which enables a man to magnify his joy, and his happiness, and to forget, if only for a little while, life's great tragedies, and heartaches, and sorrows; if you mean that drink the sale of which pours into our treasuries untold millions of dollars, which are used to provide tender care for our little crippled children, our blind, our deaf, our dumb, our pitiful aged and infirm; to build highways and hospitals and schools—then certainly I am for it.

This is my stand. I will not retreat from it. I will not compromise.[1]

Society is repeatedly challenged to find a balance between party and quiet, drinking and temperance, control and liberty, speedy justice and caution. Society is challenged to limit the spread of risky situations and to manage those which are present. Society seeks to contain disputes and sexual urges, to protect property and youths. This is a highly imperfect trial-and-error process. Societies and periods of history vary in the way these problems are addressed, and the diversity of legal systems proves that point. Yet the criminal justice system has an important role in backing up the other institutions of society. To understand criminal justice, we must keep reminding ourselves that its role is only one part of a larger picture, as society seeks to maintain peaceful relationships among its citizens. In Part 2, we will present four types of control that society uses to address these challenges.

Main Points of Part 1

- Part 1 began with the general philosophical "problem of order," stated by Thomas Hobbes in 1651.

- We broke that problem down into four challenges facing every society. We then made it clear that society must contain the problems that challenge it. These problems are not "solvable," but they can be contained or limited. Failure to do so means that risky situations can lead to criminal events that interfere with the enjoyment of life.

- Society's first challenge is to contain disputes and prevent them from escalating into something more serious, including a criminal event.

- The second challenge is to limit acting on sexual temptations and assure that citizens do not harm others sexually.

- Society's third challenge is to minimize conflicts over property, often using civil law, but occasionally depending on criminal law as well.

- Society's fourth challenge is to make sure children grow up safely, avoiding offending and victimization. This includes avoidance of alcohol and drug abuse and a variety of dangerous behaviors.

Note

1   Quoted in: Safire, W. (1997). *Lend me your ears: Great speeches in history*. New York: W. W. Norton & Company; p. 955.

PART 2

Four Types of Crime Control

Part 1 noted the sorts of harms that society seeks to minimize. We now review four methods that society uses to minimize those harms. In presenting these four types of control, we also introduce some important criminological theories.

Some political leaders proclaim a "zero-tolerance policy," promising that they will prosecute "to the fullest extent of the law." Such promises are impossible to keep for these reasons:

- Real people have strong incentives and opportunities to depart from rules.

- Police and the justice system cannot enforce all laws all the time.

- Modern social life includes far too many rude incidents, sexual infractions, property challenges, and youth difficulties to allow perfect enforcement.

That's why society has to give up utopian promises and do its best in an imperfect world.

Society's control methods can be summed up in four categories,[1] depicted in Figure 2a as a series of dams that seek to hold back the daily flow of temptations, annoyances, and harms. As problems "flow" from left to right, social institutions seek to hold them back in the sequence depicted:

1. *Personal controls* are depicted by the first "dam." This involves teaching self-control to every individual. It also involves teaching people the basic moral standards of society.

2. When personal controls fail, society tries to restrain misbehavior using **social controls**, as depicted by the second dam. These controls require a social bond to other people.

3. When personal and social controls fail, society can employ **situational controls**, as depicted by the third dam. These controls discourage rule-breaking on a very practical basis in everyday settings.

4. When personal, social, and situational controls all fall short, society turns to its last resort. The **formal controls** of the justice system become applicable.

Figure 2a sums up a good deal of information about how society seeks to contain its problems and meet its challenges.

Delivering these four types of control is a huge task involving diverse institutions of society. Personal and social controls are instilled by families, small groups, and schools. Situational controls emerge as businesses, architects, builders, and government agencies design and manage stores, buildings, and public places. Formal controls are applied by criminal justice agencies, which may call on other organizations to help.

Formal controls, including police actions, are expensive and intrusive. That's why society uses formal controls sparingly—a last resort after the other major techniques

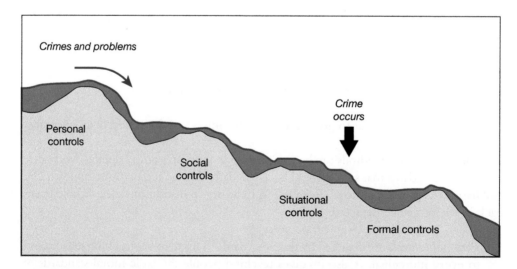

FIGURE 2A
Society's Four Control Processes

have failed. *Crime represents a **failure of personal, social, and situational controls**.*[2] The prior sentence is very important, for it helps you understand that the justice system fits into a much larger control process. As you learn more about the justice system, try to think of it within this broader perspective. Again, the justice system only applies after the first three types of control have failed. For another example, consider the incest taboo discussed in Part 1. Society uses personal, social, and situational controls to prevent family members from having sex with one another, hoping that the criminal justice system will never be asked to step in.

Society injects crime controls at several stages of the human life cycle. Problems can be traced to each stage. Figure 2b presents *five stages of crime and control* to help organize our discussion. Reading from left to right:

1. The stage *before birth* involves prenatal damage to fetuses and genetic factors that could contribute to crime.

2. The *early childhood* stage is the period between birth and puberty. This is when personal controls are instilled.

3. *Adolescence* includes the teenage years from puberty to the onset of adulthood. This is when social controls are front and center.

4. *Near the time of the crime* refers to the day or hour a crime might occur. This is the period in which situational controls most apply.[3]

5. *After the crime event* refers to the period after a crime has been committed. That's when formal controls are asserted.

These four control processes and five stages cover quite a bit of theoretical ground. Yet they have something in common. All four processes seek to make crime inconvenient. Another way to put it is that society tries to make compliance with its

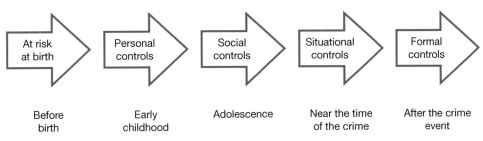

FIGURE 2B
Crime Control over Five Stages of Life

rules relatively convenient and normal. It teaches everybody its moral rules, hoping to constrain people to follow them. It teaches them self-control so they can comply on their own. It builds social bonds and then uses a social control strategy so people check and balance one another. Society institutes situational designs that make it difficult to circumvent the rules and easier to comply with them. Society creates a justice system to add further inconvenience for those who will not comply.

We now turn to Unit 2.1, which details the influences of the prenatal period and early development of personal controls. Then, Unit 2.2 will discuss the importance of social controls for checks and balances that are especially important during the teen years. Unit 2.3 will look at situational controls against crime. Finally, Unit 2.4 will look at formal controls applied after a crime occurs.

FLASHCARD LIST FOR PART 2: FOUR TYPES OF CRIME CONTROL

- Failure of control processes
- Five stages of crime and control
- Formal controls
- Personal controls
- Situational controls
- Social controls

QUESTIONS ADDRESSED IN PART 2

1. How does society try to instill controls during childhood?

2. What control processes apply most during adolescence?

3. Why is the period near the time of the crime important?

4. Which control processes become most relevant *after* a crime has occurred?

Notes

1   For perspective, see Kornhauser, R. R. (1978). *Social sources of delinquency: An appraisal of analytic models*. Chicago: University of Chicago Press. Weisburd, D., Groff, E. R., & Yang, S. M. (2014). Understanding and controlling hot spots of crime: The importance of formal and informal social controls. *Prevention Science, 15*(1), 31–43.

2   Reiss, A. J. (1951). Delinquency as the failure of personal and social controls. *American Sociological Review, 16*(2), 196–207. Groff, E. R. (2015). Informal social control and crime events. *Journal of Contemporary Criminal Justice, 31*(1), 90–106. Braga, A. A., & Clarke, R. V. (2014). Explaining high-risk concentrations of crime in the city: Social disorganization, crime opportunities, and important next steps. *Journal of Research in Crime and Delinquency, 51*(4), 480–498.

3   Newman, G., & Clarke, R. V. (2016). *Rational choice and situational crime prevention: Theoretical foundations*. Abingdon, U.K.: Routledge.

Unit 2.1 Personal Controls

Controls begin the first time a parent says "no-no-no" to a toddler and continue with teachers monitoring and scolding school children, with adults chiding teenagers, and with police officers telling a group of youths to quiet down. Controls are not always negative—they also employ human warmth and kindly guidance. Whatever the methods, controls are always imperfect.[1]

Were these tasks easy, society would have little to worry about. Children would do their homework, go to school on time, and remain there until dismissal. People would tell no lies, and they would eat the right foods. Substance abuse would vanish. Public places would be well managed. Nobody would steal. Sexual misbehavior would be absent. The justice system would not be needed. Unfortunately, this ideal is far from the reality, requiring society's control processes to work hard every day.

Before Birth

A child's criminal potential might begin before birth. As noted in the introduction to Part 2, the first stage of the life course, the stage *before birth*, covers the prenatal period—the period before birth when genetic makeup is determined and prenatal exposures take place. That period sets up the reality at birth, how each of us starts out in life.

More than a century ago, an Italian physician named **Cesare Lombroso** offered a theory of crime based on the "***born criminal***," whose congenital defects also produced physical differences from other people.[2] Early genetic theories were linked to racism, and they falsely portrayed offenders as a distinct population separate from the rest of humanity. Lombroso himself soon realized that he needed to elaborate beyond a simple genetic theory. Over time criminologists have learned that there are numerous pathways towards crime.

Modern biosocial approaches are much more specific than in the past. Possible pathways to crime before birth include fetal damage[3] and genetic predisposition. A fetus can be damaged by lead poisoning or by the mother's alcohol intake or other substance abuse.[4] That's why beer cans and whiskey bottles have warning labels for pregnant women, for fear that the fetus will be harmed and behavioral problems could result.

Genetic Factors

Today's genetic research views crime as an individual *disorder* influenced in part by genes.[5] Genetic research *accepts the strong role of social environments* and avoids racial attributions and grand theorizing. It recognizes ***genetic misconceptions*** about crime, including these four:

1. *First misconception.* A single gene is directly responsible for criminal behavior.

2. *Second misconception.* All crime is genetically determined.

3. *Third misconception.* Each person's criminal acts can be predicted genetically.

4. *Fourth misconception.* Genetic factors replace environmental explanations of crime.[6]

Recent brain research supports this argument that at least some young adolescents with serious antisocial behavior problems have different brain structures than other youths.[7] However, you will learn in Part 4 that brain development during adolescence also tends to produce risky behaviors for most youths of all races and socioeconomic groups. Risky behavior is a normal possibility for adolescence, even though a subset of youths may face extra risks.

Alcohol researchers offer us another possible genetic pathway towards crime for some people. ***Genetic background*** probably accounts for a good deal of the risk for becoming an alcoholic.[8] To be sure, not all alcoholics commit crime; not all crime is committed by alcoholics; and not all excess drinking is carried out by alcoholics. It appears that hundreds of genes are associated with excessive drinking behavior. It seems impractical to apply gene therapy or to develop a pill to stop alcoholism given this complexity.[9]

Although fetal and genetic factors play a role for at least some offenders, this textbook places much more emphasis on social pathways emerging after birth. ***Simply being human*** may be the most important risk factor for crime. "Normal" people can still be tempted to steal something, get angry, drink too much, or misbehave during adolescence or later on in life. When faced with strong temptations, normal human beings are capable of breaking rules.[10] However, some people create extra problems for society.

Psychopaths

Psychopaths are people who cannot establish relationships or love other people. They are egocentric and manipulative. Their characteristic trait is lack of empathy—they cannot feel for the suffering of others. That makes it easier for them to harm others and ignore the suffering they inflict.[11] Psychopaths engage in amoral and criminal behavior and are often more violent than other offenders.

Except in extreme cases, it is difficult to classify people as psychopaths or to use that category to predict their crime patterns.[12] Most criminal behavior, including violence, is probably committed by people who cannot be classified as psychopaths and, indeed, are not seen as belonging to any special population.

However, special populations are important for prisons and local jails. About one in four state prison inmates have a recent history of a diagnosed mental problem, and more than half have some history or symptoms of mental issues. Such problems are even more prevalent in local jails.[13] Criminologists have long tried to predict crime participation from mental health symptoms. Unfortunately, a large portion of the *general* population also has symptoms of poor mental health at some point in life without necessarily committing crime. This has been confirmed in the United States,[14] Australia,[15] Germany,[16] and the Netherlands.[17] It is difficult to predict crime participation in advance based on mental health issues. That's why criminologists study crime and control processes in the larger population, starting at a young age.

Early Childhood

Criminologists have long paid attention to sources of crime causation that occur during early childhood. Their inquiries consider whether the adult world mistreats children and whether that world instills personal controls at an early age. The mistreatment issue has received a good deal of attention. Children who have been abused or neglected during early childhood are especially likely to become violent later. This is called the **cycle of violence**, because it passes violence from generation to generation in a nongenetic fashion.[18]

Personal controls are instilled in early childhood. These controls help a person withstand temptations and to act with the future in mind. They include **moral teachings** and **self-control**. Moral teachings set the standards that are used by society's other control processes. Religion and morality are intertwined, but rules of proper behavior go beyond religion. They include many instructions about how we are supposed to behave in daily life.

Moral Teachings

Parents, teachers, and other adults try very early to teach children both specific and general rules of behavior. They tell young children to get to school on time, sit quietly, learn, do homework, and play well with other kids. They instruct them not to use bad words, tell lies, steal things, or hit other children. They say to eat vegetables first, ice cream later. They teach both specific rules and general moral principles. Shouldn't that be enough guidance for life?

Unfortunately, researchers have found that moral *teachings* do not simply produce moral *behavior*. An important psychological study found that many people faced with temptation violate their own rules; after that violation, they begin to loosen those same rules.[19] Part 4 explains why moral teachings are often insufficient for withstanding the influences and temptations of delinquency. Yet moral rules are important for society to impart.

Morality can influence behavior through two quite different mechanisms, internal and external. By the internal mechanism, society teaches people moral rules when they are very young. Society hopes these rules will become internalized and compel good behavior throughout the life cycle. (This internal mechanism is discussed in Part 4, which considers the learning theories of Sutherland and Akers.)

Moral teachings also can control behavior externally, with people pushing each other to follow the rules. In other words, moral teachings can create a *checks and balances* system in everyday life. Everybody knows they are not supposed to do certain things, and people can put social pressure on one another to follow the rules. Individuals who violate rules when they are on their own may follow those same rules when others are watching. Later in Part 2 we present social control theory, which reflects this idea. Yet society hopes that people will learn to regulate themselves. That's why society seeks to instill personal controls in early childhood, hoping people will take these rules with them through the life cycle.

Resisting Temptations

Every day we might be tempted to go back to sleep and skip class or work, to eat fattening foods, to say or do something harmful to another person. Faced with temptation, each of us might forget the larger picture or future consequences. Fortunately, self-control is possible, as we shall see. One illustration has to do with forbidden speech, "when the brain tames the tongue."[20] In an experimental study, subjects apparently were able to censor their use of swear words before uttering them. However, some people were unable to hold back before saying something forbidden under some circumstances. We shall be exploring how self-control processes apply to different aspects of life, but especially crime and delinquency. The idea of self-control will help us address rule-breaking within a larger perspective. Why does anybody keep studying or working without heading out to play? ***Resisting temptation*** is an important skill, even at a young age, since children are expected to sit quietly in school and play well with other children. Adult society tries to teach young children patience.

The Marshmallow Experiment

In 1960, ***Walter Mischel*** carried out a simple experiment with small children that helps us understand self-control—the ***Stanford Marshmallow Experiment***.[21] Mischel offered each child a choice of one marshmallow *now* or two marshmallows *if you can wait 15 minutes*. Some children quickly took the one and gave up the other. Other children held out as long as they could, then gave in and settled for only one marshmallow. Some managed to resist the full 15 minutes and receive a second marshmallow—their reward for patience and self-control.

Self-control is imparted by age six or seven and is clearly associated with better school performance. Mischel also learned that self-control helped predict success much later in life.[22] As Part 2 progresses, you will see how self-control inhibits various bad behaviors, including crime and delinquency. The importance of self-control reaches even further and wider.

A General Theory of Self-Control

Criminological theorists ***Michael Gottfredson and Travis Hirschi*** subsumed criminal behavior within a ***general theory of self-control***.[23] (We will talk about earlier work by Hirschi in the next unit.) Low self-control not only makes a person more likely to commit a crime, but also contributes to bad performance in school and family life. It leads to bad eating habits, substance abuse, and sexual risk-taking.[24] In many aspects of life, lack of self-control keeps a person from performing well.

Additional negative outcomes are also likely. Low self-control makes it harder to control one's thoughts, manage emotions, handle unwanted impulses, drive a car safely, sustain attention, make good decisions, give a good impression to others, turn the other cheek when others are nasty, keep calm when a customer is rude, or avoid overreaction to a partner's bad behavior. More broadly, low self-control interferes with the ability to hold a job, to complete a university degree, or to avoid unwanted pregnancies.[25] Most important for this book, low self-control has been linked to crime in 32 different nations across the world.[26]

Self-control directly applies to the four challenges facing every society, as discussed in Part 1. People low in self-control are more likely to

- get into disputes and to escalate those disputes;

- give in to their sexual urges and violate society's taboos;

- steal or vandalize property or trespass on the rights of others; and

- have trouble growing up safely and helping their own children to do the same.

Self-control also applies to reading the books assigned in a college class and showing up for all the lectures. Indeed, self-control theory tells us a lot about ourselves and others. It also shows that relatively minor "infractions" (having an extra scoop of ice cream) and major crimes (committing murder) are part of a larger control process. Extreme criminals are not from a different species, but rather have more failures in controlling human weaknesses that apply to all of us.

The concept of self-control is clear, simple, and general. Self-control theory organizes a vast range of information for a wide variety of human behaviors and shortcomings. Yet self-control theory offers no panacea for society. Society can try to teach self-control at an early age, but cannot magically instill self-control for all.

Pleasure Now, Harm Later

Two basic imbalances impair the control process. First, society's rewards and punishments are out of sync. Many behaviors produce pleasure in the short run, but harm people in the long run. Drinking alcohol produces immediate pleasure, but alcoholism arrives slowly and liver damage might take decades to become manifest.[27] Pizza and beer taste good at the table, but it may take a month to notice you are getting fat. Drug abuse starts small and does little harm at first, but can become addictive later. The ultimate example is for those who believe in the afterlife: Few people consider daily what St. Peter would decide after they die.

Society's second basic imbalance is that rewards come much more often than punishments.[28] You can drive home influenced by alcohol 100 times before getting picked up by the police or having an accident. A burglar can enter myriad houses before finally getting caught. Someone can make obnoxious statements for a year before getting punched in the nose. This holds for many behaviors, making it easy for people to disregard the rules. You can see why self-control has so much work to do.

Self-Control Is Work

Roy Baumeister and his psychologist colleagues greatly sharpened our understanding of self-control as the ability to *control or override* one's thoughts, emotions, and urges.[29] Baumeister explained self-control as

- a very beneficial part of personality, allowing a person the flexibility necessary to attain goals; and

- an executive process, requiring a person to exert *extra effort* to override what may be very natural urges.

Self-control is hard work. Baumeister's research concluded that *self-control is like a muscle that gets tired in the short run.* If we tire out our self-controlling muscle, the resulting fatigue makes self-control more difficult to apply soon after. Baumeister carried out experiments that had two steps. In the first step, the subject of the experiment was confronted with a tiring self-control task, such as solving a difficult puzzle. In the second step, the subject was given another self-control task, such as resisting tasty chocolate. The results were clear: Depleting willpower in the first task leaves less self-control remaining for second task.[30] The Baumeister team also gave people lemonade to sip during their tasks, discovering that self-control goes up in the short run when glucose level rises.[31]

Imagine yourself with a long shift at work, an obnoxious boss, and many unpleasant customers. At the beginning of the shift, you are polite and follow all the rules. As your shift wears on, the job wears you down. You get tired and perhaps your glucose levels fall. Your self-control energy is depleted and finally you blurt out the wrong words, getting yourself in trouble with others, perhaps with co-workers or your boss. That is how daily life tests a person's self-control level. Yet we cannot assume self-control to be fixed for each person.

Variability in Self-Control

University students (like other populations) vary in their self-control levels. Some undergraduate students are especially low in self-control, drinking far too much and skipping class far too often.[32] These students may fail their classes and have to leave university. At the other extreme are super-students who take honors courses and go on to achieve advanced degrees.

Most students are not so extreme. Many do some studying and try to attend most classes, but cannot resist a late evening out with friends. Self-control is a human process,

Time spent at different self-control levels

FIGURE 2C
Comparing Two Students and How Their Self-Control Varies over the Week

hence an inconsistent process. Figure 2c depicts two students, each with mixed levels of self-control. Jane spends more time than Janice at high levels of self-control. Jane is able to study more *consistently*, but Janice can control herself long enough to cram for a test. At least she can spend *some* time studying.[33] Jane parties only on weekends, while Janice parties several nights a week and then crams the night before an exam. The two students differ, but still overlap.[34]

Summing up, self-control helps people perform better, but it is not a perfect process. It is subject to fatigue and depletion, and is challenged anew. Real social situations draw people away from their own rules and goals, and they cannot easily avoid all tempting situations or all social life. That's why our study of society's controls must look beyond discrete individuals.

FLASHCARD LIST FOR UNIT 2.1

- Baumeister, Roy
- Born criminal
- Cycle of violence
- General theory of self-control
- Genetic background

- Genetic misconceptions
- Gottfredson, Michael and Travis Hirschi
- Lombroso, Cesare
- Mischel, Walter
- Moral teachings

- Psychopaths
- Resisting temptations
- Self-control
- Simply being human
- Stanford Marshmallow Experiment

DISCUSSION QUESTIONS

1. How do marshmallows relate to crime?

2. Why is self-control so broadly important?

Notes

1   Ross, E. A. (2009 [1903]). *Social control: A survey of the foundations of order*. Piscataway, NJ: Transaction Publishers.

2   Lombroso, C. (2006 [1899]). *Criminal man*. Durham, NC: Duke University Press.

3   Beaver, K. M., & Wright, J. P. (2005). Evaluating the effects of birth complications on low self-control in a sample of twins. *International Journal of Offender Therapy and Comparative Criminology, 49*(4), 450–471.

4   Behnke, M., & Smith, V. C. (2013). Prenatal substance abuse: Short- and long-term effects on the exposed fetus. American Academy of Pediatrics Technical Report. *Pediatrics, 131*(3), e1009–e1024.

5   Raine, A. (2002). Biosocial studies of antisocial and violent behavior in children and adults: A review. *Journal of Abnormal Child Psychology, 30*(4), 311–326. Raine, A. (2013). *The anatomy of violence: The biological roots of crime*. New York: Vintage.

6   Raine, A. (2013). *The psychopathology of crime: Criminal behavior as a clinical disorder*. Amsterdam: Elsevier.

7   Fairchild, G., Toschi, N., Sully, K., Sonuga-Barke, E. J., Hagan, C. C., . . . & Passamonti, L. (2016). Mapping the structural organization of the brain in conduct disorder: Replication of findings in two independent samples. *Journal of Child Psychology and Psychiatry, 57*(9), 1018–1026.

8   Tawa, E. A., Hall, S. D., & Lohoff, F. W. (2016). Overview of the genetics of alcohol use disorder. *Alcohol and Alcoholism, 51*(5), 507–514.

9   Lo, C.-L., Lossie, A. C., Liang, T., Liu, Y., Xuei, X., . . . & Muir, W. M. (2016). High resolution genomic scans reveal genetic architecture controlling alcohol preference in bidirectionally selected rat model. *PLOS Genetics, 12*(8), 1–23.

10   Pinker, S. (2002). *The blank slate: The modern denial of human nature*. New York: Viking.

11   Jolliffe, D. (2014). Empathy and offending. In G. Bruinsma & D. Weisburd (Eds.), *Encyclopedia of criminology and criminal justice*, pp. 1338–1344. New York: Springer.

12   Jones, S. (2008). Juvenile psychopathy and judicial decision making: An empirical analysis of an ethical dilemma. *Behavioral Sciences and the Law, 26*(2), 151–165.

13   James, D. J., & Glaze, L. E. (2006). *Mental health problems of prison and jail inmates*. Washington, DC: Bureau of Justice Statistics.

14   Kessler, R. C., McGonagle, K. A., Zhao, S., Nelson, C. B., Hughes, M., . . . & Kendler, K. S. (1994). Lifetime and 12-month prevalence of DSM-III-R psychiatric disorders in the United States: Results from the National Comorbidity Survey. *Archives of General Psychiatry, 51*(1), 8–19.

15   Henderson, S., Andrews, G., & Hall, W. (2000). Australia's mental health: An overview of the general population survey. *Australian and New Zealand Journal of Psychiatry, 34*(2), 197–205.

16   Jacobi, F., Wittchen, H. U., Holting, C., Höfler, M., Pfister, H., . . . & Lieb, R. (2004). Prevalence, co-morbidity and correlates of mental disorders in the general population: Results from the German Health Interview and Examination Survey (GHS). *Psychological Medicine, 34*(4), 597–611.

17   Bijl, R. V., Ravelli, A., & Van Zessen, G. (1998). Prevalence of psychiatric disorder in the general population: Results of The Netherlands Mental Health Survey and Incidence Study. *Social Psychiatry and Psychiatric Epidemiology, 33*(12), 587–595.

18   Widom, C. S. (1989). The cycle of violence. *Science, 244*(4901), 160–166.

19 Mills, J. (1958). Changes in moral attitudes following temptation. *Journal of Personality, 26*(4), 517–531.

20 Severens, E., Janssens, I., Kühn, S., Brass, M., & Hartsuiker, R. J. (2011). When the brain tames the tongue: Covert editing of inappropriate language. *Psychophysiology, 48*(9), 1252–1257.

21 Mischel, W., Shoda, Y., & Rodriguez, M. L. (1989). Delay of gratification in children. *Science, 244*(4907), 933–938.

22 Mischel, W. (2014). *The marshmallow test: Understanding self-control and how to master it*. New York: Random House.

23 Gottfredson, M., & Hirschi, T. (1990). *A general theory of crime*. Stanford, CA: Stanford University Press. Beaver, K. M., Wright, J. P., & DeLisi, M. (2007). Self-control as an executive function: Reformulating Gottfredson and Hirschi's parental socialization thesis. *Criminal Justice and Behavior, 34*(10), 1345–1361.

24 Barlow, H. D. (1991). Explaining crimes and analogous acts, or the unrestrained will grab at pleasure whenever they can. *Journal of Criminal Law and Criminology, 82*(1), 229–242.

25 Baumeister, R. F., Heatherton, T. F., & Tice, D. M. (1994). *Losing control: How and why people fail at self-regulation*. New York: Academic Press. Hirschi, T., & Gottfredson, M. R. (2000). In defense of self-control. *Theoretical Criminology, 4*(1), 55–69.

26 Rebellon, C. J., Straus, M. A., & Medeiros, R. (2008). Self-control in global perspective: An empirical assessment of Gottfredson and Hirschi's general theory within and across 32 national settings. *European Journal of Criminology, 5*(3), 331–361.

27 Reynolds, B., & Schiffbauer, R. (2005). Delay of gratification and delay discounting: A unifying feedback model of delay-related impulsive behavior. *The Psychological Record, 55*(3), 439–460.

28 Matsueda, R. L., Kreager, D. A., & Huizinga, D. (2006). Deterring delinquents: A rational choice model of theft and violence. *American Sociological Review, 71*(1), 95–122.

29 Vohs, K. D., & Baumeister, R. F. (Eds.). (2011). *Handbook of self-regulation: Research, theory, and applications*. New York: Guilford. De Ridder, D., Lensvelt-Mulders, G., Finkenauer, C., Stok, F. M., & Baumeister, R. F. (2012). A meta-analysis of how trait self-control relates to a wide range of behaviors. *Personality and Social Psychology Review, 16*(1), 76–99.

30 Baumeister refers to this process as "ego depletion."

31 For a challenge to Baumeister's findings, see: Carter, E. C., Kofler, L. M., Forster, D. E., & McCullough, M. E. (2015). A series of meta-analytic tests of the depletion effect: Self-control does not seem to rely on a limited resource. *Journal of Experimental Psychology: General, 144*(4), 796–815. We have decided to stick with the greater body of diverse evidence amassed by Baumeister and colleagues.

32 Gibbs, J. J., & Giever, D. (1995). Self-control and its manifestations among university students: An empirical test of Gottfredson and Hirschi's general theory. *Justice Quarterly, 12*(2), 231–255.

33 Schouwenburg, H. C., & Groenewoud, J. (2001). Study motivation under social temptation: Effects of trait procrastination. *Personality and Individual Differences, 30*(2), 229–240.

34 Hartwig, M. K., & Dunlosky, J. (2012). Study strategies of college students: Are self-testing and scheduling related to achievement? *Psychonomic Bulletin and Review, 19*(1), 126–134.

UNIT 2.2 Social Controls

Charles–Louis Montesquieu explained in 1748 that "every man invested with power is apt to abuse it . . . it is necessary from the very nature of things that power should be a check to power."[1]

Montesquieu's theory was used to build ***checks and balances*** into the United States Constitution. We can also find checks and balances in everyday life, as people prompt one another and remind one another to follow the rules. These ***reminders*** are especially important during the teenage years, when youths increase their autonomy and encounter additional temptations and opportunities to break rules. That's why additional controls are attempted by society. While society reduces these tangible controls and ongoing supervision, it increasingly relies on intangible controls, such as the ***social bonds*** youths have with parents and others.

Social control theory considers how people influence one another, thereby discouraging delinquent behavior. It begins by rejecting the basic question asked by many criminologists: Why do criminals commit crime? Instead, social control theorists believe that every person experiences temptations and could commit a crime. They ask a second question instead: Why doesn't *everybody* commit crime? Everybody likes to get something for nothing. Every small child in the store quickly reaches for candy without paying the cashier. Every teenager discovers illicit possibilities. Every adult likes something fattening, is tempted to drive fast, drink more, or get angry. Temptations come at us fast every day.[2]

Professor ***Travis Hirschi***—the most important social control theorist—answers the second question as follows: Normally a person is entwined in relationships with others, which can be summed up as "the social bond."[3] Someone with a strong social bond is less likely to break society's rules. Someone with a weak social bond is more likely to break those rules. (You recall we talked about Hirschi's later work with Gottfredson in the previous unit.) So the question to ask is: How strong is a person's social bond? The social bond includes these elements:

- *commitments* to the future;

- *attachments* to other people;

- *involvements* in conventional activities; and

- strength of *beliefs* in conventional rules.

An example of a *commitment* to the future is the wish to graduate from university. Finishing high school, going to college, getting on the basketball team, getting a good job—all of these are examples of future goals. These commitments give society a handle with which it can "control" you. For example, your university can pressure you to pay library fines by withholding course credits that you need for your future.

An example of an *attachment* to another person is the fear that your mother will find out what you did, or that a favorite teacher, friendly adult, or friends will disapprove. An example of an *involvement* in conventional activity is being so busy with school and job that there's no time left for partying. Working mothers find themselves so busy with job, family, and the man in their lives that little time remains to break rules or laws.

Hirschi's fourth element, *belief*, does not claim that delinquents have their own value system. They believe the same rules (and that crime is bad), but they feel a weaker commitment to those rules. Professor Hirschi was not very clear on this topic, but in Part 4 we further explain how youths circumvent their own rules.

To sum up, the social bond is strong when somebody combines future commitments, personal attachments, conventional involvements, and more commitment to conventional rules. The social bond is weak for someone free from these obligations, making it easier to break those rules. When the social bond is weak, the checks and balances system in society cannot function very well.

Temptation vs. Bonding

We can understand individual offending in terms of a tug of war: Temptations pull a person towards crime, while the social bond pulls in the other direction. If the social bond is strong enough, the crime does not occur. If the temptation is strong enough, the social bond can be overcome. However, society can reassert its rules for those with a strong bond.

What about those with a weak bond to society? Suppose that a youth in secondary school is caught drinking in the park nearby during school hours. Box 2a imagines a dialogue that could take place afterwards between a school official and the youth. The school official has a difficult youth whose weak social bond makes it hard to

> **BOX 2A Fictional Dialogue between School Official and Youth Who Violated School Rules**
>
> | Dialogue elements | Theoretical implications |
> | --- | --- |
> | *Official*: You won't graduate if you keep misbehaving. | Official trying to invoke future commitments as social control. |
> | *Youth*: What do I care about graduating? | Youth clearly not responding to social control effort. |
> | *Official*: You've been very bad. I'm going to call your mother. | Official trying to invoke attachment to others for social control purposes. |
> | *Youth*: Go ahead and call her. I don't care. | Again, this youth is not responding to the usual social control mechanisms. |
> | *Official*: You won't be able to participate in any school sports or activities. | Official is invoking conventional involvements as a social control method. |
> | *Youth*: I don't plan to anyway. | Official is not getting anywhere in trying to invoke informal social control. |

deliver social control. Read the dialogue and imagine yourself in both roles. A more controllable student would have worried about graduation, begged the school official not to call home, and dreaded exclusion from school sports or other desired activities.[4]

To understand social control theory, you should *think small*. Usual daily activities occur in rather small groups of people who know each other rather well. Even within a larger school or workplace, people interact in small groups. Each person has specific ties to others, has specific goals for the future, and is absorbed in specific localized activities. Ask yourself: Is there anybody I must not disappoint? Is there any goal or activity I must not ruin? The answers will help you recognize your own social bond.

This raises an interesting set of questions: Is the social bond powerful enough to control a youth *even when adults are absent*? Or does social control depend on the *proximity* of relevant adults? Your textbook authors believe the latter to be true for more youths than not. We believe that the social bond is important but that proximity of parents is even more important. We will discuss this in greater detail in Part 4. The next section illustrates how Japanese society seeks to apply social control to teenagers.

Teenagers in Japan vs. the United States

Japanese society really knows how to keep teenagers busy. Japanese youths spend an average of 42 more days in school per year (220 vs. 178 in the United States). After formal school is over in the afternoon, nine out of ten Japanese youths begin a second school day. They spend approximately four additional hours each day in other "cram schools" to prepare for rigorous entrance exams, as shown in Figure 2d.

You can see from the figure that the *teenagers in Japan* (upper bar) have their afternoons filled with extra schooling, while those in America (lower bar) are unassigned when school is over. Better Japanese students are sent to advanced programs; others go to remedial programs; others focus on learning piano, sports, or other skills or clubs. Japanese students stay with the same skill program or club year after year. With stable and prolonged participation under adult control, parents know where they are most of the day. Many Japanese youths even go to extra classes on Saturday.[5]

Figure 2d understates how occupied Japanese youths can be. To get to school and to cram school, and later to get home, they often have to take long train and bus rides, often with several changes.[6] Many youths leave home before 7:00 am and arrive home 12 hours later, occupied for most of the time in between.[7] They ride public transportation with people of different ages (in contrast to American students who would ride school buses dominated by adolescents). Japanese youths wear distinct uniforms to identify their specific school so misbehavior can be reported back. Of course, they might become rowdier as they move farther from where their school uniform would be recognized.[8]

Figure 2d shows that American youths often have a four-hour gap between the end of school and time at home.[9] Although Japanese youths are far from perfect—often smoking cigarettes and avoiding homework—the adult world has monopolized much of their time and hence contained their delinquent tendencies.

The impact of school time on crime can be demonstrated in other ways and for other nations.

- Those American states that have elevated their minimum school dropout age have experienced declines in both property and violent crime arrest rates for ages 16 through 18.[10]

- When Sweden extended compulsory schooling from seven to nine years, that directly increased attendance at high-crime ages. This reform strongly reduced the probability of committing property crimes but not violent crimes.[11]

- The Kobe earthquake decimated parts of Japan in 1995, damaging 3,885 schools and thousands of homes and resulting in many parent or teacher casualties. It took a year or more to restore schooling for some youths, whose violent crime

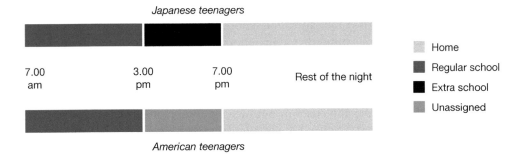

Japanese teenagers

7.00 am   3.00 pm   7.00 pm   Rest of the night

Home
Regular school
Extra school
Unassigned

American teenagers

FIGURE 2D

Comparing Japanese and American Teenagers, How Weekday Activities Are Assigned by Adults

participation increased over those who were quickly put back in school. There was no impact on property crime.[12]

- In England and Wales, significant property crime reductions resulted from raising the mandatory age for remaining in school.[13]

- When the Chilean government extended schooling from half days to full days, youth crime declined and girls from poor families were less likely to get pregnant.[14]

- Other American studies have examined days when teachers were in training[15] or on strike,[16] measuring the impact on juvenile crime. Interestingly, these studies found that the level of reported property crimes committed by juveniles decreased on school days. However, violent crimes went up on school days, indicating that access to peers can make crime worse.

The last finding reminds us to pay close attention to adult presences and ability to control or influence adolescent situations. Adult control varies form one segment of the school day to another, which in turn can influence levels of crime and delinquency. The next section links two theories—social control theory and routine activity theory,[17] considering adults' trial-and-error process as they seek to keep their teenagers out of trouble.

American Parents Also Try to Guide Teenage Situations

Theoretically, American parents could follow the Japanese pattern, scheduling their teenagers so tightly that they have no room or time to hang out together or to escape adult influence. However, most American parents are less systematic than Japanese parents in managing their teenagers' time. They often try to encourage a safer mix of friends[18] as well as part-time jobs and after-school participation in approved activities and sports.[19] Many parents hope that after-school activities will enhance responsible development and reduce problem behaviors.[20] However, the results of criminological research are quite a bit more pessimistic.[21] Teenagers involved in after-school programs can still find ways to evade adult supervision. They leave football practice as a pack and violate adult rules after the coach is out of sight. When afternoon activities have ended—but before parents return home—they find the right time to evade adult supervision. They tell parents there is an extra practice, using the time to do something parents would not approve.

The impact of sports participation on delinquency in the short run and long run is also disappointing. High school athletes are *more* likely than other youths to be arrested for drunk driving and shoplifting, even a decade after graduation from high school.[22] American researchers have also found disappointing evidence that extracurricular activities make bullying risk even worse.

> [I]nvolvement in extracurricular activities leaves adolescents vulnerable to victimization by influencing their exposure and proximity to motivated offenders and the level of guardianship available. Adolescents who are involved in extracurricular activities spend more time unsupervised with their peers, thereby increasing their exposure and proximity to motivated offenders and their risk of victimization. In addition, adolescents' involvement in extra-curricular activities reduces the level of guardianship provided by the school by allowing adolescents on campus during off hours.[23]

Once more we see evidence that American efforts at social control of teenagers are often feeble in comparison to the Japanese strategy. Adults have long held out hope that after-school jobs would reduce delinquency. Yet "[t]he preponderance of evidence from the studies on work and delinquency, including our national study, suggests that work as teenagers experience it has little or no effect on delinquency."[24] Perhaps teenagers use their work schedules as opportunities for evading parental controls or spend the extra money from part-time jobs in forbidden ways.

Traditional studies of parental monitoring asked parents to report on how closely they monitored their children, then compared these reports to evidence of delinquency. The research often concluded that parental monitoring serves to reduce delinquency. More recent evidence indicates that parents might be overstating their monitoring activities and successes and underestimating the ability of their teenagers to find times and places to break parental rules. The newer evidence indicates that teenage children do not reveal to parents their comings and goings.[25]

A systematic effort to increase adolescent supervision would probably require a longer school day and a longer school year. It would require more organization, stability, and supervision in recreational programs. In short, it would cost money and require very clear thinking and coordination. Such a shift in educational policy would not only improve education, but also help to "squeeze" the age–crime curve, producing a shorter period of delinquency and less crime. (We will discuss the age–crime curve in Part 4.)

Routine Activities

In a modern metropolis, most parents will not necessarily receive timely reports about their children. That provides an opening for many teenagers to live a "double life"—following parental rules in some settings but breaking those same rules elsewhere. When parents and teachers are out of sight, teenagers find additional opportunities to break rules, as we will see in Part 4.[26]

The *routine activity theory* was developed in the late 1970s, by the senior author of this textbook, and has since evolved.[27] The theory began with three elements: *offender*, *target*, and *the absence of a guardian*. In 1995, three more elements were added to routine activity theory, producing the crime triangle depicted in Figure 2e and discussed below.[28] Routine activity theory focuses on how conventional everyday activities create crime opportunities.[29] In general, the theory looks at how a likely offender finds a suitable crime target, with guardians against crime absent.

- *Guardians* are normally not police or security guards, but rather ordinary citizens whose proximity discourages a crime from happening.

- *Targets* include lightweight goods that are high in value as well as persons who are highly vulnerable to robbery or assault.

   Likely *convergences* of offenders and targets in the absence of guardians results from:

- routine conventional activities, such as work or school; or

- nightlife, barrooms, or entertainment zones.

You recall from research reported in Part 1 that going to and from school is at least 20 times riskier than being home. In Part 4 you will learn that offending is greatly enhanced while teenagers are together without parents near. You will learn that time spent in unstructured peer activities is at least 50 times more likely to produce crime as family, school, or work activities. These findings tell us that social control often depends on more than intangible social bonds, that the proximity of parents is also important.

The Crime Triangle

Escaping parents and other adults is only the first step towards committing a crime. A potential offender also needs some direct crime opportunities. The process of finding crime opportunities is summed up in the "*crime triangle*,"[30] presented in Figure 2e. The triangle reorganizes the original three elements of routine activity theory, adding three new elements. The convergence of potential offenders and targets is represented in the inner triangle as the new element *place*, or *setting*. The inside triangle thus presents *three main elements needed for a crime to occur*—a potential *offender*, a *place* or *setting* hospitable to crime, and a suitable *crime target*. A place or setting is better for crime if it hides illegal action or contains good targets for crime.

Compared to the original routine activity approach, the crime triangle is more specific about the process of guardianship, the ways that people supervise people and things and prevent crime while they do so. Some people are guardians of property, such as their own purses or homes. Other people supervise places—we call them managers. Other people supervise other people—we call them "*handlers*." The outer triangle thus illustrates *three types of supervision* that prevent a crime from occurring, making a setting less risky:

Figure 2e

The Crime Triangle, Summarizing How a Potential Offender Escapes Supervision and Finds Crime Opportunity

1. A potential offender cannot commit a crime very easily if a handler is present. That includes a parent, teacher, or anybody else who can exert social control. This is where control theory applies.

2. After evading the handler, a potential offender must find a place that offers crime opportunity. But such a place is much less suitable for a crime when a *place manager* is present. This might include a homeowner still at home or a receptionist watching the entry to an office suite.

3. After evading parents and finding a place with no manager, a potential offender needs to find a crime target lacking a guardian. For example, a purse left in an empty office provides a crime opportunity.

Any situation with adequate supervision of people, places, and targets is unlikely to produce a crime. That gives a community extra options for preventing crime. Potential offenders can be informally supervised on a daily basis. Places can be supervised by place managers. Fewer crime targets can be provided. Existing crime targets can be supervised more often. Indeed, a community can reduce crime opportunity in unobtrusive ways without increasing arrests or punishments. We will talk about these ways in the next section. Most of this supervision is incidental to ongoing social life[31] and enables avoidance of arrests and formal actions. That provides an opening for additional crime controls when personal and social controls have reached their limits.

FLASHCARD LIST FOR UNIT 2.2

- Attachments
- Beliefs
- Checks and balances
- Commitments
- Convergences
- Crime triangle
- Guardians
- Handlers

- Hirschi, Travis
- Involvements
- Montesquieu, Charles-Louis
- Offender
- Place, setting
- Place managers
- Reminders

- Routine activity theory
- Social bonds
- Social control theory
- Supervision, three types
- Targets
- Teenagers in Japan

DISCUSSION QUESTIONS

1. Give an example of a youth strongly subject to social control and another youth subject to very little social control.

2. Which is more powerful for preventing crime, strong self-control or strong social control?

3. Describe the routine activities of one teenager who will find it easy to commit a crime and then another teenager who will find it hard to do so.

Notes

1   De Montesquieu, C. (1989 [1748]). *Montesquieu: The Spirit of the Laws*. Ed. and trans. by A. M. Cohler, B. C. Miller & H. S. Stone. Cambridge: Cambridge University Press. Book XI, Chapter 4.

2   Fishbach, A., Friedman, R. S., & Kruglanski, A. W. (2003). Leading us not into temptation: Momentary allurements elicit overriding goal activation. *Journal of Personality and Social Psychology*, *84*(2), 296–309.

3   Hirschi, T. (1969). *Causes of delinquency*. Berkeley, CA: University of California Press.

4   Jenkins, P. H. (1997). School delinquency and the school social bond. *Journal of Research in Crime and Delinquency*, *34*(3), 337–367.

5   Not all accounts of Japanese secondary education are favorable. See: Yoneyama, S. (2012). *The Japanese high school: Silence and resistance*. Abingdon, U.K.: Routledge.

6   Russell, N. U. (1997). Lessons from Japanese cram schools. In N. U. Russell (Ed.). *The challenge of Eastern-Asian education: Implications for America*, pp. 153–170. Albany, NY: State University of New York Press.

7   Roesgaard, M. H. (2006). *Japanese education and the cram school business: Functions, challenges and perspectives of the* Juku. Nordic Institute of Asian Studies Monograph No. 105. Copenhagen: NIAS Press. www.diva-portal.org/smash/get/diva2:858563/FULLTEXT01.pdf (retrieved June 5, 2016).

8   Tanioka, I., & Glaser, D. (1991). School uniforms, routine activities, and the social control of delinquency in Japan. *Youth and Society*, *23*(1), 50–75.

9   Mahoney, J. L., Harris, A. L., & Eccles, J. S. (2006). Organized activity participation, positive youth development, and the over-scheduling hypothesis. *Social Policy Report*. *20*(4), 3–30.

10   Anderson, D. M. (2014). In school and out of trouble? The minimum dropout age and juvenile crime. *Review of Economics and Statistics*, *96*(2), 318–331.

11   Aslund, O., Gronqvist, H., Hall, C., & Vlachos, J. (2015). *Education and criminal behavior: Insights from an expansion of upper secondary school*. IZA Discussion Paper No. 9374. Bonn: Institute for the Study of Labor.

12   Aoki, Y. (2014). More schooling, less youth crime? Learning from an earthquake in Japan. IZA Discussion Paper No. 8619. Bonn: Institute for the Study of Labor.

13 Machin, S., Marie, O., & Vujić, S. (2011). The crime reducing effect of education. *The Economic Journal*, *121*(552), 463–484.

14 Berthelon, M. E., & Kruger, D. I. (2011). Risky behavior among youth: Incapacitation effects of school on adolescent motherhood and crime in Chile. *Journal of Public Economics*, *95*(1), 41–53.

15 Jacob, B. A., & Lefgren, L. (2003). Are idle hands the devil's workshop? Incapacitation, concentration, and juvenile crime. *American Economic Review*, *93*(5), 1560–1577.

16 Luallen, J. (2006). School's out . . . forever: A study of juvenile crime, at-risk youths and teacher strikes. *Journal of Urban Economics*, *59*(1), 75–103.

17 Felson, M. (1995). Those who discourage crime. In J. E., Eck & D. Weisburd (Eds.), *Crime and place*. Crime Prevention Studies Vol. 4, pp. 53–66. Monsey, NY: Criminal Justice Press. www.popcenter.org/library/crimeprevention/volume_04/03-Felson.pdf (retrieved May 14, 2017).

18 Warr, M. (2005). Making delinquent friends: Adult supervision and children's affiliations. *Criminology*, *43*(1), 77–106.

19 Shannon, C. S. (2006). Parents' messages about the role of extracurricular and unstructured leisure activities: Adolescents' perceptions. *Journal of Leisure Research*, *38*(3), 398–420.

20 Mahoney, J. L., Larson, R. W., Eccles, J. S., & Lord, H. (2005). Organized activities as developmental contexts for children and adolescents. In J. L. Mahoney, R. W. Larson, & J. S. Eccles (Eds.), *Organized activities as contexts of development: Extracurricular activities, after school and community programs*, pp. 3–22. New York: Psychology Press.

21 Gottfredson, D. C., Gerstenblith, S. A., Soulé, D. A., Womer, S. C., & Lu, S. (2004). Do after school programs reduce delinquency? *Prevention Science*, *5*(4), 253–266.

22 Hartmann, D., & Massoglia, M. (2007). Reassessing the relationship between high school sports participation and deviance: Evidence of enduring, bifurcated effects. *The Sociological Quarterly*, *48*(3), 485–505.

23 Popp, A. M., & Peguero, A. A. (2012). Social bonds and the role of school-based victimization. *Journal of Interpersonal Violence*, *27*(17), 3366–3388.

24 Gottfredson, D. C. (1985). Youth employment, crime, and schooling: A longitudinal study of a national sample. *Developmental Psychology*, *21*(3), 419–432; p. 430.

25 Kerr, M., & Stattin, H. (2000). What parents know, how they know it, and several forms of adolescent adjustment: Further support for a reinterpretation of monitoring. *Developmental Psychology*, *36*(3), 366–380.

26 Osgood, D. W., & Anderson, A. L. (2004). Unstructured socializing and rates of delinquency. *Criminology*, *42*(3), 519–550. Osgood, D. W., Wilson, J. K., O'Malley, P. M., Bachman, J. G., & Johnston, L. D. (1996). Routine activities and individual deviant behavior. *American Sociological Review*, *61*(4), 635–655.

27 Felson, M. (2016 [2008]). Routine activity approach. In R. Wortley & M. Townsley (Eds.), *Environmental criminology and crime analysis*, 2nd edition, pp. 87–97. Abingdon, U.K.: Routledge. Chamard, S. (2010). Routine activities. In E. McLaughlin & T. Newburn (Eds.), *Sage handbook of criminological theory*, pp. 210–224. Thousand Oaks, CA: Sage Publications. Miró, F. (2014). Routine activity theory. In J. M. Miller, (Ed.), *The encyclopedia of theoretical criminology*, pp. 734–741. New York: John Wiley & Sons.

28 Felson, Those who discourage crime.

29   Felson, M. and Eckert, M. (2016). *Crime and everyday life*. Thousand Oaks, CA: Sage Publications.

30   Clarke, R. V., & Eck, J. E. (2005). *Crime analysis for problem solvers in 60 small steps*. Washington, DC: Center for Problem Oriented Policing.

31   Jacobs, J. (1961). *Death and life of great American cities*. New York: Random House.

Unit 2.3 Situational Controls

Suppose you are a teacher giving a multiple-choice test to your high school class. You do not want them to cheat on the test. You hope their personal and social controls will keep them honest, but your experience as a teacher tells you that many of them will try to cheat anyway. Your experience also tells you that it is a nuisance to catch people cheating and try to punish them, especially when cheating is common.[1]

Instead you use your computer to produce two forms of the same test, then pass out the test so that students next to each other will not see the same test form. They will then find it difficult to cheat. This is a type of *situational control*—using very practical techniques to minimize bad behavior. It makes much more sense to design out cheating than to let people cheat and then try to catch them.[2] This situational prevention approach can also be applied to reduce crime. According to our life stages of crime and control, these techniques apply near the time of the crime.

Professor **Ronald V. Clarke** is the father of *situational crime prevention*—a systematic set of techniques for slicing away at crime. His work has been used around the world by police, local agencies, and private industries, all seeking to control illicit behavior.[3] In 2015 he received the Stockholm Prize for Criminology for his efforts, which have been credited with spearheading the major crime reductions in modern nations over the past decade.[4]

Situational prevention operates by denying the offender *easy crime opportunities*. Every crime event needs a place. It needs a time. It depends on some people being absent and others present. It may require tools, illegal substances, or even weapons. These requirements give society an extra set of situational controls that can be applied *near the time of the crime*. These control methods are also very specific in the types of crime stopped and the methods used to stop it. Researchers find very positive and substantial results in many different settings.[5]

Some Interesting Examples

Here are some interesting and diverse examples of situational crime prevention:

The motorcycle helmet story. Many motorcycles are stolen on the spur of the moment for joyriding. Motorcycle helmet laws make it more difficult to steal a motorcycle without planning. States where helmet laws have been enacted saw dramatic declines in motorcycle theft rates.[6]

Controlling cell phone fraud. After cell phones were programmed to require passwords, thefts of phones and services declined markedly.[7]

Redesigning car locks. Car theft greatly declined when old door locks were replaced by ones that a car thief could not reach in and pull up and steering wheel locks were added. This may be one of the major reasons for declines in car theft internationally.[8]

Cleaning up graffiti right away. This removes the incentive for painting more graffiti, since the painter no longer feels "famous" as nobody sees what was painted.[9]

Fixing bad parking lots. Many cars are stolen from insecure parking lots and structures. Working with parking lot managers, criminologists have reduced car thefts by trimming hedges, increasing lighting and visibility. Parking structures suffer less theft when access is controlled.[10]

Reducing piracy on the high seas. Somali pirates preyed on the narrow shipping lanes in the Gulf of Aden and the Indian Ocean. Then shipowners began constructing reinforced *safe rooms*, allowing the crew to shut down the ship and send out distress signals, giving time for help to arrive.[11]

Controlling sports crowds. Many sports venues manage liquor sales, thereby reducing aggressive words, vandalism, fights, and the tendency to throw things. They also manage pedestrian flows in order to minimize conflicts and arguments.[12]

Often situational prevention is very local. It tends to be highly effective when suitably focused and works best with the help of good crime analysts who figure out when, where, and how crime is carried out. Situational prevention often relies on businesses and public agencies, not just the police, to help reduce specific crime problems.

The application of situational prevention has helped with a very diverse set of problems. These efforts have produced reductions in:

- barroom violence;
- child sexual abuse;
- corruption;
- crowd violence;
- drug crime networks;
- election disruption;
- elephant killings;
- homicide;
- identity theft;
- illegal fishing;
- incivilities in libraries;
- internet crimes;
- livestock theft;
- misbehavior in prisons;
- ocean pollution;
- organized crime;
- ransom kidnaping;
- suicide;
- terrorism; and
- tiger killings.[13]

Drinking on Campus

From one-fourth to one-third of students admit to driving under the influence of alcohol.[14] Student alcohol consumption is also related to aggressive behavior, including intimate partner violence. Based on 7,775 daily electronic diary reports, students engaged in 3.6 times as much physical aggression on drinking days relative to non-drinking days.[15] Men were seven times more likely to be verbally aggressive on drinking days than on non-drinking days. Crime victimization risks are also related to drinking behaviors.[16] Excess drinking contributes to the failure to complete a college degree, as we mentioned earlier in the textbook.[17]

H. Laurence Ross wrote the classic work explaining why arrests and punishments are so ineffective for controlling drunk driving and other drinking violations in an automotive society.[18] His argument was that drinking is embedded in social life and difficult to contain or control. He also pointed out that most drunk drivers are never arrested for it. Similarly, most underage drinking never results in arrest, and excessive drinking generally goes unpunished.

On the other hand, alcohol regulation has achieved substantial success using situational prevention methods when it sets **reasonable goals** and targets key actors and processes in the alcohol "delivery system."[19] For example, licensing and service regulations can reduce the flow of alcohol and contain the locations in which people drink. Those who depend on their liquor licenses are subject to civil regulation and punishment, which do not require that the state prove their misbehavior "beyond a reasonable doubt."[20] An example of an **unreasonable goal** is the total banning of alcohol in a modern society that has ample opportunities for evasion. However, people are highly responsive to environmental cues that can affect their levels of drinking and their misbehavior in alcohol settings.[21]

Table 2a lists 34 situational prevention methods that can lower the levels of excess drinking on or near university campuses.[22] Students may be highly responsive to the price of alcohol, and drinkers are influenced by size of containers and serving practices. Hours and locations have long been shown to have an influence on the quantities that people drink and the trouble they get into. Bar owners have also proven that they can get people to drink considerably more with drinking contests, specials, and sale of pitchers and larger containers. They can also gain considerable profit in flaunting liquor laws, serving those who are already drunk or otherwise violating administrative rules and terms of their licenses. Given that they are subject to civil law, their licenses can be suspended or revoked without proving guilt beyond a reasonable doubt. In general, situational prevention has proven effective for containing alcohol and barroom problems.

The Situational Crime Prevention Strategy

Situational prevention does *not* focus on imprisonment or other long-term risks. Rather it focuses on the offender's *immediate* rewards, risks, and difficulties, as shown in Figure 2f. The strategy is to **increase the risks** for the offender, to **increase the effort**

TABLE 2A Situational Prevention Methods to Reduce Alcohol Consumption in and around College Campuse

Type of situational preventative method	Specific tactics
Administrative and planning	Enact liability laws
	Have alcohol-free parties & events
	Hold hosts liable for misbehavior
	Increase cost of alcohol license
	Limit size of drinking parties
	Monitor privatization of community events
	Prevent parties at hotels & motels
	Reduce density of alcohol establishments
	Require server training & licensing
	Restrict days and hours of sale
	Set minimum age for servers
	Penalize badly managed establishments
	Use administrative law
Influence where drinking occurs	Create dry campuses & residence halls
	Create separate & distinct drinking areas
	Enact noisy assembly ordinance
	Enforce against public alcohol use
	Prohibit sales on or near campus
	Remove the heavy drinking locations
	Restrict consumption to specific areas
	Restrict or ban home alcohol deliveries
Reducing the flow of alcohol	Cut off service to intoxicated individuals
	Drop alcohol discounts and free alcohol
	Eliminate last-call announcements
	Eliminate self-service
	Increase price of alcohol or excise tax
	Limit quantity per request
	Limit total quantity of alcohol at events
	Promote alcohol-free drinks & food
	Register or ban beer kegs
	Restrict happy hours & price promotions
	Serve drinks with low alcohol content
	Use quota for drinks per person
	Use smaller glasses, ban pitchers

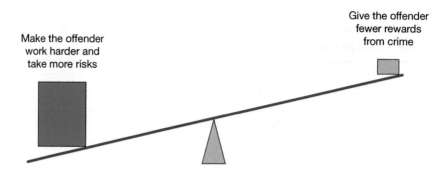

FIGURE 2F

Force the Offender to Work Harder and Take More Risks for Fewer Rewards from the Criminal Act

that an offender must make to carry out a crime, and to **reduce the rewards** an offender gets from carrying out the crime. These three actions together make it pointless for the offender to commit the crime, which is no longer worth the trouble.[23]

Situational crime prevention is closely related to **problem-oriented policing**, which we give substantial attention to in Unit 3.2. Whether applied by police or others, situational crime prevention focuses on particular problems—such as incidents in and around barrooms or thefts of women's handbags from bars and restaurants. Then the crime analyst figures out how to lessen that problem. There is an entire website (www.popcenter.org) describing situational crime prevention applications and problem-oriented policing efforts. The website presents many hundreds of prevention examples. It also offers many opportunities for student papers. However, some critics claim that situational prevention merely shifts crime from one place to another.

The Displacement Hypothesis

The **displacement hypothesis** argues that specific crime prevention produces no *overall* benefit to society. Instead (the argument goes), a specific crime prevented here is *simply displaced* to other places nearby.[24] Advocates of this hypothesis insist that society can only reduce crime by solving its "root causes." This hypothesis is important as it implies that situational crime prevention cannot be effective for overall crime prevention. This is not just a practical matter, but also a philosophical question. Does crime occur because of deep-seated features of society or individuals? Or is it a more practical matter, responding to temptations and situations?

We now have a fair amount of evidence that the displacement hypothesis is wrong, or at least largely wrong. A 2009 survey of 574 situational crime prevention measures found that 426 cases of crime reduction did not result in displacement.[25] Some displacement was observed, but only about one-fourth of the time. In many cases crime prevention produced a ***diffusion of benefits***—crime reduction in one place spilled over to nearby places. For example, better surveillance at a university parking structure resulted in fewer thefts not only there but also in other parking structures. Thus, crime can be reduced in local situations without making it worse down the street or over the hill.[26] If these studies are correct, crime reduction does not require us to transform all of society; we can work on it step by step. In Part 5 we will revisit the displacement effect and discuss whether crime reduction in one community pushes it to another. Like personal and social controls, situational controls cannot promise universal success. That leaves a formal justice system as the "last resort."

FLASHCARD LIST FOR UNIT 2.3

- Clarke, Ronald V.
- Diffusion of benefits
- Displacement hypothesis
- Easy crime opportunities

- Goal, reasonable, unreasonable
- Increase the effort
- Increase the risk
- Problem-oriented policing

- Reduce the rewards
- Ross, H. Laurence
- Situational control
- Situational crime prevention

DISCUSSION QUESTIONS

1. When is situational control applied in relation to the time of the crime?

2. How does situational control differ from social control?

Notes

1   Staats, S., Hupp, J. M., Wallace, H., & Gresley, J. (2009). Heroes don't cheat: An examination of academic dishonesty and students' views on why professors don't report cheating. *Ethics and Behavior, 19*(3), 171–183.

2   Carroll, J., & Oxford Centre for Staff Development. (2007). *A handbook for deterring plagiarism in higher education.* Oxford, U.K.: Oxford Centre for Staff and Learning Development.

3   Clarke, R. V. (1980). Situational crime prevention: Theory and practice. *The British Journal of Criminology, 20*(2), 136–147.

4   Cornish, D. B., & Clarke, R. V. (Eds.). (2014). *The reasoning criminal: Rational choice perspectives on offending.* Piscataway, NJ: Transaction Publishers.

5   Guerette, R., Johnson, S., & Bowers, K. (2016). *Situational crime prevention.* Abingdon, U.K.: Routledge.

6   Mayhew, P., Clarke, R. V., & Elliott, D. (1989). Motorcycle theft, helmet legislation and displacement. *The Howard Journal of Criminal Justice*, *28*(1), 1–8.

7   Clarke, R. V., Kemper, R., & Wyckoff, L. (2001). Controlling cell phone fraud in the US: Lessons for the UK "Foresight" prevention initiative. *Security Journal*, *14*(1), 7–22.

8   Ekblom, P. (2014). Designing products against crime. In G. Bruinsma & D. Weisburd (Eds.), *Encyclopedia of criminology and criminal justice*, pp. 948–957. New York: Springer.

9   Uittenbogaard, A., & Ceccato, V. (2014). Safety in Stockholm's underground stations: An agenda for action. *European Journal on Criminal Policy and Research*, *20*(1), 73–100.

10 Clarke, R. V., & Goldstein, H. (2003). Thefts from cars in center-city parking facilities: A case study in implementing problem-oriented policing. In J. Knutsson (Ed.), *Problem-oriented policing: From innovation to mainstream crime prevention studies*. Crime Prevention Studies, Vol. 15, pp. 257–298. Monsey NY: Criminal Justice Press.

11 Bryant, W., Townsley, M., & Leclerc, B. (2014). Preventing maritime pirate attacks: A conjunctive analysis of the effectiveness of ship protection measures recommended by the international maritime organization. *Journal of Transportation Security*, *7*(1), 69–82.

12 Madensen, T. D., & Eck, J. E. (2008). *Spectator violence in stadiums*, Problem-Specific Guides Series, No. 54. Washington, DC: Center for Problem-Oriented Policing.

13 Clarke, R. V. (2005). Seven misconceptions of situational crime prevention. In N. Tilley (Ed.), *Handbook of crime prevention and community safety*, pp. 39–70. London: Routledge.

14 Clapp, J. D., Johnson, M., Voas, R. B., Lange, J. E., Shillington, A., & Russell, C. (2005). Reducing DUI among US college students: Results of an environmental prevention trial. *Addiction*, *100*(3), 327–334.

15 Moore, T. M., Elkins, S. R., McNulty, J. K., Kivisto, A. J., & Handsel, V. A. (2011). Alcohol use and intimate partner violence perpetration among college students: Assessing the temporal association using electronic diary technology. *Psychology of Violence*, *1*(4), 315–328.

16 Fisher, B. S., Sloan, J. J., Cullen, F. T., & Lu, C. (1998). Crime in the ivory tower: The level and sources of student victimization. *Criminology*, *36*(3), 671–710.

17 Martinez, J. A., Sher, K. J., & Wood, P. K. (2008). Is heavy drinking really associated with attrition from college? The alcohol–attrition paradox. *Psychology of Addictive Behaviors*, *22*(3), 450–456.

18 Ross, H. L. (1994). *Confronting drunk driving: Social policy for saving lives*. New Haven, CT: Yale University Press.

19 Graham, K., Bernards, S., Osgood, D. W., Homel, R., & Purcell, J. (2004). Guardians and handlers: The role of bar staff in preventing and managing aggression. *Addiction*, *100*(6), 755–766. Homel, R., Carvolth, R., Hauritz, M., McIlwain, G, & Teague, R. (2004). Making licensed venues safer for patrons: What environmental factors should be the focus of interventions? *Drug and Alcohol Review*, *23*(1), 19–29. Scott, M. S., & Dedel, K. (2006). *Assaults in and around bars*, 2nd edition. Washington, DC: Office of Community Oriented Policing Services.

20 Graham, K., & Homel, R. (2012). *Raising the bar*. Abingdon, U.K.: Routledge.

21 De Andrade, D., Homel, R., & Mazerolle, L. (2016). Boozy nights and violent fights: Perceptions of environmental cues to violence and crime in licensed venues. *Journal of Interpersonal Violence*. Published online July 5. https://doi.org/10.1177/0886260516657910.

22 Toomey, T. L., Lenk, K. M., & Wagenaar, A. C. (2007). Environmental policies to reduce college drinking: An update of research findings. *Journal of Studies on Alcohol and Drugs*, *68*(2), 208–219.

23 Cornish, D. B., & Clarke, R. V. (Eds.). (2014). *The reasoning criminal: Rational choice perspectives on offending*. Piscataway, NJ: Transaction Publishers.

24 Reppetto, T. A. (1976). Crime prevention and the displacement phenomenon. *Crime & Delinquency*, *22*(2), 166–177.

25 Guerette, R. T., & Bowers, K. J. (2009). Assessing the extent of crime displacement and diffusion of benefits: A review of situational crime prevention evaluations. *Criminology*, *47*(4), 1331–1368.

26 Weisburd, D., Wyckoff, L. A., Ready, J., Eck, J. E., Hinkle, J. C., & Gajewski, F. (2006). Does crime just move around the corner? A controlled study of spatial displacement and diffusion of crime control benefits. *Criminology*, *44*(3), 549–592.

Unit 2.4 Formal Controls

When the other three control processes fail, society often turns to the formal controls offered by the criminal justice process. These controls generally come in only *after* a crime is committed, the very last stage in Figure 2b. We urge you to take a course in criminal justice process in the future. Our only purpose here is to familiarize you with the basic complexities of the justice process.

The *official procedures* of law and justice are complicated enough. The reality has even more to it. As one legal scholar explained:

> Many books leave the false impression that an understanding of the formal law and major structures of the court is all that one needs to know about the criminal courts. This kind of analysis provides only a limited view of how the courts administer justice. The law is not self-executing. It is a dynamic process of applying abstract rules to concrete situations.
>
> In making decisions about charges to be filed, the amount of bail to be required, and the sentence a convicted person will receive, judges, prosecutors, and defense attorneys must make choices for which the formal law provides few precise guidelines.
>
> [. . .] An examination of law in action reveals a gap between how the law is supposed to operate and how it is applied.[1]

Multiple Steps

Any democratic nation takes the rule of law seriously and does not wish to deny human rights. It does not wish to take away property without due process of law. These lofty principles lead to many grubby procedures. Figure 2g shows how many *procedural steps* might be necessary to prosecute a crime in Canada.[2] Over 100 steps

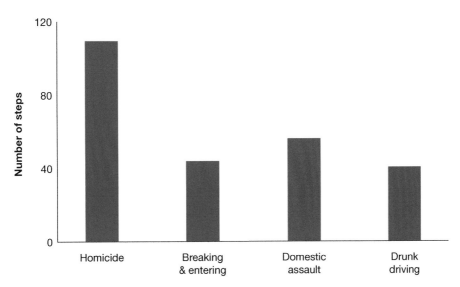

FIGURE 2G

Maximum Number of Procedural Steps by Type of Crime, Illustrating Complexity of the Justice System (Canadian Study)

Source: Data drawn from A. Malm, N. Pollard, P. Brantingham, P. Tinsley, D. Plecas, P. Brantingham, I. Cohen, & B. Kinney (2005). *A 30 year analysis of police service delivery and costing, "E" Division.* Vancouver: Simon Fraser University, Institute for Canadian Urban Research Studies.

might be needed for a homicide case, and about 40 steps for a drunk driving case (driving under the influence of alcohol). The same study found that procedural complexity had increased quite a bit over time, producing additional costs and inefficiencies in the Canadian justice system. Although procedures vary among the 50 American states and the federal system, similar levels of paperwork and *legal complexity* can easily emerge. You can see that in a modern democratic society, criminal justice is a complicated process. That makes formal control difficult to deliver within the confines of the law.[3]

System Complexities in the United States

The U.S. Department of Justice produced a complicated chart including 70 common subprocesses that can apply to a case going through the American justice system. Often repeated in textbooks, the chart starts with cases entering that system, continues with prosecution and pretrial processes, and then proceeds with adjudication, sentencing, and sanctions. That chart does not even capture the full set of procedural complexities, much less the differences among jurisdictions, but it is worth going to the reference and looking at it.[4] Our textbook is not about criminal procedure, which you can learn about elsewhere.[5] However, you should know how complicated that procedure is and why its complexity limits the potential of a justice system in a free society.

The U.S. legal framework derives from England, and it is referred to as "the *common law*." As we mentioned at the beginning of this textbook, common law grows case by case, with previous cases setting precedents for future cases.[6] Over time, tens of thousands of cases accumulate to produce *case law*, which continues to grow every day. In contrast, *statutory laws* are passed by a legislative body and signed into law by the executive. Each of 50 states and the federal government has its own statutes. Statutory laws include the punishment to be doled out when they are not followed. An American judge examines both *case law* and *statutory law*, then makes a legal ruling.

This system is most complicated for civil cases, which rely mainly on bookshelves and computers filled with case law. Criminal cases lean more on statutes, yet these are not always clear or succinct when applied in certain circumstances. Even though the U.S. Constitution prohibits "vague" laws, this does not mean that all laws are crystal clear. So American judges have a lot of work to do. They rule on what the law is and on procedural issues. If there is a jury, it will rule on the facts of the case. If there is no jury, the judge has to rule both on law and on facts. From the defendant's viewpoint, this process might well be the worst experience.[7] (Of course, most cases are never tried at all, as you will see in Part 3.)

Had the French and Indian War (1754–1763) taken a different turn, Americans might now be using Napoleonic law, and the American "system" would be more organized. Emperor Napoleon was a very orderly and systematic general, who dominated France and the European continent from 1804 to 1814. His government standardized, centralized, and routinized law.[8] Four eminent jurists drafted the Napoleonic Code, and the code spread wherever French influence prevailed. However, American justice reflects the complexities of many cases and the codes of the 50 states and the federal system.

Summarizing Principles of Formal Criminal Justice

Despite these complexities, *six summarizing principles* span the formal criminal justice process:

1. A crime must come to the attention of authorities.[9]

2. Authorities must declare a case against someone, stating exactly what that case is.[10]

3. At any time, authorities can end a case and kick it out of the system.[11]

4. Authorities must decide whether to move a case forward to the next stage.

5. Authorities are often allowed to delay a case.[12]

6. Authorities have a good deal of leeway or **discretion at most stages** of the justice process.

These six principles tell us that the justice system often ends up making a very large number of decisions. Yet the criminal justice system can't get involved unless officials know a law was broken. Later in the textbook, we will address issues in reporting crimes. For now, we focus on the period after the crime is known. Many of the decisions made by the justice system have severe consequences, such as whether somebody's freedom will be taken away. Even revoking a driver's license threatens someone's economic position and social freedom. Many of the most important decisions are made well before a trial might occur. Officials make the following **decisions before trial**:

*   whether to drop the case;[13]

*   whether a case is a felony or a misdemeanor;

*   whether a case is for juvenile or adult court;[14] and/or

*   whether to set bail.[15]

Officials may decide to release the suspect or to proceed with the case. Even if they proceed, they may decide to reduce charges and the suspect may offer to plead guilty.

Officials at every level have a considerable degree of discretion to decide among options.[16] These decisions can be very important. An individual can easily lose freedom for many months without being convicted, depending on the bail decision. A delayed decision hangs over the offender and often the victim too. For cases that go all the way through the process in court, a judge or jury has to decide on the punishment, hopefully in a manner that is viewed as fair by society.

What the Public Expects

Public expectations of the justice system range from minimal to ideal. **Minimal expectations** are that extreme cases lead to arrest, conviction, and incarceration of the guilty person. The public is very displeased when guilty parties go unpunished and when innocent persons are wrongfully convicted. Many members of the public have *ideal expectations* of the justice system—expecting most crimes to be solved and most offenders to be arrested quickly and punished. Many people have ideal expectations of rehabilitation or deterrence—expecting that the punishment will fit the crime—but lack a consensus about how much punishment should apply to each type of case, and many people are less punitive when confronted with specific examples.[17] Public views about justice also vary from one community to another and even within the same community.[18]

De Minimis

In Part 5 you will learn that the public often gets upset about small crimes and disorderly behaviors near where they live. These concerns put the public in direct conflict with a fundamental concept of the law, **de minimis**. The full Latin phrase is *Maxim de minimis non curat lex*. It means that "the law does not care about trifling matters."[19] In practical terms, it means that judges do not want to hear about minor arguments over trivial matters. The term is used in both the civil and criminal courts. In civil courts, the doctrine helps weed out frivolous lawsuits. In criminal courts, it means that big-city judges do not want to hear about every urban annoyance from panhandling to littering. In Part 5, you will learn that citizens often care very much about urban annoyances. *De minimis* creates a conflict between communities and the justice system. Community disorder concerns are often considered trivial by judges, who are used to dealing with very serious felonies, such as burglary, robbery, and aggravated assault. Indeed, every police officer and prosecutor keeps *de minimis* in mind with every decision.

> These officials can hardly proceed in every case in which a person is thought to be violating the literal terms of a law, and thus have little choice but to use their judgment about which conduct is worth arresting and prosecuting.[20]

You can see why officials will probably **decide not to act** in situations they assess to be *de minimis*. Yet the larger public expects to be protected from all disorder, and what is a small matter to the justice system is not so small to ordinary citizens.

Procedural Justice

Justice system officials are in a tricky situation. In using discretion, they need to make sure that the public feels they have been fair, that no social group or community has been either unjustly targeted for police action or unjustly excluded from police protection. Regardless of legal outcome, the public expects fair treatment. Even if no action results, it expects that its grievances will be heard. The term "*procedural justice*" (or fairness) summarizes what we mean. To achieve procedural justice, four elements need to be present when the public deals with formal authorities—people need

- to have their side of the story heard, to feel they have a voice;

- to feel that the authorities are neutral;

- to perceive their treatment by authorities as polite, that their rights are respected and their dignity preserved; and

- to perceive authorities as trustworthy.[21]

When these elements are present, the public usually accepts its justice system and believes in its legitimacy.[22] We will return to this concept in Part 3.

Some types of enforcement are especially taxing on procedural justice. For example, problems emerge from excess criminalization of behaviors, that cannot be fully regulated in practice.[23] Spotty enforcement of laws against marijuana use creates conflict with youths and perceptions of racial profiling. In Part 3, you will see that the justice process has difficulty meeting even minimal public expectations given the costs and complexities with which it must deal and the need to maintain its legitimacy.

FLASHCARD LIST FOR UNIT 2.4

- Case law
- Common law
- Decide not to act
- Decisions before trial
- *De minimis*
- Discretion at most stages

- Legal complexity
- Official procedures
- Procedural justice
- Procedural steps
- Public expectations, ideal, minimal

- Six summarizing principles [of criminal procedure]
- Statutory laws

DISCUSSION QUESTIONS

1. How fast does the justice system act?

2. What do you infer about the limits of the justice system?

Notes

1   Neubauer, D. W., & Fradella, H. F. (2015). *America's courts and the criminal justice system*. Boston: Cengage Learning; pp. xxii–xxiii.

2   Malm, A., Pollard, N., Brantingham, P., Tinsley, P., Plecas, D., . . . & Kinney, B. (2005). *A 30 year analysis of police service delivery and costing, "E" Division*. Vancouver: Simon Fraser University, Institute for Canadian Urban Research Studies.

3   Posner, R. A. (1990). *The problems of jurisprudence*. Cambridge, MA: Harvard University Press.

4   Criminal justice system flowchart [online]. Bureau of Justice Statistics. Revised July 20, 2017. www.bjs.gov/content/largechart.cfm (retrieved August 1, 2017).

5   Allen, R. J., Stuntz, W. J., Hoffmann, J. L., Livingston, D. A., Leipold, A. D., & Meares, T. L. (2016). *Comprehensive criminal procedure*, 4th edition. New York: Wolters Kluwer.

6   Holmes, O. W. (2009 [1881]). *The common law*. Cambridge, MA: Harvard University Press.

7   Feeley, M. M. (1979). *The process is the punishment: Handling cases in a lower criminal court*. New York: Russell Sage Foundation.

8   Lyons, M. (1994). *Napoleon Bonaparte and the legacy of the French Revolution*, Vol. 1. London: Macmillan.

9   Skogan, W. G. (1977). Dimensions of the dark figure of unreported crime. *Crime & Delinquency*, *23*(1), 41–50.

10 Keil, G. & Poscher, R. (Eds.). (2016). *Vagueness and law: Philosophical and legal perspectives*. Oxford, U.K.: Oxford University Press.

11 Goldstein, J. (1960). Police discretion not to invoke the criminal process: Low-visibility decisions in the administration of justice. *The Yale Law Journal*, *69*(4), 543–594.

12 DiVita, G. (2010). Production of laws and delays in court decisions. *International Review of Law and Economics*, *30*(3), 276–281. Chappe, N. (2012). Demand for civil trials and court congestion. *European Journal of Law and Economics*, *33*(2), 343–357.

13 Shermer, L. O. N., & Johnson, B. D. (2010). Criminal prosecutions: Examining prosecutorial discretion and charge reductions in U.S. federal district courts. *Justice Quarterly*, *27*(3), 394–430.

14 Kupchik, A. (2006). *Judging juveniles: Prosecuting adolescents in adult and juvenile courts*. New York: NYU Press.

15 Goldkamp, J. S., & Gottfredson, M. R. (1979). Bail decision making and pretrial detention: Surfacing judicial policy. *Law and Human Behavior*, *3*(4), 227–249.

16 Gottfredson, M. R., & Gottfredson, D. M. (2013). *Decision making in criminal justice: Toward the rational exercise of discretion*. New York: Springer Science & Business Media.

17 Cullen, F. T., Fisher, B. S., & Applegate, B. K. (2000). Public opinion about punishment and corrections. *Crime and Justice*, *27*, 1–79.

18 Skogan, W. G. (2006). Asymmetry in the impact of encounters with police. *Policing & Society*, *16*(2), 99–126. Skogan, W. G. (2006). *Police and community in Chicago: A tale of three cities*. Oxford, U.K.: Oxford University Press.

19 De Minimis. (2008). *West's encyclopedia of American law*, 2nd edition [online]. http://legal-dictionary.thefreedictionary.com/De+Minimis (retrieved May 10, 2017).

20 Husak, D. (2009). The de minimis "defense" to criminal liability. Presentation at University of California, November 20, p. 6. www.law.berkeley.edu/files/De_Minimis2_DHusak.pdf (retrieved May 10, 2017).

21 Tyler, T. R., Jackson, J., & Bradford, B. (2014). Procedural justice and cooperation. In G. Bruinsma & D. Weisburd (Eds.), *Encyclopedia of criminology and criminal justice*, pp. 4011–4024.

22 For example, see: Gold, E. with Bradley, M. (2013). The case for procedural justice: Fairness as a crime prevention tool. *Community Policing Dispatch*, *6*(9) [online newsletter]. https://cops.usdoj.gov/html/dispatch/09-2013/fairness_as_a_crime_prevention_tool.asp (retrieved June 1, 2017).

23 Smith, S. F. (2012). Overcoming overcriminalization. *Journal of Criminal Law and Criminology*, *102*(3), 537–591.

PERSPECTIVE ON PART 2

In Part 2 we mapped out the four processes by which society seeks to contain misbehavior: personal control, social control, situational control, and formal control. Each process is imperfect. We also outlined five life stages and how they relate to crime and control. Starting before birth, genetic and prenatal environment may influence future development of a child. Self-control starts in early childhood. Social control manifests itself more during the adolescent years. Situational control of risky settings occurs near the time of the crime. Formal control occurs after the crime occurs—and as a last resort. In short, society devises a multi-method effort to keep people on the right track and away from criminal behavior.

Instilling self-control is inconvenient. Supervising teenagers at all times is inconvenient. Situational prevention cannot cover all public space. Apprehension and punishment of offenders is an impractical task. The various controls mentioned in Part 2 sometimes apply best in small systems. When people know and can monitor each other, it is harder to evade control processes. Personal controls work best if people can provide checks and balances for each other. As the number of people rises or they become more anonymous, controls are more easily evaded. This is especially true for social controls. Social controls seem to work best when people know one another and to work worst in anonymous situations and very large groups.

Formal controls are also more difficult to apply in very large cities with millions of people coming and going. Moreover, it is often quite convenient to break the law. When in a hurry to get to class or work, it is easy to speed on the highway and then park illegally. It is easy in a self-service store to take something without paying. Even when it is against one's better judgment, it is easy to cut corners. It is convenient for the bartender to pour another drink. Society tries to make all types of crime less convenient, yet it produces some risky situations where those efforts fail. We have reviewed quite a range of efforts by society to minimize risky situations. Part 3 next considers in detail how the justice system faces challenges when the public asks it to do something.

Main Points of Part 2

There are four types of control in society helping to maintain the society's rules: personal controls, social controls, situational controls and formal controls.

- Crime occurs when personal, social, and situational controls have failed.

- The four types of control map to five life stages in terms of crime and control:

   a. Before birth, genetic predispositions are set that may affect the development of personal controls.

   b. Early childhood emphasizes the development of personal controls.

   c. Social controls become more prominent in adolescence.

   d. Situational controls come into play near the time of a potential crime.

   e. Formal controls are applied by the criminal justice system only after a crime has been committed.

- Early criminologists such as Lombroso looked to find people who were "born criminal," assuming outward physical characteristics reflected a criminal "gene."

- Hirschi and Gottfredson posited a general theory of crime, which is better described as a general theory of self-control.

- Routine activity theory studies how daily routines create crime opportunities.

- The crime triangle helps summarize the convergence of offenders and targets, and demonstrates the importance of others as handlers, guardians, and place managers for supervision and preventing crime.

- Situational crime prevention can make potential crime targets more secure and place management more effective.

- Formal controls are complex, costly, and take a long time to implement.

PART 3

Realistic Justice

Our justice system is extremely expensive and overburdened.[1] Caseloads and paperwork can increase quickly.[2] The general public expects a great deal from police and other officials, even in years when crime rates are lower. The whole justice system process is labor-intensive, involving heavy use of trained people. Rehabilitation and drug programs are also labor-intensive and unmechanized, hence costly. Incarcerating offenders for long periods of time is even more costly.

Most of the modern criminal justice system is no more efficient than it was 50 years ago. It is not easy to change because of the *inability to automate* the busiest parts of the system. Economists use the term "Baumol's cost disease"[3] to explain any industry that cannot put modern technology to sufficient use. We currently have no robot police, judges, prison guards, teachers, or social workers. Even though our advanced society gives us super-efficient microchips and factories that can make a million products, it is inefficient in administering justice or helping people in trouble.

In fact, advanced society can make justice even more expensive than in the past. With automated 9-1-1 systems and cell phones, more people are calling police demanding services. After seeing television shows with expensive crime scene investigations, burglary victims are disappointed that police lack sufficient personnel and budget to do the same for them.[4] Any mistakes that police make are also widely advertised.[5] Thus modern society multiplies the tasks of the justice system without helping it to automate its most tedious tasks. Indeed, the justice system has great difficulty holding most offenders accountable for most of their ill deeds.

Unit 2.4 briefly described the cumbersome *official system* of formal controls. Now we offer you a more *realistic account* of what happens in the pursuit of justice. When faced with a troublesome event, officials have these choices:

1. Avoid the issue and walk away.

2. Resolve the issue on the spot.

3. Divert a case to other organizations.

4. Initiate an official criminal case, but find a way to speed it up or move it to the side.

5. Adjudicate a criminal case formally and slowly.

If somebody commits a murder, officials have no choice but to institute formal action. However, for most crimes and disorderly behaviors, police have many options about what to do—or not to do. In other words, they have a good deal of *official discretion*, having decision points built into their daily work. Officials often make decisions that seek to lighten the load on the system and to avoid slow and costly formal processes. However, they also may have to go beyond formal decisions and act informally. That's why Part 3 covers *unofficial discretion*; that is, informal decisions made by officials to streamline their workload, avoiding formal processes. This is not a matter of laziness. The justice system simply does not have the capacity to do what is demanded of it. You will learn in Part 3 that officials have a good deal of discretion at many levels of justice and can't bother with issues they determine to be *de minimis*.

We hope you will take additional courses in which you learn the ins and outs of the criminal justice system. This textbook cannot cover these many details. However, we hope you will learn here why the justice system can't do it all. Unit 3.1 discusses how society tries to assign accountability for harmful acts. Then Units 3.2 and 3.3 explain what we can realistically expect from our police and courts, respectively. Units 3.4 and 3.5 address the theories and realities of punishment and its alternatives, also discussing the numerous efforts made to punish offenders over the years and the reality of those efforts. Unit 3.6 explains how we learn about crime, how we collect crime data, and what the data are likely to miss.

FLASHCARD LIST FOR PART 3: REALISTIC JUSTICE

- Discretion, official, unofficial
- Inability to automate
- Official system
- Realistic account

QUESTIONS ADDRESSED IN PART 3

1. How much crime can the formal justice system handle?

2. How does the justice system try to lessen its load?

3. Why do societies punish?

4. Can we tell which punishments are effective?

5. What are some of the ways we measure crime?

6. How much crime is known to police?

Notes

1   Yang, C. S. (2016). Resource constraints and the criminal justice system: Evidence from judicial vacancies. *American Economic Journal: Economic Policy*, *8*(4), 289–332.

2   Wooldredge, J. D. (1989). An aggregate-level examination of the caseload pressure hypothesis. *Journal of Quantitative Criminology*, *5*(3), 259–283.

3   Baumol, W. J. (2012). *The cost disease: Why computers get cheaper and health care doesn't*. New Haven, CT: Yale University Press. Towse, R. (1997). *Baumol's cost disease: The arts and other victims*. Cheltenham, U.K.: Edward Elgar Publishing.

4   Huey, L. (2010). "I've seen this on CSI": Criminal investigators' perceptions about the management of public expectations in the field. *Crime, Media, Culture*, *6*(1), 49–68. Walker, S. E., & Archbold, C. A. (2013). *The new world of police accountability*. Thousand Oaks, CA: Sage Publications.

5   Greer, C., & McLaughlin, E. (2010). We predict a riot? Public order policing, new media environments and the rise of the citizen journalist. *British Journal of Criminology*, *50*(6), 1041–1059.

Unit 3.1 Assigning Responsibility

A central task in every society is to assign responsibility for good and bad things that people do. On the good side, society tries to reward achievements at school and at the workplace. On the bad side, society tries to figure out the harms that people do, then hold them accountable. We focus here on the bad side.

The unpleasant tasks can fall on the justice system. That system must deal with people harming others too much or too often. That task is very difficult in practice. Responsibility for harm is not easy to assign, even in theory. That's why states and nations differ so much in their general approach and struggle so much with specific cases. When is somebody old enough to be treated as a criminal? When is a misbehavior handled as a *civil case* (based on non-criminal law and regulations) as opposed to a *criminal case*? When is an accidental outcome still considered a criminal act?

Sometimes *accountability* is easy to handle. To quote Justice Oliver Wendell Holmes, "Even a dog distinguishes between being stumbled over and being kicked."[1]

Perhaps a dog's instincts work better than large human institutions that make decisions about past events reported inconsistently by others. Assigning responsibility for harm can become difficult. Taking offender goals into account, we can classify *four categories of harm* to other people,[2] as indicated in Figure 3a.

Reading the figure from left to right, we start with someone harming someone else. That could have occurred by accident or by intent. For example, reckless drivers *harm others unintentionally* (category A). In contrast, violent offenders or property offenders *harm others intentionally* (category B). Intentional crime has two subcategories:

- B^1—Sometimes intentional harm is merely *a means to another end*, not itself the goal sought by the offender. For example, a robber is usually *indifferent* to the harm he does you; he just wants your money.

- B^2—In other cases, the offender's *goal is to harm* the victim. After an argument, one man punches the other, delivering harm for its own sake.

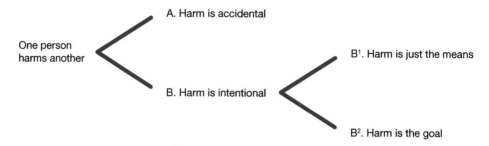

FIGURE 3A
Four Categories of Harm against Another Person

Figure 3a teaches us that harm-doers do not always intend the harm they do and that not all intended harm was done for its own sake. These categories come from the social psychology of harm-doing. In practice, the legal system struggles to classify **offender intent**. How do we determine *what the offender had in mind* at the time of the crime? It is difficult even in theory to understand levels of criminal responsibility, especially when harm is not fully intended.

Sorting Out Accidental Harm

Accidental harm (A) has many nuances. For the accidental harm-doer, society needs to **assign blame**. Sometimes society assigns no blame whatever, sometimes mild blame, sometimes strong blame. Suppose you get into a car accident. Authorities might decide nobody is to blame. Even if they decide one driver is to blame, they might assign mild blame and let the insurance agency handle it. In other cases, blame is more serious—but not serious enough for a **criminal court**. Such cases can end up in **civil court**, but are likely settled out of court by attorneys. Their job is to strike a bargain and resolve disputes. Civil courts and attorneys are far more numerous than criminal attorneys for a reason—most legal blame does not involve threat of incarceration or personal punishment.

Yet some types of serious accidental harm are the province of criminal law. A high-speed drunk driver who kills another person will likely face criminal charges. Legal systems usually distinguish between different types of homicide.[3] For example, **involuntary manslaughter** is the unlawful killing of another human being without intent to kill. If you are planning to go to law school, you should look up how your state defines these diverse forms of homicide and the levels of blame for each:

1. Justifiable homicide

2. Involuntary manslaughter

3. Voluntary manslaughter

4. Negligent homicide

5. Non-negligent homicide

6. Second-degree murder

7. First-degree murder

Pay close attention to the presence or absence of an intent to kill, and the offender's ability to foresee the victim's death. You can see why assigning responsibility for harm-doing is a real and recurring challenge. Any given legal system might take a slightly different approach to dealing with the issues depicted in Figure 3a, but all societies have decisions to make about how much harm an offender intended. The answer to that question influences the way criminal law is written as well as the **discretion** used by justice officials in administering those laws.

Suppose that an employee, after being fired from his job, angrily sets fire to the boss' building. The employee did not realize that the janitor was working late in the building. The offender did not intend to kill the janitor, only to hurt the boss' business. His excuse is unlikely to carry much weight in the legal system. Society has little patience for killing innocent people and often holds defendants accountable for the **worst outcomes** of a criminal act, despite a less nasty initial intent.[4] This disgruntled employee is likely to be charged with murder or with non-negligent homicide. Every society tends to blame and punish people for serious harm they do to others. That's not always easy to do in practice. A legal system must pay some attention to the state of mind of the accused.

A Criminal State of Mind

Mens rea is the Latin term for a "criminal state of mind,"[5] making a harm-doer criminally responsible.[6] As we've noted, an ordinary traffic accident normally does not involve a criminal state of mind and is not treated as a criminal act. However, an ordinary burglar meets the *mens rea* test the moment he enters uninvited, knowing it is someone else's home. Not all cases of criminal intent are as clear-cut as a burglary. That's why many legal codes distinguish different levels of responsibility for criminal actions. No single definition of *mens rea* is found in American states or in other nations. The following categories are commonly used, starting with the worst criminal state of mind:[7]

1. *Purposively.* The defendant undertakes his action intending to do harm.

   Example: Shooting someone with the hope of killing.

2. *Knowingly.* A defendant knows his conduct will almost surely result in harm.

   Example: Shooting at an enemy in a crowd, but accidently killing someone else.

3. *Recklessly.* A defendant knows his actions produce substantial risk of harm.

   Example: Not telling a disliked driver that his car has no brakes.

4. *Negligently.* A defendant should have been aware of a substantial and unjustifiable risk.

   Example: Taking archery practice in an area of high urban density; the arrow misses the target, and a person is injured.

How can we really determine what's in someone's mind when they do harm? How can we tell how much blame to assign? Sometimes a reckless driver harms others without intending to do so. Sometimes a person's action does more harm than initially intended, such as when an assailant does not realize how hard he is hitting the victim. Sometimes someone did not intend harm but **should have known** harm could result, such as the drunk driver who injures a pedestrian. Figure 3b depicts the general problem with the aid of billiard balls.[8]

FIGURE 3B
Depiction of Indirect Harm Resulting from an Initial Action

When a person strikes the first ball to the left, that sets in motion a sequence of impacts, knocking the ball to its right out of place, and so on. By analogy, human actions can set in motion a series of events, indirectly harming others. If that harm is totally unforeseeable, blame is not appropriate. If I invite you to meet me for a cup of coffee, I am not responsible for the accident you have along the way. However, if the harm is likely or obvious, the justice system may blame me. Officials might need to figure out how much blame to assign.

Now we continue from the earlier discussion of "worst outcomes." Once someone has committed a clear criminal act, the criminal justice system usually blames that person for the worst results emerging from that initial criminal act. Consider a pair of offenders robbing a store, with one of the robbers shooting and killing the store clerk. The other robber did not even know his partner had a gun with him, much less that the partner would kill the clerk. Yet the justice system will probably blame him, too, for the death resulting from that robbery.[9] The term ***accomplice liability*** means that an accomplice in a crime is responsible for what was done by his partner in crime.[10] A robbery accomplice who did not intend for his partner to shoot a gun is still liable for the outcome, even for a murder.[11] At least in the United States, such offenders "should have known" that participation in a robbery sets in motion potential outcomes that are more serious than the robbery itself. In terms of the billiard balls in Figure 3b, a store robber is threatening force and should have known that violence could result and that this could be lethal.

Legal scholars use phrases like these:

"The defendant should have *foreseen* the negative outcome" (acted knowingly).

"The defendant should have been aware of the risk" (acted negligently).

"***Any reasonable person*** would know this could happen"[12] (acted recklessly).

These are all attempts to assign responsibility, even when a bad outcome is partly accidental.

You can see that the blaming process is challenging. *Mens rea* is especially difficult to determine for special segments of the population. Do we fully blame a person with a learning disability? What about someone who is psychotic? Do we treat a child differently for harming others?[13] Many discretionary features are built into the law in general, especially for juveniles. The discussion of modern brain research in Part 4 raises the issue that juveniles may be less in control of their actions than adults. Can a criminal state of mind exist among juveniles? Can society hand them a license to harm others with impunity? These recurrent controversies play out in the justice system.

Juvenile Justice Tries Another Approach

For centuries, legal systems treated offenders alike, regardless of age. This started to change in the Middle Ages when English Chancery Courts intervened to look out for the property interests of children. The notion of ***parens patriae***—the state acting in the role of parent—was established.[14] That concept expanded in the mid 19th century. In 1825, the New York House of Refuge became the first American institution to house juveniles in a separate section from adults.[15] Social reformers of the era looked to help juveniles they felt were in extremely harmful neighborhoods and households; they looked to take them away from their impoverished situations, hoping to protect them and society as whole.[16] Yet many reform efforts backfired. Impoverished juveniles were transferred to facilities that were not always improving their lives or prospects.

The first juvenile court formed in 1899 after Chicago social workers pushed for a separate judicial system for juveniles. In many states, juvenile justice is part of the family court system, which handles other matters concerning juveniles.[17] Whether you call them juvenile courts or family courts, juveniles are treated somewhat differently from adults. Outcomes in the juvenile system are negotiated—with the idea that a child is not capable of having a criminal mind. That's why the juvenile system thinks in terms of providing services, not punishment, seeking to protect youths from future trouble. Juvenile systems have great leeway and can even have authority over youths for non-criminal acts, acting in the "best interest of the child."[18]

In modern legal systems, *very* young people cannot be judged to have a criminal state of mind. In Australia those under age 10 cannot be charged with a criminal offense, while blameworthiness at ages 10 through 14 is debatable in court.[19] In American states, the age cutoff for charging varies from 6 to 12, depending on the state. Even after these ages, juveniles are usually handled separately from adult courts.

Since the 1970s, American juvenile courts increasingly follow formal procedures and allow attorney representation. Yet judges and juvenile court social workers remain empowered to figure out the needs of youths and monitor their progress, exerting a good deal of discretion. Juvenile courts often use non-criminal justice terms that sound like negotiated outcomes of disputes in civil courts. Instead of saying "guilty," they might issue a "finding" that the youth committed the delinquent act and is blame-worthy. Juvenile detention facilities are called "homes," "ranches," or "schools." These facilities are quite diverse in size and type. Yet youths, held against their will, will probably consider their assignment as punishment.[20] A few juvenile facilities are secure, resembling prisons more than the public likes to admit.

Still, the juvenile justice approach differs from the adult system. By far the most common juvenile court outcome is probation, as opposed to denial of freedom. A juvenile court can deal with status offenses, actions that are permitted for adults but illegal for juveniles, as we spoke about in Unit 1.4. This means the court could con-sider chronic truancy, running away from home, being out late at night, or being uncontrollable. Drinking alcohol underage is a common status offense that (at least in theory) is subject to juvenile court response. Youths can also enter the juvenile system if their parents abandon or abuse them. This fits the idea that juvenile justice is designed to protect the young. Although the juvenile system is supposed to engage in child protection, it is often so overrun with serious cases that it has little time to act early; it may only become involved after problems have already become serious.[21]

Societies cannot agree about what age criminal responsibility begins. Nor can they agree on the age when juvenile court supervision ends and adult courts take over. Yet each society *tries* to solve the problems. Sometimes this age of adulthood is fixed in law, but some jurisdictions allow it to be decided case by case. For example, a very immature adult might be treated as a child, or a very mature youth might be treated as an adult. In the United States, using adult courts for young offenders is especially common for homicide and other very serious offenses. Also, some juveniles are transferred to adult prisons, and sometimes in the other direction.[22] Yet these discretionary decisions are not necessarily carried out with any consistency.[23] During the 1990s, with a high rate of violent juvenile offending, the list of such crimes increased, while the age for charging in the adult court went down.[24] Since 2005, the Supreme Court and the states have started reversing that trend, recognizing the scientific advances in the understanding of brain development. The age for assessing adult responsibility has been raised to at least 18 years.[25]

So far, we've seen that assigning criminal responsibility is fundamentally difficult and poses many dilemmas. A single and coherent theory of blame is elusive. That's why nations vary and people disagree on what to do. It is difficult not only to write sensible laws assigning blame, but also to apply those laws. That requires figuring out what a harm–doer really intended and then what punishment fits. If there was a *single* answer to these questions, all societies would have found it by now.

Legal theorists have discussed *mens rea* for centuries, but busy justice officials cannot wait around for legal theory. They must decide now! Every day people call on the civil or criminal system to *do something*. Police and judges in all nations face the difficult and expensive task of assessing criminal responsibility and intent, including for young offenders. Numerous disputes and sexual transgressions occur every day. Many property issues arise. Many youths require protection, but also harm others. The best way for society to deal with this onslaught is to find simpler ways to contain problems, usually through families, schools, and small groups, using the justice system as a last resort. When the justice system must get into the act, the first thing it looks for is a way out.

FLASHCARD LIST FOR UNIT 3.1

- Accomplice liability
- Accountability
- Any reasonable person
- Assign blame
- Civil court, case
- Criminal court, case

- Discretion [official, unofficial]
- Four categories of harm
- Harm as a means to another end, as the goal
- Harm others intentionally, unintentionally

- Involuntary manslaughter
- *Mens rea*
- Offender intent
- *Parens patriae*
- Should have known
- Worst outcomes [of a criminal act]

DISCUSSION QUESTIONS

1. Why is *mens rea* important?

2. When is accidental harm also a crime?

Notes

1   Holmes, O. W. (2009 [1909]). *The common law*. Cambridge, MA: Harvard University Press; p. 5.

2   Felson, R. B. (2009). Violence, crime, and violent crime. *International Journal of Conflict and Violence*, *3*(1), 23–39.

3   Blom-Cooper, L. (2011). *Fine lines and distinctions: Murder, manslaughter and the unlawful taking of human life*. Sherfield-on-Loddon, U.K.: Waterside Press.

4   Husak, D. (2014). Abetting a crime. *Law and Philosophy*, *33*(1), 41–73.

5   Malle, B. F., & Nelson, S. E. (2003). Judging *mens rea*: The tension between folk concepts and legal concepts of intentionality. *Behavioral Sciences and the Law*, *21*(5), 563–580.

6   Simons, K. W. (2003). Should the Model Penal Code's *mens rea* provisions be amended? *Ohio State Journal of Criminal Law*, *1*(1), 179–205.

7   National Paralegal College. (n.d.). Model Penal Code's *mens rea* [online]. https://national paralegal.edu/public_documents/courseware_asp_files/criminalLaw/basicElements/ModelPenal CodeMensRea.asp (retrieved May 20, 2017).

8   Alicke, M. D. (2000). Culpable control and the psychology of blame. *Psychological Bulletin*, *126*(4), 556–574.

9   Sayre, F. B. (1930). Criminal responsibility for the acts of another. *Harvard Law Review*, *43*(5), 689–723.

10 Mueller, G. E. (1987). Mens rea of accomplice liability. The *Southern California Law Review*, *61*, 2169.

11 Morris, N. (1956). The felon's responsibility for the lethal acts of others. *University of Pennsylvania Law Review*, *105*(1), 50–81.

12 Ginther, M. R., Shen, F. X., Bonnie, R. J., Hoffman, M. B., Jones, O. D., . . . & Simons, K. W. (2014). The language of *mens rea*. *Vanderbilt Law Review*, *67*(5), 1327–1372.

13 Steinberg, L. (2013). The influence of neuroscience on U.S. Supreme Court decisions about adolescents' criminal culpability. *Nature Reviews Neuroscience*, *14*(7), 513–518.

14 Kurlychek, M. C. (2014). History of juvenile courts. In G. Bruinsma & D. Weisburd (Eds.), *Encyclopedia of criminology and criminal justice*, pp. 2181–2191. New York: Springer.

15 Peirce, B. K. (1969). *A half century with juvenile delinquents: The New York House of Refuge and its times*. Montclair, NJ: Patterson Smith.

16 Platt, A. M. (1977). *The child savers: The invention of delinquency*. Chicago: University of Chicago Press.

17 Rosenheim, M. K. (2002). *A century of juvenile justice*. Chicago: University of Chicago Press.

18 Kohm, L. M. (2008). Tracing the foundations of the best interests of the child standard in American jurisprudence. *Journal of Law and Family Studies*, *10*(2), 337–376.

19   Urbas, G. (2000). *The age of criminal responsibility*. Trends and Issues in Crime and Criminal Justice, No. 181. Canberra: Australian Institute of Criminology. www.aic.gov.au/media_library/publications/tandi_pdf/tandi181.pdf (retrieved August 19, 2016).

20   Hockenberry, S., Sickmund, M., & Sladky, A. (2015). *Juvenile Residential Facility Census, 2012: Selected findings*. Washington, DC: Office of Juvenile Justice and Delinquency Prevention, U.S. Department of Justice.

21   Howell, J. C., & Lipsey, M. W. (2004). A practical approach to evaluating and improving juvenile justice programs. *Juvenile and Family Court Journal, 55*(1), 35–48.

22   Johnson, B. D., & Kurlychek, M. C. (2012). Transferred juveniles in the era of sentencing guidelines: Examining judicial departures for juvenile offenders in adult criminal court. *Criminology, 50*(2), 525–564.

23   Marshall, I. H., & Thomas, C. W. (1983). Discretionary decision-making and the juvenile court. *Juvenile and Family Court Journal, 34*(3), 47–59.

24   Unfortunately, no national data set tracks the number of juvenile cases waived to adult criminal courts. The 13 states that publicly report all juvenile transfers vary in their documentation. See: Griffin, P., Addie, S., Adams, B., & Firestine, K. (2011). *Trying juveniles as adults: An analysis of state transfer laws and reporting*. Washington, DC: Office of Juvenile Justice and Delinquency Prevention; pp. 20–21.

25   Laird, L. (2017). States raising age for adult prosecution back to 18 [online]. *ABA Journal*, February 1. www.abajournal.com/magazine/article/adult_prosecution_juvenile_justice (retrieved May 20, 2017).

Unit 3.2 Realistic Policing

Police are society's ongoing agents of control and confrontation. Their job includes telling you to stop doing something you want to do. Despite this confrontation, most policing is more ordinary than its televised version.[1] Later in this unit we fill in some details about routine police work. Although we hear a lot about police and citizens shooting at one another, you will learn how rarely that happens. You will learn that the real problem is rudeness, going in both directions, and that a central challenge is to maintain a *civil society* with satisfactory relationships between officials and citizens, and among various groups of citizens. Before proceeding, we explain that police officers are diverse individuals with different ideas about what to do or what they can accomplish.

Authority and Control

Some police have an expansive view of their challenge and responsibility to protect the laws and morals of larger society. These officers view themselves as *asserting control* over the streets in the areas they patrol. Yet their goal cannot really be achieved since they cannot control the streets in a whole city or at all hours. That leaves them with a never-ending game of hide and seek.[2]

Other police officers are much more practical; they scale down their expectations and seek to *contain* problems. They are less concerned with maintaining their authority and more concerned with solving problems and *keeping the peace*. They see their first duty as calming people down, "working the beat," and avoiding arrests whenever possible.[3] Even when arresting people, some officers can do so neatly, while others widen the conflict and make things worse.

Female officers are often better than male officers at calming down agitated people and minimizing unnecessary confrontation. An Australian study found that while female officers constituted 24 percent of the police force, only 16 percent of complaint files related to them.[4] Women officers are more likely to bypass aggressive styles and to gain compliance from the public, thus making police work more efficient.[5] The contrast between "asserting control" and "keeping the peace" reflects the police struggle with the realities of a society much larger than themselves.

Police Use of Force

The *police use of force* can be defined as the amount of effort required by police to compel compliance from an unwilling subject.[6] At best, local departments give guidance on when and how much force is considered reasonable.[7] Thus it is not surprising that police use of force generates very different perceptions, depending on whom you ask.

- Citizens often underestimate the amount of force that police need to arrest someone.[8]

- Police often defend one another, even when they are wrong.[9]

- Public attitudes about police use of force reflect the racial and ethnic fissures in society.[10]

Nonwhite and Hispanic adults have consistently more negative perceptions of police and police behavior. In addition, youths of all ethnic and social groups have increasing encounters with police as they proceed through adolescence, with favorable youth attitudes towards the police beginning to decline around age 12, even among white youths.[11]

As this textbook was being written, several very scary murders of police officers occurred in major American cities. Several upsetting police shootings of citizens also occurred. These well-publicized incidents are very harmful to police–community relations,[12] but do not reflect the national arithmetic. The statistics tell us there is very little risk that police will die from gunshots on the job. Based on reports about more than half a million officers in 2015, only 41 officers died from injuries during felonious assaults, and about the same number from traffic accidents.[13] Considering the number of officers at risk, it is quite unusual for them to die in a gun attack or even to face an attack with a gun.

When guns are fired or when other weapons and physical maneuvers that can cause death are used by the police, it is considered *police use of deadly or lethal force*. Most police officers in the United States never fire a gun at anybody and are not fired at by suspects.[14] Again, police reality differs from the televised version. From diverse sources, *The Washington Post* found just under 1,000 police shootings of citizens in 2015.[15]

Not all use of force by police is a use of deadly force. Use of force is now best viewed on a continuum with different levels from verbal interventions and other non-lethal methods up to the use of deadly force. Police policies match these levels to the solving of certain situations involving citizens.[16] A study of several thousand **police–citizen encounters** shows us that police mainly avoid the use of guns.[17] Although police officers usually began by avoiding confrontation, in half of these encounters police used a verbal instruction, usually a command but sometimes a threat. In one of five encounters police used some sort of physical action (such as a pat-down or handcuffing). Additional recent research on lethal force reaffirms its infrequent use and that it is most likely when suspects are resisting arrest.[18] Concerns about deaths and injuries in police custody have led to development and use of weapons that are less lethal, including disabling sprays and **TASERs**, which are one example of conducted energy devices (CEDs) that immobilize a person with a discharge of high-voltage electricity at a distance. Although people have been injured or even have died from police use of these devices, alternative weapons are usually safer than firearms.[19]

The most complete national study of police use of force was carried out 20 years ago, showing much lower rates of use of force than one would expect. For every thousand sworn officers, one civilian was shot, and neck constraints were seldom used. Only one in eight officers had unsnapped the holster or taken the weapon out of it. About 4 percent of officers reported having taken a firm grip of a suspect or twisted a wrist or arm. Just under half had handcuffed a suspect or used a leg restraint.[20] Clearly most police work is nonviolent. However, we cannot dismiss the confrontational nature of an arrest or how difficult it can be to overcome a strong and resistant suspect.[21] About 1 in 11 officers was assaulted in 2015, usually in a minor way. Some 50,212 officers were assaulted while performing their duties.[22] Even though most of these assaults did not require medical treatment, they still serve to poison police experience with citizens. Later in this unit, we discuss how rudeness in both directions fouls police–community relationships.

Ordinary Police Work

Most policing involves paperwork, patrolling, giving traffic tickets, and responding to calls from citizens. This is **ordinary police work**. You will remember that we developed our four challenges every society faces from reviewing calls for service. Most calls from citizens involve annoyances and complaints, not felonies. These are mainly reported by citizens directly dialing 9-1-1 or some other emergency number. Most of these calls for police service are not about crime itself, as Figure 3c tells us. The diagram presents data from Albuquerque, New Mexico,[23] but similar patterns are found in many cities. Some 37 percent of calls are about traffic issues. A dozen percent are about

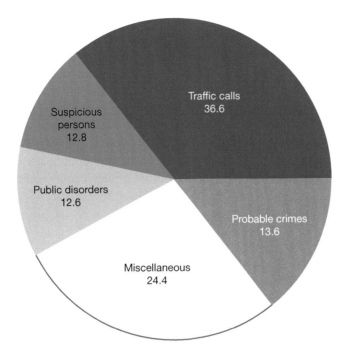

FIGURE 3C
Non-Crime Burdens on Police Based on Responses to Calls for Service (%)
Source: Adapted from D. Pathey & P. Guerin (2009). *Analyzing calls of service to the Albuquerque Police Department.* University of New Mexico, Institute for Social Research.

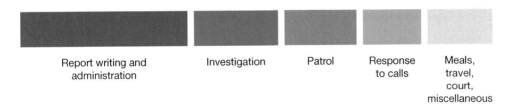

FIGURE 3D
Police Service Costs by Category of Service Provided: An Illustration of Routine Burdens on Police (Canadian Study)
Source: Adapted from A. Malm, N. Pollard, P. Brantingham, P. Tinsley, D. Plecas, P. Brantingham, I. Cohen, & B. Kinney (2005). *A 30 year analysis of police service delivery and costing, "E" Division.* Vancouver: Simon Fraser University, Institute for Canadian Urban Research Studies.

suspicious persons or public disorders. Other calls are to lend medical or other assistance or responding to alarms—usually false alarms. Many are unclassified. Only one in six calls for service appears to be about crimes, in the usual sense of the word. In many cities, barking dogs and noisy neighbors dominate the calls for service.

Police are so busy taking care of these complaints that they have little time left for direct crime intervention, except when emergencies demand it. Figure 3d sums up police time allocation as found in a Canadian study.[24] Much more time is spent writing reports and doing administration than is spent "catching crooks." American police probably spend more time in court than their Canadian counterparts depicted in this chart. Much of that court time deals with routine misdemeanors and traffic cases.

The Decision to Arrest

On occasion, law enforcement officers do make arrests. Under the worst circumstances, they have no choice but to arrest the suspect. More often they have *discretion*—an option whether to arrest or not. We have talked a lot about discretion in the criminal justice system already. A well-known study of police summed up the cost–benefit analysis going through an officer's head in deciding what to do with a suspect in a realistic situation:[25]

1.   Has anyone been hurt or deprived?

2.   Will anyone be hurt or deprived if I do nothing?

3.   Will the arrest improve the situation or only make matters worse?

4.   Is a complaint more likely if there is no arrest, or if there is an arrest?

5.   What does the sergeant expect of me?

6.   Am I getting near the end of my shift?

7.   Do I need to go to court on my day off?

8.   Will the charge stand up, be withdrawn, or be dismissed by the prosecutor?

9.   Will my partner judge me favorably or unfavorably if I arrest?

10. Will this guy do something worse if I let him go?

One of the main features of policing is its *decentralization*. Contrast a police department with a factory whose manager can watch the products being made and supervise the workers along the line. In comparison, police officers are scattered in different parts of the city, making their own decisions and readily evading supervision. Sometimes the officers in the field have better judgment than their supervisors and sometimes not. In any case, a police department does not operate with military precision or centralized control.[26] Perhaps the increasing number of police car tracking devices and cameras both on cars and on officers will eventually give police supervisors more control over what their officers do.[27]

Reactions to Police–Citizen Encounters

With or without arrest, police–citizen encounters have consequences. The general problem is that police contacts are intrinsically confrontational. An officer tells you that you are making too much noise; you are driving too fast; your seatbelt is not fastened. Or an officer tells you what to do—show me your driver's license; fix your tailgate light; go home. Or he does something negative, such as giving you a speeding ticket that costs you money or blaming you when you think the fault belongs to someone else. In each case, an officer-conflict situation exists and can on occasion escalate into something worse. Unfortunately, rudeness can often go in both directions.[28]

Psychology researchers have found that bad experiences influence people much more than good experiences.[29] According to one study, a bad experience during a contact with the police had 14 times as great an impact as a good experience.[30] Thus even if police avoid excessive force and impoliteness most of the time, they will still irritate much of the public in noticeable ways. Similarly, even if most citizens are polite to police officers, a few rude exceptions can spoil the officer's day.

This sort of conflict situation applies not just in minority neighborhoods. Interviews with college students revealed substantial antagonism towards campus police and underlying conflict.[31] These contrasting student views illustrate some of the issues:

[Student A] The police here spend too much time arresting underage drinkers, messing with intoxicated students, and busting up parties when they should be attempting to prevent more serious crimes. This is college. Kids are going to party. Hell, that's why some of us are here!

[Student B] The police suck. They just drive around looking for a party to write up. They are quick to write tickets for drinking-related matters, but don't seem to bother to pursue crimes when people's cars are broken into or vandalized. All they care about is seeing how badass they can make themselves seem by messing with drunk college kids.

[Student C] Police need to be more aggressive in the downtown area in arresting belligerent drunks. Too many students get wasted and take over. The cops seem oblivious, as does the school.

[Student D] The cops here have a very tough job. This is a college town, and college kids don't exactly care what the police say or do. I think they do the best they can. It's not easy to control nearly 20 thousand crazy college kids, most of whom are partying all the time.

Clearly students disagree about the police role. Some students appear not to know that drunkenness is linked to car vandalism. The police are caught in the middle with complaints by those breaking rules and those wanting more enforcement—sometimes the same person making both arguments on different occasions. Despite complaining, many students accept police authority.[32]

Many police encounter complaints by citizens angry over noisy neighbors, or who have come home to find their homes burgled. These citizens often get angry about the lack of police effort in resolving their concerns or pursuing the persons who offended against them.[33] They might not understand that the police cannot legally or practically accomplish what they are asking; nor can they duplicate what happens on television.

Procedural Justice and the Police

To understand public satisfaction with police, we return to procedural justice, a concept introduced in Unit 2.4.[34] The importance of procedural justice was recognized by a recent presidential task force on policing.[35] In a democratic society, citizens expect official procedures to be fair, and they expect to be treated properly as those procedures play out. They expect to receive their traffic ticket with a proper explanation and suitable politeness. They do not want to be brushed aside while reporting a crime. *Impolite encounters* are important because they undermine the legitimacy of police with citizens. Police also have a right to proper treatment by citizens.

In this section we examine what happens in real life. We consider how often police are impolite to citizens, and how frequently citizens are rude to police. Even in nations with limited ethnic variation, police can have unpleasant interactions with citizens. Yet the racial divide can intensify conflicts between police and citizens further. Keep in mind that police have a confrontational job—they tell you that you should be doing something different. They tell you to end the party or to stop drinking outside, or something else you do not want to hear. Do you respond politely? Do they tell you politely, following principles of procedural justice? Does a small incident escalate into something worse? Even the victim of a crime can become angry with the police officer, expecting more service or demanding that the crime be solved.

You already know from prior discussions that most police–citizen encounters occur without violence and certainly without guns blaring. You will be happy to know that citizens are much more likely than not to be courteous, respectful, and polite to police. This includes citizens of different races than the officer. Expert communications researchers watched many hours of videotapes of police–citizen encounters, learning that both white and nonwhite citizens were much more likely than not to be courteous, pleasant, respectful, and polite. Communications were generally more positive if the citizen and officer were of the same race, but even when they were of different races, politeness in both directions still occurred much more often than impoliteness.[36]

The problem comes from comparisons to the rest of daily interactions. To put it bluntly, most workers can expect unpleasant encounters with customers or fellow workers less than 1 in 20 times. Most customers and clients can expect courtesy almost always from service providers. Police can expect roughly one in five citizen encounters to be unpleasant. Citizens can expect a similar risk of an unpleasant encounter with police, and many citizens will experience *all* police encounters as intrusive. Moreover, we cannot rule out the evidence that police are more likely to focus on minority group members, enhancing distrust no matter what the reason for this focus. Any society with a background of racial divide ends up with extra conflict between police and their community, with a certain amount of rude behavior going in both directions.

One study observed thousands of police–citizen encounters in Indianapolis, Indiana, and St. Petersburg, Florida. Overall, although citizens were respectful in 85 percent of cases, they were disrespectful in the remaining 15 percent of encounters. The researchers identified two types of disrespect, passive and active. Passive displays of disrespect, which were more common, included ignoring an officer's request. Much less often, citizens were actively disrespectful towards police; this included name-calling, derogatory remarks, slurs, and insulting gestures.[37]

Another study, involving police officers from 12 departments in Illinois and Wisconsin, found a major problem of police stress from dealing with mistreatment by the public (compounded by mistreatment within their own departments). The study revealed "disrespectful, rude, or condescending behaviors" by the public. Officers reported that members of the public "made personal verbal attacks against me," "showed that they were irritated or impatient with me," and "made negative comments about my job performance."[38]

We interpret these results both in terms of the number of negative encounters and in terms of emotional impact. The numbers tell us that most citizen encounters with police are reasonably polite. However, even though the worst incidents are uncommon, exceptions are numerous enough; moreover, they can have very serious impacts on police.

To sum up, many citizens report negative encounters with police, and many police report negative encounters with citizens. Since, in psychological terms, bad experiences outweigh good experiences, rude encounters have significance beyond their raw numbers. The tempo of rude encounters is also important. A citizen might have a rude experience with an officer once or twice a year, or less often. However, an officer might have a rude experience with a citizen once or twice a week, or more often. Rude encounters can be amplified if community members talk about them, if police talk to one another about them, or if the media cover the worst incidents. And, as we saw in Part 1, rudeness can escalate, creating riskier situations for both the police and the public.

As noted already, police are society's agents of control and confrontation. We should be gratified that most encounters are polite, but unfortunately the worst incidents cause the most trouble. On television, "police" (that is, actors in police uniforms) use force a good deal, often drawing their guns and shooting or getting shot; yet police in real life do not even spend most of their time engaging in arrests. Each police encounter with the public gives the police the opportunity to treat citizens fairly and reinforce their legitimacy more broadly.

Service vs. Crime Reduction

Arguably, police are less a crime-fighting force than a public service agency.[39] As we've just seen, they handle traffic problems, respond to calls for service, and quiet down undergraduate parties. They give crime victims a chance to report for insurance purposes or to complain about a crime that is unsolvable. They fill out forms. They give the community a sense of police presence. Interestingly, police deal with small issues and huge issues more than with middle-level issues. They devote a lot of time to both barking dogs and well-publicized murders, with little time left for ordinary burglaries. They use discretion every day, mostly to avoid arrests.[40]

A citizen expects police to patrol, to drive by their home as often as possible. However, police patrols are hard to do in a modern American city with people spread out over considerable space. For example, Los Angeles has 1.3 million households and 9,800 officers.[41] To cover the 168 hours in a week, four shifts are needed, reducing personnel to 2,450 officers at a time. Because of regular days off, illness, training time, and vacation, less than a fourth of these officers are available for patrol at any given time. That leaves only 612 officers for 1.3 million households, so that each patrolling officer would have to cover an average of 2,124 homes. Driving by so many homes makes it impossible to know what's going on and to protect homes very well. Even a doubling of the size of the police force would be doubling of a drop in the bucket. Other cities face similar problems.

Directed Patrol and Hot Spot Policing

The bad news from researchers is that undirected police patrols are not effective in preventing crime.[42] The good news is that police patrols can be focused in ways that prove effective. There is increasing research showing that crime is heavily concentrated at particular blocks or addresses. That research is reviewed in Part 5. Such concentrations open the door for directed patrols and hot spot policing. **Directed patrols** focus at particular times on particular addresses or complexes known to generate more crime. **Hot spot policing** is similar but might include a slightly wider area—such as several blocks where problems are concentrated.[43] The research indicates that randomly arriving to police a specific place for 15 minutes reduces crime there and in the vicinity.[44]

Do Police Reduce Crime, or Merely Displace It?

You recall in Part 2 we discussed crime displacement—the hypothesis that crime reduced here simply goes there. This is a very important topic. If crime prevented in one place is merely pushed to another, our efforts to control crime will have been wasted. The issue is often raised with respect to situational crime prevention. Fortunately, the research literature shows that most efforts do not produce substantial crime displacement. In fact, there is more often real crime reduction or diffusion of benefits—crime is reduced not only in the area where prevention occurs, but also in surrounding areas.

The same issue can be raised with hot spot policing or any directed police patrols. Do these police efforts simply push crime elsewhere, resulting in no reduction in total crime? Although displacement can occur in some cases, multiple tests of hot spot policing have found noteworthy crime and disorder reductions.[45] When displacement and diffusion effects were measured, unintended crime prevention benefits emerged, with crime reductions beyond the immediate hot spot.[46]

Sometimes hot spot policing focuses on specific places or types of locations, such as bus stops, where police can show up for a very brief period and yet have a major impact in reducing crime.[47] Different methods to focus police efforts have proven to be effective.[48] Although some drug policing pushes offenders to later hours or nearby crime locations, this often forces drug dealers out of the best places and times for selling drugs so that offenders end up with fewer sales and the drug problem diminishes.[49] Moreover, closing down the best locations for selling drugs, such as an open market in a park, can remove the chance to reach new and younger consumers, causing the drug-consuming population to get older over time, without being replenished.[50]

Such strategic efforts can have greater impact in reducing crime and involve fewer personnel and lower costs. This depends on improvements in crime analysis, and it will benefit from future improvement in the ability to predict crime[51] using mapping and crime analysis to figure out how.[52] With such information, police can then focus their efforts and achieve much greater crime prevention per dollar spent. This sometimes occurs through ***intelligence-led policing***,[53] which gathers systematic information on *individual suspects*, as well as community mapping of *crime patterns and locations*. These approaches share an interest in

- gathering more information about offenders and crime; then

- organizing that information so it can be used quickly; then

- evaluating whether the police have reduced local crime.

Modern policing seeks to focus efforts and reduce crime with limited resources. Of course, patrolling is not the only technique police have available; nor do they have to stay within their own organization to reduce crime.

Problem-Oriented Policing

In Part 2 we discussed how situational crime prevention can help reduce crime. The numerous techniques of situational prevention can be used by police to focus their efforts. This is known as "***problem-oriented policing***" and was invented by ***Herman Goldstein***, a leader in policing for many decades.[54] This approach involves first identifying "the problem." A problem looks beyond any single offender or any single criminal act to the risky local situation that causes multiple incidents. For example, suppose that Joe's bar is serving people as much alcohol as they ask for, no matter how drunk they already might be. Suppose that the crime analyst maps all late crimes in the vicinity, documenting that Joe's bar is the epicenter. As Figure 3e indicates, this bar creates many crime problems. People who get drunk at Joe's then break in to cars, have traffic accidents, get in fights, urinate on neighbors' lawns, make a lot of noise, and more.[55] The map in Figure 3e shows that Joe's bar is *the problem*; it is creating risky situations beyond the barroom itself.[56] In most jurisdictions, this is contrary to liquor law and would justify revocation of Joe's liquor license, or at least threatening to do so.

That's why civil law, which regulates private matters and includes licensing and administrative rules, supplements the police and criminal justice system.[57] Police have learned to reduce criminal activity using civil law in various cities. For example, in one study, one in four property or business owners complied or made tenants comply

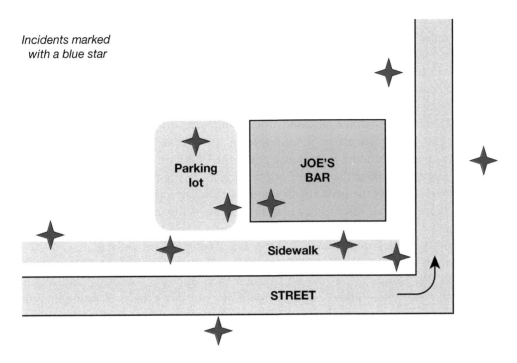

Incidents marked with a blue star

FIGURE 3E
A Single Barroom Can Generate Problems Nearby

with the law after receiving notices from the police threatening them with fines.[58] The information mapped in Figure 3e, along with evidence that liquor laws are being violated, justifies revoking Joe's license to operate the bar. Even a threat to close the bar pushes Joe and other bar owners to follow the law.

Several arguments have been used to justify this strategy:

- It is easier to punish one bar owner than to apprehend 100 customers.

- Civil law (which governs liquor licenses) requires lower levels of proof than criminal law since nobody is to be incarcerated.

- This approach allows more crime reduction with fewer arrests and prosecutions.

- This saves money and police effort.[59]

This reflects a more general issue in policing. Most police activity is reactive—citizens call and complain, police are dispatched, then they try to deal with each incident one by one. It is very difficult for police to escape this mode given public demands on their time. However, problem-oriented policing offers a much more efficient alternative. Instead of responding to each incident one at a time, the police draw upon liquor authorities, housing officials, and other local sources to mitigate the local source of the problem.

The approach in Figure 3e of mapping Joe's bar and surrounding crime problems can be generalized to other facilities; one example is mapping private apartment buildings that permit an active indoor drug market inside, which also lets crime percolate to the surrounding area. Police could then find out who owns the building and send a letter warning the owner of civil action. Without requiring arrests, that process would confront the owner with a potential loss of property, giving an incentive to handle the situation. Police have a high success rate at low cost using that method.[60] In so doing they involve other branches of government, including the code enforcement department, the health department, and the liquor enforcement agency.

This shows that police can improve their efficiency with a dual strategy of broadening and focusing.[61] They can broaden their efforts by working with other branches of government and social agencies. They can focus their efforts by finding out where and when to patrol or using crime mapping to isolate how and where a problem emerges. Patrols can be directed at places where risk is greatest, during times when crimes are most likely to occur. A good police department puts more officers around the entertainment district at night and near the secondary school in the afternoon as students are going home. A good police department learns where its crime hot spots are located and how these shift by day of week, hour of day, or even faster. That depends on good data systems and good crime analysts who know how to put the computer to work in a practical way. Such innovations are found in some police agencies, but certainly not in all, and some officers ignore any suggestions that are made. Fortunately, many officers are oriented towards doing good in a practical way and have good intuitions about how to do so.

Efforts to Avoid Arresting People

Even though police arrest citizens, they spend much more effort trying to avoid doing so. Police cannot respond formally to every event of underage drinking or substance abuse coming to their attention. As we mentioned in Unit 2.4, sometimes police determine these incidents to be *de minimis* and take no actions. Other times, they take actions short of arrest. They cannot arrest everybody drunk in public or haul to jail every late-night partygoer. They cannot prosecute every person they take to the station, much less every motorist stopped. The prosecutors and judges are already too busy and would get very angry with them if they tried to send forth all cases.

To avoid arresting people, police use their discretion and often use other methods.[62] They

- negotiate with people to get them to follow the law;

- ask other individuals to help gain compliance;

- ask other organizations to help deal with some offenders; and

- call upon other government agencies.

Police might negotiate with citizens in their homes, on the street, in bars, and even in police stations.[63] These negotiations are designed to gain compliance with laws without requiring an arrest. We might consider this to be semi-official action. It is official because the officers have the power to arrest. Their badges and uniforms give them an extra authority. However, we use the term "semi-official" because they may be very friendly, ask politely, explain, reason, or otherwise induce compliance, leaving the threat to arrest *unvoiced*. This is why we recognize police discretion as being so important.

Many of these techniques are quite conversant with criminological theory. For example, ***police–citizen negotiation*** might include reminding someone of the rules, drawing upon the personal controls instilled in their childhood. Control theory applies when reminding partygoers about the neighbors or hinting that a parent will be called. This offers us a somewhat different take on traditional theories. We usually think of personal controls and social controls as preventing people from initiating a crime. However, it may also be possible to use these methods after a crime is underway to secure a peaceful desistence.[64]

More likely than not, citizens comply with an officer's request. Often an officer can offer a simple explanation and persuade a citizen to comply. Despite famous cases to the contrary, this tendency to comply transcends race and socioeconomic status. Most minority group members comply when an officer asks them to quiet the party or to take their friend home when he has had too much to drink. The ability to arrest and punish is *implicit* in the police officer's authority, and a good officer learns how to use that authority to simplify the task. An officer might be thinking of ways to avoid a lot of paperwork. He or she might wish to avoid complaints by citizens, police superiors, prosecutors, or judges. An officer might wish to avoid bandages and trips to the hospital, not only for injuries to suspects but also injuries to their own body. An officer also wants to avoid ruining his own evening. As explained by one police chief with long experience on the street and in leadership:

- *All arrests encompass a risk of resistance.* Some issues are simply not important enough to risk aggravating a situation with an arrest when lesser means will suffice.

- *Arrests take time to process.* Custody arrests take an officer out of service for quite a while, and when things are busy, it is better to stay in service to deal with emergency and higher-priority calls than to take the time to process an arrest for some minor offense.

- *For quality of life issues, enforcement by arrest is rarely effective.* Instead, peer pressure or negotiation is more likely to resolve the issue in the long term.

- *Solving the immediate problem is often the goal.* If an officer can get compliance by simply asking for it, without the need for enforcement action, they are happy to do so. Anything more is unnecessary and could make it more difficult to gain voluntary compliance should they have to deal with that person at some later date.[65]

From reading the comments above, you can see how this officer (who later became chief of police) combined wisdom with enforcement. He further explained that most police–citizen contacts involve minor crimes and misbehaviors, and can be resolved without any overt threat to arrest. Some contacts lead to initial verbal aggression, which can peter out if officers give people time to vent. Often, an angry person just wants the catharsis of voicing a complaint. If the officer lets the person purge their emotions, that might be all it takes to calm a disturbance. Officers who avoid rushing in too quickly often discover that a situation can resolve itself. Sometimes aggressive words continue, requiring officers to warn or threaten the parties involved with enforcement action. With experience, officers learn that shouting or threatening often makes the situation worse, including for themselves.[66] Quieting down the party to maintain good relationships with neighbors works better than demanding compliance because "I am a police officer." The police shouting that is heard in television shows illustrates exactly how bad policing is carried out.

Officers can also call upon cultural or social supports in order to gain compliance without arrest, such as inviting family or friends to handle the matter peacefully. Getting another party to take responsibility for resolving the issue can be helpful; for example, allowing a sober person to take an intoxicated person home. When a youth is acting aggressively, it may make more sense to invoke a call to a parent than a visit to jail.

We have been offered these suggestions by experienced police officers: A professional demeanor is very important for calming a situation and avoiding arrests. To achieve this, an officer needs to lower the level of citizen arousal until some semblance of discussion is possible. Even if the officer is not calm inside, he or she must convey that impression, lowering the voice, calming facial muscles, appearing confident, foregoing accusations against a citizen, and avoiding an angry response to a citizen's insult. The officer usually should not move in too close too soon, thus staying out of danger while a citizen vents. In other words, officers should not join the fray unless and until they finally must.

Some officers get to be very good at quelling disturbances or otherwise gaining compliance while minimizing escalation. These officers understand well the dispute escalation process we discussed in Part 1. Inexperienced officers or those lacking "people skills" often end up producing more work for themselves and other officials than really is necessary while, at the same time, antagonizing the community and failing to resolve the ongoing problems. Of course, police negotiation has its limits, but that does not mean arrest and punishment are all that remain. When this is the case, citizens need to feel they were treated fairly.

FLASHCARD LIST FOR UNIT 3.2

- Asserting control
- Civil society
- Decentralization (of police work)
- Directed patrols
- Discretion (to arrest)
- Goldstein, Herman

- Hot spot policing
- Impolite encounters
- Intelligence-led policing
- Keeping the peace
- Negotiation, police–citizen
- Ordinary police work

- Police use of deadly or lethal force
- Police use of force
- Police–citizen encounters
- Problem-oriented policing
- TASERs

DISCUSSION QUESTIONS

1. How much time do police spend dealing directly with crime?

2. Why do police so often avoid arresting people?

Notes

1 Bittner, E. (1990). *Aspects of police work*, p. 30. Boston, MA: Northeastern University Press.

2 Herbert, S. (2006). Policing contested space: On patrol at Smiley and Hauser. In N. Fyfe, (Ed.), *Images of the street: Planning, identity and control in public space*, pp. 220–230. Abingdon, U.K.: Routledge.

3 Muir, W. K. (1979). *Police: Streetcorner politicians*. Chicago: University of Chicago Press.

4 Porter, L. E., & Prenzler, T. (2015). Police officer gender and excessive force complaints: An Australian study. *Policing and Society*, 1–19. Published online November 26, 2015. http://dx.doi.org/10.1080/10439463.2015.1114616.

5 Bergman, M. E., Walker, J. M., & Jean, V. A. (2016). A simple solution to policing problems: Women! *Industrial and Organizational Psychology*, 9(3), 590–597.

6 International Association of Chiefs of Police (2002). *Police use of force in America 2001*. Alexandria, VA: IACP. www.theiacp.org/portals/0/pdfs/publications/2001useofforce.pdf (retrieved May 20, 2017).

7   National Institute of Justice (2016). Police use of force [online], modified November 29, 2016. www.nij.gov/topics/law-enforcement/officer-safety/use-of-force/pages/welcome.aspx (retrieved May 20, 2017).

8   Terrill, W., & Mastrofski, S. D. (2002). Situational and officer-based determinants of police coercion. *Justice Quarterly, 19*(2), 215–248.

9   Correll, J. Park, B., Judd, C. M., Wittenbrink, B., Sadler, M. S., & Keesee, T. (2007). Across the thin blue line: Police officers and racial bias in the decision to shoot. *Journal of Personality and Social Psychology, 92*(6), 1006–1023.

10 Peck, J. H. (2015). Minority perceptions of the police: A state-of-the-art review. *Policing: An International Journal of Police Strategies & Management, 38*(1), 173–203.

11 Schuck, A. M. (2013). A life-course perspective on adolescents' attitudes to police: DARE, delinquency, and residential segregation. *Journal of Research in Crime and Delinquency, 50*(4), 579–607.

12 Weitzer, R. (2015). American policing under fire: Misconduct and reform. *Society, 52*(5), 475–480.

13 FBI: Uniform Crime Reporting. (n.d.). Law enforcement officers killed and assaulted, 2015 [online]. https://ucr.fbi.gov/leoka/2015/home (retrieved May 9, 2017).

14 For an idea about the relatively low risk in New York City, see: Bratton, W. J. (2014). *New York City Police Department annual firearms discharge report, 2013.* New York: New York City Police Department. www.nyc.gov/html/nypd/downloads/pdf/analysis_and_planning/nypd_annual_firearms_discharge_report_2013.pdf (retrieved August 1, 2017).

15 Source: www.washingtonpost.com/pb/policeshootings/ (retrieved August 19, 2016).

16 National Institute of Justice (2009). The use-of-force continuum [online], August 4. www.nij.gov/topics/law-enforcement/officer-safety/use-of-force/Pages/continuum.aspx (retrieved May 20, 2017).

17 Terrill, W. (2003). Police use of force and suspect resistance: The micro process of the police-suspect encounter. *Police Quarterly, 6*(1), 51–83.

18 Leinfelt, F. H. (2005). Predicting use of non-lethal force in a mid-size police department: A longitudinal analysis of the influence of subject and situational variables. *The Police Journal, 78*(4), 285–300.

19 Williams, H. E. (2008). *TASER electronic control devices and sudden in-custody death: Separating evidence from conjecture.* Springfield, IL: Charles C. Thomas Publisher.

20 McEwen, T. (1996). *National data collection on police use of force.* Washington, DC: National Institute of Justice.

21 Terrill, W. (2005). Police use of force: A transactional approach. *Justice Quarterly, 22*(1), 107–138.

22 FBI: Uniform Crime Reporting, Law enforcement officers killed and assaulted, 2015.

23 Pathey, D., & Guerin, P. (2009). *Analyzing calls for service to the Albuquerque Police Department, June 2009.* University of New Mexico: Institute for Social Research. http://isr.unm.edu/reports/2009/analyzing-calls-for-service-to-the-albuquerque-police-department.pdf (retrieved June 9, 2017).

24 Malm, A., Pollard, N., Brantingham, P., Tinsley, P., Plecas, D., . . . & Kinney, B. (2005). *A 30 year analysis of police service delivery and costing, "E" Division.* Vancouver: Simon Fraser University, Institute for Canadian Urban Research Studies; see p. 14.

25 Wilson, J. Q. (1978). *Varieties of police behavior.* Cambridge, MA: Harvard University Press; see p. 84.

26   Reiss, A. J. (1973). *The police and the public*. New Haven, CT: Yale University Press.

27   White, M. D. (2014). *Police officer body-worn cameras: Assessing the evidence*. Washington, DC: Office of Community Oriented Policing Services.

28   Sykes, R. E., & Clark, J. P. (1975). A theory of deference exchange in police-civilian encounters. *American Journal of Sociology*, *85*(3), 584–600.

29   Baumeister, R. F., Bratslavsky, E., Finkenauer, C., & Vohs, K. D. (2001). Bad is stronger than good. *Review of General Psychology*, *5*(4), 323–370.

30   Skogan, W. G. (2006). Asymmetry in the impact of encounters with police. *Policing & Society*, *16*(2), 99–126.

31   Weiss, K. G. (2013). *Party school: Crime, campus, and community*. Boston, MA: Northeastern University Press.

32   Allen, A. N. (2017). Do campus police ruin college students' fun? *Deviant Behavior*, *38*(3), 334–344.

33   Skogan, W. G. (1990). *The police and the public in England and Wales: A British crime survey report*. London: Stationery Office.

34   Goodman-Delahunty, J., Verbrugge, H., Sowemimo-Coker, C., & Kingsford, J. (2013). Procedural justice violations in police-citizen interactions: Insights from complaints about police. *Journal of the Institute of Justice & International Studies*, *13*, 1–18.

35   President's Task Force on 21st Century Policing. (2015). *Final report of the President's Task Force on 21st Century Policing*. Washington, DC: Office of Community Oriented Policing Services.

36   Dixon, T. L., Schell, T. L., Giles, H., & Drogos, K. L. (2008). The influence of race in police–civilian interactions: A content analysis of videotaped interactions taken during Cincinnati police traffic stops. *Journal of Communication*, *58*(3), 530–549.

37   Reisig, M. D., McCluskey, J. D., Mastrofski, S. D., & Terrill, W. (2004). Suspect disrespect toward the police. *Justice Quarterly*, *21*(2), 241–268.

38   Adams, G. A., & Buck, J. (2010). Social stressors and strain among police officers: It's not just the bad guys. *Criminal Justice and Behavior*, *37*(9), 1030–1040.

39   Bercal, T. E. (1970). Calls for police assistance: "Consumer demands for governmental service." *The American Behavioral Scientist*, *13*(5), 681–692.

40   Ericson, R. V. (1982). *Reproducing order: A study of police patrol work*. Toronto: University of Toronto Press.

41   FBI Uniform Crime Reporting (n.d.). Crime in the United States 2013 [online]. https://ucr.fbi.gov/crime-in-the-u.s/2013/crime-in-the-u.s.-2013/tables/table-78/table-78-cuts/table_78_full_time_law_enforcement_employees_california_by_city_2013.xls (retrieved June 4, 2017).

42   Kelling, George L., Pate, T., Dieckman, D., & Brown, C. E. (1977). The Kansas City preventive patrol experiment: A summary. In Caro, F. G. (Ed.), *Readings in evaluation research*, pp. 323–342. New York: Russell Sage Foundation.

43   Telep, C. W., & Weisburd, D. (2016). Hot spot policing. In W. G. Jennings (Ed.), *The encyclopedia of crime & punishment*. Chichester, U.K.: John Wiley & Sons.

44   Telep, C. W., Mitchell, R. J., & Weisburd, D. (2014). How much time should the police spend at crime hot spots? Answers from a police agency directed randomized field trial in Sacramento, California. *Justice Quarterly*, *31*(5), 905–933.

45   Weisburd, D., Wyckoff, L. A., Ready, J., Eck, J. E., Hinkle, J., & Gajewski, F. (2006). Does crime just move around the corner? A controlled study of spatial displacement and diffusion of crime control benefits. *Criminology, 44*(3), 549–592.

46   Braga, A. A., Papachristos, A. V., & Hureau, D. M. (2014). The effects of hot spots policing on crime: An updated systematic review and meta-analysis. *Justice Quarterly, 31*(4), 633–663.

47   Ariel, B., & Partridge, H. (2016). Predictable policing: Measuring the crime control benefits of hotspots policing at bus stops. *Journal of Quantitative Criminology*, 1–25. Published online June 29. DOI: 10.1007/s10940-016-9312-y.

48   Haberman, C. P., & Ratcliffe, J. H. (2012). The predictive policing challenges of near repeat armed street robbery. *Policing: A Journal of Policy and Practice, 6*(2): 151–166.

49   Rengert, G., Chakravorty, S., Bole, T., & Henderson, K. (2000). A geographic analysis of illegal drug markets. In M. Natarajan & M. Hough (Eds.), *Illegal drug markets.* Crime Prevention Studies, Vol. 11, pp. 219–240. Monsey, NY: Criminal Justice Press.

50   Knutsson, J. (1997). Restoring public order in a city park. In R. Homel (Ed.), *Policing for prevention: Reducing crime, public intoxication and injury.* Crime Prevention Studies, Vol. 7, pp. 133–151. Monsey, NY: Criminal Justice Press.

51   Bowers, K. J., Johnson, S. D., & Pease, K. (2004). Prospective hot-spotting: The future of crime mapping? *British Journal of Criminology, 44*(5), 641–658.

52   Harries, K. (1999). *Mapping crime: Principle and practice.* Washington, DC: National Institute of Justice, Crime Mapping Research Center.

53   Ratcliffe, J. H. (2016). *Intelligence-led policing.* Abingdon, U.K.: Routledge.

54   Center for Problem-Oriented Policing. (n.d.). Herman Goldstein [online]. www.popcenter.org/bios/goldstein (retrieved August 1, 2017).

55   Green, J., & Plant, M. A. (2007). Bad bars: A review of risk factors. *Journal of Substance Use, 12*(3), 157–189.

56   Scott, M. S., & Dedel, K. (2006). *Assaults in and around bars,* 2nd edition. Washington, DC: Office of Community Oriented Policing Services. www.popcenter.org/problems/pdfs/Assaults_in_and_Around_Bars.pdf (retrieved August 1, 2017).

57   Smith, M. (1998). Regulating opportunities: Multiple roles for civil remedies in situational crime prevention. In L. Green Mazerolle & J. Roehl (Eds.), *Civil remedies and crime prevention.* Crime Prevention Studies, Vol. 9, pp. 67–88. Monsey, NY: Criminal Justice Press. www.popcenter.org/library/crimeprevention/volume_09/Regulating_Opportunities.pdf (retrieved May 16, 2017). Scott, M. S., & Goldstein, H. (2005). *Shifting and sharing responsibility for public safety problems.* Problem-Oriented Guides for Police, Response Guide Series, No. 3.Washington, DC: Office of Community Oriented Policing Services.

58   Payne, T. C. (2017). Reducing excessive police incidents: Do notices to owners work? *Security Journal, 30*(3), 922–939. Madensen, T. D. (2007). *Bar management and crime: Toward a dynamic theory of place management and crime hotspots.* Doctoral dissertation, University of Cincinnati.

59   Reid-Howie Associates. (2003). *Liquor licensing and public disorder: Review of literature on the impact of licensing and other controls, and audit of local initiatives,* Research Findings No. 68. Edinburgh: Scottish Executive Social Research. www.popcenter.org/problems/assaultsinbars/PDFs/crf68.pdf (retrieved August 1, 2017).

60   Eck, J. (1998). Preventing crime by controlling drug dealing on private rental property. *Security Journal*, *11*(1), 37–43. Eck, J. E., & Wartell, J. (1998). Improving the management of rental properties with drug problems: A randomized experiment. In L. Green Mazerolle & J. Roehl (Eds.), *Civil remedies and crime prevention*. Crime Prevention Studies, Vol. 9, pp. 161–185. Monsey, NY: Criminal Justice Press. www.popcenter.org/library/crimeprevention/volume_09/ImprovingtheManagement.pdf (retrieved August 1, 2017).

61   Plant, J. B., & Scott, M. S. (2009). *Effective policing and crime prevention: A problem-oriented guide for mayors, city managers, and county executives*. Washington, DC: Office of Community Oriented Policing Services. www.popcenter.org/library/reading/pdfs/mayorsguide.pdf (Retrieved August 20, 2016).

62   This section draws from personal communication with Howard Williams, former Police Chief, San Marcos, Texas.

63   Miller, S., & Blackler, J. (2017). *Ethical issues in policing*. Abingdon, U.K.: Routledge.

64   Bard, M., & Zacker, J. (1976). *The police and interpersonal conflict: Third-party intervention approaches*. Washington, DC: Police Foundation.

65   Williams, H., personal communication.

66   Birzer, M. L. (2003). The theory of andragogy applied to police training. *Policing: An International Journal of Police Strategies & Management*, *26*(1), 29–42.

Unit 3.3 Realistic Court Activity

We just discussed situations where the police may negotiate a solution to a situation and avoid making an arrest. Once an arrest is made, it is up to the courts to determine the *mens rea* of the accused, examine the evidence, and ultimately assess blame by determining the guilt of the accused; if guilty, the court then imposes a sentence. At the end of Part 2, we talked about all the steps required by the court system and noted the appeal of avoiding all these steps. This unit gives you some more information about what it takes to administer justice in a modern society, considering the delays and uncertainties that are part of this process.

Delay in Court

Let's look at what really happens in court processing. Figure 3f describes "driving under the influence" (DUI) cases in an Arizona study. After 90 days, six out of ten cases remain unresolved by the justice system, and after five months, one in four cases remain open.[1] Length of time for court processing in felony cases often lasts more than a year in the United States.[2] Canadian[3] and Australian[4] court statistics indicate very similar problems.

The U.S. Constitution guarantees a **speedy trial**, but that is not the normal practice for serious cases, with felony cases taking a year or more. One reason is that courts are very busy. Another reason is that some defendants are in no hurry to be tried and sentenced, especially those out on bail. Some of those incarcerated awaiting trial agree to a plea bargain that grants time served and lets them out of jail almost immediately. Others, however, may fear a long sentence and thus decide to delay taking a plea or to take their chances with a trial. The constitutional right to a speedy trial is offset by the fact that most petitions to delay the trial are filed by the defendant.[5] Busy prosecutors and judges are only too happy to comply.

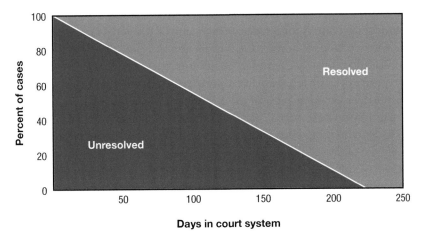

FIGURE 3F

Case Duration, Driving Under the Influence of Alcohol Cases, Flagstaff, Arizona

Source: Adapted from S. Yates (2014). *An analysis of case flow management of driving under the influence (DUI) cases in the Flagstaff Justice Court.* Williamsburg: VA. National Center for State Courts.

Although speedy adjudication is unlikely for serious cases, lower-level police courts often handle minor cases quickly, as we will discuss a bit later. Any defendant who pleads "not guilty" to a felony is in for a long wait. The best chance of speeding things up is to arrange a ***plea bargain***, as discussed in the next section. This can occur any time but is usually before a trial begins, including the period soon after arrest. This is how a defendant might greatly reduce the time needed to resolve the case—but at a price: He or she must plead guilty.

Plea Bargaining

The defendant can get it over with quickly by simply pleading guilty and accepting the punishment that the prosecutor demands and the judge is willing to impose. Defense attorneys often negotiate with the prosecutor on behalf of their client; the resulting agreement is called a plea bargain.[6] This illustrates why a knowledgeable defense attorney is very important for someone charged with a criminal offense. Researchers have believed that public defenders are more knowledgeable than private attorneys about the routines of a local court based on their daily contact. Public defenders would push for pleas in most cases, knowing the judge and prosecutor and what they wanted. Private attorneys would more often push for trials. Current research is mixed, finding in some places public defenders push for fewer pleas than private attorneys.[7]

In the United States, plea bargaining is *very* important.[8] To give you an idea, a 2004 study of state courts[9] found that 96 percent of property crime cases involved a guilty plea with no trial whatever. Of the remaining cases, three out of four led to a bench trial, handled only by the judge. A full jury trial is very rare indeed.[10] A similar pattern was shown for drug cases. Even weapons offenses, robberies, and aggravated assaults are plea bargained at rates of around 92 or 93 percent.

Two major crimes are partial exceptions. "Only" 69 percent of murders are plea bargained. Most remaining homicide cases go to a jury, not a bench trial. With forcible rape, 83 percent of cases end in a guilty plea, again with most of the rest going to a jury. However, other sexual assaults are rather like property crimes in that the tendency is for cases to be plea bargained. This applies only to cases that made it this far in the system. You can see that the justice system based on trial by jury is a rare exception to the rule: Most cases do not get to this stage, and those that do reach the courts are largely bargained out.

The plea bargain usually occurs in two stages: an ***informal negotiation*** followed by a ***formal hearing*** in which a judge ratifies the informal agreement.[11] Box 3a gives an example of what a private and informal conversation between the defense attorney and the prosecutor might sound like. Sometimes this conversation would be held in the back of the courtroom or in the judge's chamber, perhaps with the judge listening. Sometimes this even happens at the last minute, just before the jury walks in. The judge might well tell the jury to go home since the case is already settled. Some prosecutors will not allow the assistant prosecutor to reduce charges without a supervisor's permission. Some plea bargaining takes more time and effort, with the defendant agreeing to incriminate other offenders, tell the court where the loot or drugs are hidden, etc.

Defense attorneys and prosecutors often bargain over the number of charges, their severity, and type and length of the sentence. For example, three counts of assault (for hitting three people) might be reduced to one count. Aggravated assault might be reduced to simple assault. A two-year sentence might be reduced to one year plus probation. Pleas may reflect statutory limits, local practices, and the policies of the prosecutor's office, all influencing how far down in severity one can successfully plea and how minimal a sentence can be imposed. The defendant hopes to trade a guilty plea for less punishment, and the prosecutor adds a conviction to his ledger while avoiding extra work required to prepare and endure a trial.

Outside the United States, plea bargaining exists, though often unofficially. Australia, Canada, England, New Zealand, and the United States, all common-law nations, have some form of plea bargaining. In all these nations, official trials have given way in part to the "art of the deal."[12] Discretion at the pretrial stage has also been reported for France, Germany, Japan, and South Korea.[13]

Instead of going through a trial, the prosecution and defense can spend a short time negotiating (as seen in Box 3a) and then get the judge's approval (see Box 3b).

> **Box 3A Fictional Dialogue Illustrating an Informal Plea-Bargain Discussion between a Prosecutor and a Defense Attorney**
>
> *Prosecutor* [Joe]: Fred, I think he should get six months for this.
>
> *Defense attorney* [Fred]: Joe, give him a break. He's a first offender and only punched the other guy twice.
>
> *Prosecutor*: But he had a knife on him.
>
> *Defense attorney*: Witnesses said he never pulled the knife out of his pocket.
>
> *Prosecutor*: OK. I'll agree to reduce this from aggravated assault to simple assault, with a month in jail.

To prevent abuses of quick plea bargaining,[14] the procedure has become more formalized in many jurisdictions. Rules of criminal procedure help protect the due process rights of the defendant that are waived when a guilty plea is entered: the right to a trial, to see the evidence against them, to cross-examine witnesses, and to present their own defense. Pleas cannot be easily appealed unless they are improperly entered. After an oral agreement between attorneys, they might be committed to writing and then signed by the defendant.

A judge also engages in a personal discourse with the defendant, as we note in Box 3b.[15] The judge may ascertain reading and writing ability, schooling, and ask about coercion or promises made during the earlier informal negotiation. Some judges quiz the defendant to make sure they know exactly what they are pleading to; if the defendant cannot answer, the judge goes over it again. Many judges assess the defendant's ability to understand what's going on. Entering a guilty plea in court takes no more than 20 to 30 minutes, far less than a trial.

We readily see that this courtroom routine takes far less time than a real trial, allowing judge and prosecutor to move on to the next case. Given the busy trial calendar, prosecutors accept plea bargains to keep busy judges happy and to get cases off their own desks.[16] Despite the rarity of trials, in a serious or complicated case, court calendars easily fill up with pretrial motions and hearings well before a plea bargain is reached. The earlier the system can kick a case out, the less work it has to do. This is an excellent example of how informal methods save the system from itself.

Many minor criminal offenses are dealt with by *local magistrates* or *justices of the peace*, who are not always trained attorneys. These low-level judges work in small courts and deal with drunk and disorderly cases, minor thefts, misdemeanors, traffic cases, or the like. Even legally trained local judges can be rather informal and less than rigorous.

Box 3B Fictional Dialogue Illustrating a Formal Plea-Bargain Hearing Before a Judge

Judge: In the matter of the State vs. Smith, Mr. Smith, how do you plead?

Defendant Smith: Guilty, Your Honor.

Judge: Mr. Prosecutor, have you reached a plea agreement?

Prosecutor: Yes, Your Honor. We agree to time already served plus probation.

Judge: Mr. Smith, do you know that you will lose the right to a jury trial?

Smith: Yes, Your Honor.

Judge: Do you give up that right?

Smith: Yes, Your Honor.

Judge: Do you give up your right to bring in witnesses in your favor by use of a subpoena?

Smith: Yes.

Judge: You know you are waiving your privilege against self-incrimination?

Smith: Yes.

Judge: And that you are waiving the right to cross-examine your accusers?

Smith: Yes.

Judge: Do you know that the maximum sentence is 5 years in prison?

Smith: Yes.

Judge: That the minimum sanction is a $500 fine?

Smith: Yes.

Judge: Do you know that you cannot be forced to testify?

Smith: Yes.

Judge: . . . and that your decision not to testify cannot be held against you?

Smith: Yes.

Judge: Did anyone force you into accepting this settlement?

Smith: No.

Judge: Do you admit that you are guilty for this assault?

Smith: Yes.

Judge: Do you agree with the plea bargain, as stated?

Smith: Yes.

Judge: You know I don't have to accept the agreement, that I could sentence you to jail today.

Smith: Yes.

Judge: You are waiving your right to a jury trial or a bench trial by me.

Smith: Yes.

Judge: Mr. Smith, you are hereby sentenced to 3 days in jail, which you have already served, and to one year of probation.

Case ends.

This allows them to act quickly and to mete out smaller sanctions with minimal delay. The judges have a good deal of discretion, often lecturing defendants to behave better, drink less, and stay out of trouble. Big cities often have night courts that dispose of barroom fighters or drunk and disorderly persons, perhaps locking them up until morning with no further sanction.

Nonetheless, we stick by our earlier assessment—that full court processing is a very slow process. As we've shown, in America plea bargaining is prevalent for a good majority of criminal cases. To sum up, plea bargains avoid long and costly trials, reducing burdens on prosecutors, judges, and other officials. Defendants may escape the discomfort of a trial and the risk of a long sentence.[17]

Helpful Organizations

The justice system depends on other *helpful organizations* to keep cases off its own desks. These include schools, health-care facilities, and other public and private organizations. Generally, school districts and police handle minor student infractions informally, not even informing police or juvenile courts, respectively.[18]

Health-care organizations take much of the load of the criminal justice system, especially in relation to substance abuse. It is not a crime to be an alcoholic or drug addict. Nonetheless, these conditions lead many people to cross the legal line—driving under the influence, creating disturbances, or making illegal transactions. We have already offered examples of how substance abuse generates risky situations, escalating into criminal acts. When police discover these infractions, they must decide whether to treat the offender criminally or to arrange medical intervention. Police often decide to take the latter approach.

Every year, many millions of drug and alcohol cases enter the health-care system, including substance abuse, poisonings, and injuries. In 2011, approximately 850,000 young adults (aged 18–25) visited emergency rooms for drug, alcohol, or other substance abuse issues.[19] *Emergency room visits* also include many problems with illicit drugs and with mixing drugs and alcohol. Surprisingly, marijuana admissions exceed the number of emergencies involving heroin or cocaine.[20] Millions of additional patients receive more expensive acute care or are treated for chronic alcohol or substance abuse problems on a residential or outpatient basis. In 2013, some 1.8 million persons were admitted to audited treatment facilities for alcohol and drug abuse. Over 1.2 million persons were under treatment in 14,148 *substance abuse facilities*. Some 86 percent of these facilities were private, although public funding may have been involved along with health insurance money.[21]

Some primary care clinics have sought creative and inexpensive ways to counsel people with alcohol problems, avoiding arrests and long-term treatment. One example involves a brief intervention consisting of two 15-minute sessions with a physician a month apart, followed up by a nurse's visit two weeks later. These few contacts resulted in improvements that lasted a few years.[22] Perhaps some people will listen to a physician after having ignored the advice of family and friends concerned about their substance abuse.

Marrying Organizations with the Justice System

Diversion programs are alternatives or partial alternatives to conviction and punishment. Many of these programs overlap with the helpful organizations just discussed, depending on how their clients or patients are admitted. Some clients are placed in facilities to avoid arresting them, but others are sent there after an arrest has already occurred.

Diversion programs have an interesting history, dating back to the Middle Ages in England, then finding their way to the American colonies. They began with the *benefit of the clergy*, which was used to avoid the harsh corporal and capital punishments of the secular courts. Any clergy facing charges in a secular court could pray for the benefit of the clergy, then be transferred to church courts, which meted out less severe punishments. Eligibility was determined by the ability to read Psalm 51. The benefit of the clergy was extended to anyone who could read it and eventually to those who could recite it from memory, thus avoiding all punishment. The practice was banned federally before 1800 and in most states not long thereafter—except for slaves, for whom there is evidence the practice continued almost until the Civil War.[23]

As with many justice system reforms, diversion programs began with juveniles and later spread to adults. Diversion either prevents people from entering the system at all (as we saw with our discussion of helpful organizations) or arranges for them to exit early, avoiding a conviction or long incarceration (prosecutorial or court diversions).

Diversion efforts in some form can take place at many stages.[24] An officer can take someone to an alcohol treatment center instead of the police station. The sergeant on duty can arrange such treatment after an officer brings somebody to the station. A defense attorney and prosecutor can agree formally or informally to diversion outside the justice system without further trial. Judges can agree to programs in place of prison or shorter prison terms allowing for drug rehabilitation. Diversion programs are extremely varied, even including patients or clients who have never been locked up at all, nor been inside a courtroom. Various programs might treat alcoholism, drug dependence, sex offending, or anger management issues.[25] Some programs are residential, housing people for various lengths of time. Others allow clients to live at home with routine visits for classes, services, or drug testing.

Court systems have gone one step further by creating specialized courts to solve specific problems, such as drug abuse. Many of these were started by judges and prosecutors frustrated with traditional court processes that failed to meet special offender needs, overemphasizing punishment while underemphasizing rehabilitation and health assistance. For example, *drug treatment courts* started in 1989, numbered over 1,300 across the United States in 2012,[26] and continue to grow.[27] These courts oversee defendants required to attend drug treatment. With successful completion of the program, their sentences can be reduced or charges can even be dismissed. Over 300 mental health courts seek to treat the many offenders with serious mental issues, de-emphasizing punishment. Other *specialty courts* focus on drunk driving, domestic violence, or the problems of veterans. Some courts target programs after a guilty plea, but others allow offenders to avoid conviction entirely.[28] Still other courts offer the offender a chance to "restore" something directly back to the community.[29] (We further discuss these *community courts* and restorative justice programs in Unit 3.5.)

These diversion methods potentially apply to millions of events in many forms and many places, all serving to take pressure off the justice system while seeking to help offenders and minimize punishment. Unfortunately, many jurisdictions fail to offer these options, or they have too few available spots to help the many people with special problems. That leaves officials with the choice of locking someone up or doing nothing at all.

Wrongful Convictions

The justice system has great difficulty avoiding injustices. It can easily fail to provide services to offenders, as just noted. It may also have trouble correcting its own mistakes. We are left with the unpleasant fact that the wrong person is sometimes convicted and may even be executed. The appeals process will not discover all cases of *wrongful conviction*.

Most criminal cases have no grounds for appeal to a higher court. Guilty pleas usually cannot be appealed at all. *Criminal appeals* can only be made on procedural or constitutional issues. The defense has a problem: The facts of the case are usually not appealable. Of the hundreds of thousands of criminal cases in 2010, only about 70,000 were appealed in state appeals courts.[30] Appeals are mandated in death penalty cases, often with limited success. To be sure, appeals help delay executions, but reversal of convictions is less common.

Technological advances have changed the types of evidence used to establish guilt. Still, technology is not a panacea—despite these advances, experts can disagree on technical evidence, and a defense attorney can still challenge whether the evidence was appropriately obtained or analyzed. *DNA testing* and other modern investigative techniques apply mainly to more serious cases involving crime scene analysis. It is hoped that these techniques will exonerate any innocent person. Unfortunately, DNA is sometimes handled poorly, and sometimes no DNA evidence is found. Moreover, some prisoners were imprisoned or even executed before these techniques became available.

The **Innocence Project**, founded in 1992 by Barry Scheck and Peter Neufeld, is a national litigation and public policy organization dedicated to exonerating wrongfully convicted persons.[31] It began to use DNA testing for death row inmates in the United States and for other convicts believed to be wrongly convicted.[32] For example:

- Joseph Lamont Abbitt was exonerated on September 2, 2009, in Winston-Salem, North Carolina, after serving 14 years in prison for crimes he did not commit. He was misidentified by two eyewitnesses.

- Christopher Abernathy was exonerated on February 11, 2015, after serving 28 years for first-degree murder, aggravated sexual assault, and armed robbery.

- Randolph "Randy" Arledge was exonerated through DNA testing on May 3, 2013. He had been convicted of rape and murder in a Texas court.

- Joseph Buffey pled guilty to the 2001 rape and robbery of an 83-year-old woman and spent 13 years in prison before being exonerated. His attorney told him if he went to trial, he could expect a sentence of 200 to 300 years in prison if convicted.

The Innocence Project lists at least 350 wrongful conviction cases exonerated through DNA. Three out of four were misidentified by eyewitnesses. Defendants in nearly 10 percent of the DNA exonerations had pled guilty to crimes they didn't commit. Unfortunately, many doubtful convictions have occurred in cases lacking DNA evidence that would have allowed exoneration. Moreover, for every wrongful conviction, at least one real offender goes unpunished.

The Innocence Project has identified several factors leading to wrongful conviction, in order of frequency:

1. Mistaken identification

2. Police misconduct

3. Prosecutorial misconduct

4. False witness testimony

5. Bad informants

6. False confessions

Wrongful convictions can result when honest detectives make mistakes. This occurs for many reasons, including cognitive biases, errors of intuition, overreliance on rules of thumb, and biases in evaluating evidence.[33] Even if society could avoid all wrongful convictions, it still would have to face the fact that so many guilty offenders are not punished and that the punishment process is itself so complicated and expensive.

FLASHCARD LIST FOR UNIT 3.3

- Benefit of the clergy
- Courts [community, drug treatment, specialty]
- Criminal appeals
- Diversion programs
- DNA testing

- Emergency room visits [alcohol-related]
- Formal hearing
- Helpful organizations
- Informal negotiation
- Innocence Project
- Justices of the peace

- Local magistrates
- Plea bargain
- Speedy trial
- Substance abuse facilities
- Wrongful conviction

DISCUSSION QUESTIONS

1. What might a judge ask to make sure a plea bargain is legal?

2. What effect might wrongful convictions have on a community's sense of procedural justice?

Notes

1   Yates, S. (2014). *Analysis of case-flow management of driving under the influence (DUI) cases in the Flagstaff Justice Court*. Williamsburg, VA: National Center for State Courts.

2   Reaves, B. A. (2013). *Felony defendants in large urban counties, 2009 – Statistical tables*. Washington DC: Bureau of Justice Statistics, U.S. Department of Justice. www.bjs.gov/content/pub/pdf/fdluc09.pdf (retrieved August 1, 2017).

3   Dandurand, Y. (2009). *Addressing inefficiencies in the criminal justice process*. International Centre for Criminal Law Reform and Criminal Justice Policy, University of British Columbia. www.publicsafety.gc.ca/lbrr/archives/cnmcs-plcng/cn29635-eng.pdf (retrieved July 21, 2017).

4   Weatherburn, D., & Fitzgerald, J. (2015). *Trial court delay and the NSW District Criminal Court*. NSW Crime and Justice Bulletin, Contemporary Issues in Crime and Justice, No. 184. Sydney: NSW Bureau of Crime Statistics and Research. www.bocsar.nsw.gov.au/Documents/CJB/Report_2015_Court_Delay_cjb184.pdf (retrieved July 21, 2017).

5   Hopwood, S. (2014). The not so speedy trial act. *Washington Law Review, 89*, 709–745.

6   Silveira, B. S. (2017). Bargaining with asymmetric information: An empirical study of plea negotiations. *Econometrica, 85*(2), 419–452.

7   See: Sudnow, D. (1965). Normal crimes: Sociological features of the penal code in a public defender office. *Social Problems, 12*(3), 255–276. Hartley, R. D., Miller, H. V., & Spohn, C. (2010). Do you get what you pay for? Type of counsel and its effect on criminal court outcomes. *Journal of Criminal Justice, 38*(5), 1063–1070. Metcalfe, C. (2016). The role of courtroom workgroups in felony case dispositions: An analysis of workgroup familiarity and similarity. *Law & Society Review, 50*(3), 637–673.

8   For a positive view, see: Howe, S. (2005). The value of plea bargaining. *Oklahoma Law Review, 58,* 599–723.

9   Dever, L. (2004). *State court sentencing of convicted felons.* Washington, DC: Bureau of Justice Statistics.

10 In addition to the pressures we note here, some of the decline in trials is attributed to sentencing guidelines, particularly at the federal level. And many believe that the number of trials is much too small. Guidelines limited judicial discretion for sentencing and gave more influence to the charging done by prosecutors; the charge then pretty much determines the sentence. See, for example: Weiser, B. (2016). Trial by jury is more concept than reality. *The New York Times,* August 8.

11 Hessick, F. A., & Saujani, R. (2002). Plea bargaining and convicting the innocent: The role of the prosecutor, the defense counsel, and the judge. *Brigham Young University Journal of Public Law, 16,* 189–355. Bibas, S. (2004). Plea bargaining outside the shadow of trial. *Harvard Law Review, 117*(8), 2463–2547.

12 Brook, C. A., Fiannaca, B., Harvey, D., Marcus, P., McEwan, J., & Pomerance, R. (2016). A comparative look at plea bargaining in Australia, Canada, England, New Zealand, and the United States. *William and Mary Law Review, 57*(4), 1190–1225.

13 Choe, D. H. (2014). Discretion at the pre-trial stage: A comparative study. *European Journal on Criminal Policy and Research, 20*(1), 101–119.

14 Colquitt, J. A. (2000). Ad hoc plea bargaining. *Tulane Law Review, 75,* 695–776.

15 See also: Maynard, D. W. (2013). *Inside plea bargaining.* New York: Springer.

16 Alschuler, A. W. (1968). The prosecutor's role in plea bargaining. *The University of Chicago Law Review, 36*(1), 50–112.

17 Fisher, G. (2003). *Plea bargaining's triumph: A history of plea bargaining in America.* Stanford, CA: Stanford University Press.

18 Des Moines Public Schools (2009–2010). Student discipline code and procedures [online]. www.dmschools.org/wp-content/uploads/2011/11/MiddleHighDisciplineCode20091.pdf (retrieved May 15, 2107).

19 Center for Behavioral Health Statistics and Quality. (2014). *The CBHSQ report: A day in the life of young adults: Substance use facts.* Rockville, MD: Substance Abuse and Mental Health Services Administration. www.samhsa.gov/data/sites/default/files/CBHSQ-SR168-TypicalDay-2014/CBHSQ-SR168-TypicalDay-2014.htm (retrieved July 21, 2017).

20 Center for Behavioral Health Statistics and Quality, *The CBHSQ report.*

21 Mental Health Services Administration (2014). *National Survey of Substance Abuse Treatment Services (N-SSATS): 2013. Data on substance abuse treatment facilities.* Rockville, MD: U.S. Substance Abuse and Mental Health Services Administration, Department of Health and Human Services. www.samhsa.gov/data/sites/default/files/2013_N-SSATS_National_Survey_of_Substance_Abuse_Treatment_Services/2013_N-SSATS_National_Survey_of_Substance_Abuse_Treatment_Services.html (retrieved August 19, 2016).

22 Mundt, M. P. (2006). Analyzing the costs and benefits of brief intervention. *Alcohol Research and Health*, *29*(1), 34–36.

23 Sawyer, J. (1990). "Benefit of clergy" in Maryland and Virginia. *The American Journal of Legal History*, *34*(1), 49–68. DOI: 10.2307/845345. Boyd, W. K. (1923). Documents and comments on benefit of clergy as applied to slaves. *The Journal of Negro History*, *8*(4), 443–447. DOI: 10.2307/2713694.

24 Lattimore, P. K., Broner, N., Sherman, R., Frisman, L., & Shafer, M. (2003). A comparison of pre-booking and post-booking diversion programs for mentally ill substance-using individuals with justice involvement. *Journal of Contemporary Criminal Justice*, *19*(1), 30–64.

25 Clear, T. R., & Dammer, H. R. (2000). *The offender in the community*. Belmont, CA: Wadsworth.

26 Strong, S. M., Rantala, R. R., & Kyckelhahn, T. (2016). *Census of problem-solving courts, 2012*. Washington, DC: Bureau of Justice Statistics. www.bjs.gov/content/pub/pdf/cpsc12.pdf (retrieved May 11, 2017).

27 National Association of Drug Court Professionals. (2016). New report: Drug courts reach milestone [online]. www.nadcp.org/PCP (retrieved August 1, 2017).

28 Strong et al., *Census of problem-solving courts, 2012*.

29 Center for Court Innovation. (n.d.). Community court [online]. www.courtinnovation.org/topic/community-court (retrieved May 11, 2017).

30 Waters, L. W., Gallegos, A., Green, J., & Roszi, M. (2015). Criminal appeals in State Courts. Washington, DC: Bureau of Justice Statistics. www.bjs.gov/content/pub/pdf/casc.pdf (retrieved May 12, 2017).

31 Dwyer, J., Neufeld, P. J., & Scheck, B. (2000). *Actual innocence: Five days to execution and other dispatches from the wrongly convicted*. New York: Doubleday Books.

32 Innocence Project. (n.d.). The cases. www.innocenceproject.org/cases/ (retrieved May 11, 2017).

33 Rossmo, D. K. (2008). *Criminal investigative failures*. Boca Raton, FL: CRC Press.

Unit 3.4 Realistic Sanctions

As we just saw with the plea-bargaining process, courts not only assess guilt, they also impose punishment. Severity of punishment is linked to the severity of the crime (conviction charge), and legislatures incorporate the range of expected sanctions for that crime into their criminal codes. That's why the charge negotiation is so important. But how much punishment is enough? Should it involve banishing the offender from society to jail or prison, and for how long? Is a fine enough? Is community supervision likely to be a good alternative? Should we give the offender less punishment due to extenuating circumstances or the lack of a long criminal record? Should we punish the offender more due to victim injury or a long history of prior offenses? We expect a great deal from our justice system.

Theory of Punishment

Through much of history, punishment has been corporal and public, such as flogging on the town square. Even non-corporal punishments, such as shaming, were still public. In the novel *The Scarlet Letter*, Hester Primm was forced to wear the letter "A" on her clothes to let the public know about her adultery and force her to endure the shame.[1] Public hangings continued in the United States into the 1930s, but even though executions have been moved inside, the public is informed about them and representatives are present as witnesses. The idea of punishment is to provide *deterrence*—to prevent future crime. Society hopes people will decide that the costs of crime outweigh the benefits, then avoid committing criminal acts. In short, society tries to teach a lesson to the offender and to everybody else. Taken in this perspective, prisons were a kind of reform since they moved punishment away from public view. We will discuss prisons more in the next unit.

One theory of punishment was stated by ***Jeremy Bentham*** in 1789.[2] Bentham advocated punishing people *only so much* as is needed to deter crime. He was a great progressive because he insisted that punishment should not be vindictive. He also advocated abolishing capital punishment and decriminalizing homosexuality. However, he was in favor of prison as a necessary tool for society to offset crime's benefits with costs. Bentham's theory is much broader than punishment as it also reminds us that people try to maintain their good reputations and avoid ill repute.

Bentham's theory is also about much more than crime; it is the foundation of current economic theory. Known as ***Utilitarianism***, he explained that an individual makes each decision to maximize pleasure and minimize pain. He argued that society must make its decisions with that balance in mind. Bentham favored ***proportionality***— appropriate punishment for the crime, not excess punishment. "Let the punishment fit the crime" can be read as a calm proclamation, not an angry scream. For years, people have debated how much punishment is needed to fit the crime. That brings up another goal of punishment—***retribution***; namely, harming someone in return for the harm they did others. Even one of the earliest legal codes, the ***Code of Hammurabi***, had a notion of retribution for crime that was proportional—"an eye for an eye," but no more.

Bentham's theory was influenced by a prior work about reforming how much people are punished. ***Cesare Beccaria*** wrote his theory of punishment in 1764.[3] Beccaria argued that punishment must not be for retribution or revenge, but only to deter more crime. He too made clear that punishment should be proportionate to the crime committed. He passionately argued that ***severe punishment is the least effective punishment***. More important are two other factors, speed and certainty of punishment. Beccaria's central idea is to make a *clear link in each of our minds between a crime and the punishment it will lead to*. That mental link depends on delivering ***swift, sure punishment***. In advocating swiftness and certainty of punishment while discouraging severe punishment, Beccaria (like Bentham) opposed capital punishment.

Behavioral science researchers use experiments carried out in laboratories to study the effects of punishment. They might deliver a punishment (such as a small shock or denying a benefit, or reward) as a ***negative reinforcement*** to try to affect subjects' (often university sophomores') behavior. These studies repeatedly show that promptness and certainty of negative reinforcement have much more effect than its severity—just as Bentham told us.[4]

The Reality of Punishment

Unfortunately, our justice system neglects these principles, as Table 3a shows. Theory and research alike tell us to orient justice towards the theoretical ideal, with

TABLE 3A **Punishment: Comparing the Theoretical Ideal to Reality in the United States, Canada, and Europe**

Punishment feature	Theoretical ideal	United States reality	Canadian and European reality
Swift punishment	Yes	No	No
Sure punishment	Yes	No	No
Mild punishment	Yes	No	Yes

punishment being swift and sure, but also mild or moderate. The table describes violations of the ideal practice suggested by Beccaria and Bentham. In the United States, severe punishment is delivered sporadically and slowly, in total violation of the ideal, based on deterrence.[5] We have already discussed how long cases can take, even when conviction is the result of a guilty plea and not a trial. After society imposes capital punishment, death row inmates spend years there between the time of their sentencing and their execution, working through the long appeal process; those executed in 2012 spent an average of almost 16 years on death row.[6] Clearly the realities of punishment delivered in the United States do not match what we are told by punishment theory or research.

Imbalances in the justice system have serious consequences. By emphasizing severe punishment, the system fills the prisons with long-term inmates and has no room for swift, sure punishment. The protracted legal battles tie up courts and police. The great irony of "get tough" policies is that they *reduce* the number of offenders who are in fact punished. That makes an offender more certain that he will escape punishment, since the system is clogged up with heavy sentencing. *High severity makes swiftness and certainty of punishment unfeasible.* Thus, deterrence becomes an idle threat for most crimes even while prison populations are on the rise. Put another way, "the iron law of prison populations" states that the total number of prisoners behind bars is purely and simply a result of two factors: the number of people put there and how long they stay. As a result, policymakers spend too much time considering policy proposals that will have little effect on incarceration rates. If length of stay is stretched, fewer people are punished and the justice system cannot deliver swift, sure punishment.[7]

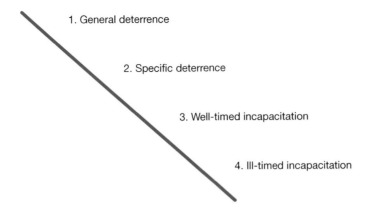

FIGURE 3G
Scale for Efficiency of Punishment

Figure 3g depicts a four-point scale that organizes *hypothetical* results of punishment from the best to worst possibility.

The best we can hope for is that punishing someone for a crime sets an example visible to *many* other people, who then are deterred from carrying out crimes themselves. Called ***general deterrence***, this is the most efficient punishment process, at least hypothetically, since punishing a few serves to deter many.

The second-best hypothetical outcome is ***specific deterrence***, which means that only the punished person is dissuaded from future crimes.[8] At best, this punishment process only dissuades one person at a time from committing crimes. Specific deterrence could be most effective if applied to highly prolific offenders before they have carried out the bulk of their likely offenses, preventing them from committing more offenses upon release from prison. Criminologists use the term ***recidivism*** to refer to an offender getting into criminal trouble again. Criminologists measure recidivism in different ways, but one way is to consider whether an offender is arrested in the three-year period following release from prison.

Suppose that punishment produces no general or specific deterrence. A third punishment process, ***incapacitation***, might still serve society in another fashion. This process keeps offenders in prison where they cannot commit crimes and, theoretically, subtracts crimes from the total that could be committed. Incapacitation neglects crimes committed within the prison walls, which are out of sight from the public's viewpoint. ***Well-timed incapacitation*** depends on long enough sentences carried out during the period when the offender would have committed the most offenses (step 3 in Figure 3g). In other words, incarceration should occur early enough to interfere with an offender's "criminal career." However, many offenders "age out" of crime simply because they have gotten too old to be active offenders. In real justice systems, *ill-timed incapacitation* is more likely to occur (step 4 in Figure 3g). That means that the offender is incarcerated after most of the damage is already done to society. Most offenders are imprisoned after their prime offending period is over—namely, around age 20 or slightly later, rather than during their mid-teenage years—and their prison sentences last long beyond the prime offending ages. In other words, the system acts too late. American society has been more effective in delivering long sentences than in imposing those sentences in a timely fashion.

Unfortunately, the justice system also induces extra criminal behavior, called *secondary deviance*. By apprehending and punishing people, the justice system labels them as criminals. That label may worsen their behavior and contribute to additional crimes. And, the label has consequences for offenders after they have completed their sentence and are returned to the community. Criminologists call this *labeling theory*. Other criminologists note that imprisonment can help introduce offenders to one another, becoming a school for additional crime and enhancing criminal networks. Prisoners may cook up crimes that they might commit upon release.

Even alternatives to prison can produce secondary deviance. Drug abusers might find buyers and sellers after being enrolled in rehabilitation programs. Unfortunately, drug treatment facilities can have notably higher violence and other crime in their vicinity.[9] These examples show that the justice process might be counterproductive. However, police and other justice officials have attempted to use existing tools more strategically to improve their efficiency.

Targeted Deterrence

Society produces too many offenders. The justice system cannot keep up with their numbers or the crimes they commit. In 2015, about 1 in every 37 adults was under some sort of correctional supervision. On any given day, almost 5 million offenders were supervised in the community and over 2 million in jails and prisons.[10] Although juveniles are incarcerated at much lower rates, this generates very high costs.[11] The *partial* taxpayer cost for corrections exceeded $50 billion in 2012, with many indirect costs not included.[12] However, authorities can use enforcement to break up specific criminal groups or to remove specialized crime settings—*targeted deterrence*. The goal is to apply society's limited criminal justice capacity with a strategic focus to maximize its impact in reducing crime.

The justice system can make **strategic arrests** and prosecutions designed to break up a criminal group or network. Some researchers have mapped organized crime and their social networks, considering how police might disrupt these networks by arresting a few well-positioned individuals.[13] Other scholars are skeptical of this approach,[14] noting, for instance, that criminal networks can often adapt after some members are arrested and incarcerated.[15] Strategic opportunities may allow authorities to arrest and incapacitate offenders who are not easily replaced, such as chemists who produce illegal drugs.[16] Local law enforcement officials have also concentrated their arrest and punishment efforts on specific problems and places. We spoke about problem-oriented policing in Unit 3.2. This includes working together to remove a drug-selling zone within a public park, to close methamphetamine labs, and to regulate and control problem barrooms or nightlife districts.[17] You can readily see that law enforcement can be highly strategic or careless and unfocused. Enforcement can be highly preventative or highly punitive.

Some of the greatest advances in strategic arrests and punishment have been made by **David Kennedy**, a Harvard University researcher who worked with police agencies to set up the **Boston Gun Project**, which has been applied in numerous other American cities.[18] The project began when Kennedy and his colleagues realized that only a few handfuls of offenders accounted for a large share of the gun violence in a tough neighborhood. If these offenders could be thwarted, dramatic reductions in violence could result. This project was based on **pulling levers**.[19] That means highly focused efforts to get offenders to stop using guns and to cut out serious violence, by specifying:

- a clear goal—to reduce gun violence in Boston;

- a definite set of known offenders (such as the 50 most violent gang members in a city);

- a clear instruction for offenders—leave your guns at home;

- tolerance for lesser crimes, even drug-selling, if the violence stops;

- meetings with offenders and their families, directly asking them to stop the gun violence; and

- swift, sure punishment for noncompliant offenders.

These gun projects have achieved swift, sure punishment by paying special attention to violent offenders on **probation** or out on **parole**. These offenders can be sent to prison without a new conviction. The terms of probation and parole usually include a ban on carrying guns and other behaviors that makes it easy to **revoke probation or parole** immediately. The police have learned to work with probation and parole officers, giving offenders a strong incentive to comply with police terms. In addition, police **banked cases**; that is, they saved evidence that could be used to convict offenders, showing each offender they had a file and could convict them at any time. Rather than punishing or over-punishing, the pulling-levers approach lets somebody know that swift, sure punishment will be imposed if they do not comply with the police demand to stay away from guns. These types of efforts have led to reductions in violence ranging from 20 to 70 percent.[20]

The Overly Rational Offender

Is it possible that our theory of punishment is wrong? Did Beccaria and Bentham overestimate the rationality and forethought of offenders? Some criminologists go to another extreme, discussing a totally irrational offender who responds to emotions, frustrations, and strains without any direction or reason. A few of these ideas are discussed in Unit 5.5.

You do not have to pick one of these two positions: the overly rational offender vs. the totally irrational offender. A field known as "decision theory" helps us understand that most human decision processes are neither perfectly methodical nor helter-skelter. Decision theorists take an intermediate position, emphasizing:

> *bounded rationality*: When people make decisions, their rationality is limited by the information they have, the limitations of their minds, and the limited time available for making a decision.[21]

This approach heavily influences situational crime controls, discussed in Unit 2.3. That approach sees most offenders making *short-term* decisions based on a *limited number of considerations*. The offender thinks, but not too much. They sometimes make bad decisions, not foreseeing the consequences of their acts or the punishment a crime may bring. They seek short-term pleasures but forget the longer-term harms. That helps explain their substance abuse and risk-taking and why the threat of punishment doesn't always deter crime.

The advances in research on decisions tell us to focus on quick, sure punishments and rewards, not on long prison terms after a long court process. We can only hope that justice policy is made with careful planning, not in response to a few widely publicized but emotional cases.

Moral Panics and the Swinging Pendulum

The history of punishment in the United States swings back and forth, responding to changes in crime rates, prison conditions, and penal philosophy. Figure 3h summarizes this process, with some periods emphasizing rehabilitation and less severe punishment, while other periods prefer long prison sentences.

The most recent swing toward more severe punishment dates from the crack epidemic of the late 1980s and 1990s. Judicial discretion in sentencing was curtailed by imposing sentencing guidelines;[22] offenders with long prior records received even longer sentences upon conviction. Mandatory minimum sentences were imposed, and with more determinate or set sentences, officials lost much of their discretion for

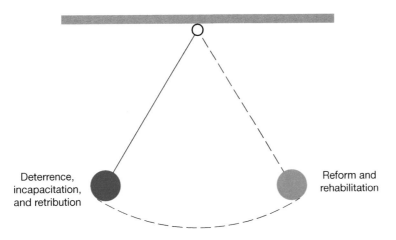

FIGURE 3H
The Swinging Pendulum between Harshness and Reform

releasing prisoners on parole for good behavior. (We will discuss this more in the next unit.)

Abolishing parole and mandating longer prison stays had major consequences for state prisons—the bulk of the U.S. corrections system. From 1982 to 2008, the number of state prison inmates more than tripled to over 1.3 million persons. The expenditures by states for prison operations quadrupled to reach $38 billion.[23] With parole curtailed, prisons no longer had a safety valve to keep from growing too much or too fast. During these decades, reform and rehabilitation fell by the wayside.

In time the ***pendulum*** returns to its previous position or somewhere in between. These swings often respond to negative events that reach public attention. Widely publicized wrongful convictions or wrongful executions might lead towards more reform. In contrast, publicity about heinous criminal acts can lead to harsher punishment. Unfortunately, most voters have little direct experience with the justice system and tend to respond to televised versions of events. The public seldom clamors for promptness of punishment or acquittal, instead being more likely to insist on increasing severity. The justice system is highly vulnerable to public outcries against crime.

Public pressure can take the form of a ***moral panic***, when fear spreads among the public.[24] Moral panics involve finger-pointing, such as attributing the crime problem to the opposing political group, to a racial minority, or to a foreign nation from which drugs might have originated. Moral panics can involve half-truths, such as highlighting drug abuse while ignoring the much larger problem of alcohol abuse. Moral panics can be based on racial prejudice or a tendency to deny local responsibility. Moral panics often focus on one type of crime or criminal receiving substantial media attention.[25]

Thus, a moral panic can lead to packing prisons with crack cocaine users, leaving no room for other drug offenders. Or a moral panic can focus on members of high-profile gangs in a few cities, ignoring other acute problems.

Scaring millions of people serves a purpose. It can get votes for a politician. It can help vendors sell identity-theft protection or other security services. It can get people to watch exaggerated movies and television shows. Unfortunately, scaring the public has negative consequences for criminal justice. Filling prisons with the wrong people for the wrong crimes; over-punishing one type of abuse while under-punishing another; giving harsher sentences to publicized cases—these are the unfortunate outcomes of moral panics. The panic process is reflected in prison costs and failure to use alternatives that could reduce those costs. Thus the panic process helps explain Table 3a. You can see why punishments in the United States today are more likely to include long prison terms for a few crimes, while neglecting many other problems. More generally, modern democracies deliver the wrong punishment—too slow and unsure to have much influence on offender behavior.

Expanding prison costs have had an impact on the funding available for other areas such as health care, housing, and education, university students being affected in terms of the extent of state funding available for higher education. (Students might ponder the fact that you might be paying several thousand dollars less per year for tuition and other costs if this money had been funneled instead into higher education.) From 1986 to 2013, the real dollar increase in expenditures for corrections was 141 percent, compared to an increase of less than 6 percent for higher education. Eleven states spent more general funds on corrections than on higher education.[26] Had the prison costs not proliferated, several thousand dollars per year could have been shaved from each student's university costs, or could have been used to improve funding for secondary education.

FLASHCARD LIST FOR UNIT 3.4

- Banked cases
- Beccaria, Cesare
- Bentham, Jeremy
- Boston Gun Project
- Bounded rationality
- Deterrence [general, specific, targeted]
- Hammurabi, Code of
- Incapacitation, ill-timed, well-timed
- Kennedy, David
- Labeling theory
- Moral panic
- Negative reinforcement
- Parole
- Pendulum
- Probation
- Proportionality
- Pulling levers
- Punishment [severe, swift, sure]
- Recidivism
- Retribution
- Revoke probation or parole
- Secondary deviance
- Strategic arrests
- Utilitarianism

DISCUSSION QUESTIONS

1. Discuss the importance of deterrence in imposing punishments.

2. Why is a pendulum a useful way to discuss the changes in sanctioning offenders over time?

Notes

1   Hawthorne, N. (1850). *The Scarlet Letter*. Boston: Ticknor, Reed & Fields. Reproduced at www.bartleby.com/83/ (retrieved August 19, 2016).

2   Bentham, J. (1789). *An introduction to the principles of morals and legislation*. London: T. Payne and Son. Reproduced at www.constitution.org/jb/pml.htm (retrieved May 16, 2017).

3   Beccaria, C. (2006 [1764]). *On crimes and punishments*. Philadelphia: Philip H. Nicklin. Reproduced at www.constitution.org/cb/crim_pun.htm (retrieved May 16, 2017).

4   Skinner, B. F. (2014 [1969]). *Contingencies of reinforcement: A theoretical analysis*, Vol. 3. Cambridge, MA: B. F. Skinner Foundation.

5   Kennedy, D. M. (2009). *Deterrence and crime prevention: Reconsidering the prospect of sanction*. Abingdon, U.K.: Routledge.

6   Snell, T. (2014) *Capital punishment, 2012–Statistical tables*. Washington, DC: Bureau of Justice Statistics.

7   Clear, T. R., & Austin, J. (2009). Reducing mass incarceration: Implication of the iron law of prison populations. *Harvard Law & Policy Review, 3*(2), 307–324.

8   Stafford, M. C. (2016). New call for assessing the effects of 21st century juvenile diversion. *Criminology & Public Policy, 15*(3), 949–952.

9   Furr-Holden, C. D. M., Milam, A. J., Nesoff, E. D., Johnson, R. M., Fakunle, . . . & Thorpe, R. J. (2016). Not in my back yard: A comparative analysis of crime around publicly funded drug treatment centers, liquor stores, convenience stores, and corner stores in one mid-Atlantic city. *Journal of Studies on Alcohol and Drugs, 77*(1), 17–24.

10 Kaeble, D., & Glaze, L. (2016). *Correctional populations in the United States, 2015*. Washington, DC: Bureau of Justice Statistics.

11 Justice Policy Institute. (2014). *Sticker shock: Calculating the full price tag for youth incarceration*. Washington, DC: Justice Policy Institute. www.justicepolicy.org/uploads/justicepolicy/documents/sticker_shock_final_v2.pdf (retrieved September 5, 2016).

12 Henrichson, C., & Delaney, R. (2012). The price of prisons: What incarceration costs taxpayers. *Federal Sentencing Reporter, 25*(1), 68–80. Travis, J., Western, B., & Redburn, S. (2014). *The growth of incarceration in the United States*. Washington, DC: National Research Council.

13 Morselli, C. (2009). *Inside criminal networks*. New York: Springer.

14 Duijn, P. A., Kashirin, V., & Sloot, P. M. (2014). The relative ineffectiveness of criminal network disruption. *Scientific Reports, 4*, Article 4238. http://dx.doi.org/10.1038/srep04238.

15 Morselli, C. (2013). *Crime and networks*. Abingdon, U.K.: Routledge.

16 Scott, M. S., & Dedel, K. (2006). *Clandestine methamphetamine labs*, 2nd edition. Problem-Oriented Guides for Police Series, Problem-Specific Guide Series, No. 16. Washington, DC: Center for Problem-Oriented Policing.

17 Monterastelli, S. (2002). Using law and law enforcement to prevent violence and promote community vibrancy near bars, clubs, and taverns. *Notre Dame Journal of Law, Ethics & Public Policy, 16*(1), 239–278.

18 Braga, A. A., & Weisburd, D. L. (2015). Focused deterrence and the prevention of violent gun injuries: Practice, theoretical principles, and scientific evidence. *Annual Review of Public Health, 36,* 55–68.

19 Braga, A. A. (2014). Pulling levers policing. In G. Bruinsma & D. Weisburd (Eds.), *Encyclopedia of criminology and criminal justice,* pp. 4174–4185. New York: Springer.

20 Braga, A. A., Hureau, D. M., & Papachristos, A. V. (2014). Deterring gang-involved gun violence: Measuring the impact of Boston's Operation Ceasefire on street gang behavior. *Journal of Quantitative Criminology, 30*(1), 113–139.

21 Yang, L., Toubia, O., & De Jong, M. G. (2015). A bounded rationality model of information search and choice in preference measurement. *Journal of Marketing Research, 52*(2), 166–183.

22 The Federal Sentencing Reform Act of 1984, which took effect in 1987; guidelines were revised by 1992, phasing out parole.

23 Kyckelhahn, T. (2014). *State corrections expenditures, FY 1982–2010.* Washington, DC: Bureau of Justice Statistics; Table 2.

24 Thompson, K. (2005). *Moral panics.* Abingdon, U.K.: Routledge.

25 Critcher, C. (2008). Moral panic analysis: Past, present and future. *Sociology Compass, 2*(4), 1127–1144.

26 Mitchell, M., & Leachman, M. (2014). *Changing priorities: State criminal justice reforms and investments in education.* Washington, DC: Center on Budget and Policy Priorities.

UNIT 3.5 Efforts and Realities

For well over a century, reformers have been offended by the cruelty of locking people up. They have proposed and experimented with a variety of alternatives. Sadly, many reforms may do little and others, more harm than good. The purpose here is to review some of those ideas, however briefly. We give you some principles that help assess more clearly what programs work better and what program expectations are realistic. First, we review a bit of history about prisons.

Jails and Prisons in America

In Unit 3.4, we noted the swing of the pendulum in penal reforms between harsher and gentler approaches. The harsher approaches emphasized deterrence, incapacitation, and retribution. The gentler approaches emphasized rehabilitation and reform. To be sure, a pendulum swing is never complete since the prior approaches to punishment continue to exist. However, policies do shift in emphasis from one era to another.

The pendulum shift in goals of incarcerating people is reflected in shifting terminology used to describe the institutions that house them. The *Online Etymology Dictionary* says "workhouse" derives from the 1650s.[1] The idea of working to pay for one's debts to society has vestiges in today's punishment systems. "Dungeons" and "gaols" ("jails") are words of the 1300s. Since punishment at that time was generally corporal, gaols were used only as temporary housing for those awaiting trial. After conviction, punishment was swiftly and publicly administered, with no further need to lock people up. *Jails* today do serve that purpose and are local (usually county) facilities that house those awaiting trial and sentence for whom bail was not set or had not yet been met. Jails now also house those sentenced to a year or less, generally on misdemeanor charges.

Today, *prisons* in the United States are run by the state and the federal governments, housing offenders convicted of felonies—those sentenced to more than one year. The word "prison" means captive, and comes to us from France in the 12th and 13th centuries. The Quakers in colonial Pennsylvania changed the purpose of prison, using it to replace corporal punishment.[2] In 1790, about one hundred years later, Benjamin Franklin was part of an organization that pushed legislation for renovating part of a gaol in Philadelphia to include a set of isolated cells where offenders were confined in silence. All work and eating were done in the single cells, and there was no contact with other prisoners or anyone else. The isolation and silence were supposed to help offenders reflect on what they had done and lead them to quickly become "penitent" for their crimes and then to return to society ready to uphold its rules. Thus, the *penitentiary* is an American invention. It was many years later before a full prison was built using this model: It didn't turn out so well—many offenders went mad from the isolation, and they didn't necessarily repent.[3]

By 1820, New York modified the Pennsylvania system in Auburn, New York, by keeping the silence and individual cells, but allowing prisoners to work and eat in congregate settings. Unfortunately, silence was strictly and forcibly enforced even in the congregate settings, introducing corporal sanctions back into the prison itself. Proponents looked to the inmates' work to support the prison itself, although self-sufficiency was rarely achieved. Most states, however, adopted the New York System.

Neither prison system did away with crime. Reformers looked next to help offenders in more concrete ways to change their ways through rehabilitation. "*Reformatory*" as a word goes back to 1758, but it did not take hold in the United States until the late 1800s, initially in relation to rehabilitating juveniles. Rehabilitation replaced repentance and work as the means to turn offenders back into law-abiding citizens. Reform was secularized; that is, detached from its religious origins. *Zebulon Brockway* experimented with and developed prison reform in New York. At the Elmira Reformatory in 1876, he introduced educational and vocational programs, a library, and a gym for younger offenders. He began inmate classification so not all were treated alike. Brockway provided incentives to improve and earn release.[4] Getting time off your sentence for good behavior was called "*good time*," deriving from the work of two other reformers, Maconochie and Crofton, who influenced American correctional history.

• In 1840, a creative British naval officer named *Alexander Maconochie* became Governor of a brutal penal island off the Coast of Australia. He instituted prison reform with the chance for prisoners to earn early release for good behavior, thus setting the stage for the development of parole (c. 1876).[5]

- In the 1850s, ***Sir Walter Crofton***, who had himself been in prison, directed the Irish Convict Prisons, inventing halfway houses, conditional release, and the equivalent of parole officers.[6]

In 1870, Brockway helped organize a conference on correctional reform in Cincinnati, Ohio, where the influence of Maconochie and Crofton was evident. This conference was the precursor to the American Correctional Association, the central association for correctional professionals today.[7] Thus, Brockway not only revamped American prisons to help rehabilitate offenders, but also helped them return to the community on parole. Brockway knew that the first return to the community might not go well; he designed a program to bring failing offenders back to the reformatory for more rehabilitation. Today we call this "revocation of parole," as discussed in the previous unit. The prisoner then sees parole as the carrot and return to prison as the stick. Parole revocation may be followed by another parole release, which may again be revoked if all conditions for living in the community are not met.

"Earning release" required a change in prison sentencing. "Fixed" or ***determinate sentences*** were replaced with ***indeterminate sentences***. Offenders had to serve the minimum sentence but, with good behavior, could avoid having to serve the maximum time. When offenders were deemed ready to go back to society (by the vote of a parole board), they were released to parole supervision, and they remained under parole supervision in the community until the maximum time of the sentence imposed. If they "messed up," they could have their parole revoked and could be sent back to prison.

Unfortunately, at Elmira, the inmate monitors became corrupt, and the facility became overcrowded with difficult inmates from other prisons. Corporal punishment was imposed. New civilian guards and procedures were mandated by the state so that by Brockway's retirement in 1900, many of his specific ideas were lost. Still, the reformatory idea remained an important part of American corrections systems.

The history of American incarceration can be summed up with the history of a single building complex at the Eastern New York Correctional Facility, which began by taking inmates from Elmira Reformatory.[8] Eastern has been used to confine people for over a century. Box 3c shows how that building changed names and functions over that period, reflecting the swing of the pendulum and certain changes in society.

Treatment gained true hold with a goal to *correct* inmates' behavior in the 1950s and 1960s. The same treatment idea was true for offenders supervised in the community during that period as well, as we will see next. Unit 3.4 detailed the more recent history of the prison and mentioned policies that lengthened prison stays and decreased use of parole to respond to the moral panic over crack in the late 1980s. This panic also changed the way supervision in the community is now carried out.

Box 3c What's in a Name?

The various words for prisons over the years reflect changes in attitudes towards punishment and reform. We will not detail all the correctional eras since 1900 and pendulum shifts in emphasis, but will give you some insight into them by detailing changes in the name of the prison closest to the hometown of the second author.

Construction for this prison began in 1894 and its first prisoners arrived in 1900. It was built as a reformatory. It has a central courtyard, with a surrounding wall containing guard towers. The central building looks like a fortress, with four wide turrets. While new buildings have been added inside and out, the fortress-look remains. It is one of the oldest prisons still in use in the United States. Here are its name changes through the years, and the populations served under those names:

1900–1921, Eastern New York Reformatory: for younger inmates;

1921–1958, Institute for Defective Delinquent Men: the first in the U.S., using advances in IQ testing, all sentences were indefinite, with no end date or set maximum time;

1958–1966, Eastern Correctional Institution: retained part for "defective delin-quents," but also had regular population inmates;

1966–1970 Catskill Reformatory: younger inmates, with mentally defective inmates moved to hospital setting;

1970–present Eastern New York Correctional Facility; maximum security prison for male felons aged 16 or older.

The early work of Brockway to classify inmates clearly broadened throughout the correctional system over the following century, with specific facilities for specific populations. Today, classification across facilities also includes security risk; reformatories are generally lower security facilities, so Eastern has been upgraded in that regard. It currently has a capacity of 1,100 and is one of just a few New York facilities that offer college courses.

Locally, the prison tended to be referred to as "the Institution," reflecting the greater part of its history with that designation as part of its name, although with different purposes: first, as a place for delinquents with IQs under 70; and later reflecting the broader treatment goals brought into the prisons, beginning in the 1950s and continuing into the 1960s when many programs were added in prisons.

For more information, see:
www.correctionhistory.org/easternny100/html/eastory.html.
www.abajournal.com/news/article/new_york_adult_criminal_prosecution_18_raise_the_age/.
www.nytimes.com/2005/02/20/magazine/uncaptive-minds.html?_r=0 and
http://bpi.bard.edu/.
White, T. W. (1989). Corrections: Out of Balance. *Federal Probation*, 53(4), 31–35.

Staying in the Community

John Augustus was a Boston cobbler and good Samaritan who in the 1840s used his own money to bail a drunk out of jail, supervised him for a couple of weeks, and helped him to re-enter society. Augustus continued such work for years, soliciting the help of others and gaining respect from judges too. His pioneering work created the foundations of how probation works today.[9] Thus, probation got its start almost 40 years before parole. Augustus initially focused on the pretrial period, deciding which offenders he would supervise. Judges trusted his judgment. Today, probation departments are responsible for preparing a pre-sentence investigation to help judges decide on sentencing and assess the risk of reoffending as well as the individual offender's service requirements. If the judge sentences the offender to probation, the probation department provides community supervision with an individualized treatment plan.

As we shall discuss below, many different *community corrections* programs supervise offenders in the community, usually those offenders who are on probation or parole. Probationers are usually less serious offenders, convicted of misdemeanors, or are considered less serious felons.[10] Parolees have felony convictions, and they have been sentenced to serve time in prison. They are generally considered the most serious offenders supervised in the community.

Probationers and parolees are told to avoid reoffending, but they might be given additional instructions by the court or the parole board. The convicted offender might be told to stay away from young children or to avoid his favorite tavern or his former cronies. He is probably banned from owning or carrying weapons or using drugs. He is denied many of the constitutional due process protections applying to other citizens, even while out in the community. No warrants are necessary to search his home.[11] If he is picked up by police in violation of the terms of parole, he might be sent back to prison with a minimal hearing—not requiring a trial or proof beyond a reasonable doubt. Sometimes these powers are used to break up activities of criminal gangs, which often have parolees in their ranks, as we saw with the Boston Gun Project. Someone out on probation or parole should be very careful not to annoy authorities.

Something Short of Prison

Intermediate sanctions fall on a continuum, ranging from something more than probation to something less than confinement in prison. Many of these programs sprang up in the 1950s and 1960s when treatment and rehabilitation were emphasized. For the most part, intermediate sanctions are part of community corrections and keep the offender in the community instead of in prison. Intermediate sanctions are not necessarily "light" punishment; they still have a retributive component because they impose conditions reducing offender freedom.[12] For example, *intensive supervision programs* (ISPs) are a family of efforts designed to provide extra supervision and surveillance, hoping to reduce *recidivism*.[13] ISPs for probationers are higher on the sanctions continuum than probation alone.

Many intermediate sanctions began as conditions seeking to help probationers or parolees. For example, easing prisoners back into the community is often assisted by *halfway houses*, which help structure the living conditions of returning prisoners, offering them a place to live that is less restrictive than prisons while providing more structure than living on one's own.[14] More recently, being placed in a halfway house has been used as a sentence itself rather than as a condition of probation or parole.[15] In contrast to halfway houses, *day-reporting centers* structure daytime activities but allow offenders to live at home. These centers provide a variety of educational, vocational, or other programs, placing intermediate limitations on offender freedom.[16]

Monetary sanctions fit onto this continuum, but are used less in the United States than in Europe. *Restitution* is payback to a victim, while *fines* are paid back to society through the courts, calibrated to the seriousness of the crime but not always to the offender's ability to pay.

Many of you were required to do "volunteer" work while in high school, giving something back to your community. Perhaps it felt more like a punishment, reducing your free time. *Community service sentences* assign offenders to perform periods of unpaid labor, with a deadline for completion, in their community. The most successful programs select offenders according to strict criteria, quickly sanctioning them for nonattendance.[17] Community service sentences have shown many benefits for juveniles, especially when supervised by an adult giving structure to the experience.[18]

Other intermediate sanctions include:

- *house arrest* (restricted ability to leave home);

- *intermittent imprisonment* (for example, spending only weekends in jail); and

- *split sentences* (a relatively short period of time in jail followed by community supervision, usually by probation).

Corrections systems have sometimes supplemented these intermediate sanctions with additional surveillance; for example, *electronic monitoring*—a technology that restricts the movement of offenders to stipulated places. Offenders are fitted with an electronic ankle bracelet to notify authorities when they leave their authorized zones.

Many alternative or intermediate sanctions include a threat to send the offender back to prison. The offender who fails a drug test or evades the limits of electronic monitoring may be detained in jail, at least for a few days as a reminder. The combination of stick and carrot is an important feature of these sanctions. However, the system is far from perfect. A single offender on release might commit a heinous crime with widespread publicity, subjecting judges, prosecutors, and justice agencies to unfair ridicule with little chance to defend themselves. On the other hand, if alternative sanctions are carefully applied, they can save a good deal of money while also reducing the extent of unnecessary incarceration. Unfortunately, the criminal justice system is not really very systematic in using its wide array of tools.

Too Many Sanctions

In the mid-1970s, **Robert Martinson** examined which correctional programs succeeded or failed. His review of several hundred studies over three decades was disheartening. The message academics and criminal justice practitioners took from his analysis was that "nothing works."[19] This assessment dampened experimentation with new programs and set the stage in the 1980s for the pendulum swing to harsher sentences. Perhaps that reflects the fact that the criminal justice system is not really a system at all, but rather a diverse set of officials with different goals and interests, often responding to political pressures.

Facing these pressures, many prosecutors and judges use alternative programs for *net-widening*, filling programs with people who would not previously have been sanctioned at all. Thus, a young man or woman caught with marijuana, instead of being released with a warning, is convicted and sent to a drug rehabilitation program. The net of justice system control is thus widened. When poorly administered, special programs do not subtract prisoners from the expensive prison system, but merely add a new layer of expenses and multiply the numbers under state supervision. European countries have the same issue.[20] Rather than reducing the burdens on government and citizens, intermediate sanctions have provided a new method for "getting tough." In many cases, intermediate sanctions were tacked on to excessive prison sentences, prolonging public expense. **Boot camps** (or shock incarceration) were very popular with the public, but they showed little, if any, effect on recidivism. Yet, in defiance of the research evidence, these programs persist for political reasons.[21]

You can see that sentencing today is complex, and that complexity makes it difficult to decide what really may work to deter new crime. Luckily, criminologists have made some progress in how to evaluate programs and look for evidence of what works. *Program evaluation research* compares offenders in a program to similar offenders not in that program. Researchers ask whether the offenders who were in the program improved. Was their recidivism lower? Did their drug abuse cease? Were they able to hold a job? With any luck, the research will show that a program did good and that the offenders committed less crime. That said, the results can be disappointing.

Yet programs to help people with substance abuse, risky sexual behavior, school misbehavior, delinquency, and violence are not doomed to failure. For example, evaluators tell us that a rehabilitation program has the best chance to succeed if it has characteristics such as these:

- comprehensive efforts;

- varied teaching methods;

- sufficient "dosage";

- a theoretical basis;

- appropriate timing;

- sociocultural relevance; and

- well-trained staff.[22]

Some people will be fortunate enough to go through such a program, and it could help them overcome a drug habit, alcoholism, or other issues. However, society will have a great deal of trouble mass-producing programs with these characteristics to help the millions of people with problems.

Different Focus on the Community

Re-entry into the community after years in prison is difficult under the best of circumstances, and returning to communities with few resources makes it even harder.

Some probation and parole supervisors form a personal attachment with released offenders and assist them in very specific ways.[23] This is done by working with handlers, place managers, and others in the community to steer them away from crime opportunities. This is called *opportunity-focused supervision*. For example, officers

- encourage the released offender to stay away from risky settings and to reduce unstructured time;

- ask the released offender questions about daily routines;

- encourage the offender to avoid specific persons and risky activities;

- develop plans with the client to help handle a risky situation, such as avoiding taking phone calls from negative peers or making these calls short; and

- "role play" with the client to help resist various temptations.

Such an approach to supervision may be more effective than a vague prohibition by the court or parole board against fraternizing with other criminals. Unfortunately, parole departments lack sufficient personnel to apply opportunity-focused supervision on a wider scale. It is also unfortunate that police are not normally informed about when offenders are coming back to the community. Police could keep an eye on re-entering offenders, helping them meet the new challenges while also protecting the local community.[24] Even better, collaboration between police, parole, and non–justice organizations can help meet the many challenges faced by returning prisoners while also addressing the risk of recidivism.[25]

Another criminal justice model assembles offenders, victims, and the community.[26] *Restorative justice* focuses on making the community and victim whole again after the harm caused by the offender. Many community courts have restorative justice in mind. The general idea is to hold the offender directly accountable to the victim and community. Some restorative justice meetings occur after sentence has been imposed,[27] while other programs are alternatives to regular court processes and the offender's punishment is determined and agreed to by all parties. When damages are smaller, restorative justice methods might make more sense; on other occasions, the victim's anger at the offender leads to excessive demands for punishment.

One restorative justice technique is known as **reintegrative shaming**, articulated by **John Braithwaite**. Its goal is to direct shaming at the offender's behavior, rather than making it personal. This is contrasted to **stigmatic shaming**, which humiliates the offender. The goal is to use the justice system in a way that avoids stigmatizing the offender, then trying to reintegrate him into society.[28] Braithwaite sought to invent ways to punish people without stigmatizing them publicly and permanently.[29] We began Unit 3.4 by talking about the scarlet letter that publicly shamed Hester Primm but did little to help her reintegrate into society. Some recent examples of public shaming that would be considered stigmatic include special license plates for DUI offenders and sex offender registries, which are often online and searchable.[30]

From more than a century of trial and error, it is quite clear that society has a difficult task as it tries to punish and reform offenders. That is especially difficult with a captive population or in a bad local environment. Evaluating the progress against crime depends on statistics on crime, punishment, and the justice system. Such statistics do not compile themselves; rather they take a lot of effort by many people. The next unit will focus on how this happens.

FLASHCARD LIST FOR UNIT 3.5

- Augustus, John
- Boot camps
- Braithwaite, John
- Brockway, Zebulon
- Community corrections
- Community service sentences
- Crofton, Sir Walter
- Day-reporting centers
- Electronic monitoring
- Fines
- Good time
- Halfway houses

- House arrest
- Intensive supervision programs
- Intermediate sanctions
- Intermittent imprisonment
- Jails
- Maconochie, Alexander
- Martinson, Robert
- Net-widening
- Opportunity-focused supervision
- Penitentiary

- Prisons
- Program evaluation research
- Recidivism
- Reformatory
- Restitution
- Restorative justice
- Sentences, determinate, indeterminate, split
- Shaming, reintegrative, stigmatic

DISCUSSION QUESTIONS

1. Why was the penitentiary an important "invention"?

2. In what ways might intermediate sanctions become incapacitative?

Notes

1 Online Etymology Dictionary. (n.d.). Workhouse [online]. www.etymonline.com/index.php?allowed_in_frame=0&search=workhouse (retrieved August 1, 2017).

2 Encyclopedia.com (n.d.). The prison reform movement [online]. www.encyclopedia.com/social-sciences/news-wires-white-papers-and-books/prison-reform-movement (retrieved May 22, 2017).

3 Smith, C. (2014). *The prison and the American imagination*. New Haven, CT: Yale University Press.

4 Brockway, Z. R. (1912). *Fifty years of prison service: An autobiography*. New York: Charities Publication Committee.

5 For biography, see: Barry, J. V. (n.d.). Maconochie, Alexander (1787–1860) [online]. *Australian Dictionary of Biography* http://adb.anu.edu.au/biography/maconochie-alexander-2417 (retrieved August 20, 2016).

6 McCafferty, J. T., & Travis, L. F. (2014). History of probation and parole in the United States. In G. Bruinsma & D. Weisburd (Eds.), *Encyclopedia of criminology and criminal justice*, pp. 2217–2227. New York: Springer.

7 American Correctional Association. (n.d.). Declaration of principles [online]. www.aca.org/ACA_Prod_IMIS/ACA_Member/About_Us/Declaration_of_Principles/ACA_Member/AboutUs/Dec.aspx?hkey=a975cbd5-9788-4705-9b39-fcb6ddc048e0 (retrieved May 21, 2017).

8 New York Correction History Society. (n.d.). Nation's first reformatory [online]. www.correctionhistory.org/html/chronicl/docs2day/elmira.html (retrieved May 26, 2017).

9   Panzarella, R. (2002). Theory and practice of probation on bail in the report of John Augustus. *Federal Probation, 66*(3), 38–42.

10   Juvenile probation is not discussed here as it works differently. It is the most common outcome for juvenile offenders.

11   *Griffin v. Wisconsin*, 483 U.S. 868 (1987).

12   Morris, N., & Tonry, M. H. (1991). *Between prison and probation: Intermediate punishments in a rational sentencing system.* New York: Oxford University Press.

13   Petersilia, J., & Turner, S. (1993). Intensive probation and parole. *Crime and Justice, 17*, 281–335.

14   For example, see: Hamilton, Z. K., & Campbell, C. M. (2014). Uncommonly observed: The impact of New Jersey's halfway house system. *Criminal Justice and Behavior, 41*(11), 1354–1375.

15   Brennan, P. (2007). An intermediate sanction that fosters the mother-child bond: A process evaluation of Summit House. *Women and Criminal Justice, 18*(3), 47–80.

16   For example, see: Boyle, D. J., Ragusa-Salerno, L. M., Lanterman, J. L., & Marcus, A. F. (2013). An evaluation of day reporting centers for parolees. *Criminology & Public Policy, 12*(1), 119–143. Spence, D. H., & Haas, S. M. (2015). Predicting client success in day report centers: The importance of risk and needs assessment. *Journal of Offender Rehabilitation, 54*(7), 502–519.

17   McDonald, D. (1986). *Punishment without walls: Community service sentences in New York City.* New Brunswick, NJ: Rutgers University Press.

18   Hopkins, G. L., & McBride, D. C., Featherston, B. C., Gleason, P. C., & Moreno, J. (2014). Decades of research shows adolescents do better with community service rather than incarceration. *The Advocate: Official Publication of the Idaho State Bar, 57*(6/7), 56–61.

19   Martinson, R. (1974). What works? Questions and answers about prison reform. *The Public Interest, 35* (Spring), 22–54.

20   Aebi, M. F., Delgrande, N., & Marguet, Y. (2015). Have community sanctions and measures widened the net of the European criminal justice systems? *Punishment & Society, 17*(5), 575–597.

21   Cullen, F. T., Blevins, K. R., Trager, J. S., & Gendreau, P. (2005). Rise and fall of boot camps: A case study in common-sense corrections. *Journal of Offender Rehabilitation, 40*(3/4), 53–70. MacKenzie, D. L. (1993). Does shock incarceration work? *Corrections Compendium, 18*(9), 5–7. Finckenauer, J. O. (2005). Ruminating about boot camps: Panaceas, paradoxes, and ideology. *Journal of Offender Rehabilitation, 40*(3/4), 199–207.

22   Nation, M., Crusto, C., Wandersman, A., Kumpfer, K. L., Seybolt, D., Morrissey-Kane, E., & Davino, K. (2003). What works in prevention: Principles of effective prevention programs. *American Psychologist, 58*(6–7), 449–456.

23   Miller, J. (2016). Keeping them off the corner: How probation officers steer offenders away from crime opportunities. *Prison Journal, 96*(3), 437–461. Miller, J. (2012). Probation supervision and the control of crime opportunities: An empirical assessment. *Crime & Delinquency, 60*(8), 1235–1257.

24   Travis, J., Davis, R., & Lawrence, S. (2014). Exploring the role of the police in prisoner reentry. *Journal of Current Issues in Crime, Law & Law Enforcement, 7*(3/4), 495–513.

25   Lutze, F. E., Johnson, W. W., Clear, T. R., Latessa, E. J., & Slate, R. N. (2012). The future of community corrections is now: Stop dreaming and take action. *Journal of Contemporary Criminal Justice, 28*(1), 42–59.

26   National Institute of Justice. (2007). Working definitions of restorative justice [online]. www.nij.gov/topics/courts/restorative-justice/pages/definitions1.aspx (retrieved May 14, 2017).

27   For interesting use of restorative justice, see a video on the journey of parents whose son was killed on 9/11 as they sought healing through mercy for one of the masterminds and eventually through sharing their experiences with convicted murderers in prison: *In our son's name*; Producer-Director, Gayla Jamison. http://inoursonsname.com/ (retrieved August 1, 2017).

28   Braithwaite, J. (2015). Respect as freedom's guarantor. *Restorative Justice*, *3*(2), 295–298. Beck, E., Lewinson, T., & Kropf, N. P. (2015). Restorative justice with older adults: Mediating trauma and conflict in later life. *Traumatology*, *21*(3), 219–226. Maruna, S. (2016). Desistance and restorative justice: It's now or never. *Restorative Justice: An International Journal*, *4*(3), 289–301.

29   Braithwaite, J. (2000). Reintegrative shaming. In R. Paternoster & R. Bachman (Eds.), *Explaining criminals and crime: Essays in contemporary criminological theory*, pp. 242–251. Los Angeles: Roxbury. Reproduced at http://johnbraithwaite.com/wp-content/uploads/2016/05/2000_Reintegrative-Shaming.pdf (retrieved May 10, 2017).

30   Bazelon, E. (2012). Shame on you! *Slate*, February 22. www.slate.com/articles/news_and_politics/crime/2012/02/shaming_drug_offenders_in_new_orleans_and_drunk_drivers_in_ohio_and_minnesota_.html (retrieved May 10, 2017).

Unit 3.6 Practical Crime Data

It would be nice if offenders filled out a form every time they committed a crime and sent the form to a central statistical office. Unfortunately, crime is measured by a variety of imperfect methods. We really do not know how much crime there is in America or any other nation. However, we have a fairly good idea how frequently *some* types of crime occur and where the general trends are heading.[1]

For many crimes, nobody has an incentive to report. If one person sells contraband to another, both parties want to keep the transaction secret from police. If a street robber demands money from a prostitute, she is unlikely to ask for police intervention because she too is on the other side of the law. A bicycle stolen from storage might not be missed until weather improves some months later. A missing piece of jewelry is not always coded as stolen, although that could very well be the case.

Many types of data help us estimate the amount of crime and the processes leading to it. Box 3d notes five types of crime data that might emerge. Crime incidents may trigger certain other events, which produce data that can then be used in studying crime. The simplest follow-up event is somebody telling the police about the crime. That produces ***police and justice data***, the oldest form of crime statistics and the one most subject to evolution. Many victims are willing to talk later about their bad experiences, contributing to a crime ***victim survey***. Many offenders are willing to describe their own crime participation or crimes they have witnessed, producing offender ***self-report data***. A crime incident could also cause injury to those involved, leading them to use medical services. ***Medical data*** on crime result from this. Alternatively, stolen products missing from a store could be measured with ***business data***. In the next several sections we discuss these data types one by one.

Box 3D How Five Types of Crime Data Are Generated

Someone tells police → Police and justice data

Victim willing to talk later → Crime victim survey data

Offender willing to talk later → Self-report survey data

Victim uses medical services → Medical data on criminal injuries

Products missing from shelves → Business data on property crime

---

Police and Justice System Data

In 1833, **André-Michel Guerry** introduced the statistical study of crime using official court data.[2] You recall our discussion of Napoleon and his centralization of government and the justice system in France. That made possible the limited compilation of reasonably consistent court statistics and helped Guerry map crime over the provinces of France. All the arithmetic was done by hand using the pencils and pens of the era, since no modern calculating machines existed. That was the beginning of crime and justice system statistics.

Around 1900, some American police departments began to compile crime data, but there were no national data. Around 1927, Donald C. Stone (then a young assistant city manager in Cincinnati) joined with several young administrators from other large cities and created the **Uniform Crime Reporting System (UCR)**. They had the approval of J. Edger Hoover, founder of the Federal Bureau of Investigation. Despite the many legal inconsistencies among states, they were able to define a common set of definitions to allow a national report of crimes reported to the police.

The UCR separated crimes into two parts. **Part I crimes** include

- willful homicide;

- (forcible) rape;

- aggravated assault;

- robbery;

- burglary;

- motor vehicle theft;

- larceny-theft; and

- arson (sometimes).

Part II crimes are more diverse, including less serious felonies and misdemeanors as well as crimes that involve police discretion and energy to enforce. However, not all these offenses are minor—drug offenses are listed as Part II and may face substantial punishment. Part II crimes are subject to substantial inconsistency in enforcement and reporting, and they are in the UCR only if cleared by arrest. Crime statistics are affected by police discretion and energy to make these arrests. Prostitution, drug, and public order offenses are especially subject to police variations. We cannot really say that a city with twice as many public drunkenness crimes on the books has more public drunkenness than the city next to it.

Table 3b presents the raw counts of Part I crimes for the United States in 2015. Note how the more minor crimes greatly outnumber homicide. For example, there are about 400 larceny-thefts reported for every reported homicide. Note also that these are raw counts of Part I crimes reported to police and compiled by the FBI—not crime rates. Raw numbers don't allow us to compare easily from one year to the next for the whole United States, nor across jurisdictions with populations of different size. *Crime rates* give us standardized measures (such as percentages) to allow for comparison across time and across places. To find out the crime rates, we need to do some extra arithmetic. Specifically, we need to divide the number of crimes by the relevant population. For example, we might divide each crime count in Table 3b by the total population of the United States to produce several crime rates.

It is easier to illustrate how we calculate a crime rate for a jurisdiction smaller than the whole United States. The traditional crime rate is calculated by dividing the number of crimes in a jurisdiction for that year by the number of people who live there. Box 3e shows how to calculate a *traditional crime rate* for a city of 116,320 people that has 3,192 crimes, or about 27 crimes per thousand residents.

Using similar arithmetic, crime rates are calculated for cities, counties, states, and nations. Note how small a crime rate usually is, since most persons report no crime at all during a usual year. That's why we multiply the fraction by 1,000 (sometimes 10,000 or 100,000). For example, there were about five murders per 100,000 U.S. population in 2015.[3]

We can use bases other than the population as the crime rate denominator. In 1965, Sarah Boggs proposed alternative crime rates and gave some examples, such as the number of cars stolen per 1,000 cars on the road.[4] More recently, researchers have been using data from Twitter and other social media to estimate rapid movement of people and to relate crime rates to shifting daily populations.[5] Some recent studies take into account how many people enter a place for work or recreation. Consider that a

TABLE 3B **Part I Crimes from the FBI Uniform Crime Reports, United States, 2015**

Part I crime types	Number reported
Homicides	15,696
Forcible rape (traditional measure)	90,185
Rape (revised measure)	124,047
Robbery	327,374
Aggravated assault	764,449
Motor vehicle theft	707,758
Burglary	1,579,527
Larceny-theft	5,706,346

Source: Federal Bureau of Investigation (2016). Uniform crime reports; Table 1. https://ucr.fbi.gov/crime-in-the-u.s/ (retrieved May 10, 2017).

Box 3E How to Calculate a Traditional Crime Rate

$$\text{Traditional crime rate} = \frac{3{,}192 \text{ crimes reported this year in this city}}{116{,}320 \text{ residential population this year in this city}} \times 1{,}000 = 27.4 \text{ crimes per thousand population}$$

---

neighborhood with a lot of bars will have more crime—the bars bring more offenders and more targets for crime. It's not really the "fault" of local residents that their crime rate is higher.

Ways of gathering and using crime data are increasingly being modified to focus more on crime incidents. The **National Incident-Based Reporting System (NIBRS)** is a very ambitious American system designed to trace crime incidents and their major features.[6] Some states and cities have implemented that system and have produced new and detailed crime data, even adding data on identity theft and cybercrime. More advanced crime data systems are already being implemented in Canada and Chile, with other nations on the way.

Police also compile "calls for service" data based on 9-1-1 calls and other citizen reports. These are not compiled into a consistent national data set, but the data can be analyzed in local areas. Calls for service include erroneous reports and multiple citizens calling to report the same incident. Even these data are useful in that they help us measure the burdens on police.

Justice system data have been compiled by the National Center for State Courts—quite an effort considering the number of states with different criminal laws and reporting systems, the vast number of independent courts, and the 17,000 police departments. In some ways, given our convoluted justice structure, the United States will never catch up with France in 1810. However, modern computer files still allow quite a bit of opportunity for students to carry out analyses. Crime and justice data are available free or at low cost via the National Archive of Criminal Justice Data in Ann Arbor, Michigan.

Victim Surveys

When the government wants to find out about more complete experiences of crime, it goes directly to the victims. The crime victim survey is one method for doing this. People don't have perfect memories, but they often remember being the victim of a crime. On the other hand, they may forget just when it happened or other specific details. In any case, crime victim surveys make data available on the wider aspects of crimes and, when carried out countrywide, provide national-level data collected in a consistent way, allowing direct comparisons between different areas.

In the United States the government uses the ***National Crime Victim Survey (NCVS)***, which asks the public about their experience of crime in the last six months—whether they had their house burgled, or had something stolen, or were hit by somebody, and various other questions. Among other aspects of the crime, respondents are asked whether they reported the incident to the police, and if not why not.[7]

The NCVS can tell us how likely a crime is to be reported by type of crime.[8] Table 3c shows the percentage of different crimes reported to police in 2015, based on NCVS data. According to the table, ordinary thefts are least likely to be reported to police, while robbery is most likely to be reported. Aggravated assaults are more likely to be reported than simple assaults.

Some basic lessons have been learned from victim surveys. People are more likely to report home intrusions by strangers and less likely to report infractions by friends or families. Victims are more likely to report when physically injured but less likely to report a crime to police if they are embarrassed. Similar lessons emerge from the English-language surveys in Britain, Canada, Northern Ireland, the Irish Republic, Scotland, New Zealand, and Australia, as well as in 66 other nations.[9] As mentioned

TABLE 3C **Crimes Reported to Police, National Crime Victim Survey, United States, 2015**

Type of crime	Respondents who say they reported the crime to police (%)
Robbery	61.9
Aggravated assault	61.9
Burglary	50.8
Domestic violence	57.7
Simple assault	41.7
Rape and sexual assault	32.5
Theft	28.6

Source: Adapted from J. L. Truman & R. E. Morgan (2016). *Criminal victimization, 2015*. Washington, DC, Bureau of Justice Statistics; Table 4.

earlier, offenders themselves often are willing to talk about their own crimes, and this is discussed next.

Self-Report Surveys

The self-report survey can be a useful way to obtain data about crimes people have carried out. They may be more willing to admit to a crime in an anonymous questionnaire than in a face-to-face interview.

The *self-report survey* asking about crimes committed was first carried out in 1943 by Professor *Austin Porterfield* at Texas Christian University.[10] He asked local delinquents to report on their own crimes and delinquent acts. Then he asked his university undergraduates to take the same survey. Porterfield discovered not much difference between the two groups. We return to that issue in Part 4. For now, an important point is that self-reports are especially useful in studying youth crime. Most of the time, youths committing a crime are not caught and punished. They drink underage, steal things, and dabble in drugs much more often than is reflected in official data.

Porterfield's idea was picked up in the 1970s. Monitoring the Future is a national survey on drug use that has been conducted annually since 1975.[11] It includes high school seniors as well as eighth- and tenth-grade students. The National Youth Survey is taken for ages 11 through 17, and other self-report surveys ask college students about their drug, alcohol, and tobacco use.[12] Self-report surveys find much more offending, including illegal drug abuse, than comes to the attention of police. However, most drug use reported in surveys involves softer drugs, such as marijuana, and does not involve daily use at high levels.

Self-report studies usually cover sporadic or occasional offending. However, other studies have used interviews with very active offenders about crime. Those studies are usually quite small, but truly fascinating. Paul Cromwell's edited volume, *In Their Own Words*,[13] collects interviews with burglars, robbers, swindlers, shoplifters, and several other categories of offender. They are very articulate in explaining how they do illegal work.

Medical Data

Vital statistics data in many nations includes homicide statistics. However, these are not the only crime statistics with a medical origin. Hospital emergency rooms and other medical organizations and facilities know a lot about the problems of society. That's why the American government created a national database by gathering data from hospital emergency rooms. The Emergency Room Statistics on Intentional Violence include data on intentional injuries, such as domestic violence, rape, and child abuse. In addition, many local emergency departments collect data on drug overdoses, alcohol poisoning, and other events that require medical help. These data are compiled in the United States by a survey called DAWN (The Drug Abuse Warning Network), offering national estimates of drug-related emergency department visits. The data show almost 2.5 million visits in 2011 for emergencies related to misuse of drugs.[14]

The old saying is that the lawyers and doctors know everybody's secrets. Although attorneys do not centralize records about their clients, medical records with no names attached tell us quite a bit. Scandinavian nations are the best for studying this since they have population registries with all health and police contacts linked by the same social identification number for individuals, meaning the data are confidential. Some of the best studies of criminal offenders, linked to health problems, have been conducted in Denmark and other Scandinavian nations. These studies help researchers in measuring the substantial overlap between mental health problems and crime problems.

Business Data

Businesses have a good deal of data on theft and other losses, but are not very inclined to make their data public. Fortunately, the National Insurance Crime Bureau

Table 3D **Top Ten Makes and Models of Stolen Vehicles, United States, 2015**

Theft rank	Make and model	Total thefts	Most targeted year
1	Honda Accord	52,244	1996
2	Honda Civic	49,430	1998
3	Ford Pickup	29,396	2006
4	Chevrolet Pickup	27,771	2004
5	Toyota Camry	15,446	2014
6	Dodge Pickup	11,212	2001
7	Toyota Corolla	10,547	2014
8	Nissan Altima	10,374	2015
9	Dodge Caravan	9,798	2002
10	Chevrolet Impala	9,225	2008

Source: National Insurance Crime Bureau (n.d.). Hot wheels 2016 [online]. www.nicb.org/theft_and_fraud_awareness/top-vehicles-stolen-by-state#States (retrieved September 18, 2016).

annually publishes the most stolen vehicles by model for the United States. Table 3d presents the 2015 statistics for the most frequently stolen vehicles.[15] Older models are much more likely to be stolen since their parts become valuable with age.

The important point is the extent of crime data that the private sector collects and compiles. Many retail chains have created excellent databases showing which of their products disappear from their shelves and warehouses. That's how we learned that items most often used for illegal drug-making are also very likely to be shoplifted.[16]

Future Crime Data: Cybercrime, Fraud, and Credit Card Abuse

Fraud and cybercrime data are not routinely compiled on a national basis, but again some sources are available. The Federal Trade Commission in the United States publishes the *Consumer Sentinel Network Data Book*, which compiled 2,582,851 *fraud complaints to the Federal Trade Commission* received during the calendar year 2014.[17]

TABLE 3E Top Six Types of Complaint to the Federal Trade Commission, United States, 2014

Complaint	Number
Identity theft	332,646
Debt collection fraud	280,998
Imposter scams	276,662
Phone and & mobile service frauds	171,809
Bank and lender scams	128,107
Prizes, sweepstakes & lotteries	103,579

Source: Drawn from Federal Trade Commission (2015). *Consumer sentinel network data book, January–December 2014.* Washington, DC: Federal Trade Commission.

Of these, the top six types of fraud complaint were: identity theft; debt collection fraud; imposter scams; phone and mobile service frauds; bank and lender scams; and prizes, sweepstakes, and lotteries. These are displayed in Table 3e with the number of complaints for each.

Other complaints included frauds based on autos, shopping, television and media, internet services, credit services, travel and vacations, foreign money offers, business opportunities, internet auctions, mortgage foreclosure, debt management, home repair, charitable solicitations, and more. Many additional forms of cybercrime are being discovered. For example, street gang members use Twitter to intimidate others, to communicate threatening imagery, and to brag about recent illegal activities.[18]

New forms of crime data have emerged in recent years. One example involves researchers using chemical analyses of wastewater to measure drug and alcohol use over time. They have been able to show how effluent levels are greater on weekends and holidays, and in urban areas with more nighttime venues.[19]

FLASHCARD LIST FOR UNIT 3.6

- Business data
- Crime rates
- Federal Trade Commission, fraud complaints
- Guerry, André-Michel
- Medical data (on injuries and drug and alcohol use)

- National Crime Victim Survey (NCVS)
- National Incident-Based Reporting System (NIBRS)
- Part I crimes
- Part II crimes
- Police and justice data
- Porterfield, Austin

- Self-report, data, survey
- Traditional crime rate
- Uniform Crime Reports (UCR)
- Victim survey

DISCUSSION QUESTIONS

1.   What do victim surveys show that official police data miss?

2.   What is the relative frequency of very serious crimes?

Notes

1   Maltz, M. D., & Frey, K. (2014). History of the statistics of crime and criminal justice. In G. Bruinsma & D. Weisburd (Eds.), *Encyclopedia of criminology and criminal justice*, pp. 2319–2326. New York: Springer.

2   Guerry, A.-M. (1833). *Essai sur la statistique morale de la France*. Paris: Crochard.

3   Federal Bureau of Investigation. (2016). Uniform Crime Reports, Table 1 [online]. https://ucr.fbi.gov/crime-in-the-u.s/ (retrieved August 1, 2017).

4   Boggs, S. L. (1965). Urban crime patterns. *American Sociological Review. 30*(6), 899–908.

5   Andresen, M. A. (2011). The ambient population and crime analysis. *The Professional Geographer, 63*(2), 193–212.

6   Addington, L. A. (2009). Studying the crime problem with NIBRS data: Current uses and future trends. In M. D. Krohn, A. J. Lizotte, & G. P. Hall (Eds.), *Handbook on crime and deviance*, pp. 23–42. New York: Springer.

7   Rennison, C. M. (2014). National Crime Victimization Survey (NCVS). In J. M. Miller, (Ed.), *The encyclopedia of theoretical criminology*, Vol. 1, pp. 564–567. Chichester, U.K.: John Wiley & Sons. Addington, L. A., & Rennison, C. M. (2014). U.S. National Crime Victimization Survey. In G. Bruinsma & D. Weisburd (Eds.), *Encyclopedia of criminology and criminal justice*, pp. 5392–5401. New York: Springer.

8   Truman, J., & Morgan, R. (2016). *Criminal victimization, 2015*. Washington, DC: Bureau of Justice Statistics. www.bjs.gov/content/pub/pdf/cv15.pdf (retrieved August 1, 2017).

9   Mayhew, P., & Van Dijk, J. (2014). International Crime Victimization Survey. In G. Bruins & D. Weisburd (Eds.), *Encyclopedia of criminology and criminal justice*, pp. 2602–2614. New York: Springer.

Other nations that have carried out at least one crime victim survey are Albania, Argentina, Austria, Azerbaijan, Belarus, Belgium, Bolivia, Botswana, Brazil, Bulgaria, Cambodia, China, Colombia, Costa Rica, Croatia, Czech Republic, Denmark, Egypt, Estonia, Finland, France, Georgia, Germany, Hong Kong, Hungary, Iceland, India, Indonesia, Italy, Japan, Kyrgyzstan, Latvia, Lesotho, Lithuania, Luxembourg, Macedonia, Malta, Mexico, Mongolia, Mozambique, Namibia, the Netherlands, New Zealand, Nigeria, Norway, Oceania, Panama, Papua New Guinea, Paraguay, Peru, the Philippines, Poland, Portugal, Republic of South Africa, Romania, Russian Federation, Slovak Republic, Slovenia, South Korea, Spain, Swaziland, Sweden, Switzerland, Tanzania, Tunisia, Turkey, and Ukraine.

10   Porterfield, A. L. (1943). Delinquency and its outcome in court and college. *American Journal of Sociology, 49*(3), 199–208.

11   Thornberry, T. P., & Krohn, M. D. (2000). The self-report method for measuring delinquency and crime. *Criminal Justice, 4*(1), 33–83.

12   Thornberry & Krohn, The self-report method for measuring delinquency and crime. Thornberry, T. P., & Krohn, M. D. (2003). Comparison of self-report and official data for measuring crime. In J. V. Pepper & C. V. Petrie (Eds.), *Measurement problems in criminal justice research: Workshop summary*, pp. 43–94. Washington, DC: National Academies Press. www.nap.edu/read/10581/chapter/4 (retrieved August 1, 2017).

13   Cromwell, P. (Ed.). (2012). *In their own words: Criminals on crime*, 6th edition. New York: Oxford University Press.

14   Center for Behavioral Health Statistics and Quality. (2013). *The DAWN report: Highlights of the 2011 Drug Abuse Warning Network (DAWN) findings on drug-related emergency department visits.* Rockville, MD: Substance Abuse and Mental Health Services Administration. www.samhsa.gov/data/sites/default/files/DAWN127/DAWN127/sr127-DAWN-highlights.htm (retrieved September 5, 2016).

15   National Insurance Crime Bureau. (n.d.). Hot wheels 2016 [online]. www.nicb.org/theft_and_fraud_awareness/top-vehicles-stolen-by-state#States (retrieved September 18, 2016).

16   Smith, B. T. (2013). *Differential shoplifting risks of fast-moving consumer goods.* Doctoral dissertation, Rutgers University.

17   Federal Trade Commission. (2015). *Consumer sentinel network data book, January–December 2014.* Washington, DC: Federal Trade Commission. www.ftc.gov/system/files/documents/reports/consumer-sentinel-network-data-book-january-december-2014/sentinel-cy2014-1.pdf (retrieved September 18, 2016).

18   Balasuriya, L., Wijeratne, S., Doran, D., & Sheth, A. (2016). Finding street gang members on Twitter. Paper presented at the *2016 IEEE/ACM International Conference on Advances in Social Networks Analysis and Mining.* August 18–21, San Francisco.

19   Ort, C., van Nuijs, A. L. N., Berset, J.-D., Bijlsma, L., Castiglioni, S., . . . & Thomas, K. V. (2014). Spatial differences and temporal changes in illicit drug use in Europe quantified by wastewater analysis. *Addiction, 109*(8),1338–1352.

PERSPECTIVE ON PART 3

We have covered a lot of ground in Part 3, but its general theme should be clear: The justice system has too much to do. Therefore, it must find ways to share the burden with other agencies of society, to avoid hyperactivity, and to do its best given the dilemmas it faces. Among those dilemmas is the problem of assigning blame, including deciding on *mens rea*, the criminal state of mind. That creates problems in theory as well as in practice. The requirements of justice are highly labor-intensive and hence expensive. What happens in the real world depends largely on how justice officials use their discretionary powers.

Although punishment should ideally be swift and certain, that does not happen in a modern justice system without taking shortcuts—ranging from plea bargaining to avoiding the system entirely. Some of these avoidance efforts are highly justifiable, but at other times important tasks are simply not performed. The system keeps trying, but it has no clear and absolute path to perfection. That helps us understand the importance of our discussion in Part 2—why society tries to contain its problems using personal, social, and situational controls, thus avoiding the need for formal controls. Any society depending on the formal system to control crime has already lost its battle for security.

We do not have a single set of data that can keep track of these processes. Official crime data do not record all crimes, much less the many disputes and issues that are handled informally. Victim surveys and self-report studies supplement official data. Business and medical statistics help as well, yet figuring out the whole process is like trying to solve a jigsaw puzzle when many pieces are missing.

Many positive efforts, both inside and outside the justice system, never generate statistics. A police officer who talks someone out of escalating a dispute might never make a report and never get credit. Neighbors and citizens resolve issues quietly without filling out forms. Avoidance of the justice system is often a good thing. Yet society cannot entirely avoid using its justice system, including its prisons and other expensive programs. Having said this, we have provided some optimistic suggestions for reducing crime while simultaneously spending less money and minimizing confrontations with citizens.

Minimizing confrontations helps maintain citizens' respect for formal controls. This is one place where we see the importance of procedural justice. We end Part 3 with some examples to illustrate its importance.

EXAMPLES

Police officer stopping a driver: An officer notices a speeding car and is about to issue a ticket. In the process of ticketing the driver, the officer uses the terms "sir" and "ma'am" with a polite tone, clearly explains that there have been a lot of accidents on this stretch of road and why police are ticketing, and at the end hands the driver a card with his own badge number and a website, inviting any comments.

Alternative: An officer uses a nasty tone, chews out the driver, and asserts his own authority as his primary focus.

Office where tickets are paid: The office is clean, extremely well ordered, and has a clear priority system for paying tickets. Anybody wishing to contest a ticket can first talk to a specialist who politely explains the ticket and citizen options for contesting it.

Alternative: The office is dirty, disorganized, full of rude people with brusque manners and grimacing faces.

Traffic court: The court process is well organized. Court personnel are polite and professional. The judge politely listens to the citizen's argument and allows reasonable time for them to make it, even if the argument makes no sense. The judge explains why he must find against the citizen this time. His judicial temperament conveys a friendly professionalism, not too personal but still human.

Alternative: Traffic cases are pushed through rudely and citizens feel cheated. Rumors fly about favoritism and prejudice. Citizens distrust the process.

When procedural justice works best, most citizens, despite having been ticketed, are convinced that the system was reasonably fair to them. Procedural justice is part of a larger idea, what political scientists call the "***civic culture***." In 1963 Almond and Verba wrote a famous book with that title.[1] Democracy depends on communication and persuasion, consensus and diversity. It depends on people feeling they are participants in the society, not just subjects of a larger authority. People must feel they will be treated fairly by government authorities. That's why procedural justice is so important. Police officers and other justice officials are more than law enforcers—they are also agents of democracy. The actions of a 22-year-old police officer are central for developing and maintaining the civic culture.

Our textbook offers you some limited optimism, but not utopianism. The fundamental problems of justice keep returning and challenging us to do the best we can. We are struck by a common thread in the best crime reduction programs. The most promising programs cut across *multiple segments* of the justice process—police, courts, probation, and parole. That applies to both the Boston Gun Project and to opportunity-focused supervision programs (a part of the probation and parole processes). These programs are not limited to punishment. They leverage different agencies and actors in the justice process and use offenders' social networks to improve their chances of avoiding getting back into trouble. These programs bring families and communities into the mix, seeking to extend informal controls and to circumscribe offending opportunities. A general principle keeps reasserting itself as we study the justice system: The best chance for reducing crime is to find strategic opportunities to do so, *focusing resources* to *keep offenders out of risky situations*. This is best accomplished by *combining multiple components* of the justice process along with environmental design and attention to daily routines after offenders are released into the community.

As we examine these efforts, we increasingly realize that the term "criminal justice system" is a misnomer because it is not really a unified system. The justice process involves many independent decisions by different people, whose discretion often leads to inconsistencies, without a strategic focus. The justice process cannot cover all offenses or offenders, or assist all victims. To make crime reduction more systematic, officials need to cooperate, combine forces, and make sure their discretion is used strategically.

Main Points of Part 3

- Implementing formal controls to prevent crime is complex, time-consuming, and expensive.

- Realistic justice involves limiting the amount the criminal justice system has to do.

- Discretion is important for the actors in the criminal justice system to handle all that is asked of them.
  - o   Police may calm things down rather than arrest.
  - o   Prosecutors may choose not to prosecute.

- o   Courts opt for plea bargains instead of trials to speed things up.

- o   Judges have the discretion to impose sentences.

- Diversion programs take offenders out of the criminal justice system altogether.

- Specialized courts attend to offenders who need special services or communities that want certain crime problems addressed.

- Punishment is most effective when it is certain, speedy, and not too severe.

  - o   Many crimes go unreported or have no arrest made, so punishment is not certain.

  - o   Trials take a long time.

  - o   The United States tends to use harsh sentences of lengthy prison terms.

- Ultimately, we hope our criminal justice system and its punishments will deter future crimes.

- There have been many efforts to achieve effective punishment, but we need realistic expectations for the outcomes.

- Crime data has many sources, but no source provides a full picture of the amount of crime.

FLASHCARD LIST FOR PERSPECTIVE ON PART 3

- Civic culture
- Combining multiple components
- Focusing resources
- Removing risky situations

Note

1   Almond, G., & Verba, S. (1963). *The civic culture: Political attitudes and democracy in five countries.* Princeton, NJ: Princeton University; p. 3.

PART 4

Risky Ages

It is a mistake to think of juvenile crime as a lower-class or minority phenomenon. As we shall see,

- Youths of all races and economic groups are vulnerable to crime's temptations.[1]

- Middle-class youths are very well represented in crime and delinquency.[2]

- Youth problems are not limited to urban areas.

Indeed, some recent studies indicate that rural youths use alcohol and methamphetamine at higher rates than urban youths.[3] By recent statistical studies, adolescents in rural areas have higher general drug use.[4] Indeed, juvenile offending is an urban, suburban, and rural problem. In addition, adolescent involvement in crime and substance abuse apply in virtually all modern nations.[5]

Part 4 explores why teenage years are so vulnerable to crime and delinquency. The age factor in crime was recognized in 1831 by **Adolphe Quetelet** (1796–1874):

Of all the causes which influence the development of the propensity to crime, or which diminish that propensity, age is unquestionably the most energetic. Indeed, it is through age that the physical powers and passions of man are developed, and their energy afterwards decreases with age. Reason is developed with age, and continues to acquire power even when strength and passion have passed their greatest vigour. Considering only these three elements, strength, passion, and judgment (or reason), we may almost say, *a priori*, what will be the degree of propensity to crime at different ages. . . . [T]he propensity to crime should be at its maximum at the age when strength and passion have attained their maximum, and when reason has not acquired sufficient power to govern their combined influence.[6]

Quetelet goes on to measure crime by age and to prove his point. He concluded that the propensity to commit crimes increases quite rapidly as youths move towards adulthood, reaching a maximum in early adulthood, and then decreasing as adults age further.[7] He saw this as a basic law of nature, and most of our evidence confirms the basic *shape* of the age curve in different nations and eras.[8] Some variations do occur.[9] Yet crime participation always seems to peak during youthful ages and then to decline.

Criminologists call this the ***age–crime curve*** or the ***crime trajectory***. For consistency, we use the first term, and in Part 4 we emphasize the teenage and young adult years, during which the curve displays the greatest shifts.

The age–crime curve is a ***general shape*** that has been found in every nation or era that criminologists have studied. It tells us that crime participation accelerates as youths proceed into adolescence, then begins to trail off as they leave adolescence and enter young adulthood. On the left of Figure 4a, you can see the ***acceleration*** of crime participation in ***early adolescence*** (around ages 12 through 14). On the right of the figure, you can see the ***deceleration*** of participation in ***late adolescence*** (around 18 and 19) and early adulthood (around 20 and 21). You can also see the ***peak participation*** in ***mid-adolescence*** (ages 15 through 17). However,

- Individuals do not fit neatly into this pattern, as you will learn later in Part 4.

- This is only a *general* shape of the age–crime curve; in different places or eras, the curve might be flatter or it might be more pronounced, or it might be skewed more to the left or to the right.

- The age–crime curve has the same basic shape for males and females, but for females, acceleration is slower and their peak is less elevated.

Researchers who study the age–crime curve admit that these curves do not represent real groups of people[10] and that they are only used to predict approximately what real people do.[11] The age–crime curve serves us well as an average description of how crime distributes over the life course, and fits in many nations and eras.[12] While the curve summarizes overall behavior, Unit 4.2 will show how individuals vary a great deal in their crime patterns.

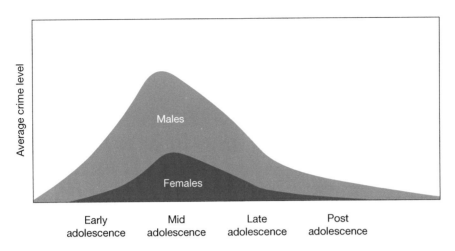

FIGURE 4A
The Age–Crime Curve for Males and Females

Society has a very strong interest in shrinking the age–crime curve. The crime problem can be reduced if society can somehow get youths to

a.   Start and accelerate delinquency at later ages (***late onset***).

b.   Commit fewer delinquent acts during mid-adolescence (***lower peak***).

c.   Decelerate and cease delinquent acts soon after the peak years (***early desistance***).

Figure 4b depicts these three improvements. It shows on the left that starting crime later in adolescence would reduce the number of crimes. It shows that less crime involvement in mid-adolescence would also reduce that number. It shows on the right that getting away from crime before the end of adolescence would also lead to less overall crime participation. Our discussion of Japanese society in Unit 2.2 described a relatively successful effort to deliver social control of adolescents. Japanese institutions successfully delay onset and lower peak participation in delinquency. Although the Japanese are less able to control delinquency in late adolescence and early adulthood, they are able to shrink the age–crime curve by keeping youths occupied most hours of the day and evening in activities that adults substantially control.

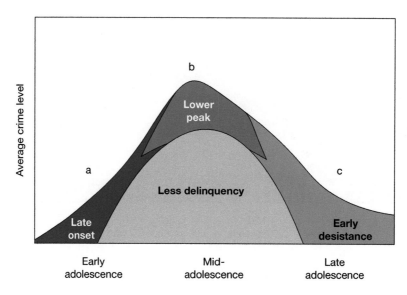

Figure 4b
Three Ways to Shrink the Age–Crime Curve

The age–crime curve helps us organize what we know and how we think about crime. Criminologists have found a similar age curve for

- having delinquent friends;[13]

- going to parties and hanging out with larger groups of peers;[14]

- general crime victimization;[15]

- sexual victimization;[16] and

- committing sexual offenses against those younger than oneself.

It is a myth that sexual offenders against children are older adults; these offenders fit the age–crime curve quite clearly, with peak offending at ages 13 through 17.[17] You can clearly see that the age–crime curve offers us a powerful summary of how crime and delinquency change. However, it is *only* a summary. In Unit 4.1 you will see that the age–crime curve reflects how the human brain develops as people move through adolescence. Unit 4.2 shows how the age–crime curve is produced and how individual youths vary from that curve. Unit 4.3 discusses peer influences over the long haul. In Unit 4.4, we discuss how various situations can induce delinquency. Unit 4.5 then continues our discussion of peers and the amount of time teens spend with them.

Evidence is growing that women are catching up to men in some violations during adolescence, including marijuana use,[18] and Part 6 will discuss the same issue in terms of alcohol consumption. Step by step, as you proceed, you will gain a growing understanding of how crime emerges and varies.

FLASHCARD LIST FOR PART 4: RISKY AGES

- Acceleration
- Adolescence, early, mid, late
- Age–crime curve
- Crime trajectory

- Deceleration
- Early desistance
- General shape (of the age–crime curve)
- Late onset

- Lower peak
- Peak participation
- Quetelet, Adolphe

QUESTIONS ADDRESSED IN PART 4

1. What are the risky ages, and how are they related to brain development?

2. How do teenagers combine or channel adult and peer influences?

3. How does time spent with teens, away from parents, influence delinquency?

Notes

1 Junger, M., & Polder, W. (1992). Some explanations of crime among four ethnic groups in the Netherlands. *Journal of Quantitative Criminology, 8*(1), 51–78.

2 Reiss, A. J., & Rhodes, A. L. (1961). The distribution of juvenile delinquency in the social class structure. *American Sociological Review, 26*(5), 720–732.

3 Pruitt, L. R. (2009). The forgotten fifth: Rural youth and substance abuse. *Stanford Law & Policy Review, 20*, 359–404. Rhew, I. C., Hawkins, J. D., & Oesterle, S. (2011). Drug use and risk among youth in different rural contexts. *Health & Place, 17*(3), 775–783. Shukla, R. K. (2016). *Methamphetamine: A love story.* Berkeley, CA: University of California Press.

4 Lambert, D., Gale, J. A., & Hartley, D. (2008). Substance abuse by youth and young adults in rural America. *The Journal of Rural Health, 24*(3), 221–228.

5 Junger-Tas, J., Marshall, I. H., Enzmann, D., Killias, M., Steketee, M., & Gruszczynska, B. (Eds.). (2009). *Juvenile delinquency in Europe and beyond: Results of the second International Self-Report Delinquency Study.* New York: Springer. Enzmann, D., Marshall, I. H., Killias, M., Junger-Tas, J., Steketee, M., & Gruszczynska, B. (2010). Self-reported youth delinquency in Europe and beyond: First results of the Second International Self-Report Delinquency Study in the context of police and victimization data. *European Journal of Criminology, 7*(2), 159–183.

6 Quetelet, L. A. J., & Smibert, T. (2013 [1842]). *A treatise on man and the development of his faculties.* Cambridge, U.K.: Cambridge University Press; p. 92.

7   Quetelet, A. (1984 [1831]). *Adolphe Quetelet's research on the propensity for crime at different ages.* Cincinnati, OH: Anderson.

8   Hirschi, T., & Gottfredson, M. (1983). Age and the explanation of crime. *American Journal of Sociology, 89*(3), 552–584.

9   Steffensmeier, D. J., Allan, E. A., Harer, M. D., & Streifel, C. (1989). Age and the distribution of crime. *American Journal of Sociology, 94*(4), 803–831.

10 Sampson, R. J., & Laub, J. H. (2005). Seductions of method: Rejoinder to Nagin and Tremblay's developments trajectory groups: Fact or fiction. *Criminology, 43*(4), 905–913.

11 Nagin, D. S., & Tremblay, R. E. (2005). Developmental trajectory groups: Fact or a useful statistical fiction? *Criminology, 43*(4), 873–904.

12 Hirschi, T., & Gottfredson, M., Age and the explanation of crime. Shulman, E. P., Steinberg, L. D., & Piquero, A. R. (2013). The age–crime curve in adolescence and early adulthood is not due to age differences in economic status. *Journal of Youth and Adolescence, 42*(6), 848–860.

13 Warr, M. (2002). *Companions in crime: The social aspects of criminal conduct.* Cambridge, U.K.: Cambridge University Press.

14 Warr, M. (1993). Age, peers, and delinquency. *Criminology, 31*(1), 17–40.

15 Truman, J. L., & Rand, M. R. (2010). *Criminal victimization, 2009.* Washington, DC: Bureau of Justice Statistics.

16 Felson, R. B., & Cundiff, P. R. (2014). Sexual assault as a crime against young people. *Archives of Sexual Behavior, 43*(2), 273–284.

17 Cotter, A. and Beaupré, P. (2014). *Police-reported sexual offences against children and youth in Canada, 2012.* Ottawa: Statistics Canada.

18 Chapman, C., Slade, T., Swift, W., Keyes, K., Tonks, Z., & Teesson, M. (2017). Evidence for sex convergence in prevalence of cannabis use: A systematic review and meta-regression. *Journal of Studies on Alcohol and Drugs, 78*(3), 344–352.

Unit 4.1 The Teenage Brain

The human brain changes greatly during adolescence.[1] This is the lesson from a decade of important research using magnetic resonance imaging (MRI). These changes are extremely important for crime and other risky behavior. Starting at puberty and continuing into the early 20s, brain development and reorganization appears in two key regions (see Figure 4c). The ***limbic region*** is in the lower center of the brain, and it is associated with the enrichment of human emotions. The ***prefrontal cortex*** covers the front part of the frontal node of the brain, and it is associated with sound judgment needed to keep these emotions in check.[2]

Uneven Brain Development

During adolescence, both regions of the brain grow rapidly. The earliest and most rapid growth occurs in the limbic region, bringing with it a dramatic enrichment of human emotions. In contrast, the prefrontal cortex lags several years behind in its maturity, making it harder for youths to control their new emotions. Figure 4d illustrates how these two regions of the brain grow during adolescence and depicts the ***risky period*** created because emotions grow faster than judgment.[3] Note that the blue line rises first, depicting the growth of the limbic region and the rich emotions it engenders. The black line (the growth of the prefrontal cortex) rises more slowly and at later ages. That tells us that *a teenager's judgment fails to develop fast enough to manage these new emotions, impulses, and urges.* The area between the two lines is filled with light blue, depicting the risky period during which teenagers are more vulnerable to participation in crime and delinquency.[4] Teenage accelerators tend to overpower their brakes.

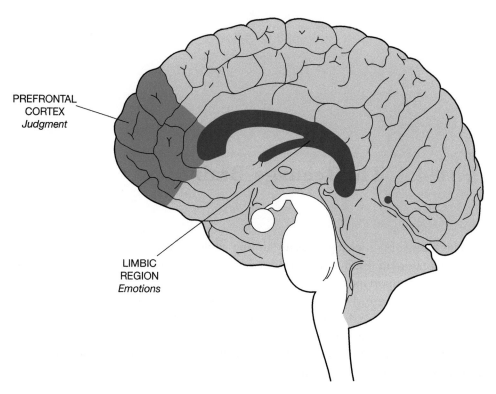

FIGURE 4C

Location of the Limbic Region and Prefrontal Cortex in the Brain

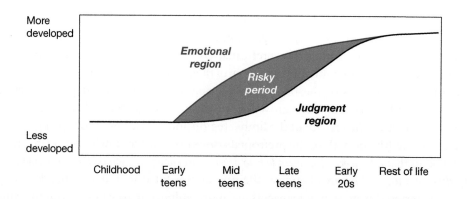

FIGURE 4D

Unequal Growth of Two Regions of the Brain during Adolescence

Source: Extension of B. J. Casey, R. M. Jones, & T. A. Hare (2008). The adolescent brain. *Annals of the New York Academy of Sciences, 1124*(1), 111–126.

Sociability, Coolness, and Sex

The limbic region's growth also enhances sociability. Thus teenagers increasingly seek the company of other teenagers. They wish to impress their peers and avoid embarrassment when peers are around. They have trouble withstanding group pressures, and they are especially apt to take risks when peers are watching.[5] They increasingly want to

- assert independence from parents;

- be seen as "cool";

- show daring and prowess;

- break rules; and

- try sex.[6]

Professor **James Coleman** noted in 1959 that adolescents show little interest in education and instead focus their attention on cars, dates, sports, popular music, and other matters unrelated to school.[7] Teens tend not to value academic performance or preparation for the future nearly as much as they value relating to other teens and participating in ***adolescent society***.[8] Those relationships also involved smoking cigarettes and drinking underage. The general involvement in ***peer culture*** persists today although the specific consumer products and music differ from 1959. Recent research on middle-class high school students reported that they try to "be cool" by using drugs and alcohol to demonstrate independence from parents.[9] Such risk-taking is associated with adolescence.[10] As milder forms of "coolness," teenagers adjust physical appearance, fashion, mannerisms, and linguistic forms to demonstrate autonomy from adults.

Consistent with modern brain research, the natural teenage process applies more generally than to just one era or one nation. However, places and times differ in how teenagers use their time. That time use in turn affects the trouble they get into, as we explain later in Part 4.

Many people think a child's misbehavior reflects on that child's parents. Parents themselves are often defensive, overstating the innocence of their own children, blaming peers for any bad behavior.[11] They may forget that their own children too are going through the same changes as peers—with increasing needs for autonomy, thrills, and socializing. Perhaps ***peer pressure*** is a mutual effect rather than bad influence in one direction.[12] Later in Part 4 we explore adult and peer influences further. We suggest that parents might have much less influence than they would like to think. But first we take a closer look at adolescent risk-taking.

Known Risks vs. Unknown Risks

Decision scientists study how people make choices in different situations.[13] People make their decisions differently when more information is available. For example, an experienced mountain climber who decides to scale a well-charted mountain on a clear day is taking a *known risk*. On the other hand, an uninformed teenager who experiments with drugs is taking an **ambiguous risk**—not knowing the odds of getting hurt.

Surprisingly, teenagers are cautious when they *know in advance* how much risk they are taking. However, teenagers are more willing than adults to take ambiguous risks with unknown chances of winning or losing. Compared to adults, teenagers appear to have a high tolerance for the unknown.[14] That makes them more willing than adults to shoplift, drink, or smoke marijuana, for which risks of getting caught or long-term damage are unclear. In terms of situational prevention (discussed in Part 2), teenagers might be discouraged from committing crimes if the community creates clear and present risks that they can see and feel.

It is possible that more experience helps enlarge their knowledge about what's risky and then makes them more cautious. A study of online adolescent behavior using social media found that between 2006 and 2009, youths learned to be more cautious about making their private information available to the public on the internet.[15] Youths can learn quickly enough from their own or their friends' bad online experiences. Yet other types of risky behavior, such as alcohol abuse, often take years to provide the negative outcome and may generate a slower learning curve.

Habit-forming substance abuse poses special problems at later ages. By the time people learn the negative consequences, they may find it difficult to pull away from the habit they formed at a younger stage of life. Past habits can linger for many years. For example, teenagers who smoke only a few cigarettes as a teenager are 16 times as likely as nonsmoking teenagers to become adult smokers.[16] The high level of adult marijuana use[17] reflects early use of marijuana during adolescence. Those who have not experimented with marijuana or other substance abuse by age 20 will probably not do so at all.[18] For some people, substance abuse becomes a lasting habit from which they may never escape. However, in many other cases, problem behaviors begin to fade as adolescence winds down.[19]

The age–crime curve has helped us organize a lot of information about offending, victimization, delinquent friends, and the social life of youths. It has helped us compare the role of youths in different societies and communities as well as changes over time in their roles. It also helps us see how changes in the adolescent brain challenge society to absorb and include millions of youths as they go through the adolescent period. We turn our attention next to the volatility and variation common in teenage years.

FLASHCARD LIST FOR UNIT 4.1

- Adolescent society
- Ambiguous risk
- Coleman, James

- Limbic region
- Peer culture
- Peer pressure

- Prefrontal cortex
- Risky period

DISCUSSION QUESTIONS

1. How do the prefrontal cortex and limbic region change during adolescence, and why is that important?

2. How long does it take for judgment to catch up with emotions?

Notes

1 Steinberg, L. (2008). A social neuroscience perspective on adolescent risk-taking. *Developmental Review, 28*(1), 78–106.

2 Giedd, J. N. (2015). The amazing teen brain. *Scientific American, 312*(6), 32–37.

3 The figure is adapted from Casey, B. J., Jones, R. M., & Hare, T. A. (2008). The adolescent brain. *Annals of the New York Academy of Sciences, 1124*(1), 111–126.

4 Spear, L. P. (2000). The adolescent brain and age-related behavioral manifestations. *Neuroscience & Biobehavioral Reviews, 24*(4), 417–463.

5 Albert, D., Chein, J., & Steinberg, L. (2013). The teenage brain peer influences on adolescent decision making. *Current Directions in Psychological Science, 22*(2), 114–120.

6 Steinberg, L., Albert, D., Cauffman, E., Banich, M., Graham, S., & Woolard, J. (2008). Age differences in sensation seeking and impulsivity as indexed by behavior and self-report: Evidence for a dual systems model. *Developmental Psychology, 44*(6), 1764–1778. Steinberg, L. (2010). A dual systems model of adolescent risk-taking. *Developmental Psychobiology, 52*(3), 216–224.

7 Coleman, J. S. (1959). Academic achievement and the structure of competition, *Harvard Education Review, 29*(4), 41–43.

8 Coleman, J. S. (1961). *The adolescent society*. New York: Free Press.

9 Jacques, S., & Wright, R. (2013). The code of the suburb and drug dealing. In F. T. Cullen & P. Wilcox (Eds.), *Oxford handbook of criminological theory*, pp. 389–404. Oxford: Oxford University Press.

10 Jonah, B. A. (1986). Accident risk and risk-taking behaviour among young drivers. *Accident Analysis & Prevention, 18*(4), 255–271.

11 Elliott, S. (2012). *Not my kid: What parents believe about the sex lives of their teenagers*. New York: NYU Press. Bogenschneider, K., Wu, M. Y., Raffaelli, M., & Tsay, J. C. (1998). "Other teens drink, but not my kid": Does parental awareness of adolescent alcohol use protect adolescents from risky consequences? *Journal of Marriage and the Family, 60* (May), 356–373.

12   Warr, M. (1996). Organization and instigation in delinquent groups. *Criminology, 34*(1), 11–37.

13   Kahneman, D., & Tversky, A. (2000). *Choices, values, and frames.* Cambridge, U.K.: Cambridge University Press.

14   Tymula, A., Belmaker, L. A. R., Roy, A. K., Ruderman, L., Manson, K., . . . & Levy, I. (2012). Adolescents' risk-taking behavior is driven by tolerance to ambiguity. *Proceedings of the National Academy of Sciences, 109*(42), 17135–17140.

15   Patchin, J. W., & Hinduja, S. (2010). Changes in adolescent online social networking behaviors from 2006 to 2009. *Computers in Human Behavior, 26*(6), 1818–1821.

16   Chassin, L., Presson, C. C., Sherman, S. J., & Edwards, D. A. (1990). The natural history of cigarette smoking: Predicting young-adult smoking outcomes from adolescent smoking patterns. *Health Psychology, 9*(6), 701–716.

17   Azofeifa, A., Mattson, M. E., Schauer, G., McAfee, T., Grant, A., & Lyerla, R. (2016). National estimates of marijuana use and related indicators – National Survey on Drug Use and Health, United States, 2002–2014. *Surveillance Summaries, 65*(11), 1–25. http://dx.doi.org/10.15585/mmwr.ss6511a1.

18   Kandel, D. B., & Logan, J. A. (1984). Patterns of drug use from adolescence to young adulthood: I. Periods of risk for initiation, continued use, and discontinuation. *American Journal of Public Health, 74*(7), 660–666.

19   Robins, L. N. (1980). The natural history of drug abuse. *Acta Psychiatrica Scandinavica, 62*(s284), 7–20.

UNIT 4.2 Teenage Volatility

We began Part 4 by introducing the age–crime curve and noting the crime information it helps summarize. In Unit 4.1, we saw how risk for delinquency fits rather well with changes in brain development. This unit further considers changes in delinquency risk over the teenage years and beyond. We note that:

- Teenagers vary greatly among themselves.

- Teenagers change a great deal as adolescence progresses.

- Many teenagers are highly volatile, even from week to week.

- Their activity pattern and risky situations vary over the hours of the day.

Throughout Part 4 we consider many of these points. We start Unit 4.2 by describing some categories of youth involvement in crime, after which we discuss teenage volatility in social life and crime participation.

Four Convenient Categories

To help sort out ideas and research on juvenile crime, Figure 4e sorts youths into four convenient categories.

a. The light blue area on the left of the diagram represents a small subset of youths who appear not to be delinquent at all; some of them are unsociable or **adult–dominated**.[1]

b. In the middle of the diagram, you see the largest group, ordinary and imperfect teenagers who are also **occasional delinquents**.[2]

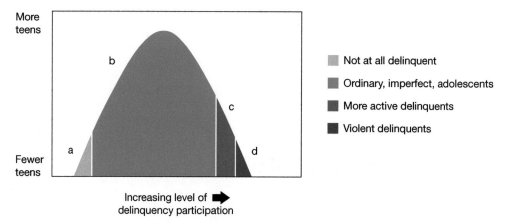

FIGURE 4E
Proportion of Teenagers at Four Levels of Delinquent Involvement

c.   A smaller group on the right represents the ***most active delinquents***, who contribute more than their share of crime, but are seldom violent.

d.   Farthest to the right is a still smaller group of ***violence-prone delinquents***—young offenders who are likely to engage in violent acts.

Groups c and d commit much more than their share of crime and receive extra attention from police. Yet the most active offenders are also greatly outnumbered by the ordinary teenagers in group b, who can do just as much harm to society through ***cumulative damage***. To understand crime, we must pay attention to all four groups.

It is easy to get lost among criminological ideas and statistics that focus on different groups of youths.

•   Subculture theory is often interested in the more violent group (d).

•   Control theory compares the more active offenders (c and d) to the more controlled youths (a).

•   Self-report studies can measure all levels of delinquency, but tend to pick up occasional but common delinquency by ordinary teenagers (b).

•   Prison studies focus on more violent offenders (d).

Thus research and theories that focus on different populations give different results.[3] We do not wish to overstate the "four groups" depicted in Figure 4e. A teenager can easily start adolescence in group b, later ending up in group c or even d.

Another teenager can have a high rate of offending in mid-adolescence, then decrease participation a year or two later. The volatile nature of teenagers is very important for understanding crime.

The Zigzags of Adolescence

Psychologists have documented the ***volatility*** and dynamics of ordinary adolescent relationships with peers.[4]

- Relationships are constantly changing.

- Fewer than half of "best friendships" survive for a year.

- Early adolescent romances last a matter of weeks or months.

- Clique memberships tend to change often.

- It is quite unusual for a clique to remain intact for a full year.

Even popular cliques can lose their popularity over the course of a school year.[5] In sum, the social patterns of ordinary adolescents are far from stable.

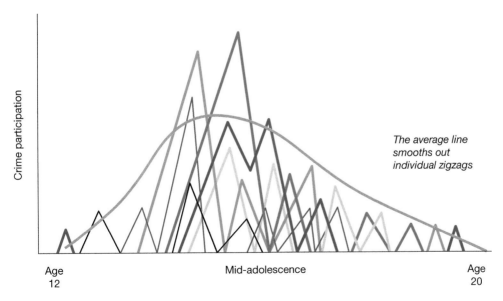

FIGURE 4F
Zigzagging through Adolescence

Instability applies to delinquency as well. Lawbreaking by youths is highly variable from week to week, month to month, and year to year. Figure 4f illustrates how several delinquent youths might **zigzag** through adolescent years, sometimes committing crimes and sometimes not. Some start earlier. Some start later. Some never commit many crimes. Some commit a lot, especially in mid-adolescence. With mathematical smoothing, these uneven shifts begin to look predictable—but we should not push that interpretation too far.[6]

Even the most active teenage offenders have their zigzags. Teens are diverse and inconsistent. *Any single individual* will tend to zigzag through adolescence, usually without a clear or smooth pattern of crime participation. Like other teenage cliques, **delinquent cliques** are themselves small and transitory. Young offenders commonly belong to multiple delinquent cliques and shift from one to another. The instigator of a delinquent act varies from one instance to the next. Offenders do not consistently assume the role of instigator or joiner over time, but instead switch from one role to the other and back again.[7]

An exceptional research study[8] shows us just how volatile teenagers can be and how this volatility influences participation in crime and delinquency. The **Teenage Networks in Schools Study (TEENS)** followed 155 students in the ninth grade in a Kentucky high school in Autumn, 2006. The students ranged in age from 14 to 16. Students were first interviewed in the second week of school, then reinterviewed *every two weeks* for five waves. To our knowledge, this is the only time researchers have re-interviewed teenagers this soon—traditionally, researchers wait a year or several years for a follow-up.

The results were stunning. As the pie chart on the left of Figure 4g indicates, in a two-week period, about half of the youths shifted friendship patterns, either breaking the earlier ties or listing new friends. In the middle chart, you see that unstructured socializing (discussed further in Unit 4.5) is also unstable from week to week. One in three has a stable pattern, and the unstable ones are equally divided between those who increase and those who decrease their unstructured socializing. Looking to the pie chart on the right, about a third of those who have been drinking alcohol are stable two weeks later, with most of the rest drinking less and some drinking more. Youths also change marijuana use, property crime patterns, and violence levels. Sometimes they go up and sometimes down, but they are not very stable—even within the course of a month. In any given interview, most report nonparticipation in crime and delinquency; but that can easily shift the next time they are interviewed. The researchers reported a "highly dynamic relation between peers, time use, and delinquent behavior in adolescence."[9] As unstructured socializing shifted, so did delinquent behavior.

Delinquent behavior appears to be more erratic than traditional research suggests, and may have a short-term "zigzag" pattern in which involvement in offending may go back and forth during periods of weeks. These data suggest that adolescents are involved in delinquent behavior during some of these periods, but abstain from it in others. This study also revealed that peer relations can be volatile resulting in very dynamic friendship networks, even within time frames of weeks.... [S]tudies employing longer time gaps between measurements may miss the dynamic nature of this life period and may fail to capture short-term relationships between peers and behavior.[10]

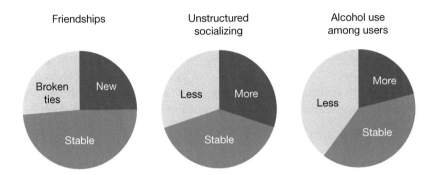

FIGURE 4G

Two-Week Shifts in Socializing and Drinking by Ninth-Grade Kentucky Youths

Source: Adapted from F. M. Weerman, P. Wilcox, & C. J. Sullivan (2017). The short-term dynamics of peers and delinquent behavior: An analysis of bi-weekly changes within a high school student network. *Journal of Quantitative Criminology*. Published online March 14. https://doi.org/10.1007/s10940-017-9340-2.

Thus, individual offender roles are situational and short-lived. You can see that it makes little sense to divide the adolescent population into "good youths" and "bad youths" considering that many youths have diverse and inconsistent behavior patterns. With all this inconsistency and irregularity *for individuals*, criminologists still discover a consistent and regular pattern for ***populations*** after individuals are averaged together.[11] Indeed, exposure to risk shifts over the life course in quite a predictable manner during adolescence and beyond—consistent with the age–crime curve. We cannot really predict what *each* person does each year, but we can describe *in general* how crime risk changes average out over the ***life course***.[12]

The Smooth Age–Crime Curve Is Just a Summary

The age–crime curve we presented in the opening to Part 4 is just a summary of the behavior of a lot of individuals, including volatile teenagers. That summary was achieved through ***mathematical smoothing*** of individual differences and zigzags. The age–crime curve sums up a good deal of information about lifetime exposure to risk of criminal activity.[13] How can we reconcile the smooth age–crime curve for the population with the individual zigzags?

We should look at the age–crime curve the way a physicist analyzes a gust of wind.[14] Wind is merely an aggregation of gas molecules. Even though wind moves in one direction, its individual gas molecules can still be moving in entirely different directions. Even though the wind is moving at one *overall* velocity, its many different gas molecules can be moving at very different velocities. Even though any one individual is erratic and largely unpredictable, the ***average shift*** of delinquents through the life course is predictable and smooth. Criminologists use mathematics and diagrams to smooth out individual behaviors and thus to summarize average crime participation changes as people move through life.[15] Researchers follow people for five or ten years, sometimes longer, to construct the age–crime curve as people move through life. You should keep the shape of the curve in mind, not forgetting that individuals have their own experiences.

FLASHCARD LIST FOR UNIT 4.2

- Adult-dominated (youths)
- Average shift
- Cumulative damage
- Delinquents, most active, occasional, violence-prone
- Delinquent cliques
- Life course
- Mathematical smoothing
- Populations
- Teenage Networks in Schools study (TEENS)
- Volatility
- Zigzags

DISCUSSION QUESTIONS

1. How smoothly do teenagers go through adolescence, as individuals vs. as a group?

2. How stable are teenage cliques?

Notes

1 Hendrix, J. A. (2016). Angels and loners: An examination of abstainer subtypes. *Deviant Behavior*, *37*(12), 1361–1379. Chen, X., & Adams, M. (2010). Are teen delinquency abstainers social introverts? A test of Moffitt's theory. *Journal of Research in Crime and Delinquency*, *47*(4), 439–468. Moffitt, T. E. (1993). Adolescence-limited and life-course-persistent antisocial behavior: A developmental taxonomy. *Psychological Review*, *100*(4), 674–701.

2   Cauffman, E., Cavanagh, C., Donley, S., & Thomas, A. G. (2015). A developmental perspective on adolescent risk-taking and criminal behavior. In F. T. Cullen & P. Wilcox (Eds.), *The handbook of criminological theory*, pp. 100–120. Oxford: Oxford University Press.

3   Thornberry, T. P., & Krohn, M. D. (2000). The self-report method for measuring delinquency and crime. *Criminal Justice, 4*(1), 33–83.

4   Brown, B. B., & Braun, M. T. (2013). Peer relations. In C. Proctor & A. Linley (Eds.), *Research, applications, and interventions for children and adolescents*, pp. 149–164. Amsterdam: Springer.

5   Eder, D. (1985). The cycle of popularity: Interpersonal relations among female adolescents. *Sociology of Education, 58*(3), 154–165.

6   Osgood, D. W. (2005). Making sense of crime and the life course. *Annals of the American Academy of Political and Social Science, 602*(1), 196–211.

7   Warr, M. (1996). Organization and instigation in delinquent groups. *Criminology, 34*(1), 11–37.

8   Weerman, F. M., Wilcox, P., & Sullivan, C. J. (2017). The short-term dynamics of peers and delinquent behavior: An analysis of bi-weekly changes within a high school student network. *Journal of Quantitative Criminology*. Published online, March 14. https://doi.org/10.1007/s10940-017-9340-2.

9   Weerman, Wilcox, & Sullivan, The short-term dynamics of peers and delinquent behavior; p. 28.

10 Weerman, Wilcox, & Sullivan, The short-term dynamics of peers and delinquent behavior; p. 26.

11 Loeber, R., & Farrington, D. P. (2014). Age-crime curve. In G. Bruinsma & D. Weisburd (Eds.), *Encyclopedia of criminology and criminal justice*, pp. 12–18. New York: Springer.

12 Osgood, Making sense of crime and the life course.

13 Sampson, R. J., & Laub, J. H. (2005). A general age-graded theory of crime: Lessons learned and the future of life-course criminology. In D. Farrington (Ed.), *Integrated developmental and life course theories of offending*, Vol. 14, pp. 165–182. New Brunswick, NJ: Transaction.

14 Maltz, M. D. (2009). Waves, particles, and crime. In D. Weisburd, W. Bernasco, & G. Bruinsma (Eds.), *Putting crime in its place*, pp. 123–142. New York: Springer.

15 Loeber & Farrington, Age-crime curve. Glueck, S., & Glueck, E. T. (1930). *500 criminal careers*. New York: Knopf. Glueck, S., & Glueck, E. T. (1950). *Unraveling juvenile delinquency*. Cambridge, MA: Harvard University Press. Sampson, R. J., & Laub, J. H. (1995). *Crime in the making: Pathways and turning points through life*. Cambridge, MA: Harvard University Press.

UNIT 4.3 Peer Influences

Criminologists have agreed for over a century that adolescent peer groups are very important for crime.[1] Yet they often disagree about how *peer influence* works and how it competes with parental influences over their teenage children. Although peers sometimes encourage adherence to society's rules,[2] criminologists mostly focus on how teenagers help one another break those rules. Peer effects can be immediate or cumulative.[3] Unit 4.4 focuses on immediate peer effects, while the current unit focuses on peer effects over longer periods of time.

Cumulative Peer Effects

Criminality is the general long-term tendency to commit crimes. Efforts to predict criminality go back at least to 1924 when Professor **Edwin Sutherland** formulated *differential association theory*. Although his work spans hundreds of pages, the most famous principle was summed up in 23 words: "A person becomes delinquent because of an excess of definitions favorable to violation of law over definitions unfavorable to violation of the law."[4]

Sutherland assumes that everybody has a general level of criminality, a general tendency to commit crime. Some people are low on the criminality scale, while others are high. Criminality is learned within intimate social groups, combining influences from

- delinquent friends;

- non-delinquent friends;

- parents; and

- other adults.

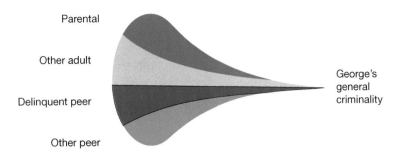

FIGURE 4H
Differential Association Theories Blend Four Sources of Influence

This ***blending model*** is depicted in Figure 4h, summing up ***multiple social influences*** on a boy named George. Different shades of blue represent different people influencing George's criminality. *These influences blend together.* If George has more delinquent peers and weaker parental influences, he will become more oriented towards crime. If he has fewer delinquent peers and stronger parental influences against crime participation, that will push him towards a lower level of criminality.

Sutherland died before modern psychologists discovered more elaborate ways that people learn. In 1966, Professor ***Ronald Akers*** extended Sutherland's differential association, taking psychological advances into account and embedding differential association within a larger ***social learning theory*** of crime.[5] Akers realized that someone can also learn criminal behavior by ***imitating peers***, such as a 12-year-old boy mimicking the behavior of a delinquent neighbor. Another youth might instead imitate a positive role model, such as an older brother who follows the rules.[6]

Differential reinforcement tells us to consider how each person's life blends positive and negative reinforcements for crime. A teenage girl shoplifts for cosmetics. Does she get something she likes without getting caught? Or does she get caught in the act and end up with no cosmetics? How do these experiences accumulate over time? Research indicates that imitation and differential reinforcement are at least as important as differential association for influencing whether youths follow rules.[7]

Figure 4i sums up these three main components of learning theory, again applied to one youth. George's general tendency to commit crime is influenced by his cumulative experiences over several years, including differential associations with other people, differential reinforcement from various experiences, and imitation of other people. These influences blend to produce a single pattern of criminality—the tendency to commit criminal acts. Will peer group research help society design programs to reinforce good behavior?

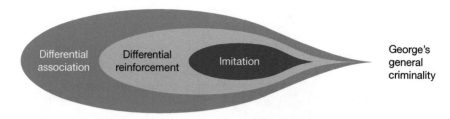

FIGURE 41
Akers' Learning Theory Blends Three Types of Influence

Research Disappointments

Parents have tried various ways to contain behaviors of their teenage children; they do not always succeed. One parental technique is to influence their ***children's choice of friends***. Such efforts tend to fail. By attempting to prohibit friendships, parents can accidently push their children into the company of delinquent friends. "Bad friends seem to become the 'forbidden fruit' that appear attractive to adolescents when their autonomy is hindered."[8]

Many researchers have devoted years of effort seeking to understand parental influences as proposed by social learning theory. One of the goals of such research is to offer advice to parents, schools, rehabilitation programs, or any other initiatives that can produce more favorable learning and thus reduce delinquency. For example, identifying early which youths are at risk of becoming delinquents might lead to supplemental programs to reduce subsequent criminality.

In 2012, three leading researchers—Professors ***David Farrington***, ***Lloyd Ohlin***, and ***James Q. Wilson***—expressed their frustrations with the level of research-based knowledge that is useful for reducing criminality:

> Whether we wish to prevent delinquency or rehabilitate offenders, whether we seek to strengthen families or improve schools, whether we believe that juvenile courts should get tougher or provide better services, we will be forced to admit, if we are honest, that we only have scattered clues and glimmers of hope (and sometimes not even that) on which to base our actions.[9]

Criminologists have tried for decades to identify a small and ***distinct group of extreme offenders*** on whom society could focus resources. That effort has not succeeded. After examining changing criminality from age 7 to age 70, Professors ***Robert Sampson*** and ***James Laub***[10] concluded that

- No distinct offender subgroup has a stable level of crime participation as they move through life.

- Individual differences, childhood characteristics, and family background cannot foretell long-term crime patterns of individuals.

- Sooner or later, crime declines with age for all offender subgroups.

These five prominent researchers ran into a barrier; namely, the difficulty in predicting individual criminal behavior. You recall from Unit 4.2 that the age–crime curve is usually smoothed mathematically because *individual* youths behave in a volatile fashion. Given that individuals might not be consistent in their behaviors, some social scientists no longer assume that a fixed level of criminality applies to all situations.

Context-Specific Socialization and Behavior

In 1995 a new and different model of learning and behavior emerged. Psychologist **Judith Rich Harris**[11] explained that learning and behavior can be highly context-specific.[12] Thus a young person learns

from parents	how to behave *at home*;
from peers	how to behave *in peer contexts*; and
from teachers	how to behave *in class*.

Importantly, youths *do not combine what they learn into a single or consistent behavior pattern for all contexts*. Rather, they learn to behave differently as the occasion requires. They learn to adjust to different contexts, facing different behavioral expectations in each. They learn to live life situationally.

Harris called this **group socialization theory**, for it states that people learn how to behave in different group contexts and do not blend these contexts together. Harris explained that parents have limited influence on behavior away from home. Although parents might influence their children in another context, such influence is not automatic. Something learned at home might be **inappropriate at school** or **inappropriate in peer settings**. According to Harris, children who imitate their parents and act that way in all settings will not have a successful childhood.

The central assumption of group socialization theory is that socialization is a highly context-specific process, with children learning how to behave in each setting from each social group. Children divide the world into categories—adults, kids, boys, girls, athletic kids, kids on my own street, etc. They decide which groups to join, and they take on those groups' behaviors and attitudes.[13] They also learn to hop from one context to another, shifting behaviors accordingly. As youths proceed through adolescence, their social skills may increase considerably, and many of them do an even better job of shifting among groups. Those who shift poorly will have trouble getting along in society. Vast cultural differences can make it more difficult to shift from one context to another,[14] yet, as Harris explained, children often learn to bridge these gaps:

> The clearest illustration of context-specific socialization is offered by the child of immigrant parents. If the language used in their home is different from the language of the community, the child will learn the local language in order to communicate with her peers. . . . By the time she is in first or second grade she will be a competent speaker of both languages, using one language in her home and the other outside of it. She will switch back and forth between them with ease—a process known as *code switching*—as though her mind contained two separate language modules controlled by the flip of a toggle.[15]

We can sum up group socialization theory with these propositions:

- Children learn separately how to behave at home and how to behave in other contexts.

- Children transfer behavior learned at home to the peer group *only* if the home behavior is approved by the peer group.

- Children's peer groups create their own culture by selecting and rejecting various aspects of adult culture and by making cultural innovations of their own.

- During childhood, children move through a series of these child-created cultures.

- As children get older, outside-the-home behavior takes precedence.

This **context-specific model** tells us that behavior is not constant or monolithic. An individual's behaviors range widely. The same person can be quiet in some settings and noisy in others. The same person uses different language with basketball friends than with school friends and also speaks differently to parents or to teachers.

Figure 4j depicts this alternative model, again using George as our example. He is influenced by parents, teachers, and peers. However, in this model, the alternative influences *do not blend together into a single behavior pattern*. George's parents influence his home behavior; his teachers affect his classroom behavior; and his peers govern how he acts in peer settings. After leaving peers and returning home, he again begins to follow parental teachings and expectations.

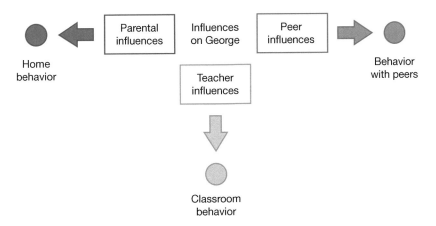

FIGURE 4J
Context-Specific Socialization Produces Different Behaviors in Different Settings

When youths from different households converge at the same place to hang out, they may follow somewhat similar behavior patterns. Although each youth maintains a personality and reflects some family influence, he or she must adjust to fit this peer context. Youths generally *enjoy* time spent with peers more than time spent with their families.

Researchers gave teenagers pagers and signaled them randomly to learn their feelings at that moment.[16] Teenagers reported their **time with friends** to be the best time of the day. They joked, received positive feedback, and felt open and free. Their moods were much better.

Whether in pairs or groups, with same-sex or opposite-sex friends, they had fun together, sharing comic routines and common activities. Teens described their enjoyment at being rowdy, crazy, or out of control. They saw their time together as a spirited, contagious group experience with freedom to say or do almost anything. In contrast, they experienced interactions with family to be rigid and constrained. They were more subject to negative feedback in family settings, inhibiting fun. Researchers have also learned that teenagers were considerably happier on weekends, planning all week for weekend activities with other teens.[17]

It is easy to see why parental teachings can fall by the wayside whenever teenagers have fun together. Indeed, Judith Rich Harris explained that context-specific behaviors apply even before the teenage years:

The child's job is a complex one, but the child's mind is up to the task. Children must learn how to behave in a variety of social contexts; they can get into trouble if they assume that what worked at home will work equally well somewhere else. In particular, displays of emotion that are acceptable inside the home are unacceptable outside the home. Children are not constrained to drag along with them, wherever they go, what they learned at home. To assume that they do so is to underrate them.[18]

We mentioned earlier the differences in use of language as young people shift from one context to another. Even younger children learn to save their cuss words for when parents are out of earshot.[19] To quote an expert on the language use of children:

> Parents and siblings go to great lengths to teach young children to say *please, thank you, may I be excused,* or *pardon me.* Politeness is a linguistic ritual that operates on a number of different social levels from casual to formal. One learns not only when to be polite but what degree of politeness is warranted in a given social setting. Learning to use dirty words [is similar to] learning to be polite. The child learns the proper way to curse, the proper place, and how to change the style of cursing in context. . . . In other words, there is also a dirty word etiquette.[20]

Children learn which words to avoid saying when mother is in earshot. Teenagers also tend to talk with one another situationally, using different vocabulary, pronunciation, and grammar than they do with adults.[21] Of course, teenagers know what not to say when parents are present and how to deceive parents.[22] Teenage deception is an ongoing topic in the literature on adolescence.[23]

These context-specific points also apply to university students, who swear a lot but learn where, when, and with whom swearing is appropriate.[24] Their cursing is most frequent in dormitories and apartments; occurs frequently in gyms and recreation settings; and occurs least often in campus offices (except for the university security office).[25] They also know to avoid certain topics and vocabulary when parents are visiting the campus or when they are in the classroom setting. An important part of growing up is to learn to shift behavior appropriately from one context to another, even at a moment's notice. The context-specific model does not deny that individuals have a personality. It merely states that a person has a range of behaviors available for different contexts. The next unit will consider immediate peer effects that lead to criminal acts.

FLASHCARD LIST FOR UNIT 4.3

- Akers, Ronald
- Blending model
- Children's choice of friends
- Context-specific model
- Criminality
- Differential association theory
- Differential reinforcement
- Distinct group of extreme offenders

- Farrington, David
- Group socialization theory
- Harris, Judith Rich
- Imitating peers
- Inappropriate at school
- Inappropriate in peer settings
- Multiple social influences
- Ohlin, Lloyd

- Peer influences
- Sampson, Robert & Laub, James
- Social learning theory
- Socialization, group, context-specific
- Sutherland, Edwin
- Time with friends
- Wilson, James Q.

DISCUSSION QUESTIONS

1. Why are Sutherland's and Akers' theories each classified as a "blended model"?

2. How does the blending model of peer effects contrast with the context-specific model?

Notes

1 Green, C. D. (2015). Hall's developmental theory and Haeckel's recapitulationism. *European Journal of Developmental Psychology*, *12*(6), 656–665. Abbott, E., & Breckenridge, S. (1912). *The delinquent child and the home*. New York: Charities Publication Committee.

2 Van Hoorn, J., Fuligni, A. J., Crone, E. A., & Galván, A. (2016). Peer influence effects on risk-taking and prosocial decision-making in adolescence: Insights from neuroimaging studies. *Current Opinion in Behavioral Sciences*, *10*, 59–64.

3 Hoeben, E. M., Meldrum, R. C., & Young, J. T. (2016). The role of peer delinquency and unstructured socializing in explaining delinquency and substance use: A state-of-the-art review. *Journal of Criminal Justice*, *47*, 108–122.

4 Sutherland, E. (1947). *Principles of criminology*, 4th edition. Philadelphia: Lippincott; pp. 6–7. See also: Matsueda, Ross L. (1988). The current state of differential association theory. *Crime & Delinquency*, *34*(3), 277–306.

5 Akers, R. L. (2011). *Social learning and social structure: A general theory of crime and deviance*. Piscataway, NJ: Transaction.

6 Greenberger, E., Chen, C., & Beam, M. R. (1998). The role of "very important" nonparental adults in adolescent development. *Journal of Youth and Adolescence*, *27*(3), 321–343.

7 Warr, M., & Stafford, M. (1991). The influence of delinquent peers: What they think or what they do? *Criminology*, *29*(4), 851–866. Hochstetler, A., Copes, H., & DeLisi, M. (2002). Differential association in group and solo offending. *Journal of Criminal Justice*, *30*(6), 559–566.

8   Keijsers, L., Branje, S., Hawk, S. T., Schwartz, S. J., Frijns, T., . . . & Meeus, W. (2012). Forbidden friends as forbidden fruit: Parental supervision of friendships, contact with deviant peers, and adolescent delinquency. *Child Development, 83*(2), 651–666; p. 12

9   Farrington, D. P., Ohlin, L. E., & Wilson, J. Q. (2012). *Understanding and controlling crime: Toward a new research strategy.* New York: Springer; p. 1.

10   Sampson, R. J., & Laub, J. H. (2003). Life-course desisters? Trajectories of crime among delinquent boys followed to age 70. *Criminology, 41*(3), 555–592.

11   See article about her: Gladwell, Malcolm. (1998). Do parents matter. *The New Yorker*, August 17, 52–64.

12   Harris, J. R. (1995). Where is the child's environment? A group socialization theory of development. *Psychological Review, 102*(3), 458–489.

13   Harris, J. R. (2000). Socialization, personality development, and the child's environments: Comment on Vandell. *Developmental Psychology, 36*(6), 711–723.

14   Phelan, P., Davidson, A. L., & Yu, H. C. (1998). *Adolescents' worlds: Negotiating family, peers, and school.* New York: Teachers College Press.

15   Harris, Where is the child's environment?; p. 462.

16   Larson, R. W. (1983). Adolescents' daily experience with family and friends: Contrasting opportunity systems. *Journal of Marriage and Family, 45*(4), 739–750.

17   Larson, R., & Richards, M. (1998). Waiting for the weekend: Friday and Saturday night as the emotional climax of the week. *New Directions for Child and Adolescent Development, 1998*(82), 37–52.

18   Harris, J. R. (1998). The trouble with assumptions. *Psychological Inquiry, 9*(4), 294–297; p. 296.

19   Hartmann, L. (1973). Some uses of dirty words by children. *Journal of the American Academy of Child Psychiatry, 12*(1), 108–122.

20   Jay, T. (1992). *Cursing in America: A psycholinguistic study of dirty language in the courts, in the movies, in the schoolyards, and on the streets.* Philadelphia: John Benjamins Publishing; p. 30.

21   Stenstrom, A. B., & Andersen, G. (1996). More trends in teenage talk: A corpus-based investigation of the discourse items cos and innit. In C. E. Percy, C. F. Meyer & I. Lancashire (Eds.), *Synchronic corpus linguistics: Papers from the sixteenth International Conference on English Language Research on Computerized Corpora*, pp. 189–203. Amsterdam: Rodopi.

22   Bristol, T., & Mangleburg, T. F. (2005). Not telling the whole story: Teen deception in purchasing. *Journal of the Academy of Marketing Science, 33*(1), 79–95. Knox, D., Zusman, M. E., McGinty, K., & Gescheidler, J. (2001). Deception of parents during adolescence. *Adolescence, 36*(143), 611–614.

23   Smetana, J. G., Metzger, A., Gettman, D. C., & Campione-Barr, N. (2006). Disclosure and secrecy in adolescent–parent relationships. *Child Development, 77*(1), 201–217.

24   Jay, T., & Janschewitz, K. (2008). The pragmatics of swearing. *Journal of Politeness Research: Language, Behaviour, Culture, 4*(2), 267–288. See also: Beers Fägersten, K. (2012). *Who's swearing now? The social aspects of conversational swearing.* Cambridge, U.K.: Cambridge Scholars Publishing.

25   Jay, *Cursing in America*; p. 86.

UNIT 4.4 Situational Inducements

We have learned that:

- Teenagers are highly volatile in their delinquency patterns.

- Individual criminal behavior is difficult to predict.

- Adolescents are happiest when with their peers.

- Youths often shift behaviors from one context to another.

Yet delinquency does not occur randomly. That leaves us with a puzzle to solve: Why do individuals commit criminal acts in one situation but not another?

Situational Inducement Theory

A half-century ago, Professors **Briar and Piliavin** addressed that very issue. They realized that:

- Most youths, at one time or another, engage in delinquency to some degree— regardless of race or social origin.

- Most early delinquents outgrow delinquency; they eventually conform to conventional morality, becoming law-abiding in late adolescence and early adulthood.[1]

Briar and Piliavin also realized that many disadvantaged youths they had *expected* to be delinquents did not *actually* become delinquent; and that many middle-class youths they had *not expected* to be delinquents *still became so*. Again, predicting delinquency proved to be problematical, leading these criminologists to take a new approach. They formulated *situational inducement theory*, which can be summed up in five propositions:

1. Youths should *not* be **dichotomized** into "delinquent" and "non-delinquent" segments.

2. Delinquent acts are *not* mainly based on special **long-term motivations** or cumulative tendencies originating in arenas distant from where specific crimes occur. Youths are not fixed in time.

3. Instead, a delinquent act is *situationally induced*, occurring in response to a person's *momentary* situation.

4. Crime has **episodic motives**, specific to the situation where the crime occurs.

5. These specific motives reflect very *general* desires to obtain valued goods, to display courage and loyalty to peers, to strike out at someone who is disliked, or simply to have fun. These desires apply to all races and socioeconomic groups.

Situational inducement theory emphasizes specific situations where delinquent acts take place. Diverse individuals from all social groups can get into such situations. Youths who are **most vulnerable** to delinquency do not have a monopoly over delinquent acts, since other youths in the same situations can also get into trouble. This led one researcher to characterize delinquency as a "pick-up game," casually emerging.[2]

A year before situation inducement theory was presented, Professor **David Matza** published a famous book entitled **Delinquency and Drift**, describing how youths commit delinquent acts almost by accident.[3] He recognized what researchers keep confirming—that delinquency is *not a stable or permanent condition or role*, that youths drift into and out of delinquency. Matza noted that "delinquents" spend much more of their time engaging in non-delinquent behavior than they spend engaging in delinquent behavior. It takes but a few seconds to steal something or even to hit someone.[4]

Matza believed (like Briar and Piliavin) that delinquent behavior is often incidental to social life. One youth might **casually offer** marijuana to another[5] or make an offhand invitation to steal something.[6] Many of these influences are informal and inadvertent. Delinquency can be unplanned, resulting from fluid social situations, not necessarily from fixed or stable levels of criminality. This helps us understand how youths zigzag through adolescence, committing criminal acts from time to time, but returning to conventional behavior too. For this to happen, youths need a way to suspend their own moral standards every now and then.

Techniques of Neutralization

Imagine some youths hanging out together after school. They see an easy target for theft—a situational inducement to commit a crime. Yet they feel inhibited by the rules and are not quite ready to break them. Professor Matza teamed up with Professor Sykes to figure out how people break their own rules. They realized that many youths use **neutralization techniques** that allow them to *suspend* the rules temporarily.[7] Youths tell themselves that it is okay to violate the rules *on this occasion*. Five common neutralization techniques are to:

Deny responsibility:	*I was drunk and couldn't help myself.*
	It was my friend's idea.
Deny injury:	*Nobody got hurt.*
	The department store won't miss one sweater.
Deny there's a victim:	*They had it coming.*
	Nobody owned it anyway.
Condemn the condemners:	*You do the same things yourself.*
	You do more harm than I ever do.
Appeal to higher loyalties:	*I stole it for my buddies.*
	I've got to stand by my friends.

Neutralization is not limited to juveniles. College students use neutralization when they cheat on tests. Reasons include "everyone does it," "it's not my fault," "it's so easy to cheat," and finally "gotta keep up my GPA."[8] Students are also quite a bit more likely to cheat if they see other students cheating.[9] College students who use illegal drugs also apply techniques of neutralization. For example, Adderall is a prescription drug that many students use as an illegal stimulant or recreational drug, risking addiction and medical harm.[10] College students find extra neutralizations for such drug use:

My drug use is safe. It has not injured me. Everybody is doing it. It is FDA approved and prescribed by many doctors, even for children. It's like coffee or an energy drink. Other students are worse than I am, using much more serious drugs. Doctors are the real deviants, giving out ... unnecessary prescriptions.[11]

Student sex offenders are also known to neutralize misbehaviors.[12] Indeed, people of all ages can use techniques of neutralization to ease their conscience and proceed to break the law. Both male and female domestic violence offenders use socially desirable explanations of their behavior, attributing greater blame to their partner than they acknowledge for themselves. They often minimize an incident's severity. In one study, some 83 percent of males involved stated the situation "got blown way out of proportion," and 71 percent said that "the police made this incident sound much worse than it was." Two-thirds said "nobody really got hurt" or that it was "not a big deal." Half said that "anyone in my situation would have done the same thing I did."[13]

Sometimes public policy efforts backfire by providing extra neutralizations. Programs promoting designated drivers provide an excellent example. Hoping to reduce drunk driving, these programs often induce nondrivers to drink more than they otherwise would.[14] Although road danger might decrease, other potential harms from alcohol can easily increase (see Part 6). In effect, the designated driver helps neutralize inhibitions against drinking too much.

Neutralization techniques help us understand how ordinary adolescents might drift into and out of delinquency by suspending the rules from time to time. They also help us understand that no clear line divides offenders from non-offenders. Many people can be induced to commit a crime on occasion and might find a way to justify this departure from their own normal rules. These departures are consistent with a variety of philosophical and religious doctrines. In Greek philosophy, the word *akrasia* is used to define weakness of will and action against one's better judgment. A recurrent theme in philosophy and theology is basic human frailty—the fact that human beings are weak and susceptible to negative enticements, influences, and pressures.[15] Indeed, the Judeo-Christian doctrine of original sin presumes that people are weak and vulnerable to temptations and inducements.

Aggressive Peer Pressure

We have noted some gentler influences and the process of drifting into delinquency. Peers can also exert **aggressive pressures** to participate in illegal acts.[16] A study of 771 middle-school children asked about dares or illicit challenges they received from other children.[17] These researchers asked,

"What did they try to get you to do?"

"How did they try to get you to do that?" and

"What did you say or do?"

This research showed that dares are part of a larger set of techniques for inducing social pressure, some involving ridicule or even threats of physical attack for not joining in. Some 36 percent of eighth graders reported they complied with the dare, and only 28 percent directly said no. Most of the others made excuses, called a name back, and sometimes used rather sophisticated evasions.

Peer effects occur at many ages and in many forms, often near the time of the crime. That is why situational inducement theory emphasizes the immediacy of crime and the motives to commit it.

Getting Up the Nerve

Researchers in the offender decision-making tradition find that offenders experience considerable tension in the moments leading up to a crime and while it is committed.[18]

Offenders need to **get up the nerve** to carry out a criminal act, especially if they face considerable danger in the process. Committing crime, especially violent crime, often takes a lot of nerve,[19] even for somebody with substantial criminal propensity. "We can think of no other conduct in the daily realm of life, where death, injury, institutionalization, loss of freedom, and future deprivation of privacy are all in play at the same time."[20]

Ethnographers find that offenders are often very anxious when committing an overt crime, and they cannot do so easily. Offenders often need to "psych each other up" prior to committing a crime.[21] Often peer pressures are necessary to propel reluctant accomplices to join in.[22] Using alcohol or drugs prior to committing a crime helps offenders get up their nerve.[23] The group process is integral to committing crimes, especially in early and middle adolescence,[24] as we will discover in Unit 7.1. Group processes can also involve contests to show nerve and daring to other youths.[25]

> Because so much crime develops serendipitously or even conversationally, offenders must routinely develop nerve on the fly. Perhaps one reason why so much predatory crime unfolds in sprees is because nerve is portable in a temporal sense: Nerve generated at an earlier moment in time is usable later, so long as the delay between time A and time B is reasonably short.[26]

That's why some offenders go on a fast crime spree while they still have the nerve to continue. Youths together probably vary in their disposition to commit criminal acts, yet an individual disposition to avoid crime might be overwhelmed by group processes. More time spent with peers may serve to produce more criminal acts, helping youths to push ahead with crime (see Unit 4.5).

Overcoming Moral Inhibitions

A long tradition of psychological research has proven that rule-breaking can be induced in experimental situations and that youths can often overcome their own inhibitions. In 1928, Professors Hartshorne and May placed 10- to 13-year-olds in situations that invited them to lie, cheat, and steal.[27] They found that it was easy to induce dishonest behavior and that those who complied with rules at home still might cheat on a test at school or in a playground game. Many studies of have confirmed that in the right situations, youths *overcome inhibitions* and proceed to lie and cheat.[28] Youths at various ages have a very high tendency to cheat when enticed, and youths attending religious schools are no better.[29] Researchers have established how readily university students cheat on exams or plagiarize papers. The problem applies, for example, to students in chemistry[30] and law school.[31] These patterns apply not only in the United States, but also in other nations, including Canada[32] and Britain.[33]

Researchers have also learned that active street offenders in a very dangerous neighborhood, expecting an early death, tend to believe in religion, the afterlife, redemption, and punishment.[34] In contrast to the idea that religion will dissuade people from committing crimes, these offenders see religion as absolving them of their sins and neutralizing their fear of death. In fact, religion helps them commit more crime.

Psychological research has shown that people faced with temptation often violate their own moral rules, after which they begin to loosen those rules when responding to attitude questions. Psychologists explain such attitude change as "reducing *cognitive dissonance*."[35] People are uncomfortable with inconsistencies and seek to reconcile them. We might imagine a teenager going through this thought process:

I was taught smoking marijuana is wrong, and I believed that myself, but

Some of my friends have started smoking it;

I don't want to cut off my friends, so

I tried some marijuana myself and nothing bad happened, so

I guess it's okay to smoke a little weed sometimes.

These imaginary thoughts show how a young person experiencing cognitive dissonance might resolve the inconsistency by relaxing moral attitudes, bringing them closer to actual behavior. Research generally finds that moral attitudes against crime have a weak ability to control behavior.[36] Interestingly, causation often goes in the opposite direction from what's expected. That is, after seeing your friends break rules or doing so yourself, you tend to change your moral attitudes and become less critical of misbehavior. Drinking alcohol underage or smoking marijuana seems much worse to 10-year-olds than to 18-year-old youths. One reason for the increasing acceptance is the rapid acceleration in delinquency among friends. One study found that by age 18, almost 80 percent of youths had friends who smoked marijuana.[37] Clearly, as adolescence proceeds it is increasingly difficult to shut oneself off from exposure to marijuana, alcohol, and other delinquent experiences.

Similar issues arise with teen attitudes towards having sexual intercourse. Researchers have followed adolescents over time to learn whether attitudes against having sex would decline with age and dating experience.[38] Dating teenagers are exposed to greater sexual opportunity and tend to set aside their restrictive attitudes and religious upbringing. Being in any dating relationship augments the probability of having sex, followed by more permissive attitudes towards sex. Perhaps we should think of restrictive social norms as a tactic used by adult society to stall adolescents from having sex for a few years. Indeed, teenagers become increasingly tolerant of sexual rule-breaking as they move from early to middle teens and onward.[39]

An interesting effort by conservative churches in the United States sought to secure virginity pledges from youths; that is, promises to abstain from sexual behavior until marriage. Millions of young teenagers signed such pledges. A study of teenage pledgers five years after their pledge found that 82 percent denied ever having pledged abstinence from sex. Pledgers did not differ from non-pledgers in premarital sexual involvement, age of first intercourse, or accumulated number of sex partners. Nor did pledgers have fewer sexual diseases or avoid anal or oral sex.[40] However, those who pledged abstinence used condoms and other contraceptives less consistently than other youths.[41] Other research found that some pledgers delayed their sexual experience if they made the pledge to themselves (rather than simply to third parties).[42] Abstinence pledges represent a concerted and organized effort by adults to influence teenage sexual behavior. In practice, many teenagers find ways to dilute adult influences as they drift through adolescence.

Diversity of Substance Abuse Behaviors

A part of adolescence is conformity and mutual influence. That does not rule out individual variations in approaching a rule-breaking situation. According to British research, *diverse youths socialize together* even though they differ in their approach to marijuana or other drugs. Adapting this idea to smoking marijuana, teenagers will tend to vary along this scale:

Least involved with marijuana

1. Keep away from marijuana or anybody else smoking it.

2. Abstain yourself, but accommodate others who smoke it.

3. Only smoke marijuana when offered in a safe setting, but do not seek it.

4. Smoke marijuana and share the cost, but do not buy it directly yourself.

5. Only buy marijuana from somebody you know and only for yourself.

6. Buy from drug dealer you know, reselling to friends or acquaintances.

7. Use any drug and buy it from anybody willing to sell it.

Most involved with marijuana[43]

Those youths at the top of the list are so averse to marijuana that they may end up with few friends and no parties to attend. It makes more sense socially to go to parties or hang out with others who smoke marijuana, even if abstaining or smoking only a little. A youth can also have access to marijuana without ever buying it from a dangerous drug dealer, instead working through intermediaries.

The same scale shown above helps us understand the marijuana supply chain. Some youths are dealers who buy marijuana in dangerous settings, then sell it to those they know. These buyers may resell smaller packets of marijuana to friends or acquaintances. This shows how marijuana moves from more dangerous settings to less dangerous settings. This also shows how marijuana can cross racial, ethnic, and socioeconomic boundaries. It can move from overt drug sales in dangerous neighborhoods to covert drug sales in middle-class neighborhoods. It can move from intermediate dealers to sharing arrangements, perhaps at a party or other youth hangout.

We reported earlier that many acts of crime and delinquency do not involve consistent instigators. Drug dealing can be an exception. A youth who is more advanced in drug use has an incentive to recruit others who might help cover his own costs. Once others take a puff, they have an incentive not to report what happened while they were together. As adolescents spend more time together, they are more likely to be exposed to these opportunities to break rules.

Linking Social Learning to Situational Inducements

Social learning theory emphasizes the accumulation of delinquent tendencies through differential association, differential reinforcement, and imitation. In contrast, situational inducement theory emphasizes the immediate circumstances that give rise to criminal acts. However, in practice, social learning theory and situational inducement theory look at many of the same processes—peer influences, social approval, group processes, imitation of others.[44]

We can put these processes on a single time line, depicted in Figure 4k. It depicts an individual starting at age 12 (on the left) and moving towards age 18 (on the right). At several points while growing up, events occur that reinforce or induce *more* crime— marked with a plus sign (+). These may include positive experiences committing a crime, successful completion of a crime, or a friend encouraging a criminal act. These might also include invitations to commit a crime or specific crime opportunities. At other points along the way from age 12 to 18, a youth may have experiences or encounters discouraging crime, marked by a negative sign (–). These could include a failed criminal act, getting sick from underage drinking, getting yelled at, meeting someone who discourages delinquent acts, or any aversive experience from breaking rules. With more data on an individual, we could imagine a much more detailed timeline, inserting each influence favoring or discouraging criminal action for that person.

In analyzing the timeline depicted in Figure 4k, learning theorists such as Akers would emphasize the cumulative learning that favors delinquency or discourages it. Other criminologists (such as Briar, Piliavin, and Matza) would emphasize the episodic and short-term inducements to break a rule. These episodes point towards analyzing how teenagers spend their time and whether the circumstances of their activities favor rule-breaking.

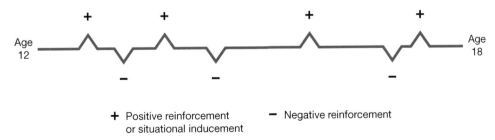

Figure 4k
Crime Reinforcements and Inducements while Moving through Adolescence

---

FLASHCARD LIST FOR UNIT 4.4

- Aggressive (peer) pressures
- Briar and Piliavin
- Casual offer
- Cognitive dissonance
- *Delinquency and Drift*
- Dichotomized (youths)
- Diverse youths socialize together

- Get up the nerve
- Matza, David
- Most vulnerable
- Motivations, long-term
- Motives, episodic
- Neutralization techniques, appeal to higher loyalty, condemn the condemners, deny

injury, deny responsibility, deny there's a victim
- Overcome inhibitions
- Situational inducement theory

DISCUSSION QUESTIONS

1. How might religion affect delinquent behaviors?

2. Compare social learning theory with situational inducements.

Notes

1   Briar, S., & Piliavin, I. (1965). Delinquency, situational inducements, and commitment to conformity. *Social Problems*, *13*(1), 35–45.

2   Gold, M. (1970). *Delinquent behavior in an American city*. Belmont, CA: Brooks/Cole.

3   Matza, D. (1964). *Delinquency and drift*. New York: Wiley.

4   Felson, M. (2006). *Crime and nature*. Thousand Oaks, CA: Sage Publications.

5   Parker, H. (2000). How young Britons obtain their drugs: Drugs transactions at the point of consumption. In M. Natarajan & M. Hough (Eds.), *Illegal drug markets*. Crime Prevention Studies, Vol. 11, pp. 59–81. Monsey, NY: Criminal Justice Press.

6   Cello, B. J., & Hope, T. L. (2016). *Peer pressure, peer prevention: The role of friends in crime and conformity*. Abingdon, U.K.: Routledge.

7   Sykes, G. M., & Matza, D. (1957). Techniques of neutralization: A theory of delinquency. *American Sociological Review*, *22*(6), 664–670.

8   King, D. L., & Case, C. J. (2014). E-cheating: Incidence and trends among college students. *Issues in Information Systems*, *15*(1), 20–27. Polding, B. E. (1995). *The extension of neutralization theory to the academic dishonesty of college students*. Doctoral dissertation, University of Florida.

9   Rettinger, D. A., & Kramer, Y. (2009). Situational and personal causes of student cheating. *Research in Higher Education*, *50*(3), 293–313.

10 Varga, M. D. (2012). Adderall abuse on college campuses: A comprehensive literature review. *Journal of Evidence-Based Social Work*, *9*(3), 293–313.

11 Paraphrased from Cutler, K. A. (2014). Prescription stimulants are "a okay": Applying neutralization theory to college students' nonmedical prescription stimulant use. *Journal of American College Health*, *62*(7), 478–486.

12 Boyle, K. M., & Walker, L. S. (2016). The neutralization and denial of sexual violence in college party subcultures. *Deviant Behavior, 37*(12), 1392–1410.

13 Henning, K., Jones, A., & Holdford, R. (2005). "I didn't do it, but if I did I had a good reason": Minimization, denial, and attributions of blame among male and female domestic violence offenders. *Journal of Family Violence, 20*(3), 131–139; p. 135.

14 Rivara, F. P., Relyea-Chew, A., Wang, J., Riley, S., Boisvert, D., & Gomez, T. (2007). Drinking behaviors in young adults: The potential role of designated driver and safe ride home programs. *Injury Prevention, 13*(3), 168–172.

15 Thero, D. P. (2006). *Understanding moral weakness.* Amsterdam: Rodopi.

16 Reed, M. D., & Rountree, P. W. (1997). Peer pressure and adolescent substance use. *Journal of Quantitative Criminology, 13*(2), 143–180.

17 Lewis, C. E., & Lewis, M. A. (1984). Peer pressure and risk-taking behaviors in children. *American Journal of Public Health, 74*(6), 580–584.

18 Cherbonneau, M., & Copes, H. (2006). "Drive it like you stole it": Auto theft and the illusion of normalcy. *British Journal of Criminology, 46*(2), 193–211.

19 The offender's need to control nerves leads us to ask whether people with the least self-control are ill-suited to committing crime – contrary to the theory presented in Unit 2.1.

20 Jacobs, B. A., & Cherbonneau, M. (2017). Nerve management and crime accomplishment. *Journal of Research in Crime and Delinquency, 54*(5), 583–616; p. 586.

21 Cromwell, P. F., & Olson, J. N. (2004). *Breaking and entering: Burglars on burglary.* Belmont, CA: Wadsworth.

22 Hochstetler, A. (2001). Opportunities and decisions: Interactional dynamics in robbery and burglary groups. *Criminology, 39*(3), 737–763.

23 Indermaur, D. (1995). *Violent property crime.* Sydney, Australia: Federation Press.

24 Felson, M. (2009). The natural history of extended co-offending. *Trends in Organized Crime, 12*(2), 159–165.

25 Hochstetler, A., & Copes, H. (2003). Managing fear to commit felony theft. In P. Cromwell, (Ed.), *Their own words: Criminals on crime,* 2nd edition, pp. 87–98. Los Angeles: Roxbury.

26 Jacobs & Cherbonneau, Nerve management and crime accomplishment.

27 Hartshorne, H., & May, M. A. (1928). *Studies in deceit.* New York: Macmillan.

28 Schab, F. (1991). Schooling without learning: Thirty years of cheating in high school. *Adolescence, 26*(104), 839–847.

29 Bruggeman, E. L., & Hart, K. J. (1996). Cheating, lying, and moral reasoning by religious and secular high school students. *Journal of Educational Research, 89*(6), 340–344. Guttmann, J. (1984). Cognitive morality and cheating behavior in religious and secular school children. *Journal of Educational Research, 77*(4), 249–254.

30 Murphy, K. L., & Holme, T. A. (2015). What might cell phone-based cheating on tests mean for chemistry education? *Journal of Chemical Education, 92*(9), 1431–1432.

31 Hansen, R. F., & Anderson, A. (2015). Law student plagiarism: Contemporary challenges and responses. *Journal of Legal Education, 64*(3) 416–427.

32 Christensen, J. M., & McCabe, D. L. (2006). Academic misconduct within higher education in Canada. *Canadian Journal of Higher Education, 36*(2), 1–21.

33   Adams, R. (2015). Cheating found to be rife in British schools and universities. *The Guardian*, June 14.

34   Topalli, V., Brezina, T., & Bernhardt, M. (2013). With God on my side: The paradoxical relationship between religious belief and criminality among hardcore street offenders. *Theoretical Criminology, 17*(1), 49–69.

35   Festinger, L. (1957). *A theory of cognitive dissonance.* Evanston, IL: Row & Peterson. Festinger, L. (1962). Cognitive dissonance. *Scientific American, 207*(4), 93–107.

36   Menard, S., & Huizinga, D. (1994). Changes in conventional attitudes and delinquent behavior in adolescence. *Youth & Society, 26*(1), 23–53. Rebellon, C. J., & Manasse, M. (2007). Tautology, reasoned action, or rationalization? Specifying the nature of the correlation between criminal attitudes and criminal behavior. In K. T. Froeling (Ed.), *Criminology: Research focus*, pp. 257–276. New York: Nova Science Publishers.

37   Warr, M. (2002). *Companions in crime: The social aspects of criminal conduct.* Cambridge, U.K.: Cambridge University Press. Warr, M. (1993). Age, peers, and delinquency. *Criminology, 31*(3), 17–40.

38   Meier, A. M. (2003). Adolescents' transition to first intercourse, religiosity, and attitudes about sex. *Social Forces, 81*(3), 1031–1052.

39   For a broader review of adolescent literature on moral reasoning, see: Eisenberg, N., Morris, A. S., McDaniel, B., & Spinrad, T. L. (2009). Moral cognitions and prosocial responding in adolescence. In R. M. Lerner & L. Steinberg (Eds.), *Handbook of adolescent psychology*, pp. 155–188. Hoboken, NJ: John Wiley & Sons.

40   Rosenbaum, J. E. (2009). Patient teenagers? A comparison of the sexual behavior of virginity pledgers and matched nonpledgers. *Pediatrics, 123*(1), e110–e120.

41   Paik, A., Sanchagrin, K. J., & Heimer, K. (2016). Broken promises: Abstinence pledging and sexual and reproductive health. *Journal of Marriage and Family, 78*(2), 546–561.

42   Williams, S., & Thompson, M. P. (2013). Examining the prospective effects of making a virginity pledge among males across their 4 years of college. *Journal of American College Health, 61*(2), 114–120.

43   Parker, How young Britons obtain their drugs.

44   Kobus, K. (2003). Peers and adolescent smoking. *Addiction, 98*(s1), 37–55.

Unit 4.5 Time with Peers

Crime events are more likely to occur when teenagers spend more time together in the absence of adults.[1] That exposes them to greater risk of victimization and offending. Teenagers do not always have such time. In Unit 2.2 we showed that Japanese youths have little time in purely peer settings. We should not forget that most of American history provided limited time spent in settings dominated by teenagers.

Teenage Time-Use Changes from the Early 1900s to the 1980s

For about a century, social scientists have been asking people how they use their time.[2] Modern governments around the world carry out *time-use surveys*. These data prove very important for evaluating how much time people spend in risky places—exposed to crime victimization while also enticing crime participation.[3]

In 1984, researchers asked people of all ages to think back to when they were 17 years old. Although the answers often depended on having long memories, respondents loved answering the questions and provided a picture of how the life of teenagers has changed over the 20th century.[4] Older respondents clearly indicated that their own adolescence during the early 20th century allowed *little free time together with peers* without parental proximity. They reported that those who were 17 years old had *much less* freedom than teenagers did by the 1980s.

- Most males and females had afternoon chores.

- Required dinner together was normal for most families all week.

- Five out of six females had bedtimes before 11.00 pm.

- Teenage automotive access was much more limited than today.

Box 4A Questions about Supervision at Age 17

When you were 17, on weekdays did you have any regular household chores or duties to perform in the afternoon? • Always, • Most of the time, • Some of the time, or • Never? ✓✓	When you were 17, did you ride after dark in automobiles driven by other teenagers? • Almost every night, ✓✓ • A few times a week, ✓ • Once a week, or • Never?
Between 3 and 6 pm on weekdays, were you at home? • Always, • Most of the time, • Some of the time, or ✓ • Never? ✓✓	When you went out with your friends after dark, how often was an adult present or nearby? • Always, • Most of the time, • Some of the time, or ✓ • Never? ✓✓
When you were at home between 3 and 6 pm on weekdays, was an adult there with you? • Always, • Most of the time, • Some of the time, or ✓ • Never? ✓✓	When you were 17, was a parent or another adult relative with you on Saturdays? • Always, • Most of the time, • Some of the time, or ✓ • Never? ✓✓
Did all of the members of your household usually eat their evening meal together on weekdays? • Yes • No ✓✓	When you were 17, by what time were you usually expected back home on Friday or Saturday nights? • By 11 pm • By midnight • By 1 am ✓ • By 2 am ✓✓ • Whenever ✓✓
When you were 17, during the daytime did you ride in cars driven by other teenagers? • Almost every day, ✓✓ • A few times a week, ✓ • Once a week, or • Never?	Total your check marks (✓) to get your score. _____ Maximum 18 points.

Source: Derived from M. Felson & M. Gottfredson (1984). Social indicators of adolescent activities near peers and parents. *Journal of Marriage and Family, 46*(3), 709–714.

Only 1 in 20 of the respondents who were 17 years old in the early 1900s reported going around often after dark with other teens. According to older female respondents, as girls, they were expected home by 10:30 pm on Fridays and 15 minutes later on Saturday nights. These survey data clearly revealed there was ***less freedom for young women***. Overall, women who were teenagers in the early 20th century reported that parents allowed them almost no freedom at all. We invite you to think back to when you were 17 years old, filling out the questionnaire contained in Box 4a. You should compare how much freedom or control you experienced to the historical patterns related above. By the 1970s, teenage autonomy from parents appears to have increased substantially for males, but the female experience changed even more.[5] Further changes have occurred since the 1980s and continue to the present day.

Further Teenage Evasion of Parental Controls

Modern American teenagers spend increasing numbers of nights out as they proceed through adolescence. Even in sixth grade (approximate age 11), more than half are out with peers two or more evenings a week, and one in six is out with peers five to seven nights a week. By tenth grade (around age 15), these numbers increase, with three out of four out with peers at least two nights a week, and one in four out five to seven nights per week. Youths spending the most evenings out with peers were twice as likely to become involved in one or more problem behaviors.[6]

The leeway that parents allow their children shifts greatly during adolescence. One study found that children are allowed to go farther from home without supervision as adolescence commences and progresses:

- Age 11—allowed to go about five or six blocks from home;

- Ages 12–13—allowed to go almost a mile from home;

- Age 14—can go over a mile from home, but not much farther;

- Age 15—permitted to go nearly three miles from home; and

- Age 16 and older—can go three or more miles from home.[7]

Parents also allowed their children increasing amounts of time without checking on them. At age 14, a child was not yet allowed three hours unsupervised. By age 15, that time exceeded three hours, reaching six hours by age 16. At age 18, the period of autonomy was about eight hours. Although these measures are approximations, they give us an idea how adult supervision declines over adolescence in the modern United States.

The traditional family meal together is almost a "thing of the past." A study of 4,746 adolescents from diverse socioeconomic and ethnic groups found that less than one in five had a family meal every night. One in seven adolescents never have family meals together.[8] Similar findings are replicated in other studies, confirming that 20th-century trends are continuing.[9] Family meals are associated not only with fewer delinquent acts, but also with better nutrition and health behaviors.

Adults sharing time with their children (or not doing so) is also important for younger teens. A middle-school study found that *latchkey youths* (those who are home alone several days per week) were four times more likely to have gotten drunk in the past month compared to youths with a parent around most of the time.[10] A review of the literature summarizes what's known about adult supervision:

- For early adolescents, the greatest substance abuse opportunity occurs immediately after school when home with a sibling or friend and with no adults nearby. Some early substance abuse occurs near school or community centers where adult supervision is inadequate.

- After entering high school, youths can more readily evade parents and go to weekend parties with less adult supervision, and can move their substance abuse to later hours. Those spending evenings and weekends with peers tend to use more alcohol.

- As adolescents age, they diversify their drinking contexts to include automobiles, public parks, beaches, and homes of others.[11]

Although parents generally monitor males less than females, absence of parental supervision facilitates substance abuse for both. Delinquency research continues to confirm the importance of adolescent time use and its relationship to parental supervision.

Calculating Time at Risk

We are learning more and more about teenagers and how they use time. One way is to give teenagers beepers or else apps on their cell phones, then get them to record what they are doing at the time. That method is increasingly used by health and delinquency researchers seeking to understand how and when teenagers make risky choices.[12]

The overwhelming evidence tells us that adolescent risks of getting in trouble vary greatly from context to context. That in turn leads us to consider a different type of crime risk rate. You recall that we described how to calculate a traditional crime rate

> ### Box 4B How to Calculate Time-Based Crime Risk
>
> (a) 52 people spend 100 hours   =   5,200 person-hours going
>   going home from school   home from school
>
> (b) Time-based   = $\dfrac{\text{240 crime victimizations while going home from school}}{\text{5,200 person-hours spent}}$ × 1,000 = 46.2 crimes per thousand person-hours going home from school
>   crime risk

(refer back to Box 3e). A traditional crime rate divides the number of crimes by the number of people living in the area where the crimes occur. However, people move around a good deal—even within a period of 24 hours. They leave their home territory to work, go to school, go shopping, or enjoy recreation. Sometimes they are victimized by crime while there or in transit. Some people also commit crimes away from their home ground. That's why we calculate time-based rates that consider how much time people spend in any given area or activity. Box 4b shows how to calculate a time-based *victimization* rate—dividing the number of crimes by the amount of time spent in an area or activity. (The same can be done for a time-based *offending* rate.)

Imagine 52 students report, over the year, spending 100 hours going home from school—a total of 5,200 person-hours. Suppose that they also report, collectively, 240 instances of being victim to crime on the way home from school. Box 4b shows how to calculate their risk of being victimized by dividing 240 by 5,200. That gives them a risk rate of about 46 crime victimizations per thousand person-hours going home from school.

These calculations can be very important because they tell us where and when risks are the greatest. Have a look at Figure 4l, which shows time-based risks of a violent victimization during five different activities at ages 15 through 19. Hour for hour, the risk when *going to and from school* is more than seven times greater than the risk while at school itself. That means that much of the effort by schools to locate police officers inside may be missing where the risk is greatest and could represent a misallocation of funds.[13] Another dramatic finding emerges from Figure 4l: Hour for hour, time spent going to and from school is 20 times more risky than time spent in home activities during waking hours. You will see shortly that differences are even greater for risks of *committing* crimes.

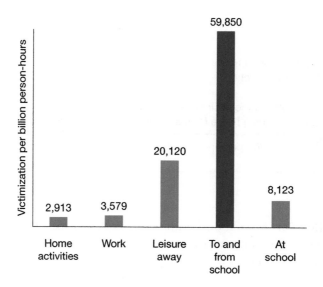

Risk of Violent Victimization per Billion Person-Hours Spent in Different Activities, Ages 15–19

Source: Adapted from A. M. Lumieux (2011). *Risk of violence in major daily activities, United States 2003–2005.* Doctoral dissertation, Rutgers University.

Delinquency and "Hanging Out"

The significance for crime of "hanging out" is increasingly documented by research.[14] **Wayne Osgood** and colleagues proved that youths are much more likely to break rules during periods of **unstructured socializing**—when teens are together but authority figures are absent.[15] Convergences of youths with adults absent can be highly criminogenic. Osgood's team found *time spent* with peers is not only extremely important for delinquency, but also has more impact than the normative influence of peers.[16] "[T]he risks of hanging out stem from the nature of hanging out as an activity, not the nature of adolescents' companions . . . hanging out is a context for friends' mutual reinforcement of preexisting characteristics."[17] Osgood's findings are quite consistent with the Judith Rich Harris context-specific model (discussed in Unit 4.3), with youth behavior adjusting to the specific contexts in which they find themselves.

Osgood's findings are based on and consistent with the routine activity approach, which emphasizes time spent and exposure to risk. Extremely powerful support for that approach also emerges from Peterborough, a city 100 km north of London, U.K.,

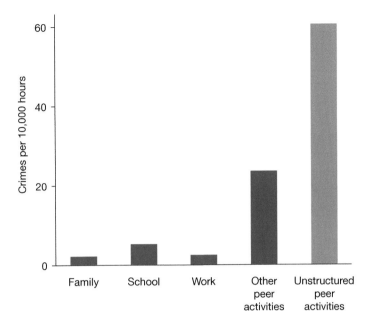

FIGURE 4M

Crimes Teenagers Commit per 10,000 Hours Spent in Different Activities, Peterborough, U.K.

Source: Adapted from P. O. Wikström, D. Oberwittler, K. Treiber, & B. Hardie (2012). *Breaking rules: Social and situational dynamics of young people's urban crime*. Oxford: Oxford University Press. Calculated from tables on pp. 330–331.

where researchers linked crime participation to teenage time use.[18] Figure 4m recalculates and sums up the most important evidence, that youths are much more likely to commit crimes during unstructured peer activities. For every 10,000 hours spent in family activities or in school activities, youths committed a miniscule number of crimes.

By far the greatest risk occurred in unstructured activities with peers—60 crimes per 10,000 hours. That means that if a thousand teens spend ten hours in unstructured peer activities, we can expect 60 crimes to occur. Hour for hour, adolescents are far more at risk when with their peers in the absence of adult supervision and control. The risk is about 30 times as great in unstructured peer activities as in family activities— a difference of *3,000 percent*! This offers powerful evidence for routine activity thinking and the crime triangle explained in Unit 2.2.

Even stronger results emerge from a study in the Netherlands. Teens were even more likely to get in trouble if their peer activities away from parents occurred near the city center or other *locations rich in crime targets*.[19] These dramatic findings reinforce that we should pay close attention to where youths are and what they are doing—especially where youths are hanging out without supervision from parents. Although American youths are more likely to hang out near malls or mini-malls (rather than town centers), the same principle applies.[20] Additional research shows active nightlife (any time after 6:00 pm) had a strong effect on victimization for boys, and that adolescents who frequented public places at night increased their risk of victimization by people they knew as well as strangers. Much of the risk was alcohol-related.[21]

Research repeatedly shows that *informal* teenage activities produce far more delinquency, hour for hour, than do other activities. The research also shows rule-breaking to be strongly associated with going to parties, as well as "hanging out with friends" or "doing nothing in particular" with peers present but adults absent. This does not mean that most of these activities involve crime and delinquency on most days. But it does mean that delinquency, illegal drug and alcohol use, and dangerous driving are much more likely to occur with peers present and adults absent. Moreover, the impact of unstructured socializing on criminal offending applies to all socioeconomic and racial groups, to high-risk and low-risk populations alike, and across different nations.[22]

School Effects on the Timing of Delinquency

Within a single day, teenage activities undergo remarkable situational shifts, with schooldays differing from other days.[23] As shown in Figure 4n, on school days, teenagers fall victim to assault on a very different timescale than on non-school days. On school days, their risk begins to increase around 1:00 pm, peaking sharply after school lets out around 3:00 pm. School day risk declines sharply at night. The pattern is *entirely* different on weekends and other non-school days. That's when risk shifts to the evening and nighttime hours. Accordingly, crime mappers have found that crime hot spots shift in space: near high schools on school days, but shifting to entertainment districts or "magnetic settings" when school is not in session.[24] Clearly, we must pay a lot more attention to where youths are located and with whom.

From "Ordinary" Delinquency to Something Worse

Offenders do not have systematic and incremental criminal careers in the same way that academics move from instructor to assistant professor to associate professor to full professor.[25] However, their minor offenses *might* lead them onward to something worse. Time exposures help us understand how bad things might happen and how they might get worse.

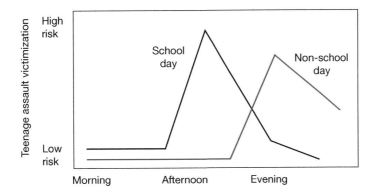

FIGURE 4N

Comparing Hourly Assaults of Teenagers, School Days vs. Non-School Days

Source: Idea based on H. N. Snyder & M. Sickmund (1999). Violence after school. *Juvenile Justice Bulletin*, National Report Series. Washington DC: Office of Juvenile Justice and Delinquency Prevention.

- Time with teens, not parents, exposes youths to more risk of crime participation.

- Time drinking exposes people to extra risk of illegal drug use.[26]

- Time spent drinking exposes people to extra risk of getting completely drunk.

- Time drunk creates extra risk of victimization and offending against others.

- Time committing minor delinquency creates extra risk of major delinquency.

As you see, criminology cannot predict when any one event will burst forth. But we can sort out the patterns of risk and take note of the ages, places, times, and activities during which risks are especially great.

FLASHCARD LIST FOR UNIT 4.5

- Free time together with peers
- Latchkey youths
- Less freedom for young women
- Locations rich in crime targets

- Osgood, Wayne
- Time-use surveys
- Unstructured socializing

DISCUSSION QUESTIONS

1. How important is adolescent time spent with peers away from parents?

2. How does school day behavior differ from weekend behavior for teenagers?

Notes

1   In addition to the Osgood papers cited later, see: Oetting, E. R., & Beauvais, F. (1987). Peer cluster theory, socialization characteristics, and adolescent drug use: A path analysis. *Journal of Counseling Psychology, 34*(2), 205–213.

2   Hoeben, E. M., Bernasco, W., Weerman, F. M., Pauwels, L., & van Halem, S. (2014). The space-time budget method in criminological research. *Crime Science, 3*(1), Article 12. Published online December 19. DOI: 10.1186/s40163-014-0012-3.

3   This approach to calculating exposure to risk was first proposed by Professor Sarah Boggs: Boggs, S. L. (1965). Urban crime patterns. *American Sociological Review, 30*(6), 899–908.

4   Felson, M., & Gottfredson, M. (1984). Social indicators of adolescent activities near peers and parents. *Journal of Marriage and Family, 46*(3), 709–714. So far as we know, this is the earliest time-use study that focused on teenage activity near peers and away from parents.

5   Every indication is that teenage autonomy from parents grew even more in the past few decades. However, recent trends towards living with parents during young adult years might tell us that the autonomy of youths is now declining.

6   Gage, J. C., Overpeck, M. D., Nansel, T. R., & Kogan, M. D. (2005). Peer activity in the evenings and participation in aggressive and problem behaviors. *Journal of Adolescent Health, 37*(6), 517e7–517e14. https://doi.org/10.1016/j.jadohealth.2004.12.012.

7   Osgood, D. W. (2008). Hanging out and up to no good: The link between time use and delinquency, and its implications for youth programs. Paper presented at the *Seventh Annual Youth Violence Prevention Conference*, April 17, University of Missouri-St. Louis. Spreadsheet data graciously provided by Professor Osgood. Responsibility for interpolation and approximation of data is ours.

8   Eisenberg, M. E., Olson, R. E., Neumark-Sztainer, D., Story, M., & Bearinger, L. H. (2004). Correlations between family meals and psychosocial well-being among adolescents. *Archives of Pediatrics and Adolescent Medicine, 158*(8), 792–796.

9   Berge, J. M., Wall, M., Hsueh, T. F., Fulkerson, J. A., Larson, N., & Neumark-Sztainer, D. (2015). The protective role of family meals for youth obesity: 10-year longitudinal associations. *The Journal of Pediatrics, 166*(2), 296–301.

10 Mulhall, P. F., Stone, D., & Stone, B. (1996). Home alone: Is it a risk factor for middle school youth and drug use? *Journal of Drug Education, 26*(1), 39–48.

11 Goncy, E. A., & Mrug, S. (2013). Where and when adolescents use tobacco, alcohol, and marijuana: Comparisons by age, gender, and race. *Journal of Studies on Alcohol and Drugs, 74*(2), 288–300.

12 Garcia, C., Hardeman, R. R., Kwon, G., Lando-King, E., Zhang, L., . . . & Kinder, E. (2014). Teenagers and texting: Use of a youth ecological momentary assessment system in trajectory health research with Latina adolescents. *JMIR mHealth and uHealth, 2*(1), e3. DOI: 10.2196/mhealth.2576.

13 Na, C., & Gottfredson, D. C. (2013). Police officers in schools: Effects on school crime and the processing of offending behaviors. *Justice Quarterly, 30*(4), 619–650.

14 Anderson, A. L. (2013). Adolescent time use, companionship, and the relationship with development. In C. L. Gibson & M. D. Krohn (Eds.), *Handbook of life-course criminology*, pp. 111–127. New York: Springer.

15 Osgood, D. W., Wilson, J. K., O'Malley, P. M., Bachman, J. G., & Johnston, L. D. (1996). Routine activities and individual deviant behavior. *American Sociological Review, 61*(4), 635–655. Osgood, D. W., & Anderson, A. L. (2004). Unstructured socializing and rates of delinquency. *Criminology, 42*(3), 519–549.

16 Haynie, D. L., & Osgood, D. W. (2005). Reconsidering peers and delinquency: How do peers matter? *Social Forces, 84*(2), 1109–1130.

17 Siennick, S. E., & Osgood, D. W. (2012). Hanging out with which friends? Friendship-level predictors of unstructured and unsupervised socializing in adolescence. *Journal of Research on Adolescence, 22*(4), 646–661; p. 646.

18 Wikström, P. O. H., Oberwittler, D., Treiber, K., & Hardie, B. (2012). Breaking rules: The social and situational dynamics of young people's urban crime. Oxford, U.K.: Oxford University Press. Calculated from tables on p. 330 and p. 331.

19 Hoeben, E., & Weerman, F. (2014). Situational conditions and adolescent offending: Does the impact of unstructured socializing depend on its location? *European Journal of Criminology, 11*(4), 481–499. Hoeben, E. M. (2016). Hanging out and messing about: Elaborating on the relationship between unstructured socializing and adolescent delinquency. Netherlands: Ridderprint.

20 Bichler, G., Malm, A., & Enriquez, J. (2014). Magnetic facilities: Identifying the convergence settings of juvenile delinquents. *Crime and Delinquency, 60*(7), 971–998. Andresen, M. A., & Felson, M. (2010). The impact of co-offending. *British Journal of Criminology, 50*(1), 66–81. Roman, C. G. (2004). *Schools, neighborhoods, and violence: Crime within the daily routines of youth.* Boston: Lexington Books.

21 Felson, R. B., Savolainen, J., Berg, M. T., & Ellonen, N. (2013). Does spending time in public settings contribute to the adolescent risk of violent victimization? *Journal of Quantitative Criminology, 29*(2), 273–293.

22 Siennick, S. E., & Osgood, D. W. (2008). A review of research on the impact on crime of transitions to adult roles. In A. M. Liberman (Ed.), *The long view of crime: A synthesis of longitudinal research*, pp. 161–187. New York: Springer.

23 Derived from Snyder, H. N., & Sickmund, M. (1999). Violence after school. *Juvenile Justice Bulletin*, 1999 National Report Series. Rockville, MD: Office of Juvenile Justice and Delinquency Prevention. www.ncjj.org/pdf/178992.pdf (retrieved July 3, 2016). Gottfredson, D. C., Gottfredson, G. D., & Weisman, S. E. (2001). Timing of delinquent behavior and its implications for after-school programs. *Criminology & Public Policy, 1*(1), 61–86.

24 Soulé, D., Gottfredson, D., & Bauer, E. (2008). It's 3 pm. Do you know where your child is? A study on the timing of juvenile victimization and delinquency. *Justice Quarterly, 25*(4), 623–646. Bichler, Malm, & Enriquez, Magnetic facilities.

25 Luckenbill, D. F., & Best, J. (1981). Careers in deviance and respectability: The analogy's limitations. *Social Problems, 29*(2), 197–206.

26 Kandel, D. (1975). Stages in adolescent involvement in drug use. *Science, 190*(4217), 912–914. Kirby, T., & Barry, A. E. (2012). Alcohol as a gateway drug: A study of US 12th graders. *Journal of School Health, 82*(8), 371–379.

PERSPECTIVE ON PART 4

You recall from Part 1 the four challenges facing society—to contain disputes and sexual urges, and to protect property and children growing up. These four challenges especially come to the fore with adolescents. Their development can clash with larger society and with one another, leading to disputes that can escalate at a higher rate than at other ages. Their rapid growth and shifting emotions require extra efforts for society. Youths are often involved in property thefts. They can easily become involved in substance abuse that interferes with their preparation for adult roles.

All four of the control mechanisms highlighted in Part 2 apply especially to adolescence. Although socialization and preparation for life commences in early childhood, the real test often arrives during adolescence. That is when social bonds conflict with the growth of sexual desire and clash with peer influences. Situational factors are tested by adolescence, and contact with justice officials is likely.

We showed in Part 4 how changes in crime participation are difficult to predict for *individuals*, but when the average is considered, there is a rather smooth age–crime curve for youths as a whole. The basic age–crime curve can be narrow or wide, depending on onset of delinquency and on time spent with peers away from parents. That thinking is aligned with delinquency and drift, described by Matza, with situational inducements influencing crime. These inducements include the mutual effects of teenagers whose time away from parental supervision can be highly criminogenic. Time-use surveys prove extremely useful for understanding exposure to risk of crime involvement, indicating that crime participation can be 60 to 100 times riskier, hour for hour, when teenagers are together with peers and in the absence of parental controls.

Researcher frustrations in predicting and unraveling individual delinquency patterns were noted. Parental limitations in controlling teenage behaviors outside their range of supervision were also noted. This is consistent with evidence presented earlier (Unit 2.2) that jobs and afternoon activities tend to be unsuccessful in reducing delinquent behavior in an American context. We have shown that adolescent crime participation is concentrated in certain times, places, and settings. Concentrated risk is a recurrent theme in our textbook. In Part 5 we show how metropolitan life can enhance and concentrate risks of crime and disorder, and in Part 6 we consider how that happens especially for women.

Main Points of Part 4

- The development of the teenage brain and the age–crime curve largely coincide.

- The age–crime curve is a useful summary, but we should not forget that adolescence is a period of volatility and zigzagging.

- Society hopes that youths will start experimenting with delinquency late and stop early.

- Two models distinguish theoretical approaches to peer and adult influences:
  - o   The *blending model* is based on social learning (differential association).
  - o   The *context-specific model* is based on the psychology of Judith Rich Harris, who emphasized shifting behaviors from one context to another, bringing adolescent time use to the forefront.

- Offending is closely linked to hanging out with other teens, absent parents.

- Time with peers shifts from early to late adolescence, and the pattern has changed from the past century to this century.

- Offending shifts over the course of the day and from school days to weekends.

- Crime is often situationally induced and is influenced by activities with peers.

- Teens learn neutralization techniques to justify their rule-breaking.

PART 5

Overt Crime Areas

We now shift our attention to neighborhoods. A "good" neighborhood hides its bad behavior. A "bad" neighborhood reveals its bad behavior to itself and others. We call the latter an ***overt crime area***, emphasizing its inability to contain its local problems.[1] Overt crimes differ from covert crimes and play a different role in community life.

- An ***overt crime*** occurs in public places; a ***covert crime*** is hidden behind closed doors.

- An overt crime is seen and heard by many people; a covert crime directly harms rather few people.

- An overt crime scares a whole neighborhood; a covert crime only impinges on those directly affected.

- An overt crime is more likely to draw police attention; a covert crime is seldom noticed by police unless a citizen calls to report it.

To determine whether a given criminal act is overt, ask yourself:

1. Does it occur in public space?

2. Can it be seen or heard by an appreciable number of local people?

3. Does it produce an ugly residue, visible after it is completed?

4. Might police see this criminal event in progress?

Note that we define overt crime from the *neighborhood* viewpoint, not the perspective of the victim or the offender.

Most of society's crimes are covert, occurring behind closed doors or as quiet thefts or quick burglaries, seen and heard by very few people and scarcely noticed at all by the larger neighborhood. Even if police are called in to take a burglary report or to quell a dispute between two households, the rest of the neighborhood might not know about it. Of course, covert victimizations accumulate, and we cannot dismiss the harm they do. Yet an overt crime does much more damage by impinging on so many people. Arguably, a single overt crime does as much local harm as ten covert criminal acts.

Our distinction between overt and covert crimes **cuts across legal categories**. Here are some examples of how people can violate the *same* law either overtly or covertly:

- Illicit drug sales are overt if they occur in a public park, but covert if they are transacted in a private apartment.[2]

- A car stolen from a public street is overt, but a car could also be stolen covertly from a personal garage or carport.[3]

- An assault is overt if it occurs in a public park, but covert if it is located inside a private home.

- A forcible rape is overt next to a public street at night, but covert if occurring indoors.[4]

- Truancy is overt if truant youths hang out in public places, but covert if teenagers quietly sneak out of school and converge out of sight.[5]

From a legal viewpoint, these paired acts are equivalent. From a **neighborhood viewpoint**, overt crime is far worse—impinging on, scaring, and irritating many more people while harming those most directly involved.

Some crimes are *committed* secretly and yet become overt because their neighborhood impact is soon noteworthy. An arsonist usually sets a fire when nobody is looking, but the burned-out cars or buildings are quite visible. Boys vandalize park furniture at night, but the damage becomes public in the morning. A tagger team paints late at night, but their graffiti soon becomes evident. We consider these overt crimes because they **damage a whole neighborhood**.[6] Upsetting more people, overt crimes can undermine use of public places[7] as well as producing extra demands for police action and more frustration with public officials for not stopping the problem.

In 1925, Ernest W. Burgess recognized that people tend to break rules outside their own residential zone.[8] A Montreal study shows the dramatic local effects when daytime and nighttime activities draw visitors from other parts of the metropolitan area.[9] Thus some neighborhoods import bad behavior from other parts of the city and some

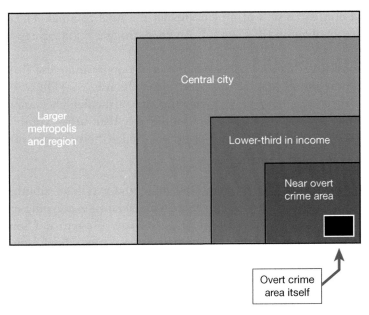

FIGURE 5A
Overt Crime Area Nested within the Larger Metropolis and Region

export their own bad behavior. A neighborhood appearing to be tranquil and secure might not be revealing the whole truth about the people living there. Not only might local offenders commit crimes outside their residential zone, but local crimes can easily be concealed. Many victims are ashamed to tell neighbors or police about problems. Within-household drunkenness, drug abuse, sexual transgressions, or assault clearly harm people in their private worlds, but might remain hidden.

A metropolis and a city contain a lot of crime variation, all of which deserves our attention as criminologists. Figure 5a depicts a larger metropolis and region, within which a central city is found. Within that, a lower-income area is nested, and that contains another area which itself contains an overt crime area.

The people in the larger metropolis and region can easily misperceive the whole central city as an overt crime area. The people in the central city can easily mistake the entire low-income part of the city with an overt crime area. These misperceptions arise because overt crime gets so much more attention than covert crime. Moreover, these misperceptions interfere with crime control.

The metropolis and region might not realize that they too have a crime problem. For example, many types of crime in rural areas are only slightly lower than in urban areas.[10] Rural drug abuse and interpersonal violence are more common than meets the eye, including the spread of methamphetamine in the wide-open regions of the United

States.[11] Illicit drug use is similar in metropolitan and rural counties. The exception is the greater metropolitan use of Ecstasy.[12] An even stronger finding is reported below:

> Rural youth have higher alcohol use and methamphetamine use than urban youth and the more rural the area, the higher the use. . . . [T]hose living in the most rural areas have nearly twice the rate of methamphetamine use as urban young adults. Rural youth are more likely than urban youth to have engaged in the high-risk behavior of driving under the influence of alcohol or other illicit drugs.[13]

Even studies showing higher urban drug abuse find very high suburban and rural involvement as well.[14] We can no longer rely on the old images assigning rule-breaking to cities and innocence to suburbs and rural areas. Many Western and Southern states have illicit drug use greater than the states with the largest cities.[15] For example, Arizona, Oklahoma, Arkansas, and Mississippi are four of the leading states for abuse of drugs more risky than marijuana. They well exceed New York, Pennsylvania, Michigan, Ohio, Massachusetts, and New Jersey. The Sunbelt of the United States in general has the highest rates of drug abuse.

However, both rural and suburban crime problems are largely covert. As the next unit indicates, overt crime is more likely to occur in tough urban neighborhoods, giving people a *perception of danger* and insecurity. Harmful outcomes go beyond perceptions since crime can grow and take over the area. Part 5 explains many parts of the problem, including tough neighborhoods (Unit 5.1); neighborhood cohesion and intimidation (Unit 5.2); the exclusion of people and activities from a neighborhood (Unit 5.3); concentrated problems (Unit 5.4); how residents accommodate to local problems (Unit 5.5); and the pathway to decay—after problems are allowed to fester for too many years (Unit 5.6). We close by explaining how modern crime maps have changed how we think about metropolitan crime (Unit 5.7).

FLASHCARD LIST FOR PART 5: OVERT CRIME AREAS

- Covert crime
- Cuts across legal categories
- Damage a whole neighborhood
- Neighborhood viewpoint
- Overt crime
- Overt crime area
- Perception of danger

QUESTIONS ADDRESSED IN PART 5

1. How do characteristics of neighborhoods generate crime and disorder?

2. Why are social cohesion, intimidation, and social exclusion important?

3. How do people adjust to adverse circumstances and high-crime neighborhoods?

4. How do neighborhoods deteriorate?

5. What have changes in crime mapping taught us about local crime?

Notes

1   Braga, A. A., Welsh, B. C., & Schnell, C. (2015). Can policing disorder reduce crime? A systematic review and meta-analysis. *Journal of Research in Crime and Delinquency, 52*(4), 567–588.

2   Curtis, R., & Wendel, T. (2000). Toward the development of a typology of illegal drug markets. In M. Natarajan & M. Hough (Eds.), *Illegal drug markets*. Crime Prevention Studies, Vol. 11, pp. 121–152. Monsey, NY: Criminal Justice Press. Knutsson, J. (1997). Restoring public order in a city park. In R. Homel (Ed.), *Policing for prevention: Reducing crime, public intoxication and injury*. Crime Prevention Studies, Vol. 7, pp. 133–151. Monsey, NY: Criminal Justice Press.

3   Webb, B., & Tilley, N. (2005). Preventing vehicle crime. In N. Tilley (Ed.), *Handbook of crime prevention and community safety*, pp. 458–485. Devon, U.K.: Willan Publishing.

4   Beauregard, E., Proulx, J., & Rossmo, K. (2005). Spatial patterns of sex offenders: Theoretical, empirical, and practical issues. *Aggression and Violent Behavior, 10*(5), 579–603.

5   McAra, L., & McVie, S. (2005). The usual suspects? Street-life, young people and the police. *Criminal Justice, 5*(1), 5–36.

6   Ceccato, V., & Haining, R. (2005). Assessing the geography of vandalism: Evidence from a Swedish city. *Urban Studies, 42*(9), 1637–1656.

7   McCormack, G. R., Rock, M., Toohey, A. M., & Hignell, D. (2010). Characteristics of urban parks associated with park use and physical activity: A review of qualitative research. *Health & Place, 16*(4), 712–726.

8   Burgess, E. W. (1925). Can neighborhood work have a scientific basis? In R. E. Park, E. W. Burgess, & R. D. McKenzie (Eds.), *The city: Suggestions for investigation of human behaviors in the urban environment*, pp. 142–155. Chicago: University of Chicago Press.

9   Felson, M., & Boivin, R. (2015). Daily crime flows within a city. *Crime Science, 4*(1), 31.

10 Donnermeyer, J. F. (Ed.). (2016). *The Routledge International Handbook of Rural Criminology*. Abingdon, U.K.:Routledge.

11 Shukla, Rashi. (2016). *Methamphetamine: A love story*. Oakland, CA: University of California Press.

12 Gfroerer, J. C., Larson, S. L., & Colliver, J. D. (2007). Drug use patterns and trends in rural communities. *The Journal of Rural Health, 23*(s1), 10–15.

13 Lambert, D., Gale, J. A., & Hartley, D. (2008). Substance abuse by youth and young adults in rural America. *The Journal of Rural Health, 24*(3), 221–228; p. 221.

14   Substance Abuse and Mental Health Services Administration. (2014). *Results from the 2013 National Survey on Drug Use and Health: Summary of national findings.* Rockville, MD: Substance Abuse and Mental Health Services Administration; Table 2.14. www.samhsa.gov/data/sites/default/files/ NSDUHresultsPDFWHTML2013/Web/NSDUHresults2013.pdf (retrieved July 19, 2016).

15   Substance Abuse and Mental Health Services Administration. (2015). *2013–2014 National Survey on Drug Use and Health national maps of prevalence estimates, by state* [online]. www.samhsa.gov/data/ sites/default/files/NSDUHsaeMaps2014/NSDUHsaeMaps2014.pdf (retrieved July 19, 2016).

UNIT 5.1 Tough Neighborhoods

Criminologists use the term *social disorganization* to describe places where various social problems coincide with crime. That occurs most often in the toughest areas of a central city. Neighborhood problems might include unemployment, poverty, dilapidated buildings, high levels of suspicion, concentrated poverty, mental problems, alcoholism, drug addiction, or more. You might think of social disorganization the way physicians and nurses think of a "syndrome"—several adverse conditions occurring together.

The idea for social disorganization came from the *Chicago School* of sociology, which thrived at the University of Chicago from 1915 to 1942.[1] The professors there treated their *city as a social laboratory*, with special emphasis on the poorest parts of town.[2] Professors *Shaw and McKay* are especially famous for trying to explain how crime concentrates in the "delinquency area" near the center of large American cities (see Unit 5.7).[3] These areas are

- *disorganized neighborhoods*, with
- low levels of *neighborhood cohesion*, and
- a pattern of *concentrated disadvantage*.

These three points help us organize what we know about overt crime areas. We discuss neighborhood cohesion in Unit 5.2. and concentration in Unit 5.4. Here, we discuss how places can be hospitable for crime.

Disorganized Places

In the 1920s and 1930s, Chicago School sociologists discovered a pattern of ethnic transition called *invasion* and *succession*.[4] Impoverished ethnic groups would move into the delinquency area, while prior residents from other ethnic groups gradually moved to better sections of town as their income increased. In Unit 5.3 you will learn how white Protestant neighborhoods resisted and tried to exclude racial and non-Protestant minorities. However, the invasion–succession process varied by city. During the Great Depression, many impoverished white Southerners flooded into Cincinnati, Columbus, Detroit, and other northeastern American cities,[5] also facing conflicts with the larger community.[6]

One of the most interesting lessons of the Chicago School research is that each group participates in more crime *while living in the delinquency area*, but its crime participation *declines as it moves on to better neighborhoods.*[7] That led social scientists to ask how a neighborhood crime rate could remain so high after its population had completely turned over. In an excellent synthesis of ideas drawn from the Chicago School, **Rodney Stark** noted that it no longer makes sense to attribute a high-crime neighborhood to the **kinds of people** who live there. Instead the data require us to look at the **kinds of places** that produce more crime risk, even as new people move in.[8]

Criminologists increasingly learn to focus on *places* where people live.[9] Stark started with poverty, but four other urban features also make an urban zone dangerous:

- **Population density**;

- **Mixed land use**;

- **Transiency**; and

- **Dilapidation**.

Stark went on to explain that *high population density* makes it more difficult for "good kids" to avoid "bad kids" who live very near. He noted that crowded living pushes teenagers outside the home, away from parental supervision. Stark also noted that crowded living makes it difficult to shield discreditable acts and information from neighbors.

Mixed land use is important for making low-income areas more suitable for crime. It brings youths close to commercial zones with street corners, bars, warehouses, and other locations making it easier to escape parental supervision. Stark explained too that

> [m]ixed-use neighborhoods offer increased opportunity for congregating outside the home in places conducive to deviance. It isn't just stores to steal from that the suburbs lack. . . . [I]n dense, poor, mixed-use neighborhoods, when people leave the house they have all sorts of places to go, including the street corner.[10]

Although middle-class teenagers can use cars to gain access to hangout locations, mixed land use in low-income areas allows such access at younger ages.

Transience refers to moving in and out, which disrupts school rosters and produces neighbors who do not know one another. Poor, dense, mixed-use neighborhoods have high transience rates. Chicago School sociologists recognized in the 1920s that the slums were the most mobile sections of the city, with inhabitants coming and going continuously. Stark pointed out that transience weakens social ties between households while making it very difficult to organize or maintain neighborhood associations. Moreover, transience reduces levels of community surveillance. As Stark explained:

> In areas abounding in newcomers, it will be difficult to know when someone doesn't live in a building he or she is entering. In stable neighborhoods, on the other hand, strangers are easily noticed and remembered.[11]

Finally, *dilapidation* interferes with neighborhood control. Neighborhoods with high population density and few homeowners also tend to be dirty and littered and have more deteriorating buildings. They have inferior public services, so streets are cleaned less often and less carefully. Dilapidation creates a social stigma for residents, conferring lower status on them. Sociologists have argued that people living under these conditions have less ***stake in conformity*** than those living in better circumstances. This leads to a simple question: What do you have to lose if you are detected committing a deviant act? If your status is high, you have more to lose. If your status is low, you have less to lose, making you more willing to take the risk. The stigma of living in the slums gives people less stake in conformity and less to lose if caught committing a crime.[12] Those who can do so will move away from the deteriorated area as soon as they can, leaving the neighborhood to deteriorate further. Stigmatized neighborhoods tend to be overpopulated by the most demoralized people, including the mentally ill, chronic alcoholics, and others unable to cope with society. These people make excellent victims of crime too. In Unit 5.6 we talk about the growing decay that these social forces create. Next, we discuss overt crime, especially selling illicit drugs.

Open-Air Drug Markets

Crime, conflict, and misbehavior can occur

- within households;

- between households; or

- in public places, impinging on an entire neighborhood.

Most Americans live in places where misbehavior is rather private, occurring either within households or as a conflict between two households. A tough neighborhood supplements ***private problems*** with ***neighborhood problems***. This reflects the presence of overt crime and ***public disorder***. We call such a neighborhood an "overt crime area" to reflect the simple fact that local problems dominate public space. An overt crime area contains not only overt crime but also a considerable amount of public disorder that might not qualify as illegal. We later discuss such public disorder and its negative impact on neighborhoods where it prevails. Even if their own homes are tranquil inside, local people cannot insulate themselves and their families from insecurity outside. Prolonged and repetitive misbehaviors in public places amplify neighborhood fear and discomfort. This is especially true when drug selling occurs in plain view.[13]

Open-air drug markets are the hallmark of a tough neighborhood. Any given drug transaction can occur quickly, yet dealers hang out in public for hours on end.[14] Their presence looms, other drug dealers may join them, and illicit customers come and go. These open-air drug transactions are usually confined to very limited spots within a city, yet may be witnessed by others living near them. A remarkable study compared drug use to drug sales for neighborhoods at different income levels.[15] Respondents were asked

- whether they had used illicit drugs *themselves* during the past year, and

- whether they had *seen* drugs sold in their neighborhood.

As the lighter bars in Figure 5b indicate, drug use in the areas with the lowest income was about the same as in high- to middle-income neighborhoods. Now look at the darker bars. Compared to the most prosperous neighborhoods, residents of the poorest neighborhoods were ten times more likely to report *seeing* drugs sold.

Figure 5b tells a powerful story. High- and middle-income areas successfully *conceal* most of their drug problems from neighbors and from police, preserving a clean reputation. In contrast, in impoverished neighborhoods, drug problems become obvious to residents, police, and outsiders.

Illicit drugs are sold in two ways, ***person-specific drug markets*** or ***place-specific drug markets***. In person-specific markets, drugs are sold through personal ties.[16] This method predominates in prosperous areas, where drug transactions are hidden from public view, protecting personal and ***neighborhood reputations***. In contrast, drug dealing in low-income areas includes more place-specific drug markets, with sales located at identifiable and predictable locations and times. In a place-specific drug market, anybody who looks like a plausible buyer—including a stranger from outside the area—can easily secure drugs.[17] The buyer knows where to go, the price tends to be cheaper, and the seller has access to more customers.[18] Impoverished neighborhoods are more suitable for place-specific drug markets because

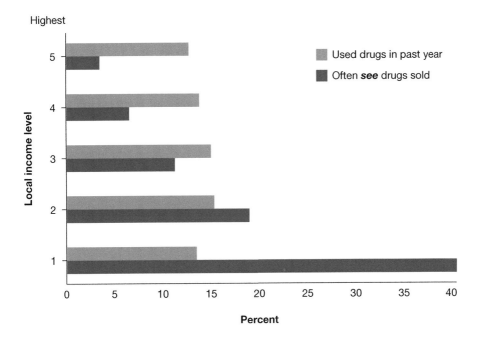

FIGURE 5B

Open-Air Drug Sales vs. Neighborhood Drug Use by Neighborhood Income Type

Source: Data drawn from L. Saxe et al. (2001). The visibility of illicit drugs: Implications for community-based drug control strategies. *American Journal of Public Health, 91*(12), 1987–1994.

- Residents have little political power and cannot control public space or get help from city hall.

- Offenders can draw from the local concentration of risky settings—liquor establishments, unattended parks, public transit hubs, busy highways, homeless shelters, and poorly managed apartment buildings.[19]

Overt drug markets have very negative consequences for a neighborhood.[20] Drug buyers are more likely to steal things in the area to feed their drug habits.[21] Emergency services are more likely to show up when drugs or weapons harm people.[22] Outdoor prostitutes are likely to be present,[23] and they are considerably more likely than indoor prostitutes to use hard drugs, to experience violence, to be raped, and even to be kidnaped.[24] Directly and indirectly, outdoor drug dealing makes a neighborhood considerably more dangerous than neighborhoods whose drug sales are hidden from view.

Outdoor Drug Sales Produce More Violence

Disputes arise when drug dealers cheat customers or one another; such disputes cannot be resolved through the legal system, so disputants often resort to violence.[25] These problems are found also with indoor drug dealers, but street dealers face especially high risk of involvement in *violent disputes and retaliations*.[26] They often use threats of violence to manage their risk.[27] Street dealers or customers are also more likely to be robbed, yet are unlikely to report their victimizations to police.[28] Many of them would prefer to take justice into their own hands, retaliating violently to redress their grievances.[29]

Significantly higher violent and property crime occurs at corners used for open-air drug distribution, especially if more than one criminal clique works the same corner.[30] Open drug markets are also associated with high levels of gun carrying.[31] The widespread use of guns by drug sellers encourages others in the neighborhood to arm themselves for self-defense or to settle disputes.[32] The impact of overt drug markets shows up in statistics for aggravated assault,[33] robbery,[34] and homicide.[35] Clearly, good drug markets are bad neighbors.[36]

Overt drug sales and related crime mean that residents are likely to *witness violence* even if not a party to it themselves. This applies not only to adults, but also to adolescents[37] and younger children.[38] In one study, in the previous year,

* 90 percent of adolescents had heard gunshots;

* 70 percent had witnessed a beating;

* 57 percent had seen a robbery in progress; and

* 46 percent had observed a shooting.[39]

Such overt crime impinges greatly on those who live in its midst.

> In most cases, however, they will adopt a "bunker mentality." They will decrease their outside activities as the local streets become less safe. They will especially limit to the barest minimum their young children's use of outside spaces. The neighborhood will become a much less satisfactory place for family life.[40]

These residents are like the prehistoric cliff dwellers in the American southwest, who pulled up their ladders for nighttime security.[41]

In a tough neighborhood, fearful parents may confine their children at home or reduce their activity space, also interfering with exercise and enjoyment of life.[42]

Overt crime creates risk that children will be unintended victims of stray bullets.[43] Most gunfire incidents are not even reported to police.[44] Even though only 1 percent of homicides fit this category,[45] that suffices to terrify local parents. Failure to call police[46] tells us how far deterioration has proceeded.

Outdoor Drug Sales Produce More Arrests

Unlike drug transactions in private places, public drug sales are especially likely to draw police attention and intervention.[47] This point is best understood by first recognizing how unlikely a drug arrest is for the larger population. A population might smoke marijuana 3,000 to 6,000 times before a single arrest occurs.[48] Dealers also have ways to avoid arrest most of the time. Researchers estimated the risks of arrest for a population of marijuana dealers in Quebec, Canada; dealers could be 95 percent sure they would not get arrested, and 99.8 percent sure that multiple arrests would not occur.[49] Of course, buying or selling drugs in the open produces greater risks, with police better able to enforce laws. Even indoor markets located near major streets expose customers and sellers to greater risks from police and from other offenders.[50]

Drug use mainly occurs in private settings, including private parties.[51] However, outdoor purchases expose people to the greatest risks of arrest. Black Americans do *not* consume more marijuana than whites, but are considerably more likely than whites to be arrested for drug sales and possession. Evidence tells us that racial discrimination plays a role in this discrepancy.[52] However, another factor is important: Black youths are twice as likely as white youths to buy marijuana *outdoors* and three times as likely to buy *from strangers*.[53] Outdoor purchases from strangers help explain their greater risk of being arrested.[54] When drug trafficking occurs in public, it becomes more visible to police, who are then more likely to intrude and interrupt. Sirens blare. Lights flash. Police rush in. People are handcuffed. The justice system makes a lot of noise in dealing with outdoor crimes.

Outdoor socializing and drinking has significance outside the United States. In Glasgow, Scotland, it was found that youths who were drinking outdoors drew extra police attention and were considerably more likely to be arrested than other youths. The quality of police contact was worse if youths were from lower-status cultural backgrounds. Youths drinking outdoors also faced extra risk that police would discover drugs or find other reasons to arrest them.[55]

Fear and Public Disorder

A tough neighborhood not only suffers overt crime but also faces a wide range of public nuisances—also known as disorder. Crime and disorder are not the same thing, as we discussed at the beginning of the textbook. Crime requires a direct violation of criminal law. Disorder includes many behaviors that are not illegal. Disorder also includes the residue of illegal acts and aversive **environmental cues**. Thus,

Selling illegal drugs is a crime.
Standing around before and after the drug sale is disorder.

Committing arson is a crime.
The presence of burned-out buildings is disorder.

Assault is a crime.
Violent youths hanging out on street corners is disorder.

Drinking in public is a crime.
Hanging out in public after getting drunk in private is disorder.

Injecting illegal drugs is a crime.
Seeing littered hypodermic needles is disorder.

Public drinking is a crime.
Noticing littered beer cans is disorder.

Dumping illegally is a crime.
Presence of junk after dumping is disorder.

Even though we distinguish disorder from crime, that does not mean every citizen will make such a distinction. In 1928, W. I. Thomas and Dorothy Thomas stated a famous theorem: "If [people] define situations as real, these perceptions are real in their consequences."[56]

The **Thomas theorem** tells us that human perceptions can create their own reality even if those perceptions are not fully objective. Disorderly sights tend to evoke a perception of crime that people experience as real. This helps us understand why many people fear crime more than crime statistics seem to warrant.[57] **Fear of crime** derives from more than crime statistics or observed crime incidents; it also reflects environmental cues that can scare people, including the cues we related above.

This is illustrated by the **rattlesnake example**. Imagine yourself hiking in the woods and seeing a rattlesnake in the grass. It can scare you without having to bite you. Even a non-poisonous snake can scare you by *reminding you* of a rattlesnake. The next time you hike you might fear the spot where you saw the snake even if there is no snake this time. You might even be afraid of similar terrain miles away from where you saw

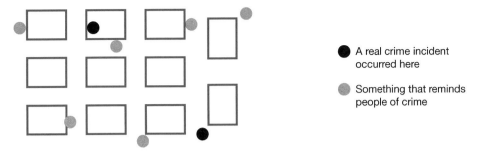

● A real crime incident
   occurred here

● Something that reminds
   people of crime

FIGURE 5C
Reminders of Crime Have Real Effects when Concentrated in Space

the rattlesnake. These environmental cues extend the rattlesnake's intimidation beyond its actual presence, much less its real bites.

City residents also respond to environmental cues, especially those that remind them of crime. These reminders tell people they are in a risky situation. Figure 5c illustrates the point by mapping a neighborhood with only two real crime incidents but six situations that *remind* people of crime. Notice the powerful impression that these additional reminders create when you look at the map from above. An even stronger negative impression probably occurs on the ground when people walk by what they perceive as danger spots.

Such environmental cues convey a sense of *disorder*.[58] In the late 1970s the United States was in the midst of a crime wave, with growing fear within and between neighborhoods. Criminologists began to understand that neighborhood fear of crime is mostly not generated by crime itself, but rather by disorder—***crime reminders***.[59] Criminologists use the general term ***neighborhood disorder*** to sum up local environmental cues that people "code" as indicating high risk of crime. Neighborhood disorder includes both social and physical disorder. Social disorder includes public arguing and drinking, rowdy teenagers, sexual harassment on the street, and public drug dealing. Physical disorder includes garbage, junk, graffiti, litter, abandoned buildings, vacant lots, and vandalized property.[60] (In Unit 5.6, we elaborate on these examples and consider how neighborhood disorder contributes to crime and further decay.) These environmental cues are interpreted as risky situations, leading residents to fear crime even when no criminal act is in progress.

The Effect of Abandoned Buildings

The link between environmental cues and crime is powerful. Many environmental conditions make crime easier to carry out. Neighborhoods wish to avoid those conditions with good reason. We have no better example than abandoned homes, businesses, factories, or warehouses. Chicago sociologists of the 1930s were well aware that delinquency areas contained more than their share of ***abandoned buildings***.[61] Today, large portions of Philadelphia, Baltimore, Detroit, and Chicago are dominated by abandoned properties. Serious and related disorder issues are reported for multiple American cities.[62] Other nations are not exempt: Substantial disorder problems can be found in Spain[63] and Canada;[64] and some 40 percent of large European cities are currently shrinking, especially in Eastern Europe and other places that lost their industrial base.[65]

Abandoned properties are helpful for criminal offenders but harmful to other neighbors and a headache for police. Urban studies have shown a number of examples. One study found that 83 percent of abandoned buildings were used by prostitutes, drug dealers, or other offenders. Another showed that homeless youths often slept in abandoned buildings.[66] It has also been found that gang members take advantage of abandoned properties to escape supervision and control.[67] Blocks with abandoned buildings have been shown to have twice as many crimes as matched blocks without such abandonment.[68] Another analysis found 11 ways that abandoned buildings feed crime.[69] Abandoned buildings provide criminal activity with opportunities and cover. Criminals are drawn to abandoned properties because nobody regulates behavior.[70] These buildings have no visible owners or place managers.[71] Inside, people can use drugs, get drunk, have sex, or whatever else they want. Teenagers can evade parents. Drug dealers can hide a stash. Burglars can conceal their loot. The properties are indicators of blight that symbolize no one cares about the neighborhood; the message to onlookers is that this is an ***ungovernable area***, no one is willing to challenge another's behavior, and the risk of being caught is low.

When police appear on the scene, local offenders can duck into abandoned buildings until they leave. Abandoned buildings also remove guardians who would otherwise be watching the street, making it easier for crime to occur in the vicinity. Abandonment further erodes the sense of caring and ownership for a neighborhood. Building owners have little incentive to fix properties whose value is largely gone. Crime grows even more, and the neighborhood becomes increasingly lost. Without rehabilitation or replacement of abandoned properties, recovery of old parts of old cities is unlikely.[72] Have another look at Figure 5c; imagine walking amid garbage, litter, abandoned buildings, drunks hanging out in public, overt drug sellers, and prostitutes walking back and forth. Even when you see no crime, you might well be afraid given that so many bad environmental cues surround you.

Chronic Street Nuisances

Even small annoyances can make a neighborhood less livable if repeated a thousand times.

> Chronic street nuisances occur when a person regularly behaves in a public space in a way that annoys—but no more than annoys—most other users, and persists in doing so over a protracted period.[73]

Residents of tough neighborhoods face *chronic street nuisances* within their own residential zone. While trivial on any one occasion, repetitive nuisances accumulate their annoyance power as hours blend into days and weeks. This gets worse if people become more aggressive, block sidewalks, or take over public space for private use. A park bench is meant to seat two or three people for a few minutes at a time and to serve a few dozen people over the course of the afternoon. A single homeless person sleeping across the bench blocks this general usage. Inadequate programs for mental health, homelessness, or substance dependency push people onto streets, where they run into conflicts with the larger neighborhood. You can see that tough neighborhoods are not just areas with high crime rates. Public disorder and multiple problems and nuisances contribute to fear of crime—beyond the actual numbers of criminal acts that occur. Overt crime brings police attention, yet covert crimes also flourish and abandoned properties foster additional problems, as the next few units indicate.

FLASHCARD LIST FOR UNIT 5.1

- Abandoned buildings
- Chicago School
- Chronic street nuisances
- City as a social laboratory
- Concentrated disadvantage
- Crime reminders
- Dilapidation
- Disorganized neighborhoods
- Drug markets, open-air, person-specific, place-specific
- Environmental cues
- Fear of crime
- Invasion
- Kinds of people
- Kinds of places
- Mixed land use
- Neighborhood cohesion
- Neighborhood disorder
- Neighborhood reputations
- Population density
- Problems, neighborhood, private
- Public disorder
- Rattlesnake example
- Shaw and McKay
- Social disorganization
- Stake in conformity
- Stark, Rodney
- Succession
- Thomas theorem
- Transiency
- Ungovernable area
- Violent disputes and retaliations
- Witness violence

DISCUSSION QUESTIONS

1.   How does transiency relate to public disorder?

2.   Why would outdoor drug sales be any worse for the neighborhood than indoor drug sales?

Notes

1   Becker, H. S. (1999). The Chicago school, so-called. *Qualitative Sociology, 22*(1), 3–12.

2   Bulmer, M. (1986). *The Chicago school of sociology: Institutionalization, diversity, and the rise of sociological research.* Chicago: University of Chicago Press.

3   Shaw, C. R., & McKay, H. D. (1931). *Social factors in juvenile delinquency: A study of the community, the family, and the gang in relation to delinquent behavior.* Report of the National Commission on Law Observance and Enforcement. Washington, DC: U.S. Government Printing Office. Shaw, C. R., & McKay, H. D. (1942). *Juvenile delinquency in urban areas.* Chicago: University of Chicago Press.

4   Burgess, E. W. (2008). The growth of the city: An introduction to a research project. In J. M. Marzluff (Ed.), *Urban ecology,* pp. 71–78. New York: Springer.

5   Gregory, J. N. (2006). *The southern diaspora: How the great migrations of black and white southerners transformed America.* Chapel Hill, NC: University of North Carolina Press. Kirby, J. T. (1983). The Southern exodus, 1910–1960: A primer for historians. *Journal of Southern History, 49*(4), 585–600.

6   Collins, W. J., & Wanamaker, M. H. (2015). The great migration in black and white: New evidence on the selection and sorting of southern migrants. *The Journal of Economic History, 75*(4), 947–992.

7   Cressey, P. F. (1938). Population succession in Chicago: 1898–1930. *American Journal of Sociology, 44*(1), 59–69.

8   Stark, R. (1987). Deviant places: A theory of the ecology of crime. *Criminology, 25*(4), 893–910.

9   Weisburd, D. (2015). The law of crime concentration and the criminology of place. *Criminology, 53*(2), 133–157.

10   Stark, Deviant places; p. 899.

11   Stark, Deviant places; p. 900.

12   Toby, J. (1957). Social disorganization and stake in conformity: Complementary factors in the predatory behavior of hoodlums. *Journal of Criminal Law, Criminology & Police Science, 48*(1), 12–17.

13   Lupton, R., Wilson, A., May, T., Warburton, H., & Turnbull, P. J. (2002). *A rock and a hard place: Drug markets in deprived neighbourhoods.* Home Office Research Study No. 240. London: Home Office.

14   Piza, E. L., & Sytsma, V. A. (2016). Exploring the defensive actions of drug sellers in open-air markets: A systematic social observation. *Journal of Research in Crime and Delinquency, 53*(1), 36–65.

15   Saxe, L., Kadushin, C., Beveridge, A., Livert, D., Tighe, E., . . . & Brodsky, A. (2001). The visibility of illicit drugs: Implications for community-based drug control strategies. *American Journal of Public Health, 91*(12), 1987–1994.

16   Eck, J. E., & Gersh, J. S. (2000). Drug trafficking as a cottage industry. In M. Natarajan & M. Hough (Eds.), *Illegal drug markets.* Crime Prevention Studies, Vol. 11, pp. 241–272. Monsey, NY: Criminal Justice Press.

17   Eck, J. (1995). A general model of the geography of illicit retail marketplaces. In J. Eck & D. Weisburd (Eds.), *Crime and place.* Crime Prevention Studies, Vol. 4, pp. 67–93. Monsey, NY: Criminal Justice Press.

18   Harocopos, A., & Hough, M. (2005). *Drug dealing in open-air markets.* Problem-Oriented Guides for Police, Problem Specific Guides Series, No. 31. Washington, DC: Office of Community Oriented Policing Services.

19   Rengert, G., Ratcliffe, J. H., & Chakravorty, S. (2005). *Policing illegal drug markets: Geographic approaches to crime reduction.* New York: Criminal Justice Press.

20   Berg, M. T., & Rengifo, A. F. (2009). Rethinking community organization and robbery: Considering illicit market dynamics. *Justice Quarterly, 26*(2), 211–237.

21   Sutton, M., Schneider, J., & Hetherington, S. (2001). *Tackling theft with the market reduction approach.* London: Home Office.

22   Weisburd, D., & Green, L. (1995). Policing drug hot spots: The Jersey City drug market analysis experiment. *Justice Quarterly, 12*(4), 711–735.

23   May, T., Edmunds, M., & Hough, M. (1999). *Street business: The links between sex and drug markets.* London: Home Office.

24   Church, S., Henderson, M., Barnard, M., & Hart, G. (2001). Violence by clients towards female prostitutes in different work settings: Questionnaire survey. *British Medical Journal, 322*(7285), 524–525.

25   Jacobs, B. A., & Wright, R. (2006). *Street justice: Retaliation in the criminal underworld.* New York: Cambridge University Press.

26   Topalli, V., Wright, R., & Fornango, R. (2002). Drug dealers, robbery and retaliation: Vulnerability, deterrence and the contagion of violence. *British Journal of Criminology, 42*(2), 337–351.

27   Jacobs, B. A., Topalli, V., & Wright, R. (2000). Managing retaliation: Drug robbery and informal sanction threats. *Criminology, 38*(1), 171–198.

28   Jacobs, B. A. (2000). *Robbing drug dealers: Violence beyond the law.* Piscataway, NJ: Transaction Publishers.

29   Topalli, Wright, & Fornango, Drug dealers, robbery and retaliation.

30   Taniguchi, T. A., Ratcliffe, J. H., & Taylor, R. B. (2011). Gang set space, drug markets, and crime around drug corners in Camden. *Journal of Research in Crime and Delinquency, 48*(3), 327–363.

31   Allen, A. N., & Lo, C. C. (2012). Drugs, guns, and disadvantaged youths: Co-occurring behavior and the code of the street. *Crime & Delinquency, 58*(6), 932–953.

32   Blumstein, A. (1995). Youth violence, guns, and the illicit-drug industry. *Journal of Criminal Law and Criminology, 86*(1), 10–36.

33   Martinez, R., Rosenfeld, R., & Mares, D. (2008). Social disorganization, drug market activity, and neighborhood violent crime. *Urban Affairs Review, 43*(6), 846–874.

34   Berg & Rengifo, Rethinking community organization and robbery.

35   Ousey, G. C., & Lee, M. R. (2002). Examining the conditional nature of the illicit drug market-homicide relationship: A partial test of the theory of contingent causation. *Criminology, 40*(1), 73–102.

36   Reuter, P., & Pollack, H. A. (2012). Good markets make bad neighbors. *Criminology & Public Policy, 11*(2), 211–220.

37   Farrell, A. D., & Bruce, S. E. (1996). Impact of exposure to community violence on violent behavior and emotional distress among urban adolescents. *Journal of Clinical Child Psychology, 26*(1), 2–14.

38   Osofsky, J. D. (1995). The effects of exposure to violence on young children. *American Psychologist, 50*(9), 782–788.

39   Rasmussen, A., Aber, M. S., & Bhana, A. (2004). Adolescent coping and neighborhood violence: Perceptions, exposure, and urban youths' efforts to deal with danger. *American Journal of Community Psychology, 33*(1–2), 61–75.

40   Rengert, G., & Wasilchick, J. (1989). *Space, time, and crime: Ethnographic insights into residential burglary.* Final Report to the National Institute of Justice, U.S. Department of Justice. Washington DC: National Institute of Justice; p. 71.

41   Rengert, G. F. (1996). *The geography of illegal drugs.* Boulder, CO: Westview Press.

42   Foster, S., Villanueva, K., Wood, L., Christian, H., & Giles-Corti, B. (2014). The impact of parents' fear of strangers and perceptions of informal social control on children's independent mobility. *Health and Place, 26* (December), 60–68. Loebach, J. E., & Gilliland, J. A. (2016). Free range kids? Using GPS-derived activity spaces to examine children's neighborhood activity and mobility. *Environment and Behavior, 48*(3), 421–453.

43   Sherman, L. W., Steele, L., Laufersweiler, D., Hoffer, N., & Julian, S. A. (1989). Stray bullets and "mushrooms": Random shootings of bystanders in four cities, 1977–1988. *Journal of Quantitative Criminology, 5*(4), 297–316.

44   Carr, J. B., & Doleac, J. L. (2016). The geography, incidence, and underreporting of gun violence: New evidence using ShotSpotter data. Unpublished manuscript. www.brookings.edu/wp-content/uploads/2016/07/Carr_Doleac_gunfire_underreporting.pdf (retrieved May 23, 2017).

45   Sherman et al., Stray bullets and "mushrooms."

46   Carr & Doleac, The geography, incidence, and underreporting of gun violence.

47   Beckett, K., Nyrop, K., & Pfingst, L. (2006). Race, drugs, and policing: Understanding disparities in drug delivery arrests. *Criminology, 44*(1), 105–137.

48   Ramchand, R., Pacula, R. L., & Iguchi, M. Y. (2006). Racial differences in marijuana-users' risk of arrest in the United States. *Drug and Alcohol Dependence, 84*(3), 264–272.

49   Bouchard, M., & Tremblay, P. (2005). Risks of arrest across drug markets: A capture-recapture analysis of "hidden" dealer and user populations. *Journal of Drug Issues, 35*(4), 733–754.

50   Sampson, R. (2001). *Drug dealing in privately owned apartment complexes.* Problem-Oriented Guides for Police Series, No. 4. Washington, DC: Office of Community Oriented Policing Services.

51   Duff, C. (2014). The place and time of drugs. *International Journal of Drug Policy, 25*(3), 633–639.

52   Murakawa, N., & Beckett, K. (2010). The penology of racial innocence: The erasure of racism in the study and practice of punishment. *Law & Society Review, 44*(3–4), 695–730.

53   Ramchand, Pacula, & Iguchi, Racial differences in marijuana-users' risk of arrest in the United States.

54   Nguyen, H., & Reuter, P. (2012). How risky is marijuana possession? Considering the role of age, race, and gender. *Crime & Delinquency, 58*(6), 879–910.

55   Galloway, J., Forsyth, A., & Shewan, D. (2010). Young people's street drinking behaviour: Investigating the influence of marketing and subculture. Glasgow, U.K.: Glasgow Centre for the Study of Violence.

56   Thomas, W. I., & Thomas, D. S. (1928). *The child in America: Behavior problems and programs.* New York: Knopf; p. 572.

57   Fattah, E. A., & Sacco, V. F. (2012). *Crime and victimization of the elderly.* New York: Springer.

58   An alternative term is *incivility*.

59   Hunter, A. (1978). *Symbols of incivility: Social disorder and fear of crime in urban neighborhoods*. Report to Law Enforcement Assistance Administration. Evanston, IL: Northwestern University. www.ncjrs.gov/pdffiles1/nij/82421.pdf (retrieved February 24, 2017).

60   Taylor, R. B. (1999). *Crime, grime, fear, and decline: A longitudinal look*. Washington, DC: National Institute of Justice.

61   Stark, Deviant places.

62   Welsh, B. C., Braga, A. A., & Bruinsma, G. J. (2015). Reimagining broken windows: From theory to policy. *Journal of Research in Crime and Delinquency, 52*(4), 447–463.

63   Marco, M., Gracia, E., Tomás, J. M., & López-Quílez, A. (2015). Assessing neighborhood disorder: Validation of a three-factor observational scale. *European Journal of Psychology Applied to Legal Context, 7*(2), 81–89.

64   Martin-Storey, A., Temcheff, C., Ruttle, P., Serbin, L., Stack, D., . . . & Ledingham, J. (2012). Perception of neighborhood disorder and health service usage in a Canadian sample. *Annals of Behavioral Medicine, 43*(2), 162–172.

65   Haase, A., Athanasopoulou, A., & Rink, D. (2016). Urban shrinkage as an emerging concern for European policymaking. *European Urban and Regional Studies, 23*(1), 103–107.

66   Greenblatt, M., & Robertson, M. J. (1993). Life-styles, adaptive strategies, and sexual behaviors of homeless adolescents. *Psychiatric Services, 44*(12), 1177–1180.

67   Tita, G. E., Cohen, J., & Engberg, J. (2005). An ecological study of the location of gang "set space." *Social Problems, 52*(2), 272–299.

68   Spelman, W. (1993). Abandoned buildings: Magnets for crime? *Journal of Criminal Justice, 21*(5), 481–495.

69   Felson, M. (2006). *Crime and nature*. Thousand Oaks, CA: Sage.

70   Shane, J. M. (2012). *Abandoned buildings and lots*. Problem-Oriented Guides for Police. Problem-Specific Guide, No. 64. Washington, DC: Center for Problem-Oriented Policing.

71   Brantingham, P. L., & Brantingham, P. J. (1995). Criminality of place: Crime generators and crime attractors. *European Journal on Criminal Policy and Research, 3*(3): 1–26.

72   Pagano, M. A., & Bowman, A. O. M. (2000). *Vacant land in cities: An urban resource*. Washington DC: Brookings Institution, Center on Urban and Metropolitan Policy.

73   Ellickson, R. C. (1996). Controlling chronic misconduct in city spaces: Of panhandlers, skid rows, and public-space zoning. *Yale Law Journal*, 1165–1248; p. 1169.

Unit 5.2 Cohesion vs. Intimidation

Neighborhood cohesion is the tendency of neighbors to know and help one another, acting for the good of the whole neighborhood. This unit explores how neighborhood cohesion serves to reduce crime. We also explore how local intimidation can reduce neighborhood cohesion and undermine neighborhood security.

- When neighborhood conditions are satisfactory, local intimidation is minimal, neighborhood cohesion grows, and overt crime is kept in check.

- When neighborhood conditions are unsatisfactory, local intimidation impairs neighborhood cohesion, making it easier to commit crimes overtly.

Neighborhoods use three methods to make themselves more secure:

- *Within-household influences*. Each household tries to keep its own household members out of trouble.

- *Between-household influences*. Neighbors assist and pressure one another to supervise children and follow rules.

- *Civic cooperation*. Local citizens group together to enhance neighborhood security, often seeking police help or political assistance.[1]

Civic cooperation requires neighborhood cohesion; it depends on neighbors willing to cooperate to make a difference in their own lives. Psychologist *Albert Bandura* defined this confidence as *collective efficacy*.

People do not live their lives as social isolates. Many of the challenges and difficulties they face reflect group problems requiring sustained collective effort to produce any significant change. The strength of groups, organizations, and even nations lies partly in people's sense of collective efficacy that they can solve their problems and improve their lives through concerted effort.[2]

Collective efficacy and neighborhood cohesion mean about the same thing, implying that people can work together for the ***general good***. Collective efficacy is an idealistic concept, referring to the better angels of human cooperation, not to fear and loathing of outsiders.

In the previous unit, we discussed social disorganization syndrome as described by Professors Shaw and McKay in Chicago. In socially disorganized neighborhoods, cohesion is low, the ability to work for the good of the neighborhood is weak, and crime control is lacking.

Robert Sampson suggested that neighborhood cohesion helps neighbors cooperate to report crime, seek outside resources, and confront misbehavior. Sampson's research team showed that more cohesive neighborhoods had less crime.[3] They also found that tough neighborhoods had very low levels of cohesion. Professor Sampson advocated *building up neighborhood cohesion* within high-crime neighborhoods to help them improve their local security.[4] For many years, social workers have sought to do just that.

Trying to Strengthen Neighborhoods

Social service workers and researchers have tried for many years to take Sampson's advice to build up neighborhood cohesion. But the effort began long beforehand. In 1889, ***Jane Addams*** founded ***Hull-House*** in Chicago to provide education and social services to needy people. Since that time, middle-class social workers have worked to improve disadvantaged neighborhoods in many North American cities.[5] Following his own research on social disorganization syndrome, Professor Shaw established the ***Chicago Area Project*** in 1934, seeking to strengthen low-income neighborhoods.[6] Its goal was

to mobilize local informal social organization and social control among the law-abiding residents. If properly done, such local organization could counteract the effects of social disorganization and work against criminal values and norms. . . . Another related objective was to overcome the influence of delinquent peers and criminal adults in the neighborhood by providing more opportunities for associating with conventional adults and peers [who] were engaged to establish and run recreational programs, summer camps, athletic teams, and other groups and activities.[7]

In addition, social workers identified and contacted delinquent gangs on the streets, then tried to involve them in alternative, non-delinquent activity. Was the Chicago Area Project successful? Assessments after 25 years,[8] 30 years,[9] and 50 years[10] indicated that some areas improved, some got worse, and some stayed about the same. Disagreement about the effects on crime stem from the fact that this was a quasi-experiment, not a controlled laboratory experiment. Social and community workers probably helped certain individuals and families in important ways, but they were not clearly able to transform neighborhoods or reduce crime rates.

Despite these disappointing results, criminologists did not give up yet. In the 1980s, a team of researchers tried to build community and reduce crime in Chicago neighborhoods. These quasi-experiments were conducted carefully, but still had limitations. Unfortunately, their research also produced pessimistic results. *Community organizers* were unable to create neighborhood cohesion in those *parts of a city that need it most*.[11] Efforts to mobilize disadvantaged communities for social or political action failed. The most successful organizing occurred in neighborhoods where crime rates were *already* low.[12] Several innovative community policing projects in American cities have sought to reduce disorder, work with local citizens and organizations, build confidence in police, and reduce fear.[13] Many positive outcomes have resulted. However, these efforts have fallen short on the most important goal: involving those who most need to be involved. Most of the positive benefits were confined to white segments of the community and those of higher income, while lower-income and black members of the community did not participate or benefit from the efforts. Local organizing efforts in Chicago and Minneapolis failed to achieve their goals. "[I]t seems that the more these programs were needed, the less successful they were. This was true even though the neighborhood *effort* was disproportionately directed towards neighborhoods in need."[14]

Further research by another team of researchers underscores the disappointing efforts at community organizing against crime. The Ford Foundation funded a rigorous community prevention program in Chicago neighborhoods, with *evaluation research* to measure its effectiveness.[15] Experienced community workers sought to organize residents in selected neighborhoods using block meetings and other participation opportunities. *Neighborhood watch organizations* sought to increase security. These efforts were a definite failure, even increasing fear of crime.[16] Another program and evaluation in Minnesota was similarly unsuccessful.

Often criminologists envision community policing as a means to develop neighborhood cohesion and to encourage community organizations to form. In a recent study, city managers from 1,300 cities and counties reported no gains in neighborhood cohesion or community participation, except in communities that already had low crime rates.[17]

Disappointing reports have also emerged from public health community organizers; in seeking to improve health behaviors, they were unable to mobilize disadvantaged neighborhoods.[18] A review of 26 studies found no pathway for improving public health through neighborhood cohesion.[19] Programs designed to provide health services to the poor often end up reaching those who are in a better position, while missing those at the bottom who most need help. This problem is called ***coverage inequality***[20]— a general issue in the helping professions. Programs designed to enhance neighborhood cohesion, efficacy, and self-esteem among youths in the least advantaged communities have also produced disappointing results.[21] Efforts to involve these youths in boys' and girls' clubs and other youth programs tend to fall far short of their goals.

> [Recruiting] young people to these structured settings is a constant battle.
>
> There are also issues related to retention. Participation in youth development programs tends to decline as youth age, and only one in four adolescents enrolled in these programs actually attends [the program] on a regular basis. When youth do participate, their involvement is most often characterized by engagement in less structured, less outcomes-oriented activities such as gameroom activities and pick-up recreational sports, not in structured programs intentionally designed to develop and promote skills and competencies.[22]

The tendency for local people to lose interest in organized efforts is a recurrent theme in organizing for crime reduction. Programs are not managing to reach those who need the most help.[23] As explained by ***Wesley Skogan***,

> [i]t is almost an article of faith among community organizers that crime is a no-win issue, and few would be willing to bet their organization's survival on its capacity to focus exclusively on crime, much less on its ability to succeed in doing anything about it. There are several reasons for this. First, criminals are a furtive, almost invisible enemy. One of the basic "rules for radicals" is that organizers should personalize their target. While groups can picket the office of a real estate developer or march on the home of a bad landlord, criminals usually remain faceless.[24]

Skogan notes that it is more difficult to mobilize local people against crime than against more specific local objectives.

> Unlike a smelly landfill, [crime] visits individuals on a house-by-house basis, and people can keep their heads down and hope to be passed over. It is also hard to win a visible victory over crime. A successful struggle over a dangerous

intersection may result in a stop sign or crossing guard for all to see, but a victory over crime involves preventing dozens or hundreds of individual events, and keeping them from happening next year as well.[25]

Even though crime may worry residents of a tough neighborhood, that does not mean they are interested in the specific program offered by social workers to change individual crime propensities or overall community life indirectly. In addition, those entering a program tend not to complete it. Some medical researchers have stated a "law of attrition"; namely, that a substantial proportion of program participants will quickly drop out of a research or health program, including online heath training.[26] The same principle applies to social programs. It has been shown that youths who drop out of after-school programs are the ones who need those programs most. Youths who continue in the program until the end of the school year are mainly those who are unlikely to get in trouble in the first place.[27]

Community organizers and social workers can do a lot of good for disadvantaged neighborhoods. Yet they also need *reasonable expectations* about what they really can accomplish and how long it will take to do so. In 1915, a leading professor warned fellow social workers not to be "too self-confident" or "cocksure" of their ability to reform neighborhoods.

> I do not want to diminish the vigor of any attack that can be made upon poverty, ignorance, disease, selfishness; but . . . vigor cannot succeed without intelligence. The battles that social work wages will not be won by phrases which too often serve as a substitute for experience and knowledge, but by trench warfare carried on by men and women who have learned every inch of the ground over which they must fight.[28]

It is not easy to improve neighborhoods or to help people who are hurting greatly. Perhaps local people are suspicious of outsiders trying to organize them.[29] Perhaps they do not wish to confront local offenders, some of whom are friends or relatives.[30] We must also consider a darker reason for why neighborhood cohesion might be difficult to cultivate: Residents of a tough neighborhood might be afraid of their own neighbors.[31]

Intimidation

Intimidation is a problem in high-crime areas in the United States,[32] Ireland,[33] and Britain.[34] For example, the British study reports that residents of very risky neighborhoods avoided walking to the shops or using public transport at certain times of the day because of intimidation by others. [D]espite promises of anonymity, one older woman refused to sign the research consent form for fear that any complaints she had made about the state of her house would be traced back to her by the council, which she thought might then evict her. Other older adults suggested that it was pointless phoning the police because, first, they were powerless to do anything, and second, the perpetrators would find out who had "grassed" on them and would seek revenge, compromising physical safety and psychological well-being. Among younger people there was also a reluctance to act to prevent crime for fear of the consequences.[35]

Intimidation of local people can be summed up in two categories:

- *Case-specific intimidation*, when a defendant in a specific case threatens the person who called police or who plans to testify in court,[36] and

- *Community-wide intimidation*, when offenders control the neighborhood, creating general fear that discourages cooperation with authorities.[37]

Intimidators might confront witnesses verbally, use nasty looks or gestures, send rude notes, make nuisance phone calls, loiter near their homes, damage their property, threaten them or their children or other family members, or directly attack them.[38] Neighborhood dominance by offenders has a chilling impact on crime reporting and neighborhood cooperation. We noted earlier the violence of drug dealing[39] and the violent retaliation found in a tough neighborhood.[40] Similar intimidation can apply to citizens who cooperate with authorities or who confront offenders directly.[41] As one researcher explained, "[t]o expect a crime-ridden neighborhood to organize to increase security is to ask its residents to confront a fear that is often extremely well-founded."[42]

This conclusion is echoed and amplified by Professor ***Wesley Skogan***, based on extensive community action research.

[M]odern studies of high-crime neighborhoods find that crime and fear undermine support for law enforcement, stimulate withdrawal from community life, and at best favor individualistic, self-protective actions. In the face of decades of serious, life-threatening crime problems, residents are more typically distrustful of one another and have a negative view of their community and its potential.[43]

Ongoing intimidation has serious consequences within a neighborhood. It forces police to lose incentives to act. It causes prosecutors to drop cases or to lose cases with plenty of witnesses. It undermines confidence in law enforcement. It reveals to local people that the offenders are in charge. It allows offenders to escalate and consolidate their hold on a neighborhood.[44]

About any neighborhood, ask this simple question: Who has the **upper hand**? If victims have the upper hand in a neighborhood, they can turn offenders in to police, or at least force them to be covert. If offenders have the upper hand, they can intimidate the larger neighborhood, even committing overt crimes. In most tough neighborhoods, offender dominance is most evident after dark,[45] although offenders might even be able to scare people in daylight.[46] In tough neighborhoods, neighbors see other neighbors as enemies, not as allies. That prevents neighborhood cohesion from developing. According to Professor Skogan, crime is a corrosive force that undermines neighborhood trust.[47] Once trust has been undermined, social order is seriously impaired.[48]

Fear is not the only process interfering with neighborhood cohesion. Nor is full public disorder the only way that people become aware of the foibles of their neighbors. Professor Rodney Stark concluded from his research that high-density, low-income areas face extra cohesion problems.

> Survey data suggest that upper-income couples may be about as likely as lower-income couples to have physical fights. Whether that is true, it surely is the case that upper-income couples are much less likely to be *overheard* by the neighbors when they have such a fight. In dense neighborhoods, where people live in crowded, thin-walled apartments, the neighbors do hear. In these areas teenage peers, for example, will be much more likely to know embarrassing things about one another's parents. This will color their perceptions about what is normal, and their respect for the conventional moral standards will be reduced. Put another way, people in dense neighborhoods will serve as inferior role models for one another—the same people would *appear* to be more respectable in less dense neighborhoods.[49]

That does not mean that everybody in the neighborhood distrusts everybody else.

Selective Trust

Although distrust is endemic within a tough neighborhood, that does not apply to all of its human relationships. Not only can people trust those within their own homes, but they also can form mutually supportive and trusting alliances with *selected* neighbors, even if they do not trust others. They try to assist those they trust to minimize harassment and victimization. They create a ***network of reciprocity***.[50] They visit each other, chat, lend things, give rides, and monitor homes for one another. These informal ties are very important for survival. Yet people remain suspicious of *other* neighbors as well as strangers who enter. They do not trust enough people to foster formal neighborhood clubs or to produce neighborhood cohesion. Many neighbors would *like* to be "good citizens," but are too afraid to carry out that wish. Intimidation and ***selective trust*** help explain why "building cohesion" is not a very practical process where it is needed most. Later we shall offer some more optimistic ideas to counter the negative points made so far. First, we need to point out that, even in neighborhoods whose cohesion is strong, crime is not always easy to control.

Inability to Watch the Street

While people in tough neighborhoods worry most after dark, the rest of society bears its greatest crime risk during daylight. Most burglary and residential thefts occur from 10:00 am to 2:00 pm on weekdays, the very hours when much of the local population is at work or school. Even those present in the neighborhood might not be able to see what is happening on the street where they live. This is especially true when streets are wide, when traffic is speedy, and when taller buildings make street supervision difficult. A long tradition of urban research tells us to pay close attention to street design and its influence on social interaction. In Part 6 we will give detailed attention to well-designed and safe streets. Here, we talk about one aspect of safe streets.

The ***guardianship in action experiment*** carried out in the Netherlands and replicated in Massachusetts demonstrated the central importance of street monitoring.[51] Researchers went to residential addresses, nosily looking around in a provocative fashion. The goal was to learn whether residents noticed their presence and responded to it. The project checked whether local people really supervise their street. At each address, the observer noted the answers to four questions, depicted in Figure 5d: Did I see anybody? Did they see me? Did they say anything (or ask what I was doing there)? Did they call the police? These four questions predicted local crime rates in that exact order. Seeing a resident was the best predictor of local security; being seen by a local resident was the second-best predictor. Being challenged was the third-best predictor. Calling police had the weakest correlation with local crime rates. *Inadequate street monitoring* is a major problem in modern society. No matter what their levels of neighborhood cohesion and commitment, many modern people are unable or unlikely to supervise their streets very closely. However, some metropolitan places make street supervision easier.

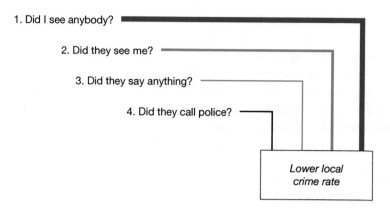

1. Did I see anybody?

2. Did they see me?

3. Did they say anything?

4. Did they call police?

Lower local
crime rate

FIGURE 5D

The Guardianship in Action Experiment

Source: Adapted from D. M. Reynald (2009). Guardianship in action: Developing a new tool for measurement. *Crime Prevention & Community Safety, 11*(1), 1–20.

Urban Villages

Cities have over time invented a solution to their security problem: the **urban village**.[52] An urban village is an enclave within a city that has

- a strong local identity;

- stable residence;

- people who know or recognize one another;

- narrow local streets;

- low-rise homes; and

- clear sight lines between homes.[53]

Urban villages are **low-income-low-crime neighborhoods**. Japanese cities offer us a good example. Tokyo is a sprawling growth of low-rise urban villages that are impairing crime.[54] Although urban villages are generally safer than the rest of the city,[55] throughout the urban world, they have been bulldozed to make room for malls or massive housing developments.[56] This has happened not only in the United States but in other countries, including modern cities in China.[57] Japan too has its movement towards anonymous high-rise living.[58] Newer forms of housing often impair the ability to see what's going on and to interact with neighbors. (Part 6 will return to this point, relating it to the safety of women.)

Mobile home communities remind us of an urban village. These neighborhoods are pejoratively called "trailer parks," and their advantages are not widely appreciated by outsiders. From a strictly socioeconomic viewpoint, the lower income and education levels of their residents create an expectancy of high crime rates. Yet statistical evidence tells us the opposite. Mobile home communities have *lower* crime rates than other low-income neighborhoods.[59] Their lower crime rates could be attributed to

- an orderly layout, with visibility from one mobile home to another; and

- locations rather distant from commercial areas that provide crime targets.[60]

We need more research on the variations among American mobile home communities, but their overall low crime rates are evident.[61] Some European mobile home parks include some residents associated with organized crime activities,[62] but we know of no research establishing that these mobile home parks have high local crime rates.

Building cohesion in high-crime neighborhoods is a great idea for reducing overall crime rates. Theoretically, all neighborhoods in the metropolis might become more cohesive and hence more secure. Unfortunately, cohesiveness is impaired by intimidation. To understand the process, Unit 5.3 examines the process of social exclusion, which then leads to a concentration of problems.

FLASHCARD LIST FOR UNIT 5.2

- Addams, Jane
- Bandura, Albert
- Between-household influences
- Chicago Area Project
- Civic cooperation
- Collective efficacy
- Community organizers
- Coverage inequality
- Evaluation research
- General good
- Guardianship in action experiment

- Hull-House (Chicago)
- Intimidation, case specific, community-wide
- Low-income-low-crime neighborhoods
- Mobile home communities
- Neighborhood cohesion
- Neighborhood watch organizations
- Network of reciprocity
- Parts of a city that need it most

- Reasonable expectations
- Sampson, Robert
- Selective trust
- Skogan, Wesley
- Upper hand
- Urban village
- Within-household influences

DISCUSSION QUESTIONS

1. Why would one neighborhood have more intimidation than another?

2. Why would one neighborhood have more cohesion than another?

Notes

1   Hunter, A. (1985). Private, parochial and public social orders: The problem of crime and incivility in urban communities. In G. D. Suttles & M. N. Zald (Eds.), *The challenge of social control: Citizenship and institution building in modern society*, pp. 230–242. Norwood, NJ: Ablex Publications.

2   Bandura, A. (1982). Self-efficacy mechanism in human agency. *American Psychologist, 37*(2), 122–147; p. 143.

3   Sampson, R. J., Raudenbush, S. W., & Earls, F. (1997). Neighborhoods and violent crime: A multilevel study of collective efficacy. *Science, 277*(5328), 918–924.

4   Sampson, R. J. (2011). The community. In J. Q. Wilson & J. Petersilia (Eds.), *Crime and public policy*, pp. 210–236. New York: Oxford University Press.

5   Davis, A. F. (1984). *Spearheads for reform: The social settlements and the progressive movement, 1890–1914.* Piscataway, NJ: Rutgers University Press. Crocker, R. (1992). *Social work and social order: The settlement movement in two industrial cities, 1889–1930.* Urbana, IL: University of Illinois Press. Sklar, K. K. (1985). Hull House in the 1890s: A community of women reformers. *Signs, 10*(4), 658–677.

6   The *CAP* still exists, and it is now a network of 40 organizations and projects promoting youth development and strong neighborhoods. See the Chicago Area Project website: www.chicago areaproject.org/.

7   Akers, R. L., & Sellers, C. S. (2013). *Criminological theories: Introduction, evaluation, and application*, 6th edition. New York: Oxford University Press; p. 169.

8   Kobrin, S. (1959). The Chicago Area Project – a 25-year assessment. *Annals of the American Academy of Political and Social Science, 322*(1), 19–29.

9   Finestone, H. (1976). *Victims of change: Juvenile delinquents in American society.* Westport, CT: Greenwood Press.

10 Schlossman, S., & Sedlak, M. (1983). The Chicago Area Project revisited. *Crime & Delinquency, 29*(3), 398–462.

11 Skogan, W. G., & Maxfield, M. G. (1981). *Coping with crime.* Thousand Oaks, CA: Sage.

12 Skogan, W. G. (2012). Collective action, structural disadvantage, and crime, *Journal of Police Studies, 25*(4), 135–152.

13 Lewis, D. A., Grant, J. A., & Rosenbaum, D. P. (1988). *The social construction of reform: Community organizations and crime prevention.* New Brunswick, NJ: Transaction.

14 Skogan, W. G. (1990). *Disorder and decline: Crime and the spiral of decay in American neighborhoods.* New York: Free Press; p. 17.

15 Rosenbaum, D. P., Lewis, D. A., & Grant, J. (1985). *The impact of community crime prevention programs in Chicago: Can neighborhood organizations make a difference?* Evanston, IL: Northwestern University Center for Urban Affairs and Policy Research.

16   Rosenbaum, D. P. (1987). The theory and research behind neighborhood watch: Is it a sound fear and crime reduction strategy? *Crime and Delinquency*, *33*(1), 103–134.

17   Barton, M. S., Weil, F., Jackson, M., & Hickey, D. A. (2016). An investigation of the influence of the spatial distribution of neighborhood violent crime on fear of crime. *Crime & Delinquency*, published online October 5. https://doi.org/10.1177/0011128716671874.

18   Cheadle, A., Wagner, E., Walls, M., Diehr, P., Bell, M., . . . & Neckerman, H. (2001). The effect of neighborhood-based community organizing: Results from the Seattle Minority Youth Health Project. *Health Services Research*, *36*(4), 671–689.

19   Zakocs, R. C., & Edwards, E. M. (2006). What explains community coalition effectiveness? A review of the literature. *American Journal of Preventive Medicine*, *30*(4), 351–361.

20   Gwatkin, D. R. (2003). How well do health programmes reach the poor? *The Lancet*, *361*(9357), 540–541.

21   Morton, M., & Montgomery, P. (2011). Youth empowerment programs for improving self-efficacy and self-esteem of adolescents. *Campbell Systematic Reviews*, *7*(5).

22   Anderson-Butcher, D. (2005). Recruitment and retention in youth development programming. *Prevention Researcher*, *12*(2), 3–6; p. 3.

23   Rosenbaum, The theory and research behind neighborhood watch.

24   Skogan, W. G. (1988). Community organizations and crime. *Crime and Justice*, *10*(1) 39–78; p. 48.

25   Skogan, Community organizations and crime; pp. 48–49.

26   Eysenbach, G. (2005). The law of attrition. *Journal of Medical Internet Research*, *7*(1), e11. doi:10.2196/jmir.7.1.e11.

27   Weisman, S. A., & Gottfredson, D. C. (2001). Attrition from after school programs: Characteristics of students who drop out. *Prevention Science*, *2*(3), 201–205.

28   Flexner, A. (2001 [1915]). Is social work a profession? *Research on Social Work Practice*, *11*(2), 152–165; p. 164.

29   Dhooper, S. S., & Moore, S. E. (2000). *Social work practice with culturally diverse people*. Thousand Oaks, CA: Sage. Rusch, L. (2010). Rethinking bridging: Risk and trust in multiracial community organizing. *Urban Affairs Review*, *45*(4), 483–506.

30   Horowitz, R. (1987). Community tolerance of gang violence. *Social Problems*, *34*(5), 437–450.

31   Rosenfeld, R., Jacobs, B. A., & Wright, R. (2003). Snitching and the code of the street. *British Journal of Criminology*, *43*(2), 291–309.

32   Jean, P. K. S. (2008). *Pockets of crime: Broken windows, collective efficacy, and the criminal point of view.* Chicago: University of Chicago Press.

33   Fitzgerald, J. (2007). *Addressing issues of social exclusion in Moyross and other disadvantaged areas of Limerick City.* Report to the Cabinet Committee on Social Inclusion. Limerick, Ireland: Limerick City Council.

34   Parry, J., Mathers, J. Laburn-Peart, C., Orford, J., & Dalton, S. (2007). Improving health in deprived communities: What can residents teach us? *Critical Public Health*, *17*(2), 123–136.

35   Parry et al., Improving health in deprived communities; p. 131.

36   Whitman, J. L., & Davis, R. C. (2007). *Snitches get stitches: Youth, gangs, and witness intimidation in Massachusetts.* Washington, DC: National Center for Victims of Crime.

37 Healey, K. (1995). *Victim and witness intimidation: New developments and emerging responses.* Research in Action Series. Washington, DC: U.S. National Institute of Justice.

38 Dedel, K. (2006). *Witness intimidation.* Problem-Oriented Guides for Police, Problem-Specific Guides Series, No. 42. Washington, DC: Center for Problem-Oriented Policing.

39 Topalli, V., Wright, R., & Fornango, R. (2002). Drug dealers, robbery and retaliation: Vulnerability, deterrence and the contagion of violence. *The British Journal of Criminology, 42*(2), 337–351.

40 Jacobs, B. A. (2004). A typology of street criminal retaliation. *Journal of Research in Crime and Delinquency, 41*(3), 295–323.

41 Jacobs, B. A., & Wright, R. (2006). *Street justice: Retaliation in the criminal underworld.* Cambridge, U.K.: Cambridge University Press.

42 Herbert, S. (2009). *Citizens, cops, and power: Recognizing the limits of community.* Chicago: University of Chicago Press; p. 55.

43 Skogan, Community organizations and crime; p. 44.

44 Chen, E. Y. (2009). Victim and witness intimidation. In H. T. Greene & S. L. Gabbidon (Eds.), *Encyclopedia of race and crime,* pp. 837–840. Thousand Oaks, CA: Sage.

45 Dedel, K. (2007). *Drive-by shootings.* Problem-Oriented Guides for Police, Problem-Specific Guides Series, No. 47. Washington, DC: Center for Problem-Oriented Policing.

46 Taylor, R. B. (1999). *Crime, grime, fear, and decline: A longitudinal look.* Washington, DC: National Institute of Justice.

47 Skogan, W. G. (1989). Communities, crime, and neighborhood organization. *Crime and Delinquency, 35*(3), 437–457.

48 Lewis, J. D., & Weigert, A. (1985). Trust as a social reality. *Social Forces, 63*(4), 967–985.

49 Stark, R. (1987). Deviant places: A theory of the ecology of crime. *Criminology, 25*(4), 893–910; p. 896.

50 Ross, C. E., & Jang, S. J. (2000). Neighborhood disorder, fear, and mistrust: The buffering role of social ties with neighbors. *American Journal of Community Psychology, 28*(4), 401–420.

51 Reynald, D. M. (2010). Guardians on guardianship: Factors affecting the willingness to supervise, the ability to detect potential offenders, and the willingness to intervene. *Journal of Research in Crime and Delinquency, 47*(3), 358–390. Hollis-Peel, M. E., Reynald, D. M., & Welsh, B. C. (2012). Guardianship and crime: An international comparative study of guardianship in action. *Crime, Law and Social Change, 58*(1), 1–14.

52 Gans, H. J. (1982). *Urban villagers.* New York: Simon and Schuster.

53 Bell, D., & Jayne, M. (2004). *City of quarters: Urban villages in the contemporary city.* Farnham, U.K.: Ashgate.

54 Bestor, T. C. (1989). *Neighborhood Tokyo.* Stanford, CA: Stanford University Press.

55 Colquhoun, I. (2004). Design out crime: Creating safe and sustainable communities. *Crime Prevention & Community Safety, 6*(4), 57–70.

56 Teaford, J. C. (2000). Urban renewal and its aftermath. *Housing Policy Debate, 11*(2), 443–465.

57 Wu, F., Zhang, F., & Webster, C. (2013). Informality and the development and demolition of urban villages in the Chinese peri-urban area. *Urban Studies, 50*(10), 1919–1934.

58 Le Blanc, R. M. (2016). What high-rise living means for Tokyo civic life: Changing residential architecture and the specter of rising privacy. *The Journal of Japanese Studies, 42*(2), 315–341.

59 Barthe, E. P., Leone, M. C., & Stitt, B. G. (2014). Trailer parks as hotbeds of crime: Fact or fiction? *Issues in Social Science*, *2*(2). https://doi.org/10.5296/iss.v2i2.6402.

60 McCarty, W. P. (2010). Trailers and trouble? An examination of crime in mobile home communities. *Cityscape*, *12*(2), 127–144.

61 McCarty, W. P., & Hepworth, D. P. (2013). Mobile home parks and crime: Does proximity matter? *Journal of Crime and Justice*, *36*(3), 319–333.

62 Kleemans, E. R., Soudijn, M. R., & Weenink, A. W. (2012). Organized crime, situational crime prevention and routine activity theory. *Trends in Organized Crime*, *15*(2–3), 87–92.

Unit 5.3 Exclusion

"Everybody wins" is an optimistic phrase. In criminology, it implies that crime can be reduced in each neighborhood without pushing problems to other neighborhoods. A considerable body of research shows that situational crime prevention (discussed in Unit 2.3) can reduce crime without such displacement.[1]

We are far less optimistic that neighborhood organization will reduce crime without displacing it to other neighborhoods. Unfortunately, neighborhoods that mobilize against crime act mainly in their own local interests with little regard for the larger community or society. Often, their focus is to push unwanted people and activities away from their own neighborhoods. Crime control then becomes a struggle among neighborhoods to exclude what they do not want in their midst. Social scientists call this a *zero-sum situation* since for every winner, there has to be a loser. Neighborhoods with the least money and power often end up with risky situations and overt crime without a path to improvement. This unit reviews various forms of neighborhood exclusion, beginning with the housing market.

Exclusionary efforts fit within a larger category: ***conflict theories*** of crime. These theories consider how crime and crime control efforts reflect conflicts among interest groups, cultural groups, and neighborhood groups. Conflict theory began with very large-scale ideas, articulated by Karl Marx, linking class conflicts to the history of law and the evolution of crime.[2] However, our focus is more modest—we consider how neighborhoods exclude unwanted people and activities, and how a zero-sum situation emerges. Conflicts between and within neighborhoods often have cultural origins,[3] also reflecting economic differences, especially in the ability to pay for housing.

Exclusion and the Housing Market

Suppose you are a metropolitan parent trying to find a place to live and raise your family. If you can afford it, you will probably seek a pleasant street with minimal traffic, good schools, and convenient shopping. You will probably not want to live next to a regional mall, the town dump, abandoned buildings, railroad yards, barrooms, or public housing.[4] You will probably try to find a stable neighborhood with more homeowners and fewer short-term renters.[5] You might check real estate websites for crime rates in that area. As you look for housing, you might also be influenced by social and ethnic prejudices. You then spend your money to buy or rent the best place you can afford and to maximize your security to the best of your ability and knowledge.

A home often costs four or five times one's annual income, so most people need to borrow money to buy one. That's why access to credit is important for escaping the riskiest neighborhoods.[6] Without such access, residents can neither stabilize their own neighborhood nor easily escape a dangerous neighborhood to buy a home elsewhere. **Mortgage access** depends on current interest rates and personal credit positions.[7] Even when interest rates are low, many people do not qualify for a home loan. Lending institutions are reluctant to provide mortgages to people who have accumulated no wealth,[8] who lack education,[9] or who have insecure jobs.[10] Will you be able to buy a home at all? Will your home be located away from overt crime and public disorder? Will you be subject to racial, religious, or ethnic prejudice and exclusion?

Box 5a details many of the methods used in American history to exclude home sales to outside groups. These techniques helped preserve white Protestant areas of cities by preventing black and Catholic entry into the local housing market. This was accomplished by interfering with free markets; for example, by preventing a white homeowner from selling a house to a black person or to an Irish or Italian immigrant—even those having sufficient funds. The courts eventually banned these methods as violating property rights. However, minority groups remained unwelcome in white neighborhoods and white schools for additional decades.

Exclusionary methods explained in Box 5a include local **segregation** laws, **restrictive covenants** in housing contracts, intimidation and other **extra-legal methods**, **red-lining** (banning home loans to certain neighborhoods), and school segregation. Perhaps the most overt method was the "**sun-down town**," which posted signs such as "No Negroes After Dark," using local police to arrest anybody who violated the exclusion. After these devices ended, localities developed another set of exclusionary methods, still with us and still making it difficult for the younger generation to buy a house.

Exclusionary Zoning

In today's world, neighborhood exclusion is often accomplished *indirectly* using **exclusionary zoning** and land-use planning. Because race is not explicitly mentioned, land-use regulations generally pass judicial tests; that is, courts consider these regulations

Box 5A Blocking Free Markets for Exclusionary Purposes, Historical Methods

Local segregation laws: On September 22, 1862, President Abraham Lincoln issued the Emancipation Proclamation. When the civil war finally ended, the freed slaves became penniless farmers and sharecroppers, and they had low crime rates. Over the next 75 years, many migrated north to take factory jobs, and their urban experience led to a crime experience. Increasingly they could afford housing in white areas, but were strongly resisted. Cities began to enact local laws explicitly designating some sections of a city "for whites only." From 1910 to 1917, many banned property sales across racial lines. In 1917, a unanimous decision by the United States Supreme Court declared these overt segregation laws unconstitutional, based on the 14th Amendment (Buchanan vs. Warley).

Restrictive, covenants: Local homeowner associations began to attach restrictive covenants to housing contracts. These covenants specifically prohibited the homeowner from selling to any member of the specific minority groups listed. Across the United States, thousands of housing associations inserted clauses into housing contracts to exclude nonwhites, Jewish Americans, Italian Americans, Irish Americans, Mexican Americans, and Chinese Americans. By 1940, some 80 percent of property in Chicago and Los Angeles carried restrictive covenants. In 1926 the Supreme Court deemed these exclusions to be legal. That stood until 1948, when the Court finally banned the widespread practice.

Extra-legal methods: After restrictive covenants were struck down by the courts, extra-legal methods were used for exclusionary purposes. Homeowner associations pressured whites not to rent or sell to minority group members. Cities closed off specific streets where black people lived. Local blacks were picketed and chased out of the neighborhood. White businesses who served black people were boycotted. Real estate licenses were revoked for agents selling to minority home buyers. These efforts helped extend ethnic segregation for several more decades.

Sun-down towns: Communities used their own police departments to reinforce racial divisions. The rules were not written into law books, but rather on signs posted at the edge of town, such as "No Mexicans After Dark;" or "No Negroes Permitted After 6 PM" Some municipalities excluded entry by Chinese, Hispanic and Jewish minorities, too. These were called "sun-down towns" because police automatically arrested any minority person seen after a certain hour. The term "exclusive area" meant what it said.

Red-lining: In 1934, the National Housing Act allowed banks to "red-line" parts of cities as unsafe zones for mortgage bankers to make loans. Black segments of a city were red-lined, so people living there could not obtain home loans even if they otherwise qualified. Federal legislation in 1968 and 1977 ended red-lining, but informal practices continued. Apartment rental agents lied about availability. Others were simply intimidated if they entered white areas.

Public school segregation: Southern schools were racially segregated by law until the 1954 Supreme Court decision (*Brown v. the Board of Education*). Northern schools were often segregated by administrative design. In addition, school segregation was applied to Mexican Americans, Chinese Americans, as well as Japanese and Native (Indian) Americans. The strong links between school and residential segregation have been documented, and help us understand the long-run difficulty in breaking the vicious cycle of crime and poverty.

A bibliography for this box is offered at the end of Unit 5.3.

legal.[11] Many local regulations are sincere and justifiable, such as mandating safe electrical work to prevent home fires; ensuring proper natural gas installations that will not blow up; and keeping toxic factories away from homes and schools.

However, many other land-use regulations serve mainly to exclude people.[12] A municipality can

- ban multifamily dwellings or confine these to limited areas;

- require that each house be placed on a large lot (that only wealthier people can afford); and

- keep nightlife, malls, warehouses, or other unwanted land uses on the other side of town.[13]

These restrictions result from politicking local government agencies, including zoning boards.[14] Exceptions to these restrictions are made for those with a good attorney[15] and political connections. People lacking education, income, power, or political skill are at considerable disadvantage in these political struggles. Zoning and other land-use decisions create a zero-sum situation, benefitting one neighborhood or one stakeholder at the expense of another.[16]

Exclusionary zoning reduces the supply of low- and moderate-income housing and drives up the price of housing.[17] Communities that aggressively apply exclusionary regulations can push housing prices to as much as 50 percent higher than for comparable communities.[18] Owners of existing homes can keep their property values artificially high, while renters cannot easily buy their own home.[19] Some American towns have zero-growth policies, to the detriment of minority populations and young white adults wishing to buy a home. Ironically, many young whites and nonwhites today face the same limitations. These impediments leave many people unable to afford homes except in or near overt crime areas.

Gates and Roadblocks

Short-term exclusion also occurs. A gated neighborhood seeks to exclude most outsiders from visiting, even for short periods of time. Such exclusion has raised considerable contemporary controversy,[20] but was widespread in Victorian London (the latter part of the 19th century), as reflected in the following directive from a local estate board:

> Notice is hereby given that there is no public thoroughfare through this estate. That no cattle are allowed to be driven through this estate. . . . That no tramps,

vagrants, organ grinders, bands of musicians, or disreputable characters are permitted on the estate. That no railway vans, coal wagons, beer trucks or carts, furniture vans, dung carts, or other heavy traffic, are allowed to pass through the gates of this estate, unless they have to deliver or take up goods on the estate. That no hackney coaches [horse taxis] are allowed on the estate, except going to or returning from the residence of any inhabitant, either to take up or set down.[21]

These 19th-century London residents sought to protect their families from annoyances and danger. Yet they met opposition. After large segments of London were blocked off from traffic, the rest of the city's residents became irritated about having to get around so many gates and through so many choke points. They pressured government to remove these interferences with their daily lives. They objected not only to the inconvenience but also to the insult of being excluded.[22]

Excluding Transients and Homeless People

After the Napoleonic wars ended in 1815, discharged military personnel generally could not find work and swelled the ranks of the urban poor. Many were penniless, living in the streets of London and other major cities. They were supplemented by destitute immigrants from Ireland and Scotland. In response, the British Parliament enacted the **Vagrancy Act** of 1824, which made it illegal to sleep in public or beg for money. The Great Potato Famine in Ireland from 1845 to 1852 augmented the street population of British cities with yet more penniless immigrants. You can imagine the strong impulse to exclude homeless strangers.

Prior to the 11th century, some nomadic tribes from north of India were cut off from returning to their native zone.[23] These tribes are known as **Roma** (also called Gypsies), many of whom remain itinerant to this day,[24] moving around Europe in search of work.[25] They have been subjected to racial stereotypes including a reputation as criminals.[26] Roma people were persecuted and several hundred thousand were exterminated by the Nazis.[27]

The American **homeless population** is not usually Roma. It is a diverse population including illegal immigrants and long-term unemployed persons mixed in with people plagued by chronic alcoholism, mental health, and drug dependency.[28] The closing of mental health facilities during the 1970s augmented the homeless population,[29] with a revolving door between local jails and local streets.[30] Hispanics are underrepresented among the homeless, perhaps reflecting strong family structures that assist those who are penniless. Homeless *individuals* are more white than black, while homeless *families* are more black than white.[31] Since unattached males tend to get into more trouble, homeless whites appear to be more involved in crime than homeless blacks.

Resistance to the homeless is a powerful force. Local governments have enacted ordinances to outlaw vagrancy, panhandling, public camping, and loitering—all directed at homeless people. Many homeless persons are white adolescent runaways,[32] lacking income, parental support, and eligibility for public welfare. Their food sources are precarious,[33] so homeless youths are quite likely to steal food or money to buy food, or to trade sex for food or temporary shelter.[34] Even though many homeless youths had committed crimes before running away, they commit *extra* crimes after becoming homeless.[35] Moreover, **street youths** provide excellent targets for crime victimization, including rape, theft, and assault.[36] Street youths receive an inordinate amount of regular attention from police, largely due to their appearance and the public places they occupy.[37] Homeless people of various ages living in downtown streets are likely to steal coins from cars, meters, and pay boxes in urban parking areas[38] or to engage in other minor thefts. Localities have some reasons to be suspicious of homeless people, who are one source of extra crime. However, their exclusion often prolongs the risky situation for the larger community. The focus on homeless outsiders also ignores homegrown crime problems and other risky situations which are often more serious.

Exclusion operates through many indirect and direct mechanisms, including housing market processes; restrictive covenants; zoning and land-use planning; aggressive barriers; and intimidation of outsiders. Exclusion is often directed at ethnic minority groups,[39] but can also apply to other social groups. Exclusion can be accidental or intentional. In any case, it gives many people no other choice but to live in an overt crime area. Exclusionary processes also create conflicts among neighborhoods.

Nimbyism

The term Nimby means "not in my backyard." **Nimbyism** is the effort by local people to exclude unwanted land uses or persons from their own neighborhood. Nimbyism is a very powerful force in the United States, but also in the United Kingdom,[40] Australia,[41] and Canada,[42] often generated by fear of crime.[43] Neighborhoods especially resist proposed land uses near where they live. Here are some examples:

"I like to go to bars, but I don't want bars in my own neighborhood."

"I shop at the mall, but don't want to live next to it."

"I believe in building prisons, but not near my family."

"I believe in wind energy but the wind turbine should not be seen from my home."

"A drug rehabilitation center might be a good thing, but not on our block."

"I believe in public housing, but not right here."

Many of these controversies are tinged with a fear of crime near home. For example, single-family dwellers might organize to resist the construction of a new apartment building in their vicinity.[44]

Nimbyism generates power struggles involving local businesses and residents, outside corporations, bureaucracies—all with different local interests. These **Nimby wars** can emerge for each land-use decision, such as the expansion of a hospital, introduction of a barroom, or construction of a public facility. A high-income area might push a problem to another high-income area or else take action to move the issue to a low-income neighborhood. A moderately low-income neighborhood might resist new public housing or unwanted barrooms or liquor stores. Support for zoning restrictions is found across races, and the **slow-growth movement** "transcends party lines and traditional differences between conservatives and liberals, with conservative Republicans willing to support liberal Democrats for city council posts, so long as they are willing to say no to developers."[45]

A neighborhood is most likely to *win* its Nimby wars if residents have extra political power, money, organizational skills, experience, and long-term commitment to the area. A neighborhood is most likely to *fail* in protecting its interests when residents are uneducated or lack political experience and are unable to develop sufficient cohesion to influence city hall.

Ethnic Heterogeneity Impairing Neighborhood Action

Many people successfully assimilate into the larger society and move into the middle class. More **homogeneous** middle-class neighborhoods contain assimilated people with a common culture. These areas are often able to cooperate to protect local political interests and to provide local assistance in case a crime occurs.

In contrast, unassimilated groups often remain poor and are stuck living in a neighborhood that concentrates disadvantaged people. We call these neighborhoods **heterogeneous** because they assemble people who lack cultural affinity with neighbors. They feel greater social distance not only from larger society, but even from the people next door. Feeling little affinity with their neighbors, they might not lend assistance if they see a crime in progress. Lacking a common sense of the neighborhood, they cannot easily politick for additional police protection or assistance from city hall to protect the street against crime.

Indeed, ethnic heterogeneity is a standard explanation for high crime levels in low-income areas, going back to Chicago School sociology. In 1938, **Louis Wirth** wrote a famous essay entitled "Urbanism as a way of life." He explained why diverse urban neighborhoods tend to undermine traditions and a feeling of common community:

> The bonds of kinship, of neighborliness, and the sentiments arising out of living together for generations under a common folk tradition are likely to be absent or, at best, relatively weak in an aggregate [with] such diverse origins and backgrounds.[46]

Even when people "look alike" to outsiders, they might in fact have very diverse cultures and origins. Thus, a Hispanic American neighborhood might include people from several different nations in Latin America, speaking different versions of Spanish, arriving in different migration waves, cooking different foods, and lacking the ability to cooperate to supervise the local area.[47] Similarly, not all black neighborhoods are homogeneous. A black neighborhood can easily contain vast heterogeneity. Black Americans differ considerably in skin tone,[48] cultural heritage, language, duration of residence, and more. A neighborhood can combine *culturally diverse* dark-skinned people from Haiti, immigrants from various Caribbean nations, Puerto Rican Americans, along with darker-skinned Hispanic Americans. Census studies indicate that from one-fourth to half of the black population in some American cities comes from the Caribbean.[49] Suburbanites might easily underestimate the diversity within a central city neighborhood and why that diversity impairs political cooperation to gain help from city hall.

This negative form of cohesiveness includes Nimbyism—working with your immediate neighbors against the interests of the larger community. Nimbyism shows us that community action can reflect selfish interests, impairing cooperation and coalition-building.[50] The literature reviewed in the current section tells us that many neighborhoods tend to exclude people and often succeed in doing so. That leaves a good share of the population concentrated in limited metropolitan space.

FLASHCARD LIST FOR UNIT 5.3

- Conflict theories
- Exclusionary zoning
- Extra-legal methods
- Heterogeneous
- Homeless population
- Homogeneous
- Mortgage access
- Nimby wars
- Nimbyism
- Red-lining
- Restrictive covenants
- Roma
- Segregation
- Slow-growth movement
- Street youths
- Sun-down town
- Vagrancy Act
- Wirth, Lewis
- Zero-sum situation

DISCUSSION QUESTIONS

1.   How does social exclusion enhance overt crime?

2.   Do you think more cohesive neighborhoods have more Nimbyism, less, or the same amount?

References for Box 5a

An historical sun-down town database is available at http://sundown.afro.illinois.edu/sundowntowns.php, allowing you to check whether your city was included.

Clotfelter, C. T. (2011). *After "Brown": The rise and retreat of school desegregation.* Princeton, NJ: Princeton University Press.

Donato, R. (1997). *The other struggle for equal schools: Mexican Americans during the civil rights era.* Stony Brook, NY: SUNY Press.

Epstein, R. A. (1998). Lest we forget: Buchanan v. Warley and constitutional jurisprudence of the progressive era. *Vanderbilt Law Review, 51*(4), 787–796.

Farley, R., & Frey, W. H. (1994). Changes in the segregation of whites from blacks during the 1980s: Small steps toward a more integrated society. *American Sociological Review, 59* (February), 23–45.

Gotham, K. F. (2000). Racialization and the state: The Housing Act of 1934 and the creation of the Federal Housing Administration. *Sociological Perspectives, 43*(2), 291–317.

Gotham, K. F. (2000). Urban space, restrictive covenants and the origins of racial residential segregation in a U.S. city, 1900–50. *International Journal of Urban and Regional Research, 24*(3), 616–633.

Hillier, A. E. (2003). Redlining and the home owners' loan corporation. *Journal of Urban History, 29*(4), 394–420.

Kluger, R. (2011). *Simple justice: The history of Brown v. Board of Education and Black America's struggle for equality.* New York: Vintage.

Kuo, J. (1998). Excluded, segregated and forgotten: A historical view of the discrimination of Chinese Americans in public schools. *Asian Law Journal, 5,* 181–212.

Loewen, J. W. (2009). Sundown towns and counties: Racial exclusion in the South. *Southern Cultures, 15*(1), 22–47.

Massey, D. S. (2007). *Categorically unequal: The American stratification system.* New York: Russell Sage Foundation.

Montoya, M. E. (2000). A brief history of Chicana/o school segregation: One rationale for affirmative action. *Berkeley La Raza Law Journal, 12*(2), 159–172.

Rice, R. L. (1968). Residential segregation by law, 1910–1917. *The Journal of Southern History, 34*(2), 179–199.

Silva, C. (2009). *Racial restrictive covenants: Enforcing neighborhood segregation in Seattle.* Seattle Civil Rights and Labor History Project, University of Washington.

Stabile, D. (2000). *Community associations: The emergence and acceptance of a quiet innovation in housing.* Westport, CT: Greenwood.

Vose, C. E. (1959). *Caucasians only: The Supreme Court, the NAACP, and the restrictive covenant cases.* Berkeley, CA: University of California Press.

Yinger, J. (1995). *Closed doors, opportunities lost: The continuing costs of housing discrimination.* New York: Russell Sage Foundation.

Notes

1   Guerette, R. T. (2009). *Analyzing crime displacement and diffusion.* Problem-Oriented Guides for Police, Problem-Solving Tools Series, No. 10. Washington, DC: Office of Community Oriented Policing Services. Johnson, S. D., Guerette, R. T., & Bowers, K. (2014). Crime displacement: What we know, what we don't know, and what it means for crime reduction. *Journal of Experimental Criminology, 10*(4), 549–571.

2   Lynch, M. J., & Groves, W. B. (1989). *A primer in radical criminology,* pp. 158–158. New York: Harrow and Heston.

3   Sellin, T. (1938). Culture conflict and crime. *American Journal of Sociology, 44*(1), 97–103.

4   Roncek, D. W., Bell, R., & Francik, J. M. (1981). Housing projects and crime: Testing a proximity hypothesis. *Social Problems, 29*(2), 151–166.

5   Friedrichs, J., & Blasius, J. (2009). Attitudes of owners and renters in a deprived neighbourhood. *European Journal of Housing Policy, 9*(4), 435–455.

6   For a more general account of position on the labor, commodity, and credit markets, see: Weber, Max. (1968 [1921–1922]). *Economy and society.* Ed. Guenther Roth and Claus Wittich. New York: Bedminster Press.

7   Barakova, I., Bostic, R. W., Calem, P. S., & Wachter, S. M. (2003). Does credit quality matter for home ownership? *Journal of Housing Economics, 12*(4), 318–336.

8   Shapiro, T. M. (2006). Race, homeownership and wealth. *Washington University Journal of Law and Policy, 20,* 53–74.

9   Gyourko, J., & Linneman, P. (1997). The changing influences of education, income, family structure, and race on homeownership by age over time. *Journal of Housing Research, 8*(1), 1–25.

10 Reid, C., & Laderman, E. (2009). *The untold costs of subprime lending: Examining the links among higher-priced lending, foreclosures, and race in California.* San Francisco: Federal Reserve Bank of San Francisco.

11 Lapping, M. B. (1978). Exclusionary land-use controls in Suburbia: Current judicial review. *State & Local Government Review, 10*(1), 16–19.

12 Hanushek, E., & Quigley, J. M. (1990). Commercial land use regulation and local government finance. *American Economic Review, 19*(2), 176–180.

13 Furr-Holden, C. D. M., Milam, A. J., Nesoff, E. D., Johnson, R. M., Fakunle, . . . & Thorpe, R. J. (2016). Not in my back yard: A comparative analysis of crime around publicly funded drug treatment centers, liquor stores, convenience stores, and corner stores in one mid-Atlantic city. *Journal of Studies on Alcohol and Drugs, 77*(1), 17–24.

14   Danielson, M. N. (1976). The politics of exclusionary zoning in suburbia. *Political Science Quarterly*, *91*(1), 1–18.

15   Shapiro, R. M. (1969). Zoning variance power-constructive in theory, destructive in practice, *Maryland Law Review*, *29*(1), 3–23.

16   Molotch, H. L. (1976). The city as a growth machine: Toward a political economy of place. *American Journal of Sociology*, *86*, 1387–1400.

17   Gerrar, M. B. (1993). The victims of Nimby. *Fordham Urban Law Journal*, *21*(3), 495–522.

18   Hamilton, B. W. (1978). Zoning and the exercise of monopoly power. *Journal of Urban Economics*, *5*(1), 116–130.

19   Dowall, D. E. (1979). The effect of land use and environmental regulations on housing costs. *Policy Studies Journal*, *8*(2), 277–288. Ellickson, R. C. (1977). Suburban growth controls: An economic and legal analysis. *The Yale Law Journal*, *86*(3), 385–511.

20   Luymes, D. (1997). The fortification of suburbia: Investigating the rise of enclave communities. *Landscape and Urban Planning*, *39*(2), 187–203. Atkinson, R., & Flint, J. (2004). Fortress UK? Gated communities, the spatial revolt of the elites and time–space trajectories of segregation. *Housing Studies*, *19*(6), 875–892.

21   Quoted in Atkins, P. J. (1993). How the west end was won: The struggle to remove street barriers in Victorian London. *Journal of Historical Geography*, *19*(3), 265–277; p. 265.

22   Atkins, How the west end was won.

23   Moorjani, P., Patterson, N,. Loh, P.-R., Lipson, M., Kisfali, P., . . . Melagh, B. (2013). Reconstructing Roma history from genome-wide data. *PLoS One*, *8*(3), e58633. https://doi.org/10.1371/journal.pone.0058633.

24   Brearley, M. (2001). The persecution of Gypsies in Europe. *American Behavioral Scientist*, *45*(4), 588–599.

25   Lucassen, L., Willems, W., & Cottaar, A. M. (2015). *Gypsies and other itinerant groups: A socio-historical approach*. New York: Springer.

26   Helleiner, J. (1995). Gypsies, Celts and tinkers: Colonial antecedents of anti-traveller racism in Ireland. *Ethnic and Racial Studies*, *18*(3), 532–554.

27   Lewy, G. (2000). *The Nazi persecution of the gypsies*. Oxford, U.K.: Oxford University Press.

28   Fazel, S., Khosla, V., Doll, H., & Geddes, J. (2008). The prevalence of mental disorders among the homeless in western countries: Systematic review and meta-regression analysis. *PLoS Med*, *5*(12), e225. https://doi.org/10.1371/journal.pmed.0050225.

29   Fischer, P. J., Shapiro, S., Breakey, W. R., Anthony, J. C., & Kramer, M. (1986). Mental health and social characteristics of the homeless: A survey of mission users. *American Journal of Public Health*, *76*(5), 519–524.

30   Belcher, J. R. (1988). Are jails replacing the mental health system for the homeless mentally ill? *Community Mental Health Journal*, *24*(3), 185–195.

31   Henry, M., Shivji, A., de Sousa, T., Cohen, R., Khadduri, J., & Culhane, D. P. (2015). *The 2015 annual homelessness assessment report (AHAR) to Congress, Part 1: Point-in-time estimates of homelessness*. Washington, DC: U.S. Department of Housing and Urban Development. http://works.bepress.com/dennis_culhane/134/ (retrieved May 24, 2017).

32   Mitchell, D. (1997). The annihilation of space by law: The roots and implications of anti-homeless laws in the United States. *Antipode, 29*(3), 303–335. Amster, R. (2003). Patterns of exclusion: Sanitizing space, criminalizing homelessness. *Social Justice, 30*(1: 91), 195–221.

33   Dachner, N., & Tarasuk, V. (2002). Homeless "squeegee kids": Food insecurity and daily survival. *Social Science and Medicine, 54*(7), 1039–1049.

34   Harding, R., & Hamilton, P. (2009). Working girls: Abuse or choice in street-level sex work? A study of homeless women in Nottingham. *British Journal of Social Work, 39*(6), 1118–1137. Heerde, J. A., & Hemphill, S. A. (2013). Stealing and being stolen from: Perpetration of property offenses and property victimization among homeless youth – A systematic review. *Youth & Society, 48*(2), 265–300. McCarthy, B., & Hagan, J. (1992). Mean streets: The theoretical significance of situational delinquency among homeless youths. *American Journal of Sociology, 98*(3), 597–627. Tyler, K. A., & Johnson, K. A. (2006). Trading sex: Voluntary or coerced? The experiences of homeless youth. *Journal of Sex Research, 43*(3), 208–216.

35   McCarthy, B., & Hagan, J. (1991). Homelessness: A criminogenic situation? *British Journal of Criminology, 31*(4), 393–410.

36   Whitbeck, L. B., & Simons, R. L. (1990). Life on the streets: The victimization of runaway and homeless adolescents. *Youth and Society, 22*(1), 108–125.

37   O'Grady, B., Gaetz, S., & Buccieri, K. (2011). *Can I see your ID? The policing of youth homelessness in Toronto.* Toronto: Canadian Homelessness Research Network.

38   Clarke, R. V., & Goldstein, H. (2003). *Theft from cars in center city parking facilities – A case study.* University of Wisconsin Legal Studies Research Paper No. 1339. Washington, DC: Office of Community Oriented Policing Services.

39   Tonry, M. (1997). Ethnicity, crime, and immigration. *Crime and Justice, 21*, 1–29.

40   Hubbard, P. (2005). Accommodating otherness: Anti-asylum centre protest and the maintenance of white privilege. *Transactions of the Institute of British Geographers, 30*(1), 52–65.

41   Mendes, P. (2001). Nimbyism vs social inclusion: Local communities and illicit drugs. *Youth Studies Australia, 20*(2), 17–22.

42   Centre for Urban and Community Studies, & Novac, S. (2002). *Housing discrimination in Canada: What do we know about it?* Toronto: Centre for Urban and Community Studies, University of Toronto.

43   Galster, G., Pettit, K., Santiago, A., & Tatian, P. (2002). The impact of supportive housing on neighborhood crime rates. *Journal of Urban Affairs, 24*(3), 289–315.

44   Saint, P. M., Flavell, R. J., & Fox, P. F. (2009). *NIMBY wars: The politics of land use.* Hingham, MA: Saint University Press.

45   Evans, H. (1986). "Slow growth" emerges as key issue in local politics. *Los Angeles Times*, November 2.

46   Wirth, L. (1938). Urbanism as a way of life. *American Journal of Sociology, 44*(1), 1–24; p. 11. www.uc.edu/cdc/urban_database/fall03-readings/urbanism_as_a_way.pdf (retrieved September 12, 2016).

47   Portes, A., & Truelove, C. (1987). Making sense of diversity: Recent research on Hispanic minorities in the United States. *Annual Review of Sociology, 13*, 359–385.

48   Keith, V. M., & Herring, C. (1991). Skin tone and stratification in the Black community. *American Journal of Sociology, 97*(3), 760–778.

49 Logan, J. R., & Deane, G. (2003). *Black diversity in metropolitan America.* New York: Lewis Mumford Center for Comparative Urban and Regional Research, University at Albany.

50 Kadushin, C., Lindholm, M., Ryan, D., Brodsky, A., & Saxe, L. (2005). Why it is so difficult to form effective community coalitions. *City & Community, 4*(3), 255–275.

UNIT 5.4 Concentration

People living throughout a metropolis have *some* problems. A middle-class neighborhood houses some sick people, some with mental health problems, some whose income has dropped dramatically, some disrupted households, and some youths who are difficult to manage. Throughout a metropolis, people have some positives as well. An area with more crime contains some strong families, some working adults, and some healthy children doing their homework. Not everybody is the same.

However, metropolitan processes can also concentrate a good deal of extreme poverty, family problems, poor health, unemployment, poor education, and crime *within a limited area.* This is called **concentrated disadvantage** and it derives directly from the social disorganization syndrome noted by Shaw and McKay and discussed in Unit 5.2. This idea is important because some problems tend to be worse and last longer when piled together. Problems reinforce one another, producing extra damage to the neighborhood. Concentrated problems last longer, catching the next generation in the same situation and preventing people from earning the money they need to escape.

Most of the city—even the inner city—is not characterized by concentrated disadvantage. Most ethnic minority areas do *not* concentrate multiple disadvantages. Yet any large city is likely to contain a corner that fits the description. Figure 5e suggests how two different social problems, unstable families and unstable residency, might be distributed over the metropolitan area. Unstable families are characterized by breakups and abandonment. Unstable residency means that people move in and out too quickly to settle down, disrupting schooling and undermining neighborhood security. These destabilizing forces are scattered across the metropolis. However, these problems are more concentrated in the zone of concentrated disadvantage in the lower right corner of the diagram. That area is also likely to have higher population density and a larger share of the teenage population, both of which make its concentrated problems more evident.

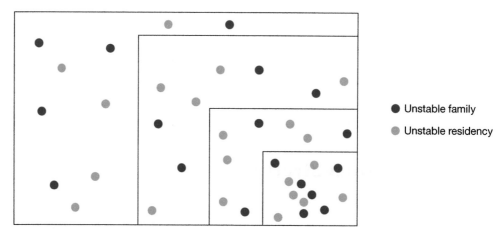

FIGURE 5E
Concentration of Unstable Family and Unstable Residency over Metropolitan Zones

It is a mistake to think that concentrated disadvantage is the only source of crime. In fact, much crime occurs in the rest of the metropolis and region—a point we have made repeatedly in this textbook. No neighborhood is immune to problems of unstable family life or unstable residency. No part of the metropolis can evade the challenges of adolescence. Yet the zone of concentrated disadvantage multiplies and intensifies problems, producing **extra crime** and putting that crime on public display. That's why society should find ways to avoid concentrating disadvantages in limited areas.

The Danish Experiment

A remarkable natural experiment emerged in Denmark when, between 1986 and 1998, thousands of refugees arrived from war zones in the Middle East, the former Yugoslavia, and other nations. Recognizing that refugee concentrations create extra youth problems, the Danish government established a special policy to *disperse* its refugee immigrants across many municipalities. Placement officers assigned families to housing without any information about educational attainment, criminal record, or family income. Officers did not meet families face to face, nor did they consider family or personal preferences at all. Refugees were simply assigned on an almost random basis, keeping social biases and economic advantages off the table. Researchers followed 4,425 immigrant youths from ages 15 through 21, checking each year for arrests and criminal convictions.[1]

- Some young males ended up in tougher neighborhoods, containing several convicted violent offenders. They got into extra trouble over the next six years, especially if members of their own ethnic group were concentrated there.

- Other young males were assigned to more suitable neighborhoods. They were unlikely to get into trouble during their adolescent years.

The negative impact of assignment to tougher neighborhoods was especially true for younger males. This **Danish experiment** illustrates how an adverse concentration can produce more crime. It also shows us that avoiding concentrated disadvantage saves society a lot of trouble overall.

The Yonkers Experiment

The **Yonkers experiment**, a quasi-experiment carried out in a city north of New York City, sought to mitigate the effects of concentrated disadvantage. A random process was used to select 147 minority families living in low-income and segregated neighborhoods.[2] Those selected then agreed to relocate to middle-class neighborhoods, where their neighborhood exposures were considerably improved. Youths who moved were interviewed two years later and compared to those remaining in the original neighborhoods. The goal was to understand whether their participation in crime declined after their removal from an area of concentrated disadvantage. The results differed by stage of adolescence:

- *Better for preadolescent children.* Moving to a middle-income area proved most helpful for families with younger children, *8 and 9 years old.* Moving them *before they entered adolescence* proved quite helpful.

- *No effect for children who had started adolescence.* Those youths who had already entered adolescence or were about to (ages 10 through 15) did no better in their new neighborhoods.

- *Youths in late adolescence got worse.* A reverse effect was found among youths aged 16 through 18, who experienced extra problems after moving from a highly disadvantaged area to a middle-class area, committing additional crime.

We can see that concentrated disadvantage begins to do lasting damage *starting very early in life*. These negative effects persist for the next several years of adolescence. That's why it is important for society to minimize the number of people entering the ages of adolescence living within areas of concentrated disadvantage. A policy to redesign and relocate low-income families with children would take time and patience, but would pay dividends. In 1835, Alexis de Tocqueville noted that Americans are restless and impatient, seeking quick solutions to problems.[3] However, sometimes American society can be systematic and committed to improvements over many years.

Public Housing De-Concentration

Many observers have argued against high-rise public housing concentrated in limited areas.[4] Instead, they are in favor of *public housing de-concentration*, suggesting that scattered-site public housing can reduce crime problems in important ways.[5] From about 1990 to around 2010, public authorities demolished hundreds of public housing projects in several American cities.[6] These were replaced with low-rise and mixed-income developments, sometimes using housing vouchers to scatter low-income families and avoid stigmatized public housing projects. A body of research found that these changes improved the housing and security of former residents.[7] That happened without making things worse for those neighborhoods that had absorbed former public housing residents.[8] Public housing is much more diverse than many people realize[9] and it works *worst* when it is

- highly concentrated in space;

- designed poorly, making crime easier to carry out; and when it

- looks so different from surrounding housing that people stigmatize it.[10]

In recent decades, many governments have learned to reduce these concentrations and thus to diminish crime, including violence.[11] However, public housing policy involving dispersal offers no panacea. Critics point out these efforts can have limited effectiveness[12] and imperfect implementation.[13] By its very nature, public housing will always concentrate people with more problems. Yet real improvements have occurred and have been well worth the effort.

The *Moving to Opportunity experiment* studied the impact of moving families living in public housing projects in the most underprivileged neighborhoods in American cities to neighborhoods with much lower poverty rates. This experiment found qualified evidence that both parents and children were safer in their new neighborhoods and their crime victimization rates declined. Youth's violent offending tended to decline; however, property offending did not decline. Clearly, relocation policies are not cure-alls; still, they are very promising policy initiatives.[14]

A Negative Experiment

The mass incarceration of the past few decades in the United States can be viewed as a kind of experiment too. Interestingly, even though other industrial nations did not go down this path, their crime patterns followed those of the United States. For example, during the 1990s, major crime reductions were observed in both the United States and Canada even though Canada did not increase its rates of incarceration.[15]

The main issue for us here is that the U.S. prison expansion had quite an impact on the neighborhoods from which prisoners were drawn. Prisoners were removed from and returned to those neighborhoods in disruptive numbers. Some observers refer to this as *cycling*—going back and forth between prison and a high-arrest neighborhood. Researchers have concluded that this process further concentrates disadvantages within limited areas.[16] This has been referred to as *penal harm* since the penal system has focused its punishments so heavily on certain areas that it goes beyond punishing the convicted individuals and also punishes families and neighbors. As we noted in Part 3, former prisoners often have difficulties reintegrating into a normal life after prison terms are completed.

Transience and Crime

At several points in Part 5 we have noted that transience creates a crime problem. Areas of concentrated disadvantage often experience more *turnover in apartments and schools*, destabilizing the neighborhood and enhancing crime risk. Transience weakens attachments among neighbors and reduces levels of community surveillance.[17] With high turnover, neighbors are strangers to one another and cannot protect the neighborhood from crime. This point applies to low-income neighborhoods, but other areas are not exempt. Some middle-class zones have high residential turnover,[18] producing the same problem in relation to community security. These middle-class neighbors do not recognize each other and have no commitment to the area. This shows up in victim surveys. For instance, based on data from the National Crime Victimization Survey for 2005, those who had lived in the same residence less than six months had *four times as much* violent crime risk as those who had lived in the same place for five years or more.[19]

Transience also affects schools.[20] Transient teenagers are more likely to produce discipline problems, to engage in crime, and to abuse alcohol and drugs. More turnover undermines the ability of schools to maintain general order and provide a good education, even for non-transient youths.[21] Teachers are less likely to relate to students, and students are less likely to relate well to one another in a school dominated by transience. Moreover, constant inflows of new students upset the status hierarchy of a school, leading to conflicts.

Nowhere is the impact of transiency more evident than with children in *foster care*; these children may shift from one family and school setting to another, with no anchor point.[22] The Adoption and Foster Care Analysis and Reporting System tells us that 415,000 American children were in foster care in 2014, typically beginning at ages six or seven.[23] Although foster care is intended to be a temporary arrangement, the average stay is two years—a substantial chunk of childhood. Some 70 percent of these children live with non-relatives, in group homes, or in institutions.

Children in foster care pose a dilemma. If they are not removed from abusive and neglectful homes, they might suffer greatly; yet if they are removed and placed in foster care settings, their new residence can be harmful too. An Illinois experiment randomly assigned children aged 5 through 15. Children placed in foster care had worse outcomes, more delinquency, and more early pregnancy. The researcher concluded that many children do better if they are not assigned to foster care, but are instead left in their original home—however flawed it may be.[24]

The important lesson is that society often does better by stabilizing neighborhoods, schools, and housing as best it can. This is a non-utopian approach. It tells us that people will continue to have problems, but that those with the greatest number of problems should not be funneled into a single corner of a city. However, as we learned in Unit 5.3, dispersing social problems leads to quite a bit of resistance since other neighborhoods do not want these people nearby.

Concentrated Disadvantage in Perspective

The link between concentrated disadvantage and crime can be misunderstood. The first mistake is to think that *most* American minority group members live in the worst areas. Despite remaining inequality and segregation, minority group members increasingly live in reasonably comfortable parts of cities and in suburbs.[25]

The inner suburban ring is much more diverse than in the past.[26] As whites moved farther from city centers, new housing opened for nonwhites.[27] A substantial share of the black population has already fled the central cities and lives in surrounding suburbs.[28] The *minority migration to the suburbs* requires us to rethink many of our old models of crime that assume the central city to be the home of all or most of the black population. Similarly, Hispanic immigrants have increasingly diversified and suburbanized, and many now live in small towns.[29] Many of the old zones of the central city face *general abandonment* by people of all races and ethnic groups: those remaining are the poorest and least able to escape poverty.

Minority populations are not nearly as disadvantaged in educational terms as in the past. Recent figures for blacks indicate that 87 percent are high school graduates; 53 percent have some college; 32 percent have an associate's degree or higher; and 23 percent have a bachelor's degree or higher. Over a third of the Hispanic American population has some college attainment.[30] To be sure, still higher educational attainments are found among white non-Hispanic Americans and Asian Americans. Despite continued gaps in education and socioeconomic status, we should not accept the naïve dichotomy between "poor, uneducated, black urbanite" and "prosperous, educated, white suburbanite." Nonetheless, noteworthy remnants of concentrated disadvantage still exist.

The second mistake is to assume that areas of concentrated disadvantage have a monopoly on crime, a point we made earlier.

• The crime problem is present well beyond the central city, including the metropolis and region.

• The unfortunate term "urban delinquency area" wrongly implies that the rest of the metropolis has no delinquency.

• Yet some parts of a city concentrate *extra* crime, especially violence and other overt crime.

The next section examines what concentrated disadvantage does to the age–crime curve.

The Elevated Age–Violence Curve

Areas of concentrated disadvantage elevate the age–crime curve, especially for violence. This was verified when researchers compared age–crime curves for different economic zones in Pittsburgh, Pennsylvania.[31] As noted in Part 4, criminologists use mathematics to smooth out individual zigzags. That produces an *average* age–crime curve. These smoothed trajectories can be compared for public housing areas, other disadvantaged areas, and average neighborhoods.

As Figure 5f suggests, areas of concentrated disadvantage (public housing or other disadvantaged areas) produce higher average participation in violence at each age of adolescence than average neighborhoods. This is most evident if you only look at the very bottom of the diagram. However, if you look at the whole diagram you readily see that most youths are not involved in violence, even at the peak ages in public housing areas. This tells us not to be too judgmental about all the people who reside in any given area. It also tells us how much damage a few violent youths can deliver. Clearly, public housing is associated with an ***elevated age–violence curve***, producing more violence participation—especially in mid-adolescence—even though most local youths try to stay out of it. Whenever you read a chart, you should always check whether the scale is at a full 100 percent or is constrained to only part of the scale, perhaps

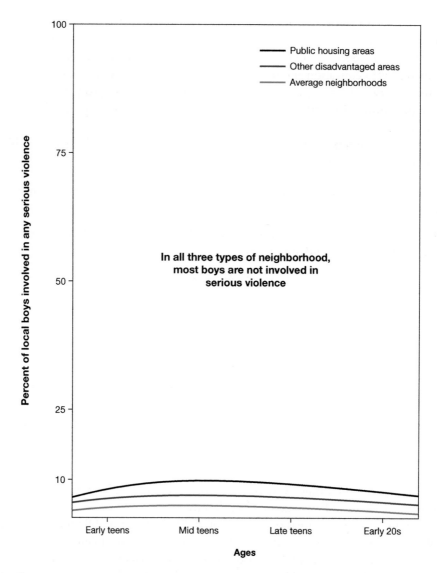

In all three types of neighborhood, most boys are not involved in serious violence

Public housing areas
Other disadvantaged areas
Average neighborhoods

FIGURE 5F

Serious Violence, Ages 13 through 24, by Neighborhood Income Level, Pittsburgh, Pennsylvania

Source: Reinterpretation and adaption of Fabio et al. (2011). Neighborhood socioeconomic disadvantage and the shape of the age–crime curve. *American Journal of Public Health, 101*(S1) s325–S332; Figure 2.

Note: Based on mathematically smoothed curves.

giving the wrong impression. You will note that all three neighborhood levels have some youths involved in some violence. Areas of concentrated disadvantage have higher levels of violence, even though most of their youths are not directly involved in it.

A Few Violent Youths Can Ruin a Neighborhood

Clearly, *a few violent youths* do far more than their share of harm, creating a difficult place to live for neighbors, for other youths, and even for themselves. The remarkable fact about tough neighborhoods is that relatively few aggressive youths can do so much damage to everyone else. In the Pittsburgh study, a small percentage of youths and a much smaller percentage of the total public housing population is the source of most of the local violence.

David Kennedy recognized this general reality in his work with the Boston Gun Project,[32] discussed in Part 3. His team learned a lesson that applies to many other American cities; only 3 percent of youths in Boston gang areas were responsible for at least 60 percent of the homicide in the entire city,[33] meaning that 97 percent of youths in gang areas were not the real problem. It is wrong to attribute all violence to these parts of the city or to assume that most youths living there are violent. Yet the concentration process generates extra violence and fear. A very small percentage of very violent youths can ruin a neighborhood, spreading fear and undermining community life. This gives us a reason not to concentrate these youths into a limited area, but rather to "divide and conquer."

Criminologists have asked whether concentrated disadvantage enhances crime. The evidence included in this chapter supports that hypothesis. This evidence appears to favor scattered public housing and enacting land use and zoning reform or other efforts to minimize concentration.

FLASHCARD LIST FOR UNIT 5.4

- A few violent youths
- Concentrated disadvantage
- Cycling (between prisons and high arrest neighborhoods)
- Danish experiment
- Elevated age–violence curve

- Extra crime
- Foster care
- General abandonment
- Minority migration to the suburbs
- Moving to Opportunity experiment
- Penal harm

- Public housing de-concentration
- Turnover in apartments and schools
- Yonkers experiment

DISCUSSION QUESTIONS

1. How does social exclusion relate to concentrated disadvantage?

2. What are some elements that could account for the elevation of the age–violence curve in areas of concentrated disadvantage?

Notes

1   Damm, A. P., & Dustmann, C. (2014). Does growing up in a high crime neighborhood affect youth criminal behavior? *The American Economic Review, 104*(6), 1806–1832.

2   Fauth, R. C., Leventhal, T., & Brooks-Gunn, J. (2005). Early impacts of moving from poor to middle-class neighborhoods on low-income youth. *Journal of Applied Developmental Psychology, 26*(4), 415–439.

3   de Tocqueville, A. (2000 [1835, 1840]). *Democracy in America.* Chicago: University of Chicago Press.

4   Jacobs, J. (1961). *Death and life of great American cities.* New York: Vintage. Newman, O. (1966). *Creating defensible space.* Collingdale, PA: Diane Publishing.

5   Goetz, E. G. (2003). *Clearing the way: Deconcentrating the poor in urban America.* Washington, DC: The Urban Institute.

6   Turner, M. A., Popkin, S. J., & Rawlings, L. (2009). *Public housing and the legacy of segregation.* Washington, DC: The Urban Institute.

7   Schmoke, K. L. (2010). *From despair to hope: HOPE VI and the new promise of public housing in America's cities.* Ed. Cisneros, H. G., & Engdahl, L. Washington, DC: Brookings Institution Press.

8   Popkin, S. J., Rich, M. J., Hendey, L., Hayes, C., Parilla, J., & Galster, G. (2012). Public housing transformation and crime: Making the case for responsible relocation. *Cityscape, 14*(3), 137–160.

9   Friedman, L. M. (1966). Public housing and the poor: An overview. *California Law Review,* 642–669.

10 Holzman, H. R., Hyatt, R. A., & Dempster, J. M. (2001). Patterns of aggravated assault in public housing mapping the nexus of offense, place, gender, and race. *Violence Against Women, 7*(6), 662–684. Haberman, C. P., Groff, E. R., & Taylor, R. B. (2013). The variable impacts of public housing community proximity on nearby street robberies. *Journal of Research in Crime and Delinquency, 50*(2), 163–188.

11 Newman, O., & National Institute of Law Enforcement and Criminal Justice. (1973). *Architectural design for crime prevention.* Washington, DC: National Institute of Law Enforcement and Criminal Justice.

12 Galster, G., & Zobel, A. (1998). Will dispersed housing programmes reduce social problems in the US? *Housing Studies, 13*(5), 605–622.

13 Epp, G. (1996). Emerging strategies for revitalizing public housing communities. *Housing Policy Debate, 7*(3), 563–588.

14 Ludwig, J., & Burdick-Will, J. (2014). Poverty deconcentration and the prevention of crime. In B. C. Welsh & D. P. Farrington (Eds.), *The Oxford handbook of crime prevention,* pp. 189–206. Oxford, U.K.: Oxford University Press.

15 Ouimet, M. (2002). Explaining the American and Canadian crime "drop" in the 1990s. *Canadian Journal of Criminology and Criminal Justice, 44*(1), 33–50.

16   Clear, T. R. (2009). *Imprisoning communities: How mass incarceration makes disadvantaged neighborhoods worse*. Oxford, U.K.: Oxford University Press.

17   Stark, R. (1987). Deviant places: A theory of the ecology of crime. *Criminology, 25*(4), 893–910.

18   Bell, C. (1998). *Middle class families: Social and geographical mobility*. London: Routledge.

19   Bureau of Justice Statistics (2006). *Criminal victimization in the United States, 2005: Statistical tables* [online]; Table 50. www.bjs.gov/content/pub/pdf/cvus/previous/cvus50.pdf (retrieved September 7, 2016).

20   Rumberger, R. W. (2003). The causes and consequences of student mobility. *Journal of Negro Education, 72*(1), 6–21.

21   Gasper, J., DeLuca, S., & Estacion, A. (2010). Coming and going: Explaining the effects of residential and school mobility on adolescent delinquency. *Social Science Research, 39*(3), 459–476. Chen, G. (2008). Communities, students, schools, and school crime: A confirmatory study of crime in US high schools. *Urban Education, 43*(3), 301–318. Hartman, C. (2003). Introduction and overview: Student mobility – how some children get left behind. *Journal of Negro Education, 72*(1), 1–5.

22   Scherr, T. G. (2007). Educational experiences of children in foster care: Meta-analyses of special education, retention and discipline rates. *School Psychology International, 28*(4), 419–436.

23   U.S. Department of Health and Human Services. (2009). *The AFCARS report* [online]. www.acf.hhs.gov/sites/default/files/cb/afcarsreport22.pdf (retrieved August 1, 2017).

24   Doyle, J. J. (2007). Child protection and child outcomes: Measuring the effects of foster care. *The American Economic Review, 97*(5), 1583–1610.

25   Hanlon, B., Short, J. R., & Vicino, T. J. (2009). *Cities and suburbs: New metropolitan realities in the US*. Abingdon, U.K.: Routledge.

26   Charles, S. L. (2011). *Suburban gentrification: Understanding the determinants of single-family residential redevelopment: A case study of the inner-ring suburbs of Chicago, IL, 2000–2010*. Cambridge, MA: Joint Center for Housing Studies of Harvard University.

27   Iceland, J., Sharp, G., & Timberlake, J. M. (2013). Sun belt rising: Regional population change and the decline in black residential segregation, 1970–2009. *Demography, 50*(1), 97–123.

28   Woldoff, R. A. (2011). *White flight/Black flight: The dynamics of racial change in an American neighborhood*. Utica, NY: Cornell University Press.

29   Massey, D. S. (Ed.). (2008). *New faces in new places: The changing geography of American immigration*. New York: Russell Sage Foundation.

30   Ryan, C. L., & Bauman, K. (2016). *Educational attainment in the United States: 2015*. Current Population Reports, No. 20. Washington, DC: U.S. Bureau of the Census.

31   Fabio, A., Tu, L. C., Loeber, R., & Cohen, J. (2011). Neighborhood socioeconomic disadvantage and the shape of the age–crime curve. *American Journal of Public Health, 101*(S1), S325–S332.

32   Kennedy, D. (1998). Pulling levers: Getting deterrence right. *National Institute of Justice Journal, 236*(2), 2–9.

33   Braga, A. A., Kennedy, D. M., Piehl, A. M., & Waring, E. J. (2000). *The Boston Gun Project: Impact evaluation findings*. Rockville, MD: National Institute of Justice.

UNIT 5.5 Accommodation

Suppose that you

- live in a tough neighborhood,

- where offenders have the upper hand,

- nested within a hostile larger society, with

- little chance to reduce local crime, and

- few opportunities to escape your own circumstances.

Criminologists would say that you live under a condition of strain, forcing you to accommodate to your undesirable situation. Three types of accommodation are important.

1. People in tough neighborhoods must accommodate to and deal with *their own dangerous neighbors*.

2. They must accommodate to *the larger society* that surrounds them.

3. They must try to deal with **aversive interpersonal experiences** that might emerge in daily life.

People sometimes respond to these strains by committing criminal acts.

Accommodating a Tough Neighborhood

Residents of a tough neighborhood need to accommodate to their nastiest neighbors. They must make the best of the worst. From a youthful viewpoint, the tough kids live in the same building, hang out nearby, and dominate the local playground.[1] The criminological literature details five options for ***accommodating*** local offenders in a high crime zone. You can:

1. ***Avoid***. Do not challenge or engage offenders, but try to steer clear of them.

2. ***Avert***. Take no flack, protect your reputation as tough, but don't join them.

3. ***Adapt***. Befriend the offenders without fully joining them.

4. ***Assist***. Help offenders from time to time.

5. ***Adopt***. Join in with delinquent groups.

These are ordered from the least involvement with neighborhood toughs to the most involvement. All levels of accommodation should be seen as trial-and-error processes as each youth tries to make the best of a bad situation.

Coping with Crime (Avoid)

The first option is to avoid offenders as best you can. You can try to put distance between yourself and neighborhood toughs by walking down safer streets and avoiding routes near bars or empty lots. You can shop in the morning, carry minimal cash, leave jewelry at home, and walk with other people. However, people living in high-crime areas cannot easily change their routine activities to avoid crime entirely.[2] Nor can young people stay inside all the time. They have trips to and from school and need to get exercise and escape home. Unable to avoid other neighborhood youths completely, they very likely must find other accommodations.

The Code of the Street (Avert)

The second coping method is also called the ***code of the street***, defined and explained by ***Elijah Anderson***:

Simply living in [a tough] environment places young people at special risk of falling victim to aggressive behavior. . . . Above all, this environment means that even youngsters whose home lives reflect mainstream values—and the majority of homes in the community do—must be able to handle themselves in a street-oriented environment.

[. . .] [P]eople become very sensitive to advances and slights, which could well serve as warnings of imminent physical confrontation.[3]

By the code of the street, being disrespected is considered dangerous since it could lead to your being bullied or attacked. You must assume that police will not be there to help you. You must stand up for yourself when challenged. In this environment, you must not tolerate rudeness that middle-class people tend not to react to. The code of the street is learned and known: Avoid saying or doing anything that would provoke someone else, but if they provoke you, don't turn the other cheek.

Unfortunately, the code of the street creates its own risks:[4] Answering every perceived insult means precipitating more fights.[5] Thus people trying to stay out of trouble might find their effort fails. Some people carry weapons with self-defense in mind,[6] but these measures can also be the source of conflict, escalation, or injury.[7] Perhaps the most interesting accommodation is in the middle of the list—getting along with offenders without joining them fully.

Sidling up to Dangerous Youths (Adapt)

Some youths socialize with the more dangerous neighboring youths. They appease these offenders as an insurance policy. They befriend and assist offenders in minor ways (short of crime), hang out with them, or stay on their "good side." They keep *a foot in both camps*. This makes sense as an adaptive strategy, but (like all accommodation attempts) carries significant risks. Youths spending more time with tough characters are themselves victimized more often and more seriously.[8] They might also be enlisted in crime and find it difficult to refuse. They might, too, be arrested by police or fall victims to drive-by shootings.

Helping Offenders Do Crimes (Assist)

Some youths begin to assist offenders actively. For example, street children in Brazilian *favelas* begin assisting drug dealers as lookouts; they progress to running errands; eventually they might begin delivering drugs to customers, and later join the criminal group fully.[9] Even without such a progression, helping offenders commit crimes is one way to accommodate living in their midst. Youths in a tough neighborhood might assist offenders by hiding contraband, warning dealers of police activity, or making illicit deliveries or pickups.

If caught by authorities, those who assist gang members and other criminals can be charged with *aiding and abetting*, which means assisting in the commission of someone else's crime. It usually requires knowing the offense is afoot, embracing it, and doing something consciously to enable the crime's success. The accomplice need not contribute to every aspect of the criminal act to be convicted and punished for aiding and abetting a crime.[10] Not every youth will recognize that assisting offenders is itself subject to prosecution. Of course, some local youths go even further. Joining a gang is the most extreme accommodation to neighborhood insecurity, adopting the riskiest posture. We are saving our discussion of gangs for Part 7.

We have reviewed five ways that individuals try to accommodate their dangerous neighbors in a tough neighborhood. They can avoid the tough guys, avert them, adapt to them, assist them, or adopt the same behavior and identity. We have described a trial-and-error process by which youths sustain social life under risky circumstances, accommodating a tough neighborhood.

Accommodating Larger Society

Residents of risky neighborhoods might need not only to accommodate dangerous neighbors but also to adjust to an unfavorable position in the larger society. A tough neighborhood could probably ignore larger society if there were no connections to it. Yet its members are exposed to the values, ideas, and prosperity of the larger world through, for example, school and mass media. Residents might yearn for a better life outside the tough neighborhood. Yet they are often ill-prepared to compete in this larger system. Criminologists use the term *strain theory* to address how people respond to bad circumstances in their society which they cannot easily handle. The idea began in 1899 when *Émile Durkheim* used the French word *anomie* to describe normlessness, a situation in which human goals could not be met in large-scale community life. Durkheim linked anomie to variations in suicide and homicide rates.

In 1938, *Robert K. Merton* offered a more specific explanation for how a general problem in society sets the stage for crime.[11] He noted that a quest for socioeconomic success is central for a modern society, yet some segments of society lack the means to achieve that success. Merton emphasized *blocked opportunities* as a central problem in society, especially for people with limited economic means. Although Merton outlined several responses to unfortunate conditions (ranging from conformity to rebellion), his most important idea for criminology was that people whose opportunities are blocked will be more likely to participate in crime. He reasoned that crime offers an *illegitimate means to achieve legitimate ends*. For example, a disadvantaged youth can steal money to buy conventional goods, such as nice clothes or cosmetics. Merton did not view low-income youths as different from any other youths, except that their opportunities for conventional achievements were blocked.

Criminologists would not realize for many years the substantial crime participation by middle-class youths; theorists confined their attention to crimes committed by the disadvantaged. In 1955, *Albert Cohen* shifted discussion of blocked opportunities from individuals to neighborhoods. He emphasized the *delinquent subculture* as a poor neighborhood's collective response to adversity.[12] A delinquent subculture not only allows residents to engage in crime, but also maintains ongoing values conducive to crime and transmits those values to others. These values defy the larger society, endanger neighbors, and represent an extreme accommodation to a negative relationship with larger society. A juvenile street gang (discussed in Unit 7.1) exemplifies a delinquent subculture.

These theorists continued to emphasize crimes committed by the poor, paying little attention to middle-class juvenile delinquency. In 1960, *Cloward and Ohlin* extended these ideas, offering *differential opportunity theory*.[13] They argued that tough neighborhoods not only block access to *legitimate opportunities*, but also provide residents with extra *illegitimate opportunities*. Thus, lower-class youths might learn how to break into cars, while middle-class youths know less about that topic. Differential opportunity theory reasoned that providing more opportunity to lower-class youths would provide them with legitimate routes to follow, and this would bring down their crime participation. During the 1960s, President Lyndon B. Johnson's War on Poverty was designed in part to reduce crime by providing more economic opportunities, enhancing legitimate means to achieve society's goals.

Yet crime in the United States grew dramatically during the very years when opportunity for the poor was expanding.[14] This called the old theories into question. This also caused criminologists to take a closer look at juvenile crime committed by middle-class youths. Writing between 1938 and 1960, Merton, and Cohen, along with Cloward and Ohlin all focused on low-income delinquent youths whose crimes they linked to blocked opportunities within larger society. These theorists also focused on juvenile gangs found in lower-class parts of large cities. As you will learn in Part 7, the old image of the gang is now obsolete. Gangs are much more diverse in location and participation, and they are not nearly as cohesive as previously believed. Youths from higher-income families are more likely to join gangs than previously believed, especially in early adolescence.[15] This surprising finding tells us that gangs are not simply a "lower-class phenomenon."

Aversive Interpersonal Experiences

The need to respond to or adjust to negative experiences applies to individuals as well as neighborhoods. Many aversive interpersonal and personal experiences could occur as the day wears on. **Robert Agnew** and colleagues have measured at least 80 negative experiences, some of which we organize below:

Family problems, including divorce, issues with children, death of family members, burden of taking care of family members, heavy childcare responsibility, low prestige in family roles, excessive family demands, childcare problems;

School problems, including problems with peers, being picked on by kids, troublesome friends, interpersonal jealousy, sports competitions at school;

Health problems, including losing medical insurance, postponing medical care, sadness and depression, sexual abuse;

Work problems, including heavy workloads, demeaning roles, verbal abuse, sexual abuse, trouble finding a suitable job, excessive work demands, job market discrimination, problems with workmates, low authority and autonomy, low prestige in work roles, unfair procedures; and

Economic problems, including the need to borrow from others, inability to meet basic needs, inability to purchase goods, demands from creditors, failure at economic goals, falling behind with paying bills, postponing major purchases, and spending beyond one's means.[16]

Criminologists have noted two different ways that negative experiences set the stage for criminal aggression, **dispute-related aggression** and **displaced aggression**. Dispute-related aggression (see Part 1) occurs when one person blames another person for a negative experience and then retaliates against the person blamed.[17] Suppose somebody knocks over your drink in the bar and does not apologize or make up for it. This creates a grievance. The grievance may escalate and lead to an attack.[18] For our analysis, it does not matter whether the attack is "justifiable" or reasonable. Nor does it matter whether those sitting in jail wish they had not gotten into so much trouble. What matters is that *at the time of the crime*, one person blamed the other for a negative experience and felt a need to retaliate. Most retaliations are verbal. Some involve property crime, such as vandalism. Sometimes they are a violent encounter. Such retaliation might seem irrational and foolish later, but at the time of the incident, it is perfectly logical, at least from a social psychologist's viewpoint. The attacker seeks to restore his self-image after perceiving an attack on it.[19] However, some social scientists emphasize how aggression is deflected elsewhere.

In 1900, the great psychiatrist **Sigmund Freud** published his most important book, *The Interpretation of Dreams.*[20] Freud presented the concept of **psychological displacement**, a defense mechanism by which the mind unconsciously substitutes a new object for goals that are unacceptable in their original form. A person transfers emotions, ideas, or wishes into another channel. In 1939, **John Dollard** developed displacement into **frustration–aggression theory**,[21] a general theory that links a variety of frustrations to a variety of aggressive acts. Any number of frustrations can be displaced to produce **seemingly unrelated aggressive acts**. The famous example is the man who is angry at his boss but afraid to retaliate for fear of losing his job; so he goes home and kicks the dog. Robert Agnew (who compiled the 80 negative experiences noted above) imported frustration-aggression theory to criminology as **generalized strain theory**. Agnew asserted that a vast range of stresses and strains over the course of a person's life produce diverse nonviolent and violent criminal behaviors. Agnew gave no particular time limits or boundaries on these effects.

The term **aversive stimuli** refers to bad experiences that people have. People and places with more *aversive stimuli* also tend to have more crime. The correlations between these bad experiences and crime have been observed in a variety of forms. The problem is that criminologists do not agree on what produces those correlations. Which of the following is the best explanation?

- Dispute-related aggression theory would tell us to look for aversive stimuli that generate conflicts, escalations, and retaliations.

- Generalized strain (and frustration-aggression theory) would tell us that all strains and all crimes could be related through unconscious displacement.

- People worn down by bad experiences may have less self-control and hence commit more crime.

It seems impossible to test these three approaches on a large scale all at once. However, social psychology laboratory experiments have addressed some of the issues in a manageable way. In a typical experiment, university sophomores are subjects as part of their introductory psychology class. One student enters a room and sees a second student, who is secretly working for the researcher. The second student insults the first. The researcher observes whether the first student answers the insult and escalates the verbal conflict. The researcher can also introduce aversive stimuli; for example, making the room uncomfortably hot, odorous, or noisy. Experiments such as this show that

- Researchers can induce the first student to counterattack the insulter.

- Aversive stimuli can enhance the aggression, but it is still *directed at the insulter.*

- Aversive stimuli have weaker effects when they are not **blameworthy**.[22]

We tentatively conclude that *directed* aggression is probably more powerful than *displaced* aggression. In other words, displacement probably has small effects, perhaps enhancing retaliations against persons blamed. It appears that aversive stimuli can produce and enhance conflicts among people, and those conflicts can lead to criminal retaliations. These patterns can apply to people in any neighborhood, but those living in environments with an extra dose of aversive stimuli probably end up with more interpersonal grievances and more frequent criminal retaliations.

Figure 5g helps us understand how these bad experiences, or aversive stimuli, can lead to aggressive behavior, sometimes including criminal acts. At the top of the figure, you see that bad experiences produce grievances *against those blamed*. In the middle of the figure, you see that bad experiences can generate psychological displacement to other people—*not* the people blamed. At the bottom of the figure you note that bad experiences can *deplete self-control*, wearing down the ability to withstand pressure and stay out of trouble. All three processes probably have some role in aggressive behavior; however, we believe that counterattacks against a blamed person offer the most direct explanation of everyday aggression.

In the course of this unit, you have seen the many ways that individuals and communities have to make accommodations and how these efforts can relate to crime.

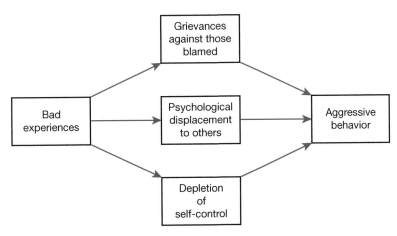

FIGURE 5G
Bad Experiences Can Enhance Aggression in Three Ways

Individuals may need to accommodate dangerous persons in their midst. Disadvantaged neighborhoods may have to accommodate their larger society. Individuals in all parts of society face annoyances and aversive stimuli to which they might respond aggressively.

FLASHCARD LIST FOR UNIT 5.5

- A foot in both camps
- Accommodating (to local offenders), avoid, avert, adapt, assist, and adopt
- Aggression, displaced, dispute-related
- Agnew, Robert
- Aiding and abetting
- Anderson, Elijah
- Aversive interpersonal experiences
- Aversive stimuli

- Blameworthy
- Blocked opportunities
- Cloward and Ohlin
- Code of the street
- Cohen, Albert
- Delinquent subculture
- Differential opportunity theory
- Dollard, John
- Durkheim, Émile
- Freud, Sigmund
- Frustration-aggression theory

- Generalized strain theory
- Illegitimate means [to achieve legitimate ends]
- Merton, Robert K
- Opportunities, blocked, illegitimate, legitimate
- Psychological displacement
- Seemingly unrelated aggressive acts
- Strain theory

DISCUSSION QUESTIONS

1. How does accommodation help us understand juvenile gangs?

2. Does overt crime force more accommodation than covert crime?

Notes

1   Stark, R. (1987). Deviant places: A theory of the ecology of crime. *Criminology, 25*(4), 893–910.

2   Skogan, W. G., & Maxfield, M. G. (1981). *Coping with crime: Individual and neighborhood reactions.* Beverly Hills, CA: Sage.

3   Anderson, E. (1994). The code of the streets. *Atlantic Monthly, 273*(5), 81–94.

4   Stewart, E. A., Schreck, C. J., & Simons, R. L. (2006). "I ain't gonna let no one disrespect me": Does the code of the street reduce or increase violent victimization among African American Adolescents? *Journal of Research in Crime and Delinquency, 43*(4), 427–458. Markowitz, F. E., & Felson, R. B. (1998). Social-demographic attitudes and violence. *Criminology, 36*(1), 117–138.

5   Felson, R. B., & Pare, P. P. (2010). Gun cultures or honor cultures? Explaining regional and race differences in weapon carrying. *Social Forces, 88*(3), 1357–1378.

6   Williams, J. S., Singh, B. K., & Singh, B. B. (1994). Urban youth, fear of crime, and resulting defensive actions. *Adolescence, 29*(114), 323–330.

7   Walsh, S. D., Molcho, M., Craig, W., Harel-Fisch, Y., Huynh, Q., Kukaswadia, A., . . . & Pickett, W. (2013). Physical and emotional health problems experienced by youth engaged in physical fighting and weapon carrying. *PLoS One*, *8*(2), e56403. https://doi.org/10.1371/journal.pone.0056403.

8   Taylor, T. J., Peterson, D., Esbensen, F. A., & Freng, A. (2007). Gang membership as a risk factor for adolescent violent victimization. *Journal of Research in Crime and Delinquency*, *44*(4), 351–380. Katz, C. M., Webb, V. J., Fox, K., & Shaffer, J. N. (2011). Understanding the relationship between violent victimization and gang membership. *Journal of Criminal Justice*, *39*(1), 48–59.

9   Inciardi, J. A., & Surratt, H. L. (1998). Children in the streets of Brazil: Drug use, crime, violence, and HIV risks. *Substance Use & Misuse*, *33*(7), 1461–1480.

10 Doyle, C. (2014). *Aiding, abetting, and the like: An overview of 18 U.S.C. 2*. Report R43769. Washington, DC: Congressional Research Service. https://fas.org/sgp/crs/misc/R43769.pdf (retrieved March 11, 2017).

11 Merton, R. K. (1938). Social structure and anomie. *American Sociological Review*, *3*(5), 672–682.

12 Cohen, A. K. (1955). *Delinquent boys: The culture of the gang*. New York: Free Press.

13 Cloward, R. A., & Ohlin, L. E. (1960). *Delinquency and opportunity: A theory of delinquent gangs*. New York: Free Press.

14 Cohen, L. E., & Felson, M. (1979). Social change and crime rate trends: A routine activity approach. *American Sociological Review*, *44*(4), 588–608.

15 Gilman, A. B., Hill, K. G., Hawkins, J. D., Howell, J. C., & Kosterman, R. (2014). The developmental dynamics of joining a gang in adolescence: Patterns and predictors of gang membership. *Journal of Research on Adolescence*, *24*(2), 204–219.

16 Agnew, R. (2016). Strain, economic status, and crime. In A. R. Piquero (Ed.), *The handbook of criminological theory*, pp. 209–229. New York: Wiley-Blackwell. Agnew, R. (2013). When criminal coping is likely: An extension of general strain theory. *Deviant Behavior*, *34*(8), 653–670. Agnew, R. (2006). *Pressured into crime: An overview of general strain theory*. New York: Oxford University Press.

17 Felson, R. B. (2004). A rational-choice approach to violence. In M. A. Zahn, H. H. Brownstein, S. L. Jackson (Eds.), *Violence: From theory to research*, pp. 71–90. Cincinnati, OH: Anderson Publishing.

18 Graham, K., Bernards, S., Osgood, D. W., Parks, M., Abbey, A., Felson, R. B., . . . & Wells, S. (2013). Apparent motives for aggression in the social context of the bar. *Psychology of Violence*, *3*(3), 218–232.

19 Felson, R. B., Osgood, D. W., Horney, J., & Wiernik, C. (2012). Having a bad month: General versus specific effects of stress on crime. *Journal of Quantitative Criminology*, *28*(2), 347–363.

20 Freud, S. (2013 [1899]). *The interpretation of dreams*. Worcestershire, U.K.: Read Books Ltd.

21 Dollard, J., Miller, N. E., Doob, L. W., Mowrer, O. H., & Sears, R. R. (1939). *Frustration and aggression*. New Haven, CT: Yale University Press.

22 Tedeschi, J., & Felson, R. B. (1994). *Violence, aggression, and coercive actions*. Washington, DC: American Psychological Association.

UNIT 5.6 The Pathway to Decay

This unit describes the **pathway to decay** that applies to parts of urban America and several cities in Europe. We discuss in this chapter how urban decay produces extra crime, which then creates even further decay. Many neighborhoods can regenerate when something bad happens. However, in decaying areas the land values are too low for recovery and regeneration. **Modern urban poverty areas** are in many ways worse than the **urban poverty areas of the past**.

Around 1850, **Henry Mayhew**—an English journalist, playwright, and social reformer—in his famous book, *London Labour and the London Poor*, described a very poor neighborhood that contained significant vice and misery.[1] Legitimate and illegitimate street activity were mixed together, but illegal activity was unable to dominate.

Mayhew's London was poor but vibrant. He described multiple stalls and vendors, selling oysters, oranges, flowers, baked potatoes, pies, herbs, coffee, spices, boot laces, dog collars, street art, walking sticks, rhubarb, nutmeg graters, and so on. He described merchants selling wet fish, dry fish, and shellfish. Others specialized in green fruit, dry fruit, vegetables, poultry, and rabbits. Second-hand sellers specialized in curtains, glass, metal trays, or weapons. Streets were active with musicians, performers on stilts, jugglers—poor people trying to make a meager living any way they could. Hanging out on the street were sailors, coal heavers, dock laborers, and others. Mixed in were prostitutes, thieves, and swindlers. The streets housed the sick and destitute and the beggars along with the working poor.

Despite the **visible human suffering**, at least Mayhew's London was alive. In contrast, some American areas are so dominated by crime that they lack any vibrancy or **visible legitimate activity**. This chapter discusses how it got that way. We describe how part of a city is ruined by the onslaught of economic and social problems. The situation gets worse and worse, and each part of the problem feeds another part.[2] Thus, abandoned properties enhance crime and disorder, while crime and disorder in turn cause more people to abandon other properties. With no positive influences countering, decay progresses. In studying that process, we introduce some important criminological ideas and some serious issues in policing. Society must try very hard to **halt the deterioration process** before it gets any worse.

When Shaw and McKay wrote their work on social disorganization, decay was already a serious problem in parts of Chicago and some other cities. Decay now dominates wide sections of Philadelphia, Chicago, Baltimore, Camden, Detroit, and beyond. Forty percent of large European cities, especially in Eastern Europe, are currently **shrinking cities**.[3] Even when the larger economy prospers, local areas can be **places left behind**.

Sociologist **William Julius Wilson** explained what happens when work disappears, augmenting the existing poor with new urban poor populations, further feeding decline in core cities while economic growth goes elsewhere.[4] He argued that race is incidental to the problem. The larger concerns are the class differences in **ability to participate** in the prosperity of the larger society.[5] As large sections of society are cut off, their parts of the city die off, producing disorder in the process.

The Importance of Disorder

Wesley Skogan has produced the best chronicle of the problem. His important book, *Disorder and Decline: Crime and the Spiral of Decay in American Neighborhoods*, includes a rich description and analysis of how many American cities have suffered:

> Disorder is evident in the widespread appearance of junk and trash in the vacant lots; it is evident, too, in decaying homes, boarded-up buildings, the vandalism of public and private property, graffiti, and stripped and abandoned cars in streets and alleys. It is signaled by bands of teenagers congregating on street corners, by the presence of prostitutes and panhandlers, by public drinking, the verbal harassment of women, and open gambling and drug use. What these conditions have in common is that they signal a breakdown of the local social order. Communities beset by disorder can no longer expect people to act in civil fashion in public places. They can no longer expect landlords to respect the character of the neighborhood.[6]

Residents may worry less about formal, named gangs than about **informal groups of youths** drinking outside, making noise, or using drugs on street corners. In disorderly neighborhoods, public parks are uncontrolled and feared, places where people sell or use drugs or get drunk.[7] Parents try to keep their children away from parks.

Neighborhood problems go beyond legal distinctions. Police define many disorders as non-criminal and *not of police concern*. Even when street behavior is clearly illegal, it is usually impractical for police to act against it. Nor do judges want to process disorder cases. Skogan continues:

> Researchers have found that perceptions of disorder have many ill effects on urban neighborhoods. Disorder not only sparks concern and fear of crime among neighborhood residents; it may actually increase the level of serious crime. Disorder erodes what control neighborhood residents can maintain over local events and conditions. . . . It threatens house prices and discourages investment. In short disorder is an instrument of destabilization and neighborhood decline.[8]

The *distinction between disorder and crime* is essential for comprehending problems in a tough neighborhood. Disorder may have a different cause than crime. Disorder may grow at a different rate than crime. Disorder requires a different policy response from crime. Many departments of government are needed to address and control disorder, and many resources are required. Yet disorder and crime are intertwined.[9] To understand the issues, we need to rethink our concept of a normal neighborhood.

The Neighborhood Ability to Heal

The world does not stand still, even in a normal neighborhood. People move in and out. People fail to pay rent or miss house payments. Some workers lose their jobs. Somebody gets sick. A crime happens. A business fails. A fire occurs and a roof collapses. Any of these events can disrupt the status quo in any neighborhood, inflicting an injury.

The *neighborhood ability to heal* from each small injury keeps it from deteriorating. When property has value, people rebuild and rehabilitate. The real estate market sees to it that vacated houses are resold and vacated apartments are re-rented. People who lose jobs have a chance to find other work. After one business fails, a new business occupies the same location. People call the city to remove debris, or the city orders a property owner to clean it up. Neighbors complain about disorderly behaviors. Homeowners have strong incentives to maintain their property values. Apartment building owners do not want to lose their tenants. In other words, the *neighborhood can adapt to change*, thus maintaining and stabilizing itself and overcoming injuries. If people hang out drinking in the park, the neighbors will complain to police; and if park furniture is broken, they will call the park authority insisting on repair. Residents are not afraid to turn in offenders. Problems do not dominate, so when one arises, it can be addressed specifically.

This is not simply a matter of neighborhood cohesion. Real estate values must be high enough to make repairs worthwhile, and disorder must be limited enough so neighbors can focus on a few problems at a time.

Every neighborhood has cuts and bruises, but not every neighborhood has the capacity to heal. In a tough neighborhood, the ability to stabilize is impaired. Real estate values are low. Homeowners are few, and they cannot afford repairs or have no incentive to make them since they cannot get the money back. Absentee landlords have little incentive to fix or maintain properties. Low-income and itinerant tenants come and go, pay rent unevenly, and have no commitment to the area. City hall considers the area to be low on its priority list for cleanups and pickups, and it cannot keep ahead of human setbacks, failures, and debris. People avoid complaining to neighbors about litter or noise to avoid risky conflicts (as discussed in Unit 5.2). *Some neighborhoods cannot recover*. Each new cut or bruise weakens them, and they lack the capacity to heal.

Simple Illustrations of Infectious Disorder

Simple experiments have long shown that disorder can be infectious and that control is feasible by stopping disorderly behaviors at the outset.[10] The *infectious nature of disorder* has been demonstrated by research on littering: As soon as one piece of litter appears, people are more likely to litter again.[11] When two pieces of litter are present, littering begins to accelerate. Frequent litter collection is important to avoid giving people the impression that "everybody litters here."[12]

The infectious nature of disorder crosses from one problem to another. A team of Dutch researchers conducted a study that demonstrated how to cultivate disorderly behavior. They also showed that one sort of disorder leads to another. For example, by painting a wall with graffiti, they could induce people to litter nearby. By attaching bicycles illegally to a fence, they could encourage people to trespass through a hole in the fence. Their results were dramatic.[13] *Each violation of rules leads to another violation of rules*. If a city and its residents fail to clean sidewalks and streets, the situation worsens. People seem to tell themselves, "If *nobody else* is following the rules, why should *I* do so?" In breaking or following rules, people are not strictly autonomous moral beings. They influence one another. They are affected by their neighbors and neighborhood conditions.

A neighborhood normally controls the infectious nature of disorder through homeownership, long-term residency, and stable businesses. Homeowners have an incentive to maintain their own properties and lawns while also looking after the area immediately in front of their homes. Long-term renters "feel" like they own their properties and have bargaining power with their landlords and the city. Established businesses have an incentive to sweep in front of the store and maintain the immediate area that impinges on their sales. Such controls are absent in areas with few homeowners but plenty of absentee landlords, unstable renters, precarious businesses, and unattended or abandoned properties.

Disorder Contributes to Serious Crime

According to **broken windows theory**, neighborhood disorder can contribute to serious crime. Presented in 1982 by **George Kelling** and **James Q. Wilson**, the theory states that police should pay much more attention to what seem to be minor local problems.[14] Kelling and Wilson argued that **minor disorder sets the stage for major crimes to occur**. Here's how it happens:

1.   Untreated local disorder produces local fear,

2.   Causing people to withdraw from neighborhood life,

3.   Reducing informal neighborhood controls, and then

4.   Allowing more serious crimes to grow.

Kelling and Wilson explained that local disorder that seems minor at first sets in motion further decay, disorder, and serious crime.[15] Later in this unit we discuss how broken windows theory can be applied or misapplied to policing.

Forces behind Disorder and Decline

Capitalism has two faces. On the one hand, it produces very high levels of productivity and prosperity for the larger society. On the other hand, capitalism destroys whole industries, whole sections of town, and sometimes whole cities. The idea is that overall level of prosperity increases for most people, but the process also produces pockets of poverty. In 1942, **Joseph Schumpeter** called this **creative destruction**,[16] a remarkable and ironic term. It tells us that our economic way of life is highly productive and effective, yet its negative effects are also powerful. Capitalism produces winners and losers, but the losers can easily end up in a worsening position. Progress is paradoxical. With capitalism, pain and gain are very closely linked, from Philadelphia, Pennsylvania, to the old mill towns of Britain, Scotland, and much of Europe. Even Manchester, England, home of the Industrial Revolution, has scarcely any heavy industry left. Rustbelt cities include Marseille (France), Adelaide (Australia),

Nottingham (England), Glasgow (Scotland), and Hamburg (Germany).[17] These declines pose a very special challenge to modern societies.

These large-scale economic changes set in motion a pathway to decay. That pathway goes through four phases, depicted in Figure 5h.[18] It begins with *deindustrialization*, the closing of factories and shift of jobs away from the central city to the suburbs or elsewhere. Many central cities in the United States lost most of their industrial jobs either to suburban areas or, more likely, to other nations. This was particularly harmful to those working mainly with their hands as unskilled or semiskilled workers. Deindustrialization was based on corporate decisions by manufacturing firms, but also responded to powerful market forces, such as the cost of labor. Two other processes go with deindustrialization:

- *Disinvestment* includes a set of decisions by landlords, homeowners, and banks not to repair and rehabilitate properties. When property values are low, further investment is not likely to be recovered in resale. In fact, many properties in the tough part of town have little or no resale value to begin with. Powerful interests and local people alike lose faith in the area. More people move out than move in, leading to further decline.

- *Demolition* is a powerful force that has undermined disadvantaged areas. Cities have routed new freeways through the worst neighborhoods, where land could be acquired cheaply. That served to destroy existing neighborhoods and destabilize whatever remained. Cities have also demolished drug properties or abandoned buildings without replacing them. These processes contribute to further negative outcomes.

The deindustrialization process is linked to national or international forces impinging on local life.

The next phase in Figure 5h is the *deterioration* that follows deindustrialization. Those persons and properties that remain face worse conditions and risks. Disorder becomes increasingly visible and the crime quite overt. Shabby buildings become shabbier, then are abandoned. Newly abandoned buildings are stripped for their copper and plumbing, which are eventually converted for illegal uses. Additional people hang out on the street, openly drinking or using drugs. The increase in disorder is related to an increase in crime. Deterioration, victimization, disorder, and fear become normal. Perhaps the most corrosive aspect of the crime increase is that residents no longer believe the perpetrators are outsiders. They *fear their own neighbors* and neighborhood youths. Neighborhood watch and community organizations make little sense in the absence of neighborhood trust. That leads to the next phase on the pathway to decay.

Withdrawal from community life (the third phase in Figure 5h) happens as people become fearful. Residents stay home after dark and even during late afternoon. They avoid strangers, talking only to those they know. They take the safest routes and do not wander around or take leisurely walks to the park. Worse still, they feel powerless to do anything about their predicament. The capacity to organize the neighborhood declines, as we explained in Unit 5.2. Researchers have found that violent crime serves to inhibit home sales and that high levels of vacancy are associated with crime.[19]

This is an indication that withdrawal is well underway. That process includes *outmigration*, especially by those who get a new job or a pay raise. That leaves behind the poorest in an already low-income neighborhood. Those moving out are attracted by a better life elsewhere and scared away by the disorder in their midst. The remaining residents are stuck there and must cope with the local problems. As real estate values drop, the chance of rehabilitating property declines and further deterioration is enhanced. If new people move in, they are likely to be lower in income than those who left, perhaps arriving from other nations and mixing poorly with those already there. Increasingly, minority populations abandon the traditional minority areas of the city, moving to better locations as their economic positions improve.

The withdrawal process includes *commercial decline*. Small retail establishments have fewer prosperous customers, and outsiders will not enter the area to shop. Any further decline in economic power leaves little chance for survival of businesses that already operate on the edge. Disorderly neighborhoods increasingly favor seedy bars and hotels along with sex-oriented businesses. Customers contribute further disorder by urinating in the street or harassing women passing by, if there are any women left.

Professor Skogan explained that these processes together produce a dramatic *demographic collapse* (the deepest part in Figure 5h). Driven out by fear, no residential population remains and no women or children can be seen. The *persons left behind* are unattached males, those who cannot fit into society—the homeless, drug addicts—living in boarded-up buildings, seedy hotels, and flophouses. Skid row saloons are the main businesses. Abandoned buildings become shooting galleries. Even street prostitution is gone since its customers are too afraid to go there. When collapse is complete, the area becomes a bombed-out residue. It is beyond recovery.

How can society resist the decay process? The ideal would be to prevent economic decline in the first place. This is very difficult to accomplish because human displacement is built into the structure of the economic system, the prosperity of which depends on the very same processes. Sometimes larger governmental and industrial forces can bring new industries in, relieving some of the local pressure. But this may not benefit all areas. An account of the deindustrialization of Pittsburgh after the dramatic decline of the steel industry also noted the growth of new jobs in other sectors

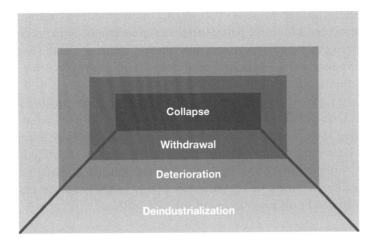

FIGURE 5H

The Pathway to Decay

Source: Adapted from Skogan, W. (1986). Fear of crime and neighborhood change. *Crime and Justice, 8,* 203–229.

of the city's economy.[20] That growth did not, however, prevent some parts of Pittsburgh from suffering. A modern society faces great pressure to improve how it polices disorder to prevent its spread.

Policing Disorder

Standard criminal justice procedures—arrest, book, prosecute, convict, and confine—are ill-suited for containing disorder or stalling a neighborhood's collapse. That does not mean they have no role, but it does mean that a better strategy is needed to police and contain disorder and prevent it from widening and deepening.

Broken windows theory helps us think about policing, but it can easily be misunderstood and misapplied. One misapplication is a ***zero-tolerance policy***, which makes a false promise to arrest everybody for every crime.[21] As we noted in Part 2, zero tolerance is unrealistic given the fact that so much crime is unreported to police and taking into account that the justice system is so expensive. Political officials who promise zero tolerance do not understand the ***limits of policing***.

Properly applying broken windows theory, ***broken windows policing*** focuses on policing disorder first and foremost, with the idea that a reduction in minor offenses and annoyances will prevent more serious crimes from following. Broken windows policing implies such actions as asking drunk men in the park to go home.

Unfortunately, broken windows policing has often produced community conflicts because it can involve additional *police–citizen confrontations*. Some police are highly skilled in managing such interactions and preventing escalations and the need for further contact. Other police are not so skilled, generating unnecessary problems and struggles with the community.

A promising approach that minimizes confrontation is problem-oriented policing, as discussed in Unit 3.2. That approach looks beyond arresting offenders one by one, or even arresting them at all. Its first task is to *identify the problem*. Looking back to Figure 3e (in Unit 3.2), note the crime and disorder incidents surrounding Joe's bar. With problem-oriented policing, officials check whether Joe is giving people alcohol when they are already drunk or allowing other illegal activities at his establishment.

Problem-oriented policing asks questions such as these:

On which corner do drug sales concentrate, and at what hours?

Is a specific small apartment building the center for local illegal activities?

Is a local public housing project poorly managed, and how can that change?

Do a few abandoned houses enhance local crimes?

After identifying the problem, police get together with other city officials and private stakeholders to figure out solutions. Often problem-oriented policing avoids arresting people, or only a few arrests are made on a very strategic basis. Often it uses civil law rather than criminal law; for example, warning Joe that he could lose his liquor license if he doesn't follow liquor regulations. Many of the situational controls mentioned in Unit 2.3 are employed by police to contain and manage crime problems.

Some of the greatest successes in policing disorder have been achieved by combining problem-oriented policing with broken windows policing. This hybrid model is called hot spot policing—again, we are following up ideas presented in Unit 3.2. To make their efforts more efficient, police use crime maps to find out where and when crime problems concentrate and then to combine any number of tactics to contain the problem. The hallmark of *hot spot policing* is that it uses broken windows thinking while minimizing the number of citizen confrontations. An experiment applied hot spot policing to each of 17 locations in Lowell, Massachusetts.[22] Prevention strategy varied with each local problem. Police learned that *avoiding confrontation* often worked better than arrests. This included

- cleaning and securing vacant lots;

- doing code inspections of disorderly taverns;

- finding social workers for those with mental health problems;

- improving street lighting;

- razing abandoned buildings;

- supplementing video surveillance;

- working out shelter for the local homeless; and

- organizing youth recreational opportunities in local parks.

The experiment produced a 72 percent reduction in loiterers, a 73 percent reduction in public drinkers, and a 61 percent reduction in drug sellers. Sixteen of 22 damaged and abandoned structures and abandoned lots or cars were corrected or removed. Most importantly, the attention to the local area's disorder led to significant reductions in assault, robbery, burglary, and total calls for police service. Police also engaged in a limited number of more aggressive tactics, including dispersing groups of loiterers, arresting public drinkers and drug sellers, and using "stop and frisk" for suspicious persons. Yet most of its success occurred without confrontation. Moreover, these reductions in crime and disorder did not result in displacing problems to other areas.[23]

In projects like this, criminologists play a very practical role in figuring out how to reduce local disorder, suggesting ideas, working closely with police, and evaluating programs.

The pathway to decay is long and tortuous, destroying people's lives, individually and collectively. That process can be stalled if interventions occur early, involve full analysis of the local problems, and include participation beyond police. However, after depopulation, commercial decline, and abandonment have ruined urban districts, it becomes difficult or impossible to recover. Some cities have gained partial recoveries in a different form, creating entertainment zones in their centers. These zones draw customers from suburban areas and smaller towns, especially on weekends, producing jobs and activity. However, these efforts can never replace the multitude of jobs lost in old cities. Moreover, the new entertainment districts are often centers for excessive alcohol consumption and related problems, which will be discussed in Unit 6.4.

Modern society has generated massive growth of jobs and prosperity in some areas, along with new forms of local decay. Many small cities, suburbs, and small towns have not been included in the new technological growth industries. Many of these places in America cannot compete with the price of labor abroad. That produces new deterioration far away from central cities. We are only beginning to understand the resulting problems, yet these changes remove any pretense that suburban areas are secure or that rural areas are idyllic.[24]

FLASHCARD LIST FOR UNIT 5.6

- Ability to participate (in prosperity)
- Avoiding confrontation
- Broken windows theory
- Capitalism has two faces
- Commercial decline
- Creative destruction
- Deindustrialization
- Demographic collapse
- Demolition
- Deterioration
- Disinvestment
- Distinction between disorder and crime
- Fear their own neighbors
- Halt the deterioration process
- Hot spot policing
- Identify the problem

- Infectious nature of disorder
- Informal groups of youths
- Kelling, George
- Mayhew, Henry
- Mayhew's London
- Minor disorder sets the stage for major crimes to occur
- Neighborhood ability to heal
- Neighborhood can adapt to change
- Not of police concern
- Outmigration
- Pathway to decay
- Persons left behind
- Places left behind

- Police–citizen confrontations
- Policing, Broken-windows, limits of
- Schumpeter, Joseph
- Shrinking cities
- Skogan, Wesley
- Some neighborhoods cannot recover
- Urban poverty areas, of the past, modern
- Visible human suffering
- Visible legitimate activity
- Wilson, James Q.
- Wilson, William Julius
- Withdrawal
- Zero-tolerance policy

DISCUSSION QUESTIONS

1. Think of a local neighborhood problem. Devise a policing and crime reduction plan that minimizes confrontation and does not rely on extra police costs.

2. A fire destroys an apartment building. What determines whether the neighborhood recovers afterwards?

Notes

1   Mayhew, H. (1861). *London labour and the London poor*. London: Dover.

2   Skogan, W. (2015). Disorder and decline: The state of research. *Journal of Research in Crime and Delinquency, 52*(4), 464–485.

3   Haase, A., Athanasopoulou, A., & Rink, D. (2016). Urban shrinkage as an emerging concern for European policymaking. *European Urban and Regional Studies, 23*(1), 103–107.

4   Wilson, W. J. (2011). *When work disappears: The world of the new urban poor*. New York: Vintage.

5   Wilson, W. J. (2012). *The declining significance of race: Blacks and changing American institutions*. Chicago: University of Chicago Press.

6   Skogan, W. G. (1990). *Disorder and decline: Crime and the spiral of decay in American neighborhoods*. New York: Free Press; p. 2.

7   Baker, T., & Wolfer, L. (2003). The crime triangle: Alcohol, drug use, and vandalism. *Police Practice and Research*, *4*(1), 47–61.

8   Skogan, *Disorder and decline: Crime and the spiral of decay in American neighborhoods*; p. 3.

9   Skogan, W. G. (2012). Disorder and crime. In B. Welsh & D. P. Farrington (Eds.), *The Oxford handbook of crime prevention*, pp. 173–188. Oxford: Oxford University Press.

10 Finnie, W. C. (1973). Field experiments in litter control. *Environment and Behavior*, *5*(2), 123–144.

11 Huffman, K. T., Grossnickle, W. F., Cope, J. G., & Huffman, K. P. (1995). Litter reduction: A review and integration of the literature. *Environment and Behavior*, *27*(2), 153–183.

12 Cialdini, R. B., Reno, R. R., & Kallgren, C. A. (1990). A focus theory of normative conduct: Recycling the concept of norms to reduce littering in public places. *Journal of Personality and Social Psychology*, *58*(6), 1015–1026.

13 Keizer, K., Lindenberg, S., & Steg, L. (2008). "The spreading of disorder." *Science*, *322*(5908), 1681–1685.

14 Wilson, J. Q., & Kelling, G. L. (1982). The police and neighborhood safety: Broken windows. *Atlantic Monthly*, *249*(3), 29–38.

15 Hinkle, J. C., & Weisburd, D. (2008). The irony of broken windows policing: A micro-place study of the relationship between disorder, focused police crackdowns and fear of crime. *Journal of Criminal Justice*, *36*(6), 503–512.

16 Schumpeter, J. A. (2013 [1942]). *Capitalism, socialism and democracy*. Abingdon, U.K.: Routledge.

17 Fasenfest, D. (2016). Rust belt cities. In *The international encyclopedia of geography*. New York: Wiley.

18 Skogan, W. (1986). Fear of crime and neighborhood change. *Crime and Justice*, *8*, 203–229.

19 Boggess, L. N., Greenbaum, R. T., & Tita, G. E. (2013). Does crime drive housing sales? Evidence from Los Angeles. *Journal of Crime and Justice*, *36*(3), 299–318.

20 Haller, W. (2005). Industrial restructuring and urban change in the Pittsburgh region: Developmental, ecological, and socioeconomic trade-offs. *Ecology and Society*, *10*(1), Article 13. http://dx.doi.org/10.5751/ES-01261-100113.

21 Kelling, G. L., & Coles, C. M. (1997). *Fixing broken windows: Restoring order and reducing crime in our communities.* New York: Simon and Schuster.

22 Braga, A. A., & Bond, B. J. (2008). Policing crime and disorder hot spots: A randomized controlled trial. *Criminology*, *46*(3), 577–607.

23 Braga, A. A. (2001). The effects of hot spots policing on crime. *The ANNALS of the American Academy of Political and Social Science*, *578*(1), 104–125.

24 Donnermeyer, J. F., & DeKeseredy, W. (2013). *Rural criminology*, Vol. 3. Abingdon, U.K.: Routledge.

UNIT 5.7 Mapping Crime

The telescope revolutionized astronomy.[1] The microscope created modern biology.[2] Similarly, new **mapping technology** is transforming criminology.[3] We are now in an exciting period with rapid growth of what we know about different types of crime, where and when it happens, and how to reduce it.

That precision was not possible in the past. In 1833 a French attorney named **André-Michel Guerry** produced the world's first crime maps, based on 86 large French provinces each averaging a population of around 370,000.[4] Guerry used a very crude calculating machine,[5] but most of his data were probably added up by hand and copied using pencils and quill pens. **Émile Durkheim** also relied on crude maps, based on **large provinces** in France and other European nations, which help explain why *anomie* theory (discussed in Unit 5.5) was so imprecise.

Crime Maps from the Great Depression

As we noted in Unit 5.1, Shaw and McKay figured out how the delinquency area fit into large American cities, starting with Chicago. They produced the first, and most famous, urban crime map based on Chicago's 77 community areas—averaging 44,000 persons each.[6] Thanks to President Roosevelt's Works Progress Administration funding, they hired an army of students to poke at clunky adding machines.[7] Shaw and McKay adapted the now famous **zonal map** of the city, devised by **Ernest W. Burgess** to describe Chicago and other American cities of that era (see Figure 5i), with residential and business zones radiating outward from the **central business district** (CBD).[8] Next comes the **zone of transition**, mixing declining factories, abandoned properties, railroad yards, commercial units, and undesirable residential buildings—also containing the delinquency area. Zones proceed outwards to residential areas, then the suburban commuter zone.

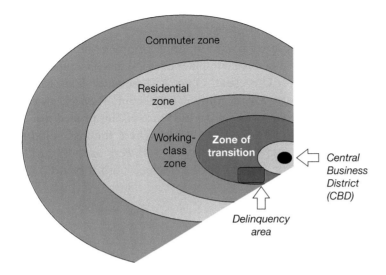

FIGURE 5I
The Zonal Model of Ernest W. Burgess
Source: Adapted from E. W. Burgess (1925). *The growth of the city*. Chicago: University of Chicago Press.

Shaw and McKay also produced a more specific **pin map** by pushing pins into the wall for the home address of each delinquent youth. A photographer with a wide-angle lens took a picture of the wall map, but there was no computer available for further analysis of specific addresses.

Crime Maps from Mainframe Computers

In the 1960s crime researchers began to use huge **mainframe computers**, as big as a classroom but with less computer power than your cell phone. At first, computer programs were hardwired like an electrician working on a huge fuse box in a garage. Crime data had to be punched digit by digit onto cards, and boxes of cards were then stuffed into the machine. Eventually programs were punched onto another set of computer cards. After boxes were hauled to the computer for card entry, analysis was slow and errors plentiful. It often took a month or more to produce a crude crime map that now takes a few seconds. These methods allowed criminologists to map crime for several hundred **census tracts** per city, containing about 4,000 people each.[9] Yet these maps could take researchers and theorists only so far.

Maps Get Closer and Closer to Crime

The most important leap forward in crime mapping was introduced in 1981 by **Dennis Roncek**. He programed the computer to assign specific crimes and specific places to *each block on the map* for Cleveland, Ohio.[10] These **block data** brought criminology closer than ever before to where crime events occur. Roncek also mapped all the barrooms in the city by block. As shown in Figure 5j, this proved that **bar blocks** have considerably more crime than non-bar blocks. These findings could not have been produced using the maps created by Shaw and McKay or those in Durkheim's era. You can see that changing map technology helped push forward our knowledge of crime.

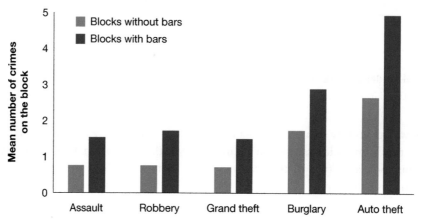

FIGURE 5J

Mean Number of Crimes on Blocks with and without Bars, Cleveland, Ohio (Classic 1981 Study)

Source: Adapted from D. W. Roncek & R. Bell (1981). The visibility of illicit drugs: Implications for community-based drug control strategies *Journal of Environmental Systems, 11*(1), 35–47.

David Weisburd and colleagues moved crime analysis even closer to specific places.[11] They mapped 323,979 calls to Minneapolis police, learning that 3 percent of places accounted for 50 percent of calls for police assistance. Robberies and rapes were even more concentrated. Researchers also transformed what we know about crime in low-income areas. The "other side of the tracks" is *far more diverse than previously believed.*

A Whole New Image of "High-Crime Zones"

Most low-income blocks have no crime at all, even in a "tough" neighborhood. Some crime hot spots are tucked away in middle-class neighborhoods. That forces us to re-evaluate our entire picture of how crime is distributed over a city or metropolis. A high-crime area is *not* riddled with crime; rather, it simply contains an ***extra share of high-crime blocks***.[12] The same observation applies to juvenile arrests, which are heavily concentrated in a few street segments.[13] These findings are verified in cities of different sizes around the United States and in other nations.

Modern crime mapping leads to three basic principles about how crime is distributed over urban space:

- ***General concentration principle***. Crime incidents are concentrated in very few blocks, intersections, and addresses. Most places have no reported crime at all.

- ***Toxic-block principle***. Even in an area with a high average crime rate, most blocks, intersections, and addresses have no reported crime at all.

- ***Tucked-away principle***. Even in an area with a low average crime rate, there are some crime hot spots tucked away.[14]

Roughly half of the crimes in a city are located at only 5 percent of the addresses. As we learn more about how crime is distributed in space and time, we are forced to discard some of our social prejudices about groups of people and the places they live.

This point is illustrated in Figure 5k, which contains four maps that show how crime mapping has developed since the 1930s:

- A map made with 1930s technology uses ***large urban districts*** and gives the impression that the East Side is dominated by crime, while the West Side is crime-free.

- A map produced with 1960s technology gives us slightly ***smaller urban districts***, but not small enough to get close to where crimes occur. It starts to show more variations on the East Side and a few crime pockets on the West Side. It still gives the impression that the East Side is overwhelmed by crime.

- A map made with 1980s technology reveals variations that the previous technologies missed, showing us that most blocks have no crime, even in the low-income zone.

- A map made with today's technology can link crime to specific addresses and problem buildings where multiple crimes are reported. This map helps local officials to focus on specific places and problems.

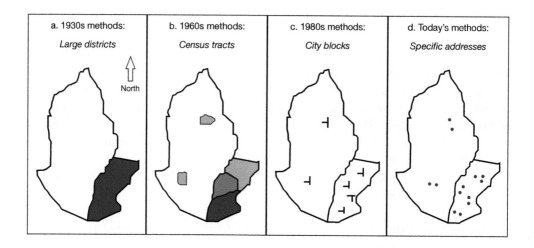

FIGURE 5K

Crime Maps for the Same City at Four Levels of Resolution, from Large Districts to Specific Addresses

Source: Adapted from P. J. Brantingham, D. A. Dyreson, & P. L. Brantingham (1976). Crime seen through a cone of resolution. *American Behavioral Scientist, 20*(2), 262–273.

Our impression of the East Side from Map (a) is completely changed as we get a closer look in Map (d). The East Side is not "crime-ridden," as previously believed. It simply has more bad blocks and bad addresses, even though most people have no crime at their addresses.

However, people living close to those toxic blocks are more sensitive to crime and more afraid. They respond to disorder and other environmental cues that remind them of crime. In addition, they are stigmatized by living near the high-crime blocks and near dilapidated and disorderly places. Thus, the bad blocks do damage to other residential zones not far away.

The new mapping techniques provide details that can help identify toxic blocks, reduce crime and disorder, and deliver better police and municipal services. Many police departments now include the ***map coordinates*** of crimes as part of their computerized data on crime incidents.[15] Today's crime maps look at much finer data, including addresses, intersections, and half-blocks. Much better ***mapping software*** can produce crime maps at low cost, helping police and researchers to learn more about risky places and times, and then use that information to prevent and contain crime. In Part 6 we consider how our additional knowledge of crime and disorder can help to protect women especially.

FLASHCARD LIST FOR UNIT 5.7

- Bar blocks
- Block data
- Burgess, Ernest W.
- Census tracts
- Central business district
- Durkheim, Émile
- Extra share of high-crime blocks

- General concentration principle
- Guerry, André-Michel
- Large provinces
- Large urban districts
- Mainframe computers
- Map coordinates
- Mapping software
- Mapping technology

- Pin map
- Roncek, Dennis
- Smaller urban districts
- Toxic-block principle
- Tucked-away principle
- Weisburd, David
- Zonal map
- Zone of transition

DISCUSSION QUESTIONS

1. Does crime theory change in response to crime mapping technology? Or do crime maps change in response to crime theory?

2. What does the concentration of crime in very few blocks tell us about delinquency areas?

Notes

1   Bud, R., & Warner, D. J. (Eds.). (1998). *Instruments of science: An historical encyclopedia.* New York: Taylor & Francis.

2   Rasmussen, N. (1999). *Picture control: The electron microscope and the transformation of biology in America, 1940–1960.* Stanford, CA: Stanford University Press.

3   Ratcliffe, J. (2010). Crime mapping: Spatial and temporal challenges. In A. R. Piquero & D. Weisburd (Eds.), *Handbook of quantitative criminology,* pp. 5–24. New York: Springer.

4   Friendly, M. (2007). A.-M. Guerry's moral statistics of France: Challenges for multivariable spatial analysis. *Statistical Science, 22*(3), 368–399.

5   Friendly, M., & de Sainte Agathe, N. (2012). André-Michel Guerry's ordonnateur statistique: The first statistical calculator? *The American Statistician, 66*(3), 195–200. It is possible that Guerry had invented or had access to a rudimentary desk calculator.

6   Shaw, C. R., & McKay, H. D. (1942). *Juvenile delinquency and urban areas.* Chicago: University of Chicago Press.

7   To see one of these machines, go to: www.youtube.com/watch?v=9Wg8iQoMy4s (retrieved November 13, 2016).

8   Burgess, E. W. (1925). The growth of the city. In R. E. Park, E. W. Burgess, & R. D. McKenzie (Eds.), *The city,* pp. 47–62. Chicago: University of Chicago Press.

9   Reviewed in: Roncek, D. W. (1975). Density and crime: A methodological critique. *American Behavioral Scientist, 18*(6), 843–860.

10   Roncek, D. W. (1981). Dangerous places: Crime and residential environment. *Social Forces, 60*(1), 74–96. Roncek, D. W., & Maier, P. (1991). Bars, blocks, and crimes revisited: Linking the theory of routine activity and opportunity models of predatory victimization. *Criminology, 29*(4), 725–753.

11   Sherman, L. W., Gartin, P. R., & Buerger, M. E. (1989). Hot spots of predatory crime: Routine activities and the criminology of place. *Criminology, 27*(1), 27–56.

12   Weisburd, D., Groff, E. R., & Yang, S.-M. (2012). *The criminology of place: Street segments and our understanding of the crime problem.* Oxford, U.K.: Oxford University Press.

13   Weisburd, D., Morris, N. A., & Groff, E. R. (2009). Hot spots of juvenile crime: A longitudinal study of arrest incidents at street segments in Seattle, Washington. *Journal of Quantitative Criminology, 25*(4), 443–467.

14   Weisburd, D. (2015). The law of crime concentration and the criminology of place. *Criminology, 53*(2), 133–157.

15   Chamard, S. (2004). The adoption of computerized crime mapping by municipal police departments in New Jersey. *Security Journal, 17*(1), 51–59. Ratcliffe, J. (2010). Crime mapping: spatial and temporal challenges. In *Handbook of quantitative criminology*, pp. 5-24. New York: Springer.

PERSPECTIVE ON PART 5

Part 5 focused on crime in neighborhoods. It made two major distinctions:

- *overt vs. covert crime*; and

- *crime vs. disorder*.

Overt crime was defined in terms of harm to the neighborhood. All neighborhoods have covert crime, harming a few people at a time. However, tougher neighborhoods supplement that with overt crime, which does greater ***neighborhood damage***.

Disorder emphasizes behaviors that fall short of crime, but harms neighborhoods. We have shown that both crime and disorder are essential for understanding neighborhood differences. Disorder is not easy to police or to handle within the justice system, yet some creative efforts to contain disorder were recounted. (We will discuss in Part 6 several additional ideas for designing safer residential and public areas to minimize disorder and deterioration.)

Extreme urban poverty areas are compared with other residential zones in Table 5a. Both have crime. The difference is that crime is mainly covert in other residential zones, while the tougher part of town has overt crime and disorder as well as a potential for open drug activity. Middle-class people also participate in overt violations of rules when they visit entertainment districts (also included in Table 5a). Such districts draw customers from surrounding suburbs and towns. Where people converge to drink and socialize, many of the rules of polite behavior can erode as alcohol flows and the night proceeds. Those with sufficient income and mobility move their misbehaviors away from their own residential zones into the entertainment zone of the city. The rightmost column of Table 5a shows how overt problems can emerge in entertainment areas. (Unit 6.4 goes into some detail on this very issue, relating it to aggression against women.)

Part 5 has covered a good deal of ground: from cohesion to intimidation; from social exclusion to concentration of poverty and other problems; from accommodation to living in tough areas to how those areas adapt to larger society. We spent a good deal of time explaining decay. We explained how a revolution in crime mapping has altered how we see cities and their high-crime zones. We have learned that in those zones, most blocks have no crime. We have also learned how it is possible for public officials to focus their efforts and thus reduce crime.

TABLE 5A **Comparing Extreme Poverty Residential Zone, Non-Poverty Residential Zone, and Entertainment Zone**

	Extreme poverty zone	Non-poverty residential zone	Entertainment zone
Covert rudeness	✓	✓	✓
Covert drunkenness	✓	✓	✓
Covert drug activity	✓	✓	✓
Covert property crimes	✓	✓	✓
Covert violence	✓	✓	✓
Overt rudeness	✓		✓
Overt drunkenness	✓		✓
Overt drug activity	✓		✓
Social disorder	✓		✓
Physical disorder	✓		✓

Ever since Mayhew's 1850 account of London, criminologists have seen a link between poverty and crime. In fact, this linkage is quite confusing. Empirical evidence continues to show too many cases where people who are not poor commit ordinary crimes, while many people who are poor commit no crime at all. Higher-income youths go through an adolescent period too, during which they break the rules of parents and larger society. How, then, do we explain the poverty–crime linkage given this evidence?

Our answer to the poverty–crime problem depends on distinguishing disorder from crime and overt crime from covert crime. We suggest that poverty does not cause covert crime or interpersonal rudeness, both of which are present in middle-class areas. However, poverty makes it more difficult for people to hide their human flaws and conceal those flaws from neighbors and from police. Poverty also makes it more difficult to escape the flaws of other people. It forces some people to live in risky situations, preventing their escape. That exposes them and their children to overt crime, along with social and physical disorder. Poverty also makes it more difficult for parents to contain the behavior of their children, who are then more likely to shift misbehavior into public view, to conflict with and join in with other youths, and to be victimized by offenders. Those neighborhoods also have trouble preventing the most aggressive youths from taking over public space. Thus, poverty causes crime and disorder to be more harmful to some neighborhoods and more obvious to all.

You have now been through much of our textbook and can take a step back to look at the larger picture. The front cover contains a summary diagram of our teaching framework, also found in the front of the book within "Our Teaching Framework." At the center of the diagram is risky situations, and the rest of the diagram examines how these situations grow and are controlled. Starting at the top of the diagram and working downwards, our teaching framework considers

- The four challenges every society must meet: To contain disputes, regulate sex, protect property, and help children develop and grow up safely. Part 1 of our book explored all four challenges.

- The four control processes that society uses in trying to meet these challenges: Personal controls, social controls, situational controls, and formal controls. Parts 2 and 3 examined these four control processes.

- The five life-cycle stages during which crime and crime control develop; Part 4 of our book emphasized these developmental processes.

Part 5 examined how neighborhood processes serve as **_crime enhancers_**. Tough neighborhoods do not _cause_ crime, which is found in other areas too. Yet tough neighborhoods _enhance_ crime, making it more overt and harmful to community life. Tough neighborhoods supplement crime with disorder. The remainder of our textbook continues to focus on crime enhancement processes. Next, in Part 6, we will examine how local crime enhancement processes harm women. The bad news is that poorly designed and mismanaged public spaces are quite harmful to the security of women. The good news is that something can be done about it.

Main Points of Part 5

- Overt crime does more harm to a neighborhood than covert crime.

- Public disorder does great local harm, even when it is not illegal.

- Middle-class people engage in a good deal of concealed criminal behavior.

- Neighborhood cohesion is difficult to introduce from outside the neighborhood.

- In high-crime areas, people are intimidated and afraid to act against crime.

- Good neighbors cannot always see when crime is happening.

- There's a long history of trying to exclude outsiders in pursuit of local safety.

- Concentrated disadvantage serves to elevate the age–crime curve.

- Residents use several methods to accommodate to dangerous neighbors.

- Adverse experiences can enhance crime, especially when blame is attributed.

- Disorder upsets more people than crime itself.

- A pathway to decay can be observed in tough neighborhoods over time.

- Crime maps have become much more precise over time, teaching us that crime is concentrated within a few blocks, intersections, or addresses.

FLASHCARD LIST FOR PERSPECTIVE ON PART 5

- Crime enhancers
- Crime vs. disorder
- Neighborhood damage
- Overt vs. covert crime

PART 6

Risky Settings for Women

In Part 5, we saw how crime and disorder can enhance local fear of crime. Part 6 details how risks apply especially to women. We believe that male students will find Part 6 especially interesting since more secure places for women would help

- make men safer and more comfortable too;

- make life more secure for their mothers, sisters, and female friends; and

- make it easier for a man to meet the right woman informally, and vice versa.

However, the main focus here is the security of women from their viewpoint.

A Female View of Crime

We can learn about victimization of both men and women by examining feminist scholarship, which seeks "a woman-centered description and explanation of human experience and the social world. It asserts that gender governs every aspect of personal and social life."[1]

Feminist criminologists examine how women fall victim to crime and are exposed to disorderly behaviors, and how women are affected by these experiences. Feminist criminologists often criticize the rest of criminology for neglecting women and failing to interpret crime in terms of gender roles. At least a dozen feminist theories of crime and justice have been propounded.[2] Many of these theories also consider how gender roles make males more aggressive and more dangerous, not only to women but also to other males.

Discussions of threats to women often focus on forcible rape, but that is only one of the aggressive encounters women face. In Part 6, we consider a wide range of aversive experiences and aggressive encounters that impinge on women. We give special attention to street harassment, nightlife harassment, and other fear-producing incidents that seldom result in legal action.[3] This broader perspective is needed to understand the vulnerability that women may feel. Part 6 focuses on the *practical* side of making women safer, offering many ways that dangers can be reduced for women. As we learned in Unit 2.3, crime prevented in one risky situation does not usually displace to another. The *absence of displacement* means that each community can improve the daily security of women living or visiting there without pushing problems to another location.

Negative Experiences for Women

Women vary greatly in how they react to crime or disorder.[4] Women also have a wide variety of *aversive experiences*, confrontations, and victimizations. In most of these incidents, no law is broken, and many confrontations contain no direct sexual content. Yet other forms of aggression are overtly sexual in nature. We try to sort out these distinctions in Figure 6a, which separates aggression from crime and *sexual aggression* from *non-sexual aggression*.

Aggression means that one person has directed hostile communication or behavior at another. Aggression can take many forms and involve many roles, but it includes male attacks on women—whether verbal or physical, sexual or non-sexual, legal or illegal. The three categories depicted in Figure 6a overlap partially, producing five types of aversive incidents for women:

- *Type A.* These incidents involve non-sexual confrontation that does not clearly cross the line into illegality.

    Example: panhandling.[5]

- *Type B.* These incidents are both illegal and confrontational.

    Example: purse-snatching.

- *Type C.* These incidents are illegal without confrontation.

    Example: ordinary theft.

- *Type D.* These incidents combine aggressive sexual confrontation with law violation.

    Example: forcible rape.

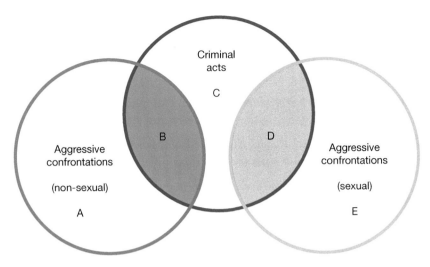

Overlapping Problems—Crime, Aggressive Sexual Confrontations, and Aggressive Non-Sexual Confrontations

- *Type E.* These incidents are aggressively sexual but avoid illegality.

    Example: **catcalling** (*shouting obscenities at women who are strangers*).

We continue to examine a wide diversity of unwanted encounters for women, ranging from "seeing men hanging around" and "manspreading" (discussed in Unit 6.2) to forcible rape. Some encounters are merely unpleasant, but others are extremely harmful. To distinguish these behaviors, we would ask ten specific questions about an aversive encounter:

1. *Is the encounter directed at her?* You might be annoyed by seeing a drunk man in the park, but it is worse if he directs his attention to you.

2. *Is the encounter proximate?* Someone shouting at you from across the street is bad, but shouting right next to you is worse.

3. *Are there sexually explicit words?* Uninvited conversation is worse if a man makes explicitly sexual remarks to you.

4. *Is a sexual threat spoken?* Sexual remarks are worse if they include an overt threat of sexual action.

5. *Is there **exhibitionism**?* It is even worse if a strange man openly rubs his crotch or pulls out his penis and shows it to an unwilling woman.[6]

6. *Is the encounter tactile?* Uninvited talk is a nuisance, but the situation is worse if a stranger touches you.

7. *Is the touching sexual?* It is even worse if the offender rubs his pelvic area or erect penis against an unwilling woman. This is known as *frotteurism*.

8. *Does the offender invade a home?* **Home invasion** is extremely threatening for a woman, even if the offender is gone by the time she returns home.[7]

9. *Is there an attempted sexual assault?* Attempted sexual assaults produce far more fear and suffering for the victim than the other examples.

10. *Is it a **penetrative sexual assault?*** A woman is most repulsed and upset by sexual attacks that penetrate her body.

These ten specific questions illustrate the wide variety of aversive experiences, sexual harassment, and sexual attack.[8] Women are even more likely to be threatened by a sexually harassing behavior in certain contexts: if the harasser is older or larger, if she is alone with him, or if the harassment occurs after dark.[9] Her fears increase further if the harasser is persistent, uses a threatening tone of voice, employs dominant or aggressive body language, or harasses in a relatively isolated location.[10] The great challenge is to reduce these risks and make women more secure.

Practical Policy Analysis

Feminist criminology includes moral analysis, legal analysis, and practical policy analysis.

- **Moral analysis** considers the wrongs that women suffer in terms of patrimony and objectification. *Patrimony* refers to male power and dominance in society and how that constrains females.[11] *Objectification* refers to males responding to females on an exclusively sexual basis.[12]

- **Legal analysis** applies the tools of the legal system in seeking to protect women from mistreatment by men.[13] This approach proposes changes in laws and how they are enforced.

- **Practical policy analysis** focuses on specific design and management of settings where women go, seeking to diminish their risks.[14]

In Part 6, we emphasize practical policy analysis, applying some of the lessons of Unit 2.3. Many distinctions that are almost irrelevant from a moral or legal viewpoint prove to be very important in making women safer from a practical viewpoint.

- From a moral or legal viewpoint, men hanging around in the park have nothing to do with forcible rape.
    - o   From a practical and policy viewpoint, men hanging out in public places can endanger, scare, and constrain women.
- From a moral or legal viewpoint, panhandlers approaching women are a minor matter.
    - o   From a practical and policy viewpoint, many women fear male strangers and avoid public places where strangers approach or pester them.
- From a moral or legal viewpoint, it does not matter whether a forcible rape occurs on or off a university campus. Both are equally bad.
    - o   From a practical and policy viewpoint, the location, timing, and *modus operandi* of crime and disorder incidents is central for prevention purposes.
- From a moral or legal viewpoint, it does not matter whether a building is designed with women's bathrooms in remote places or if homes have unsafe entries.
    - o   From a practical and policy standpoint, bad designs make women unsafe and need to be addressed.

Practical policy analysis looks beyond moral and legal discussions to distinguish the different ways that women can be endangered and how group situations influence the process.

The Social Psychological Viewpoint

Social psychology is the scientific study of how people's thoughts, feelings, and behaviors are influenced by the actual, imagined, or implied presence of others. Social psychology considers the diverse situations in which people interact *with other people*.[15] Consider the following situations:

Situation X: A man makes unwanted and crude sexual comments to a woman in public *within earshot of other men*.

Situation Y: A man makes unwanted and crude sexual comments *while alone with a woman*.

These two situations are entirely different from a social psychological viewpoint, even if they seem the same from a moral viewpoint. What makes them different is the presence or absence of other people in a face-to-face encounter. In Situation X, the man might be seeking to impress or show off to other men as he harasses a woman. In Situation Y, the man may be seeking to conceal from outsiders his effort to gain sexual access to a woman. Perhaps the first man harasses many different women as each of them passes him in the street or as he moves through the public transit train. Another man stalks and harasses the same woman over and over.[16] Both are repeat harassers, but their patterns are quite different from a social psychological point of view.

The harms from forcible rape depend on whether the perpetrator has a close relationship with the victim, is a casual acquaintance, or is a total stranger. In general, sexual violence committed by spouses or boyfriends are more coercive and produce more serious injuries than those committed by strangers or acquaintances.[17] *Psychological harm* also differs by how the victim and offender are related.[18] Victims feel a greater sense of personal betrayal when sexually traumatized within a close relationship.[19] For example, an assault by a steady boyfriend might produce a fear of building future personal relationships with other men. Feminists often call for the justice system to act against these problems, but this is not always possible.

Looking Beyond the Justice System

Parts 1 through 3 of this book explained that the justice system in general is very expensive and cumbersome. This is no less true when women are targeted. Street harassment and other incidents harmful to women are not easily reported to or processed by the justice system. Even the most serious sexual attacks often evade the legal system: An offender is unknown; proof is elusive; witnesses are missing; or the victim is too embarrassed and afraid to go forward with charges.[20] Sexual incidents small and large are usually ill-suited for legal action. That means that offenders usually go unpunished. Even women police or sympathetic male justice officials cannot easily overcome these practical difficulties. Protecting women creates a special policy challenge that goes well beyond the police and the courts. Recent efforts have used cell phone technology to combat harassment of women. Various apps allow women to report street harassment; however, there is no indication that these apps are effective in reducing that problem.[21] To increase security for women, criminologists must continue to broaden their horizons and to touch base with urban planners, geographers, architects, and designers. This has already happened in several nations, as you shall see as Part 6 unfolds.

Need for Women Architects

Why are so many places poorly designed for women? A good explanation is the longtime lack of women architects. Many U.S. architecture schools refused to admit women until the 1972 passage of a federal anti-discrimination law. Many women trained in architecture do not get hired by firms, and others have left their profession early.[22] Although the number of women architects has increased in recent years, most of the buildings, cities, and urban spaces in the United States today were designed by men, usually without considering the special security needs of women.

Winston Churchill commented: "First we design buildings; then they design us."[23] Buildings cannot alone transform people, but bad buildings and environments can enhance crime, disorder, and fear. Architectural designs have historically served to disadvantage women by producing "biased space."[24] Historically, homes were designed with woman's space separate from men's, and public spaces were designed with little concern for the interests, security, or comfort of women. Toilets had too few stalls for women and were often placed in remote and risky spots.[25] Public parks—both small[26] and large[27]—often contain blind spots that scare women away. Fortunately, researchers and designers have learned how to reduce crime and fear of crime in parks,[28] pointing the way towards making women more secure there.[29]

Unit 6.1 explains why women are more afraid when confronted with the same cues as men; it also presents five policy recommendations for making women more secure. Unit 6.2 reviews efforts to make streets and public environments safer for women. Unit 6.3 focuses on minimizing annoyances and attacks closer to home. Unit 6.4 examines some risky recreation situations and alcohol policies and practices impinging on women. Perhaps Part 6 will make you angry about some of the ways that society foolishly endangers women. However, you might feel better as you learn how these dangers can be reduced and reversed.

FLASHCARD LIST FOR PART 6: RISKY SETTINGS FOR WOMEN

- Aggression, non-sexual, sexual
- Analysis, legal, moral, practical policy
- Aversive experiences
- Catcalling

- Displacement, absence of
- Exhibitionism
- Forcible rape
- Frotteurism
- Home invasion
- Ordinary theft

- Panhandling
- Penetrative sexual assault
- Psychological harm
- Purse-snatching
- Social psychology

QUESTIONS ADDRESSED IN PART 6

1.   How does society design risky situations for women?

2.   What are the "smaller" sexual risks and annoyances that women face, and why are they important?

3.   Why do women feel greater fear of crime and disorder than men?

4.   How can society design safer environments for women?

5.   Can liquor policy protect women more effectively?

Notes

1   Danner, M. (1991). Socialist feminism: A brief introduction. In B. MacLean & D. Milanovic (Eds.), *New directions in critical criminology*, pp. 51–54. Vancouver: Collective Press; p. 51.

2   Maidment, M. R. (2006). Transgressing boundaries: Feminist perspectives in criminology. In W. S. DeKeseredy & B. Perry (Eds.), *Advancing critical criminology: Theory and application*, pp. 43–62. Landham, MD: Lexington Books. Ahrentzen, S. (2003). The space between the studs: Feminism and architecture. *Signs: Journal of Women in Culture and Society*, 29(1), 179–206. Marzbali, M. H., Abdullah, A., Razak, N. A., & Tilaki, M. J. M. (2012). The influence of crime prevention through environmental design on victimisation and fear of crime. *Journal of Environmental Psychology*, 32(2), 79–88.

3   Graham, K., Bernards, S., Abbey, A., Dumas, T. M., & Wells, S. (2016). When women do not want it: Young female bargoers' experiences with and responses to sexual harassment in social drinking contexts. *Violence Against Women*. Published online August 23. DOI: 10.1177/1077801216661037.

4   Stylianou, S. (2003). Measuring crime seriousness perceptions: What have we learned and what else do we want to know. *Journal of Criminal Justice*, 31(1), 37–56. Ignatans, D., & Pease, K. (2016). Taking crime Seriously: Playing the weighting game. *Policing*, 10(3), 184–193.

5   Lopez, K. (2016). *Neighborhood incivilities: Effects of disorder on fear of crime, perceived risk of victimization, and constrained social behavior.* Doctoral dissertation, University of Michigan.

6   Clark, S. K., Jeglic, E. L., Calkins, C., & Tatar, J. R. (2016). More than a nuisance: The prevalence and consequences of frotteurism and exhibitionism. *Sexual Abuse*, 28(1), 3–19.

7   Lane, J., & Fox, K. A. (2013). Fear of property, violent, and gang crime: Examining the shadow of sexual assault thesis among male and female offenders. *Criminal Justice and Behavior*, 40(5), 472–496.

8   Felson, R. B., & Cundiff, P. R. (2014). Sexual assault as a crime against young people. *Archives of Sexual Behavior*, 43(2), 273–284.

9   Fairchild, K. (2010). Context effects on women's perceptions of stranger harassment. *Sexuality and Culture*, 14(3), 191–216.

10   Esacove, A. W. (1998). A diminishing of the self: Women's experiences of unwanted sexual attention. *Health Care for Women International*, 19(3), 181–192.

11   Renzetti, C. M. (2013). *Feminist criminology*. Abingdon, U.K.: Routledge.

12   Szymanski, D. M., Moffitt, L. B., & Carr, E. R. (2011). Sexual objectification of women: Advances to theory and research. *The Counseling Psychologist*, 39(1), 6–38.

13 Grana, S. J. (2009). *Women and justice*. Washington, DC: Rowman & Littlefield Publishers.

14 Day, K. (2011). Feminist approaches to urban design. In T. Banerjee & A. Loukaitou-Sideris (Eds.), *Companion to urban design*, pp. 150–161. Abingdon, U.K.: Routledge.

15 Pryor, J. B., Giedd, J. L., & Williams, K. B. (1995). A social psychological model for predicting sexual harassment. *Journal of Social Issues*, *51*(1), 69–84.

16 Spitzberg, B. H. (2016). Stalking/obsessive relational intrusion. In C. R. Berger (Ed.), *The international encyclopedia of interpersonal communication*, pp. 1–9. New York: Wiley.

17 Stermac, L., Bove, G. D., Brazeau, P., & Bainbridge, D. (2006). Patterns in sexual assault violence as a function of victim perpetrator degree of relatedness. *Journal of Aggression, Maltreatment and Trauma*, *13*(1), 41–58.

18 Ullman, S. E., Filipas, H. H., Townsend, S. M., & Starzynski, L. L. (2006). The role of victim–offender relationship in women's sexual assault experiences. *Journal of Interpersonal Violence*, *21*(6), 798–819.

19 Ullman, S. E. (2007). Relationship to perpetrator, disclosure, social reactions, and PTSD symptoms in child sexual abuse survivors. *Journal of Child Sexual Abuse*, *16*(1), 19–36.

20 Zydervelt, S., Zajac, R., Kaladelfos, A., & Westera, N. (2016). Lawyers' strategies for cross-examining rape complainants: Have we moved beyond the 1950s? *British Journal of Criminology*, *57*(3), 551–569.

21 Weiss, M. (2016). An analysis of anti-gender based street harassment mobile applications. *Intersect: Stanford Journal of Science, Technology and Society*, *9*(3). http://web.stanford.edu/group/ojs3/cgi-bin/ojs/index.php/intersect/article/view/855 (accessed August 1, 2017).

22 Stratigakos, D. (2016). *Where are the women architects?* Princeton, NJ: Princeton University Press.

23 Churchill, W. S. (2003). A sense of crowd and urgency. Speech to the House of Commons, October 28, 1943. In *Never give in! The best of Winston Churchill's Speeches*, pp. 358–360. New York: Hyperion.

24 Shah, R. C., & Kesan, J. P. (2007). How architecture regulates. *Journal of Architectural and Planning Research*, *24*(4), 350–359.

25 Jeffreys, S. (2014, August). The politics of the toilet: A feminist response to the campaign to "degender" a women's space. *Women's Studies International Forum*, *45*, (July–August), 42–51.

26 Nordh, H., & Østby, K. (2013). Pocket parks for people: A study of park design and use. *Urban Forestry and Urban Greening*, *12*(1), 12–17.

27 Iqbal, A., & Ceccato, V. (2016). Is CPTED useful to guide the inventory of safety in parks? A study case in Stockholm, Sweden. *International Criminal Justice Review*, *26*(2), 150–168. Knutsson, J. (1997). Restoring public order in a city park. In R. Homel (Ed.), *Policing for prevention: Reducing crime, public intoxication and injury*. Crime Prevention Studies, Vol. 7, pp. 133–151. Monsey, NY: Criminal Justice Press.

28 Groff, E., & McCord, E. S. (2012). The role of neighborhood parks as crime generators. *Security Journal*, *25*(1), 1–24.

29 Hilborn, J. (2009). *Dealing with crime and disorder in urban parks*. Problem-Oriented Guides for Police, Response Guide Series, No. 9. Washington, DC: Office of Community Oriented Policing Services. McCord, E. S., & Houser, K. A. (2017). Neighborhood parks, evidence of guardianship, and crime in two diverse US cities. *Security Journal*, *30*(3), 807–824.

Unit 6.1 The Policy Challenge

Women learn at a young age to avoid certain places and to be home at certain times. Girls are usually more restricted than boys in terms of space, time, and activities.[1] When old enough to make their own decisions, many females continue to have a relatively narrower span of activities, often to avoid unpleasant encounters with males.[2] This unit explores how negative experiences enhance fear for women.[3] Public policy has quite a challenge—to make women more secure as they go about their daily lives.

The Structure of Fear

Feminist criminologists helped develop *victimology*, the study of how people are victimized by crime, how they fear victimization, and how they react to disorder and aversive environmental cues reminding them of crime.[4] People become fearful for many reasons beyond their statistical risk of falling victim to crime. Extra fear can result from:

- witnessing social and physical disorder;[5]

- victimization of family, friends, and acquaintances;[6]

- alarming rumors; and

- mass media accounts of crime incidents.[7]

Women perceive higher risk than men and are more sensitive to social and physical disorder, including decrepit and abandoned buildings.[8] Like men, women are especially responsive to dangers closer to home.[9] Studies in the United States and many other nations consistently show that women are much more afraid of crime than men.[10] For example, the 2014 Swedish national crime survey found that only 1 in 20 men feared attack or assault, while 1 in 3 women had such fear.[11] Women who are personally victimized are shocked to discover their vulnerability,[12] but even non-victims feel more fear than men. Fear of crime depends on three key components:

1. *Risk*. Exposure to a situation in which a harmful event might occur,

2. *Consequences*. Anticipation of serious consequences from such an event, and

3. *Lack of control*. The feeling that you are helpless and cannot escape the harmful event.[13]

A single word, **vulnerability**, sums up the problem.[14] Negative environmental cues that convey risk, serious harm, and loss of control make women feel especially vulnerable.[15] Imagine a woman is confronted by a panhandler. It is possible that he will be harmless and polite. It is also possible that his panhandling is a pretext for more aggressive behavior. Women tend to dislike approaches from males they do not know.

The Shadow of Rape

Compared to men, women face lower statistical risk of *non-sexual* aggression. However, women are exposed to quite a bit higher risk of *sexual* attack. Women who have been sexually attacked report their experience as terrifying and humiliating.[16] Women fear most being sexually attacked with penetration, as we have already noted.[17]

Even in crime situations where sexual attack is absent, women often fear the worst. This extra fear has led some criminologists to formulate the **shadow of rape hypothesis**. It tells us that diverse forms of non-sexual aggression evoke in women a fear of being raped.[18] In the back of their minds, many women think of robbery, even panhandling, as potential rape circumstances.[19] In the minds of many women, sexual assaults and non-sexual crimes are linked together. Neighborhood robberies, non-sexual assaults, auto thefts, vandalism—any of these crimes could enhance women's fear of encountering strange men who might carry out a sexual assault. This helps explain why neighborhood social and physical disorder bothers women more than men, reminding them of their sexual vulnerability.[20] Crimes involving *confrontation*, such as robbery and non-sexual assault, cause many women to think, "I could also have been raped." Arriving home to discover a burglar had been there, a woman is especially upset that her private space has been invaded. However, invasive behavior can also occur in public and social settings.

Too Close for Comfort

*"**Proxemic theory**"* relates to the psychological study of how close people get to one another and how they feel about proximity. The four types of distance between two persons are:

- *Public distance*: people minimize eye contact and stay away about 2 meters (6 or 7 feet);

- *Formal social distance*: people engage in formal interactions, do not touch, and get no closer than 1.2 meters (4 feet);

- *Personal distance*: interactions with friends occur no closer than about a half meter (1.5 feet); and

- *Intimate distance*: closer in space, with more perception of heat and smell.[21]

On a public street, each human being expects others to respect the small private zone near their bodies and to allow anonymous passage through public space without confrontation.[22] A study of 42 countries learned that women are considerably more likely than men to prefer that strangers keep their distance.[23] When male strangers approach too closely or block their passage, women may begin to worry that they cannot control what might happen.[24]

The shadow of rape makes sense for two extra reasons:

- The offender population is disproportionately male.

- Offenders are generalists, not specialists.

It is reasonable for a woman to assume that the burglar who violated her home was probably male and to worry about what he might have done to her. It is also reasonable to assume that the burglar is not a special class of offender and could also have committed rape given the opportunity. Rapists are not easy to distinguish from non-sexual offenders.[25] We should not be surprised that women are likely to arrive at a fearful response to panhandling and other non-sexual crimes. Assuming the worst is a normal human response.[26] Bad experiences have more impact on people than good experiences, and people process bad information more thoroughly than good information.[27] To make women more secure from sexual attack, society needs to attend more broadly to security on streets and in neighborhoods. Options are shown in Figure 6b.

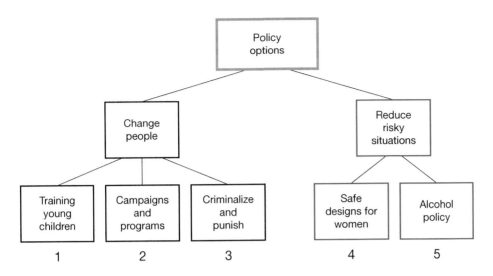

FIGURE 6B
Policy Options for Reducing Male Aggression against Females

Policies to reduce male aggression against women include:

1. *Training young children.* Reshaping early education to make males less aggressive towards females (see Unit 2.1)[28] by changing society's norms, practices, and behaviors.[29]

2. *Campaigns and programs.* Using public relations and training programs to change male attitudes and behaviors towards women.[30]

3. *Criminalization and punishment.* Using energetic law enforcement to contain male aggression.

4. *Safe designs for women.* This topic is discussed throughout Part 6.

5. *Alcohol policy.* This topic is examined in Unit 6.4.

Lacking proof that early childhood education changes subsequent sexual aggression, feminist organizations have shifted their focus to publicity campaigns, campus programs, and law enforcement.

Feminist Media Advocacy

For several decades, the feminist movement has engaged in *media advocacy*; that is, publicity campaigns against sexual attacks and abuse of women. For example, the Michigan Coalition Against Domestic and Sexual Violence provides toolkits, guides for journalists, and factsheets about how sexual violence harms women. They train female activists in mass communication planning, building media relationships, and arranging interviews with survivors of sexual attacks.[31]

Media advocacy has been present for at least a half-century, including anti-rape, anti-smoking, anti-drinking, anti-drunk-driving, and anti-gang campaigns.[32] Unfortunately, media advocacy often fails to achieve stated goals.[33] Four decades of campaigns against drunk driving have met with mixed results.[34] Well-publicized executions in the United States failed to reduce the homicide rates.[35] The massive and prolonged Drug Abuse Resistance Education (D.A.R.E.) and First Lady Nancy' Reagan's "just say no" publicity produced no measurable reductions in drug abuse.[36] Neither have broad anti-shoplifting campaigns had much impact.[37] Media campaigns can even backfire. Publicity against drugs can lead to *increases* in illegal drug use.[38] Other publicity and media exposure ends up increasing fear of a problem and distorting public perceptions, without reducing the problem itself.[39]

Media advocacy sometimes works better as one part of a larger effort.[40]

- Publicity campaigns against smoking and drinking can help if they are backed by higher prices for cigarettes and liquor. Steep increases in excise tax can lead to major reductions in cigarette smoking[41] and drinking.[42] Doubling the alcohol tax appears to reduce alcohol-related mortality by 35 percent.

- Local publicity against burglary can reduce the burglary rate when coupled with property marking.[43]

- A local publicity campaign succeeded in getting many bicycle owners to lock their bikes properly; the message was clear and simple and was combined with instructions on locking procedures.[44]

Feminists complain that the preponderance of television content *reinforces* traditional gender roles,[45] diluting their own efforts to change male attitudes and behaviors.[46] The anti-rape movement probably succeeded in changing public *policy* towards rape,[47] but there is no indication that this publicity served to reduce *rape itself*.[48]

We can imagine how a more targeted media campaign could make women safer. For example, a university organization could develop a service to take women home from bars or parties on weekends. A targeted publicity campaign could encourage women to use this service and thus avoid risk of attack.

Educating Potential Offenders

Some women's service organizations include anti-rape programs on college campuses. These programs help women avoid being raped while, at the same time, seeking to change rape attitudes of campus men. Evaluations of such programs are limited,[49] but existing evidence is disappointing. Although the anti-rape program changes men's attitudes in the short run, within a few months men revert to their pre-program attitudes.[50] Nor is it clear that changes in attitudes have any impact on actual behavior. More disturbing, anti-rape programs can easily increase one problem (fear of rape) without decreasing the larger problem (rape itself).

Criminologists have witnessed a long history of easy solutions that sound good, only to discover that they do not work. A good example is *Scared Straight!* This was a famous documentary film showing prison inmates shouting at and terrifying young offenders brought to visit the prison. The idea was to "scare them straight" so that they would avoid a future in prison.[51] Programs like this became popular with the public and were imitated elsewhere, but evaluation research demonstrated that they not only failed to reduce crime and delinquency, but even seemed to enhance it.[52] Public relations efforts generally fail to reduce crime.

Protecting Women by Enhancing Enforcement

Many feminists have advocated protecting women with more energetic law enforcement.[53] Criticizing the shortcomings of the justice system,[54] these feminists argue that officials should

- treat sexual assault victims more respectfully and fairly;[55]

- work much harder to discover and charge rapists;[56] and

- punish rapists more harshly than in the past.[57]

"Get tough" policies pose many practical problems. Consistent with Part 3, the justice system is extremely cumbersome as it seeks to apprehend, prosecute, convict, and incarcerate sexual offenders who harm women.[58] It is difficult to prove men guilty while also protecting female victims and protecting those men falsely accused.[59] Women reporting sexual attacks may themselves undergo a grueling process as a case moves through the system. "Second rape" is the term used to explain how women may suffer due to treatment by medical,[60] social service,[61] and legal agencies.[62]

The 1984 Minneapolis Domestic Violence Experiment sought an easier solution. In some cases of women calling police to report domestic violence, police *immediately* went to arrest the man and take him to jail.[63] In a control group, men were not arrested under similar circumstances. The experiment initially concluded that a compulsory arrest reduced domestic violence and protected women, without requiring long-term incarceration. This was one of the most influential and important policy research projects in the history of criminology. Police departments across the United States began arresting males accused of domestic violence and quickly jailing them.[64] That led the federal government to fund several additional studies to determine whether the policy really did work. Replications were tried in at least five other urban areas, but the results were quite mixed.[65] The quick jailing process appears to have worked best with middle-class males. In some cases, men endangered the women even more after getting home from jail. In other cases, quick arrests worked for a short period and then failed to reduce domestic violence a while later. A medical review of efforts to reduce wife abuse found no better results.

Shelters to Protect Women against Domestic Violence

Women's shelters are designed to protect women against domestic violence. These shelters may succeed in providing comfort and additional services, and as a gateway for medical care or legal advice. Woman's shelters sometimes help women avoid subsequent violence, but can also make things worse by enhancing conflict with male partners. Programs that target women or their male batterers have not demonstrated clear effectiveness in reducing recidivism. Some women who spent at least one night in a shelter and who received program assistance reported an improved quality of life without subsequent abuse. Yet, many intervention strategies did not clearly improve the situation faced by women or the behavior of men.[66] Hopefully, this will change. In the meantime, it makes sense to look for other options that could make women more secure.

Women's Risks Are Quite Concentrated

Fortunately, danger to women is extremely concentrated in time and in space as well as being linked to certain types of activities. This concentration allows each community to focus its efforts to make women safer. Women are also highly situational in their fear; for example, they are eight times as fearful of going to laundromats after dark compared to staying home. Women are substantially more afraid of night than day, and most fear inescapable, shadowy, and isolated public places. After dark, they fear public transit a lot, but bars and clubs more.[67] Not surprisingly, they fear places where they are exposed to more strangers.[68] They don't like places where strangers can lurk in the shadows. They also fear concealing bushes, low levels of lighting, dark tunnels. Two words summarize the production of fear among women:

- **Prospect** is the ability to see around yourself and thus avoid walking into danger.

- **Refuge** is the ability for somebody attacking you to escape.[69]

Women feel unsafe in places with low levels of prospect and high levels of refuge. In other words, they do not want to feel trapped by a man who can attack and then get away. At night, women are in particular danger when lighting is highly uneven and an offender in the shadows can follow a woman walking through the lighted area, finding just the right moment to attack.[70]

Criminologists are beginning to use newer technologies to map the specific streets and places where women experience the greatest fear.[71] In a London-based study, participants installed a special app on their cell phones and went about their normal daily activities; researchers pinged them and asked them to relay their levels of fear at the time and place where they were.[72] A respondent could be walking some distance with no fear at all, then suddenly report a fearful situation. Fear varied substantially over the hours of day and within very small areas.[73] Women's risk shifts greatly within a 24-hour cycle.[74] For example, a study of Ottawa, Canada, showed how crime risk was influenced by daily flows of students and faculty.[75] Activity flows within a city— for shopping, work, and leisure—caused crime risk to spike in some places and times, but not others.[76] This new evidence places special pressure on public officials (and on

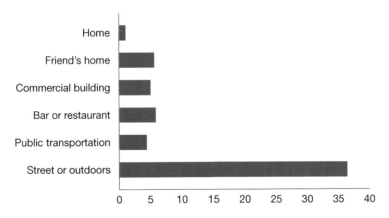

FIGURE 6C

Women's Risk of Violent Victimization per Million Person-Hours in Each Setting

Source: Adapted from A. M. Lemieux (2011). *Risks of violence in major daily activities, United States, 2003–2005*. Doctoral dissertation, Rutgers University; Table 7.5.

criminologists) to help protect women at times and places where they face the greatest dangers.

These dangers can be calculated by dividing (a) the number of victimizations in each setting by (b) the amount of time spent in that setting. As Figure 6c indicates, women face much more danger of violence for the hours they spend in streets or other outdoor environments. *Hour for hour* it is about 50 times riskier for women to be on streets or in public places compared to being at home. Risks to women can be localized even more. Some cities calculate which barrooms produce the most crime incidents, then apply liquor control policies to reduce the local problem (see Unit 6.4). Risk of violence is also greatest for teenage and young adult women, for single women, and for women recently separated or divorced.[77] Fortunately, society has the tools to reduce many of these risks for women by targeting the times, places, and activities where problems occur.[78]

Safer Design for Women

Oscar Newman was a famous architect and urban designer who figured out how to make women and men safer. Newman focused on how many people could enter an area without being noticed. Accordingly, he defined four types of space (Figure 6d):

- public space;
- semipublic space;
- semiprivate space; and
- private space.[79]

Public space allows the larger public to enter unrestricted. It includes streets, parks, and other very public places. **Semipublic space** is open to the public but is used in fewer ways. It includes sidewalks in front of your home and other areas where the public can go but often does not. **Semiprivate space** is mainly for residents, including the lobbies of apartment buildings or the yard just in front of a private home. **Private space** is reserved for residents and their invited guests.

As space becomes more private, people are more secure. As space becomes totally public, people are less secure. Newman advocated urban designs that maximize private and semiprivate access. He also advocated drawing clear lines so people know when they are entering semiprivate or private space. That does not require formidable walls and fences, guards, or other "hard" lines of demarcation. Instead it involves simple design ideas, such as flowers or lawns that give people a sense of where private space

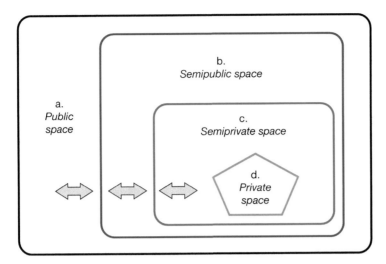

FIGURE 6D
Gradual Transitions to Private Space Make Women Much Safer

begins. Public housing complexes that use these principles experience much less local crime. That happens because of **natural surveillance**, the fact that good design makes it easier for residents to see and protect the area near their homes.[80]

Ask yourself, "How easily can strangers get to your home without anybody noticing them?" Figure 6d maps out the four types of space that can be pieced together to make people safer. The blue arrows indicate residents walking between the four types of space. With a safer design, a stranger can only get into private space after passing through semipublic and a semiprivate space. Gentle barriers and designs allow people to see that somebody is entering and to inhibit an outsider. This strategy also makes it safer for women to leave their homes, passing through semiprivate and semipublic spaces. Her risk goes up as she makes these transitions, but (at least for part of the way) neighbors might see what is happening.

Now we turn to a very unsafe design for women, as mapped in Figure 6e. This design includes no semipublic or semiprivate space. Homes are directly appended to public space, where outsiders can enter without inhibition. To make matters worse, part of the public space is hidden from view, as depicted by the grey shading. That can occur because there is no lighting or because bad building designs create nooks and crannies that endanger residents. Such hidden space makes it easier for unobserved offenders to break in or trespass on private spaces, or to ambush women as they leave for work, school, shopping, or other purposes. The blue arrows in Figure 6e show how unsafe a woman's movements can be. Worse still are designs allowing women no way to get home at night without walking through hidden space.

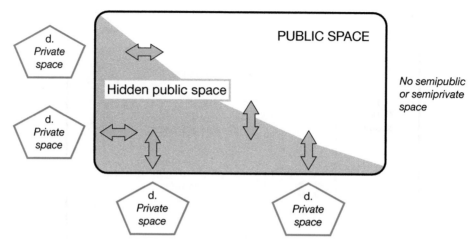

FIGURE 6E
Worst Design for Women

Women Pioneers in Safe Design

Ten years before Oscar Newman, two women figured out how cities can be designed to make people safe. In 1961 **Elizabeth Wood** suggested designing places in which people can thrive. That requires that a neighborhood and home allow active exercise, sunshine, fresh air, getting out, going somewhere, and carrying out some household tasks outdoors—such as washing a car or fixing a bike.[81] She reminded designers that for many people, these activities are the means and the excuse for social life: to see other people, to talk to other people, or to do something with other people. She understood that modern urban design was beginning to destroy many basic human needs that homes are supposed to provide.

That point was articulated the same year in a still-famous book by **Jane Jacobs**, *Death and Life of Great American Cities.* Jacobs explained how modern high-rise buildings, wide streets, and unassigned spaces serve to destroy communities. That happens because there are no longer **eyes on the street**,[82] making it very difficult for local people to live a safe life. Jacobs' observations were personal. She was a journalist, not an urban planner, and she was observant. She is the subject of a recent film, *Citizen Jane: Battle for the City*, which documents her fight to preserve her New York City neighborhood, Greenwich Village, preventing the removal of many low-rise buildings by developers who wanted to replace them with huge high-rises. Designs that interfere with local socializing and visibility make people far less secure. That insecurity has consequences in terms of diverse street harassment, social disorder, and serious sexual crimes. Poorly designed neighborhoods and mismanaged public spaces can produce a wide range of harms for women. Sadly, modern public places enhance risks for women, including risks of sexual attack.

In some contexts, women face considerable ***situational disadvantage***—specific conditions that make them especially vulnerable to harassment or harm.[83] Women can be stuck with one aggressive male and nobody else around. But they can also face situational disadvantage when greatly outnumbered by male strangers, or when in a crowded setting they cannot escape. We disaggregate the risks to women by looking separately at dangers in the street (Unit 6.2), dangers at or near home (Unit 6.3), and dangers in the night (Unit 6.4). Different dangers pose different policy challenges. Yet all three demonstrate that women can be harmed by design and management processes that disregard their security. The great irony is that a strong female presence in the architecture and planning professions would probably have made metropolitan environments safer for men as well as women.

FLASHCARD LIST FOR UNIT 6.1

- Eyes on the street
- Jacobs, Jane
- Natural surveillance
- Newman, Oscar
- Prospect
- Proxemic theory
- Refuge

- Shadow of rape hypothesis
- Situational disadvantage
- Space, public, semipublic, semiprivate, private
- Victimology
- Vulnerability
- Wood, Elizabeth

DISCUSSION QUESTIONS

1. Why do women tend to fear strangers more than men they know?

2. What is the shadow of rape, and how does it relate to panhandling?

Notes

1 Valentine, G. (1989). The geography of women's fear. *Area, 21*(4), 385–390.

2 Valentine, G. (2014). *Social geographies: Space and society*. Abingdon, U.K.: Routledge.

3 Hale, C. (1996). Fear of crime: A review of the literature 1. *International Review of Victimology, 4*(2), 79–150.

4 Fattah, E. A. (Ed.). (2016). *Towards a critical victimology*. New York: Springer.

5   Grubb, J. A., & Bouffard, L. A. (2015). The influence of direct and indirect juvenile victimization experiences on adult victimization and fear of crime. *Journal of Interpersonal Violence, 30*(18), 3151–3173.

6   Sacco, V. F. (2005). *When crime waves.* Thousand Oaks, CA: Sage Publications.

7   Sacco, V. F. (1995). Media constructions of crime. *Annals of the American Academy of Political and Social Science, 539*(1), 141–154. Heath, L. (1984). Impact of newspaper crime reports on fear of crime: Multimethodological investigation. *Journal of Personality and Social Psychology,* 47(2), 263–276. Heath, L., Patel, A., & Mulla, S. (2015). Toward a social-psychological understanding of mass media and fear of crime. In D. Chadee (Ed.), *Psychology of fear, crime, and the media: International perspectives,* pp. 79–96. Abingdon, U.K.: Routledge.

8   Loukaitou-Sideris, A. (2014). Fear and safety in transit environments from the women's perspective. *Security Journal, 27*(2), 242–256.

9   Luo, F., Ren, L., & Zhao, J. S. (2016). Location-based fear of crime: A case study in Houston, Texas. *Criminal Justice Review, 41*(1), 75–97.

10 Van Dijk, J. (2016). The criminal victimization of children and women in international perspective. In H. Kury, S. Redo, & E. Shea, E. (Eds.), *Women and children as victims and offenders: Background, prevention, reintegration,* pp. 405–425. London: Springer.

11 Statistics Sweden. (2014). *Women and men in Sweden: Facts and figures 2014.* Stockholm: Statistics Sweden.

12 Sacco, V. F., & Macmillan, R. (2001). Victimization and fear of crime: Re-thinking a classic controversy from a criminal event perspective. In R. F. Meier, L. W. Kennedy, & V. F. Sacco (Eds.), *The process and structure of crime: Criminal events and crime analysis.* Advances in Criminological Theory, Vol. 9, pp. 213–247. New Brunswick, NJ: Transaction.

13 Killias, M., & Clerici, C. (2000). Different measures of vulnerability in their relation to different dimensions of fear of crime. *British Journal of Criminology, 40*(3), 437–450.

14 Abdullah, A., Marzbali, M. H., Woolley, H., Bahauddin, A., & Maliki, N. Z. (2014). Testing for individual factors for the fear of crime using a multiple indicator-multiple cause model. *European Journal on Criminal Policy and Research, 20*(1), 1–22.

15 Loukaitou-Sideris, A., & Eck, J. E. (2007). Crime prevention and active living. *American Journal of Health Promotion, 21*(4 suppl), 380–389.

16 Ledray, L. E. (2015). *Recovering from rape.* New York: Holt.

17 Ignatans, D., & Pease, K. (2016). Taking crime seriously: Playing the weighting game. *Policing, 10*(3), 184–193. Stylianou, S. (2003). Measuring crime seriousness perceptions: What have we learned and what else do we want to know. *Journal of Criminal Justice, 31*(1), 37–56.

18 Ferraro, K. F. (1996). Women's fear of victimization: Shadow of sexual assault? *Social Forces, 75*(2), 667–690.

19 Lane, J., & Meeker, J. W. (2003). Women's and men's fear of gang crimes: Sexual and nonsexual assault as perceptually contemporaneous offenses. *Justice Quarterly, 20*(2), 337–371. Warr, M. (1985). Fear of rape among urban women. *Social Problems, 32*(3), 238–250. Fisher, B. S., & Sloan, J. J. (2003). Unraveling the fear of victimization among college women: Is the "shadow of sexual assault hypothesis" supported? *Justice Quarterly, 20*(3), 633–659.

20 Snedker, K. A. (2015). Neighborhood conditions and fear of crime: A reconsideration of sex differences. *Crime and Delinquency, 61*(1), 45–70.

21 Hall, E. T. (1966). *The hidden dimension*. New York: Doubleday.

22 Hall, E. T. (1968). Proxemics. *Current Anthropology*, *9*(2–3), 83–108. Goffman, E. (2008). *Behavior in public places*. New York: Simon and Schuster.

23 Sorokowska, A. (2017). Preferred interpersonal distances: A global comparison. *Journal of Cross-Cultural Psychology*, *48*(4), 577–592.

24 Junger, M. (1987). Women's experiences of sexual harassment: Some implications for their fear of crime. *British Journal of Criminology*, *27*(4), 358–383.

25 Harris, D. A., Mazerolle, P., & Knight, R. A. (2009). Understanding male sexual offending: A comparison of general and specialist theories. *Criminal Justice and Behavior*, *36*(10), 1051–1069.

26 Sunstein, C. R. (2009). *Worst-case scenarios*. Cambridge, MA: Harvard University Press.

27 Baumeister, R. F., Bratslavsky, E., Finkenauer, C., & Vohs, K. D. (2001). Bad is stronger than good. *Review of General Psychology*, *5*(4), 323–370.

28 Thornton, C. D., & Goldstein, L. (2006). Feminist issues in early childhood scholarship. In B. Spodek & O. N. Saracho (Eds.), *Handbook of research on the education of young children*, pp. 515–531. Abingdon, U.K.: Routledge.

29 Michigan Domestic and Sexual Violence Prevention Steering Committee. (n.d.). *Preventing intimate and sexual violence in Michigan: Prevention plan highlights for 2010–2015*. Okemos, MI: Michigan Coalition to End Sexual Violence. www.mcedsv.org/images/Document/Prevention/Prevention ReportEnglish6-2012.pdf (retrieved April 15, 2017).

30 Cooper, L. B., Paluck, E. L., Fletcher, E. K., Ryan, I. M., Branscombe, N. R., & Center, T. J. (2013). Reducing gender-based violence. In M. K. Ryan & N. R. Branscombe (Eds.), *The SAGE handbook of gender and psychology*, pp. 359–377. Los Angeles, Sage.

31 Michigan Coalition Against Domestic and Sexual Violence. (n.d.) *Working with the media: A toolkit for service providers*. Okemos, MI: Michigan Coalition to End Sexual Violence. www.mcedsv.org/images/Document/Resources/Working%20With%20the%20Media%20A%20Tookkit%20for%20Service%20Providers.pdf (retrieved April 15, 2017).

32 Mazerolle, L. (2003). The pros and cons of publicity campaigns as a crime control tactic. *Criminology and Public Policy*, *2*(3), 531–540.

33 Wallack, L. (1990). Media advocacy: Promoting health through mass communication. In K. Glanz, F. M. Lewis & B. K. Rimer (Eds.), *Health behavior and health education: Theory, research, and practice*, pp. 370–386. San Francisco: Jossey-Bass.

34 Grunig, J. E., & Ipes, D. A. (1983). The anatomy of a campaign against drunk driving. *Public Relations Review*, *9*(2), 36–52.

35 Bailey, W. C. (1990). Murder, capital punishment, and television: Execution publicity and homicide rates. *American Sociological Review*, *55*(5), 628–633.

36 Ennett, S. T., Tobler, N. S., Ringwalt, C. L., & Flewelling, R. L. (1994). How effective is drug abuse resistance education? A meta-analysis of Project DARE outcome evaluations. *American Journal of Public Health*, *84*(9), 1394–1401.

37 Sacco, V. F. (1985). Shoplifting prevention: The role of communication-based intervention strategies. *Canadian Journal of Criminology*, *27*(1), 15–29.

38 Reinarman, C., & Levine, H. G. (1997). *Crack in America: Demon drugs and social justice*. Berkeley, CA: University of California Press.

39   Glassner, B. (2010). *The culture of fear: Why Americans are afraid of the wrong things: Crime, drugs, minorities, teen moms, killer kids, mutant microbes, plane crashes, road rage, & so much more.* New York: Basic Books.

40   Johnson, S. D., & Bowers, K. J. (2003). Opportunity is in the eye of the beholder: The role of publicity in crime prevention. *Criminology and Public Policy, 2*(3), 497–524.

41   Chaloupka, F. J., Straif, K., & Leon, M. E. (2011). Effectiveness of tax and price policies in tobacco control. *Tobacco Control, 20*(3), 238–238.

42   Wagenaar, A. C., Tobler, A. L., & Komro, K. A. (2010). Effects of alcohol tax and price policies on morbidity and mortality: A systematic review. *American Journal of Public Health, 100*(11), 2270–2278.

43   Laycock, G. (1991). Operation identification, or the power of publicity. *Security Journal, 2*(2), 67–72.

44   Sidebottom, A., Thorpe, A., & Johnson, S. D. (2009). Using targeted publicity to reduce opportunities for bicycle theft: A demonstration and replication. *European Journal of Criminology, 6*(3), 267–286.

45   Gentry, J., & Harrison, R. (2010). Is advertising a barrier to male movement toward gender change? *Marketing Theory, 10*(1), 74–96.

46   Kahlor, L., & Eastin, M. S. (2011). Television's role in the culture of violence toward women: A study of television viewing and the cultivation of rape myth acceptance in the United States. *Journal of Broadcasting and Electronic Media, 55*(2), 215–231.

47   Gornick, J. C., & Meyer, D. S. (1998). Changing political opportunity: The anti-rape movement and public policy. *Journal of Policy History, 10*(4), 367–398.

48   Vladutiu, C. J., Martin, S. L., & Macy, R. J. (2011). College- or university-based sexual assault prevention programs: A review of program outcomes, characteristics, and recommendations. *Trauma, Violence, and Abuse, 12*(2), 67–86.

49   Fisher, B. S., Daigle, L. E., & Cullen, F. T. (2008). Rape against women: What can research offer to guide the development of prevention programs and risk reduction interventions? *Journal of Contemporary Criminal Justice, 24*(2), 163–177.

50   Breitenbecher, K. H. (2000). Sexual assault on college campuses: Is an ounce of prevention enough? *Applied and Preventive Psychology, 9*(1), 23–52. Daigle, L. E., Fisher, B. S., & Stewart, M. (2009). The effectiveness of sexual victimization prevention among college students: A summary of "what works." *Victims and Offenders, 4*(4), 398–404.

51   Finckenauer, J. O. (1982). *Scared straight! and the panacea phenomenon.* Englewood Cliffs, NJ: Prentice-Hall; pp. 112–152.

52   Petrosino, A., Turpin-Petrosino, C., & Buehler, J. (2003). Scared Straight and other juvenile awareness programs for preventing juvenile delinquency: A systematic review of the randomized experimental evidence. *Annals of the American Academy of Political and Social Science, 589*(1), 41–62.

53   Coker, D. (2001). Crime control and feminist law reform in domestic violence law: A critical review. *Buffalo Criminal Law Review, 4*(2), 801–860.

54   MacKinnon, C. A. (2007). Women's lives, men's laws. Cambridge, MA: Harvard University Press.

55   Tasca, M., Rodriguez, N., Spohn, C., & Koss, M. P. (2013). Police decision making in sexual assault cases: Predictors of suspect identification and arrest. *Journal of Interpersonal Violence, 28*(6), 1157–1177.

56   Avalos, L. (2016). Prosecuting rape victims while rapists run free: The consequence of police failure to investigate sex crimes in Britain and the United States. *Michigan Journal of Gender and Law, 23*(1). http://repository.law.umich.edu/mjgl/vol23/iss1/1.

57   Levit, N., Verchick, R. R., & Minow, M. (2016). *Feminist legal theory: A primer.* New York: NYU Press.

58   Temkin, J. (2002). *Rape and the legal process,* 2nd edition. Oxford: Oxford University Press.

59   Sameit, M. D. (2013). When a convicted rape is not really a rape: The past, present, and future ability of Article 120 convictions to withstand legal and factual sufficiency reviews. *Military Law Review, 216*, 77–121.

60   Campbell, R., & Raja, S. (1999). Secondary victimization of rape victims: Insights from mental health professionals who treat survivors of violence. *Violence and Victims, 14*(3), 261–275.

61   Campbell, R., Wasco, S. M., Ahrens, C. E., Sefl, T., & Barnes, H. E. (2001). Preventing the "second rape": Rape survivors' experiences with community service providers. *Journal of Interpersonal Violence, 16*(12), 1239–1259.

62   Berger, V. (1977). Man's trial, woman's tribulation: Rape cases in the courtroom. *Columbia Law Review, 77*(1), 1–103.

63   Sherman, L. W., & Berk, R. A. (1984). The specific deterrent effects of arrest for domestic assault. *American Sociological Review, 49*(2), 261–272.

64   Sherman, L. W., & Cohn, E. G. (1989). The impact of research on legal policy: The Minneapolis domestic violence experiment. *Law and Society Review, 23*(1), 117–144.

65   Garner, J., Fagan, J., & Maxwell, C. (1995). Published findings from the spouse assault replication program: A critical review. *Journal of Quantitative Criminology, 11*(1), 3–28.

66   Wathen, C. N., & MacMillan, H. L. (2003). Interventions for violence against women: Scientific review. *Journal of the American Medical Association, 289*(5), 589–600.

67   Gordon, M. T., & Riger, S. (1989). *The female fear: The social cost of rape.* Urbana, IL: University of Illinois Press.

68   Scott, H. (2003). Stranger danger: Explaining women's fear of crime. *Western Criminology Review, 4*(3), 203–214.

69   Reyns, B. W. & Fisher, B. S. (2010). Hotspots of fear. In B. S. Fisher & S. P. Lab (Eds.), *Encyclopedia of victimization and crime prevention,* pp. 463–464. Thousand Oaks, CA: Sage.

70   LeBeau, J. L. (1987). The journey to rape: Geographic distance and the rapist's method of approaching the victim. *Journal of Police Science & Administration, 15*(2), 129–136.

71   Tompson, L. A. (2016). *Explaining temporal patterns in street robbery.* Doctoral dissertation, UCL (University College London).

72   Solymosi, R., Bowers, K., & Fujiyama, T. (2015). Mapping fear of crime as a context-dependent everyday experience that varies in space and time. *Legal and Criminological Psychology, 20*(2), 193–211.

73   Solymosi, R. (2017). *Exploring spatial and temporal variation in perception of crime and place using crowdsourced data.* Doctoral dissertation, UCL (University College London).

74   Andresen, M. A. (2006). Crime measures and the spatial analysis of criminal activity. *British Journal of Criminology, 46*(2), 258–85.

75   LaRue, E., & Andresen, M. A. (2015). Spatial patterns of crime in Ottawa: The role of universities. *Canadian Journal of Criminology and Criminal Justice, 57*(2), 189–214.

76   Boivin, R., & Obartel, P. (2017). Visitor inflows and police use of force in a Canadian city. *Canadian Journal of Criminology and Criminal Justice, 59*(3) 373–296. Felson, M., & Boivin, R. (2015). Daily crime flows within a city. *Crime Science, 4*(1), Article 31. DOI: 10.1186/s40163-015-0039-0.

77 Rezey, M. L. (2017). Separated women's risk for intimate partner violence: A multiyear analysis using the National Crime Victimization Survey. *Journal of Interpersonal Violence*, Published online February 21. https://doi.org/10.1177/0886260517692334.

78 Jeffery, C. R. (1971). *Crime prevention through environmental design.* Beverly Hills, CA: Sage Publications.

79 Newman, O. (1972). *Defensible space*; p. 264. New York: Macmillan.

80 Newman, O. (1995). Defensible space: A new physical planning tool for urban revitalization. *Journal of the American Planning Association, 61*(2), 149–155.

81 Wood, E. (1961). Housing design: A social theory. *Ekistics, 12*(74), 383–392.

82 Jacobs, J. (1961). *The death and life of great American cities.* New York: Random House.

83 Gardner, C. B. (1995). *Passing by: Gender and public harassment.* Berkeley, CA: University of California Press.

UNIT 6.2 Risky Streets

Rude public behavior harms everyone,[1] but mismanaged public places endanger and exclude women even more than men by fostering **street harassment**.[2] *Any single instance* of street harassment might not be serious; yet *a **repetitive pattern*** of street harassment puts women at a disadvantage.[3] Women are quite a bit more likely than men to reduce participation in community life after aversive street experiences.[4] These fears impair social participation in multiple ways—going to meetings, walking outdoors, using public transit, or jogging in the park.[5] Women are also likely to avoid certain streets or places, or to limit their public activities to daytime or to hours when other women are around. Many women will only go out at night when accompanied by a male they know or in groups of females who offer mutual protection.[6] Those women who are repeatedly harassed are especially constrained and most likely to change their behavior patterns.[7]

Starting in adolescence, girls learn to avoid certain places where they are likely to be approached by male strangers. Most young women have had at least one frightening experience in at least one setting, or they have heard about similar encounters from others.[8] They learn that in public places, the behavior of strangers is potentially unpredictable and uncontrollable. Geographers study this issue by asking women to draw a mental map of their daily activity space and mark on the map spaces that they fear.[9] Street harassment has a different pattern in dense settings where women are most exposed to strangers.

In general, street harassment tells us that something is wrong.[10] Yet criminal and civil law are practically useless for stopping it. "[M]en who harass women on the street are not apprehended, they are not punished, the victims are not compensated, and no damages are paid. The entire transaction is entirely invisible to the state."[11]

To invoke civil or criminal law, the victim must establish the harasser's intent to inflict harm, prove the injury was severe, and then show a pattern of repeated misconduct. Prosecutors generally do not get involved unless something physical occurs or a single offender stalks the same woman repeatedly.[12] However, most street harassers find a new target each time, thus evading any legal controls. Men are probably unaware of most street harassment against women they know, since these incidents occur mainly while a woman is walking unaccompanied.[13]

The Scope of Street Harassment

Harassment is far from new, going back even to biblical times.[14] Street harassment was common in London in the 1880s[15] and in Canada at least as long ago.[16] In 1875 a young Wisconsin woman sued the Chicago and Northwestern Railroad after their train conductor forcibly kissed her.[17]

We define street harassment as a face-to-face encounter in a public place where an unacquainted person makes obscene or degrading remarks to the victim. In most cases, this involves a female being harassed by a male, but that is not the only possibility.[18]

Common street harassment includes a wide variety of negative public experiences, including wolf whistles, sexual taunts, nasty remarks, leers, catcalls, vulgar suggestions, and sexual remarks about a woman's physical appearance.[19] Street harassment can be targeted at teenage girls just after they have developed sexually. Women vary in their responses to being harassed,[20] but the greatest danger is that they begin to fear that a physical attack will follow.

Street harassment includes aggressive incidents in streets and in public transit settings—trains, metros, buses, bus stops, stations—and in walking to and from these locations. Public transit researchers have found that fear of crime and disorder reduces ridership.[21] New York City and Chicago have recently instituted campaigns to reduce incivilities on public transit through new posters. The posters are aimed at reducing: litter, hogging the pole, disorderly exits, wearing large backpacks, noise from radios, and *manspreading*—when men sit with their legs spread in a "V," taking up multiple seats.[22] Sometimes manspreading may be a form of sexual display directed at women, but this is not always the case. Some of these behaviors affect the civility of riding public transit; they also affect space on crowded trains and a passenger's ability to ride and exit safely. After the campaign was implemented in New York City, college student observers assessed behavior etiquette on subways. They examined gender differences by time of day and noted which cars women selected. Some findings are of special interest:

- Manspreading is less frequent when subway cars are crowded. The researchers concluded that the behavior was thus situational.

- Females are more likely to ride subway cars with greater density and to choose interior cars.[23]

The fact that women tend to choose crowded cars fits with other research. On crowded cars women avoid exhibitionism and manspreading; however, they face other harassment risks, such as frotteurism—touching or rubbing someone without consent, as we previously noted. Frotteurism is most prevalent on crowded public transit.[24]

Some metropolitan women forego convenient buses or trains and instead drive private cars to avoid harassment by men.[25] Arguably, street harassment indirectly adds to traffic jams, air pollution, and energy depletion by making public transit less attractive for riders. This is one more reminder that criminology can play an important role in wider society by offering practical policy ideas for increasing the security of women.

Many street harassers begin with an apparent compliment, such as a positive reference to a woman's appearance; if the woman ignores him, the harasser switches to a hostile tone, shouting an obscene insult. If the woman acknowledges him, he escalates his attention. Women learn by experience to try to get away or to avoid locations where harassment is most likely to occur. Women have no way to determine in advance which strangers have friendly vs. harmful motives. Even a relatively minor encounter with a stranger could become a serious problem.

> Rapists may harass women on the street to determine which women are likely to be easy targets, a process called "**rape-testing**" . . . some rapists carefully size up their prey, using sexual harassment to select targets that seem unlikely to fight back in an assault.[26]

Some offenders go beyond words alone, following their victim as she walks along. Some incidents clearly cross the line into illegality,[27] such as a male exhibitionist who pulls down his pants or pulls out his penis or a male who gropes women in the public transit system. Next, we consider how many women have been harassed at some point in their lives.

Exposure to Street Harassment

In a study of street harassment in the United States (Table 6a), half of the women interviewed had previously encountered men shouting sexual comments or making sexual gestures at them. One in four women had been touched or brushed by a male stranger. One in five had been followed without permission. Harassment is quite common in France,[28] Italy,[29] Finland,[30] the Netherlands,[31] and the United States.[32] However, harassment rates tend to be highest in nations with very high urban **population density** and very crowded **metro systems**. Researchers have found very high street harassment rates in Egypt,[33] Mexico,[34] India,[35] Japan,[36] China,[37] and Turkey.[38]

TABLE 6A **Street Harassment Experiences, United States, 2014**

Type of street harassment	Women experiencing harassment (%)
Shouting sexual comments, making sexual gestures	51
Talking about body parts or making obscene sounds	25
Purposely touching or brushing against you in sexual way	23
Calling a nasty sexual name	22
Following you without permission	20
Making an explicit sexual request or comment	14
Flashing, exposing genitals, public masturbation	14
Forcing you to do something sexual	9

Source: Data drawn from H. Kearl (2014). *Unsafe and harassed in public spaces: A national street harassment report*. Reston, VA: Stop Street Harassment Organization.
Note: N = 982.

In the Turkish study, two-thirds of women were exposed to public verbal abuse and one-third to public physical abuse. Like in other nations, Turkish women fear public transit at certain hours. One of the most interesting observations from the Chinese study is that higher-status women are often targeted for harassment by lower-status men. This reminds us that strangers can evade the conventions and social stratification rules that apply in more organized settings. A well-dressed, well-educated, middle-class woman can be subject to shouts of "hey baby" and comments about her anatomical features by a man of lower status.

New websites and apps allow women to record incidents in which they are harassed, and these are especially well developed in Egypt.[39] These websites confirm that street harassment is highly concentrated by intersection, offering a potential for future efforts to minimize the problem by redesigning places for greater security. That requires additional research about which sorts of street designs facilitate harassment of women.

As noted in Unit 5.3, Louis Wirth's famous 1938 paper, "Urbanism as a Way of Life," explained why large cities and high population density generate additional problems. According to Wirth: "Characteristically, urbanites meet one another in highly segmental roles. . . . The contacts of the city may indeed be face to face, but they are nevertheless impersonal, superficial, transitory, and segmental."[40]

By mixing people together in anonymous settings, a city lessens social control and makes it easier for one person to be rude to another. A highly mobile urban society provides many stranger contacts and more risk of street harassment.[41] Even nonurban people are highly mobile, often entering urban settings, shopping malls, or entertainment zones exposing them to anonymous situations.[42]

Interviews with college males who admitted harassing women indicated that that they harassed women they knew and those they did not know. However,

> college men are more likely to engage in stranger harassment when they are in a group. Participants indicated that the extra anonymity afforded in group contexts was an important motive when engaging in stranger harassment. Participants also indicated stranger harassment was more likely to occur in group contexts because these behaviors serve a group bonding function. The former finding is consistent with the literature that anonymity . . . often leads to more extreme and uninhibited behavior.[43]

An old study found that most male harassers offered no explanation when interviewed initially, but then provided a variety of neutralizations (a term explained in Unit 4.4). They said that their catcalls or sexual comments were fun and hurt nobody, or claimed they were giving women pleasure.[44] We often find in criminology that the offender and victim tell very different stories about the incident and have very different ideas about the quantity of harm that it produces.

Population Density and Proximity

We also need to consider when metropolitan life puts strangers closer to one another than most of them really wish to be. You recall from Unit 6.1 that psychologists have developed "proxemic theory," telling us that people want to be a couple of meters or yards from one another. Despite this, people tend to get just a few inches away from others while crowding to board a bus. They do not move as close together during other parts of a public transit trip.[45] Bottlenecks create special problems for women: As people push to get through, men have an extra opportunity to brush against or grope women. A few key bottlenecks and highly crowded locations generate most of the tactile risk for women in public places.

Putting together what we know, very high density and rather low density pose different problems for women.

- At *very high* public density, women risk being touched or groped.
- At *very low* public density, women risk a forcible rape.

However:

• At *moderate* public density, women face less risk of unwanted encounters with men.

Population density depends on more than where people live. Even people who live at low suburban densities can enter crowded situations when they go to cities or when they leave home for work, shopping, education, or recreation. In these settings, women may be exposed to risks. In general, those risks are minimized at moderate densities (as noted above), but that does not mean a person could not have a bad moment when the crowd is out of sight and an offender is close by.

The density–crime discussion goes back to the Chicago School in the 1930s, and the importance of street density is old as well.[46] Only recently have the tools of social media transformed our ability to measure how women's risks concentrate in time and space. A Japanese study documented how purse-snatchings are concentrated in certain spots along the streets of Osaka, providing designers and police the information they need to protect women more than in the past.[47] In addition, exhibitionism and public indecency in Kyoto, Japan, is highly concentrated in time and space. Exhibitionists look for teenagers after school in nonresidential areas, and their offenses have been clearly mapped and analyzed.[48] A British study showed risks above, below, and around public transit stations, the location and operating procedures of which greatly influence the safety of riders.[49] The compelling conclusion is that each of us can be affected by design decisions made by others. We hope those making the decisions become fully aware of the impact they have on the security of women.

Women and the Safe Cities Movement

In the 1990s, a movement began in Vienna, Austria, to make that city's public environments more hospitable and secure for women. City officials asked citizens to fill out questionnaires about how they moved around the city. Males answered the questions quickly, but women could not stop writing about their experiences. Compared to men, women make many more trips and have more elaborate ways of moving about the city as they care for children, carry out errands, and seek to avoid danger. Vienna launched a "gender mainstreaming" movement to make women safer and help them participate more in city life.[50] For example:

• City planners designed apartment buildings with courtyards allowing parents and children to spend secure time outdoors without needing to go far from home.

• City officials subdivided public parks into more secure activity areas suitable for a wider variety of activities, enhancing visibility and increasing the participation of women.

Almost immediately city officials noticed behavioral changes. Boys and girls went outdoors more and used parks more frequently. This design plan was not based on a fortress society or a gated community seeking to lock out the larger world and keep local people inside. Rather it produced a semipermeable area where visitors could enter but would be noticed, and residents could protect their neighborhood in a kinder and gentler fashion, still going outdoors.

This approach is supported and applied by several governments around the world.[51] In a housing development in Stockholm, Sweden, designers made life safer for women by:

- arranging residential layouts so streets and sidewalks became visible;

- insuring clear *sight lines* between buildings;

- locating activities to maximize safety;

- making clear what zones are public or reserved for residents.

These efforts reduced crime and fear, while making environments more livable for women and for men.[52] These ideas were picked up by the United Nations Entity for Gender Equality and the Empowerment of Women. Influenced by feminist goals, urban planners began to analyze how public spaces are used, who uses them, when, and for how long. They developed the Safe Cities program to make women more secure in urban environments by improving public designs.[53]

> Planning and designing safe public spaces for women and girls is the process whereby urban planners, designers, architects, women, grassroots and other community actors collaborate to make the physical features of public spaces safe and welcoming for women and girls. If public spaces are dark, abandoned, unclean, overgrown, or lacking certain elements like benches or emergency phones, they are potentially unsafe for everybody, but for women and girls in particular. Therefore, there is an increased chance that women and girls will not use spaces where they feel fear and/or experience violence. In a safe cities for women and girls initiative, it is necessary that the safety needs of women and girls are taken into account in planning and design. Experience shows that when a space is occupied by women and girls, it is also occupied by more people in general.[54]

Drawing from Oscar Newman (discussed in Unit 6.1), Vienna officials designed a gradual transition between public, semipublic, semiprivate, and private space—making people much more secure and allowing women and families to engage in outdoor activities near home.

Safer Designs for Women

Fear responds to surrounding land uses, such as taverns, liquor stores, bus stops, vacant lots, and abandoned buildings.[55] Certain places generate more crime, or even attract offenders. For example, crime is often enhanced in the vicinity of fast food restaurants, shopping malls, and barrooms.[56] Not only do some establishments generate more crime in the vicinity, but they produce more anonymous public space where rude behavior is more likely to occur.[57] Certain combinations of land uses can be especially harmful. Barrooms and bus stops, for example, are a harmful combination. Offenders hanging out at or in front of the barroom can find female targets walking to or from the bus stop. Schools next to parks produce a very harmful combination since teenage girls are likely to enter unsupervised park space and are subject to harassment or physical attack. Schools and shopping districts create a harmful combination as students find hangouts in or near shopping areas, increasing truancy from school and getting into more trouble after school. These combinations subject female students to more harassment, both by students and non-students. These problems are enhanced if shopping districts or malls are poorly managed, allowing harassment to grow.

In addition, two categories of spaces are particularly frightening: enclosed spaces with limited exit opportunities, such as multistory parking structures and underground pedestrian passages; and anonymous and deserted open spaces such as empty public parks.

Making Walking Routes Safer for Women

Newman's ideas have been folded into a larger approach known as ***Crime Prevention Through Environmental Design (CPTED)***.[58] That approach considers additional design ideas to help women, such as making sure people can see what's going on near their homes and as they move in public spaces. Places are safer when other people are near and have a clear view. The safest places are those supervised by the "place managers" we discussed in Unit 2.2. These include homeowners, business owners or managers, doormen or supervisors—anybody whose role includes looking after local places. Unfortunately, low-income areas have too few place managers. Even so, safety can be addressed by designers, who can minimize purely public space and maximize visibility to help protect low-income women from harassment and attack. Good designs make places safer for poor and rich alike.[59]

Using CPTED principles, public zones can be made more secure for women as they walk, jog, or engage in other activities. It is difficult to guarantee that no stranger will make a harassing remark or gesture. Society can, however, make it more difficult to carry out overt attacks on women.

Figure 6f compares two ***walking routes*** for women. The route on the left is dangerous, while the route on the right is relatively more safe. The origin could be a home or a parking lot. The destination could be a store or recreation spot. In the dangerous route, a woman walks by ***concealed space***. In the safer spot on the right, a woman walks by normal residential or commercial places (but not a tough barroom).

This figure tells us that a community can make women much safer by reclaiming abandoned spaces and avoiding concealed spaces. A community can be careful about where it locates public transit stops and stations. A community can be cautious about the route that local high school students walk to get to or from school.[60] Walking is a healthy exercise and a public health issue. However, some of the public health literature appears to miss these important facts about safe walking routes. We will address this more in the next unit.

Urban planners learn to be careful about how they mix different land uses, or "malignant mixes."[61] As has been noted, mixing large bars with residential areas becomes a problem. Mixing high schools with shopping malls creates problems for both. Mixing high schools with public parks gives teenagers more chance to skip school, while endangering them on the way to and from school. Research has verified that

- Walkable local environments can greatly enhance security for women.

- Mixing commercial and residential land uses can greatly endanger women.

- Fast traffic and dense, interconnected, streets endanger women.[62]

Interestingly, the principles that apply in central cities also tend to apply in suburban areas.[63] Designing insecure and fearful places triggers basic human responses that apply to all races and regions. That does not deny cultural variations; but it does tell us that criminologists from around the world can easily trade notes.[64]

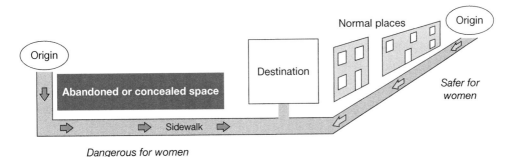

FIGURE 6F
Comparing Two Walking Routes for Women

Making Public Transit Safer for Women

In 1909, Julia D. Longfellow, a feminist leader, proposed that the last car of New York City subway trains be reserved for women. The goal was to protect women from sexual "insults and indignities." For a short time one New York subway line provided special cars for women, then discontinued the practice.[65] Japan has had women-only transit cars since 1912;[66] currently, 15 countries offer women-only options on public transportation, including Brazil, Egypt, Germany, India, Indonesia, Iran, Japan, and Malaysia.[67] You can see that harassment of women in public transit is a long-standing issue.[68]

Although separate cars for women are a matter for further discussion, transit systems can be made considerably safer for women.[69] When the metro was built in Washington, DC, engineers were determined not to repeat the New York City subway experience.[70] Washington Metro construction was consistent with the situational prevention principles presented in Unit 2.3. The idea was that possible offenders would have to exert a lot of effort to commit crimes.

Designers avoided nooks and crannies and created wide-open pathways to and from train railways to maximize *natural surveillance*. Employee surveillance is aided by Metro's very clear sight lines, alongside other design features.

- Access is controlled, with few stairways to street level. Metro closes during low-ridership hours to reduce criminal opportunities.

- Designers placed a gap between paths and walls, which were constructed with materials that impair graffiti and vandalism.

- Metro's design prevents crowds from forming, making it harder to pick pockets or for frotteurism to occur.

- Metro provides few chairs or benches in stations that men could use for loitering or for picking out women to target.

- Metro's platforms are a uniform 600 feet long, designed for eight-car trains, short enough to monitor and prevent abuse of women.

- Train platforms have minimal supporting columns so it is easy to spot bad behavior. A wide-open design provides riders unobstructed views and maximizes security for women waiting for their train.

- Trains themselves are characterized by a "straight through" design, enabling police to walk freely between cars and thus increasing formal surveillance capabilities.

Metro's planners deliberately avoided long, winding corridors and corners found in many older systems. The Washington Metro designed out hidden spots that endanger women.[71] Unfortunately, the Washington Metro has recently been starved of funds by an unfriendly Congress and declining ridership, so it no longer has full employee surveillance of its entry ways and platforms, and its safety systems are on the decline.[72]

Forcible Rape and Environmental Design

To carry out a forcible rape, a man must arrange to be alone with a woman in a hidden area where her resistance will not be noticed. He might

- find a woman already within a hidden area;
- find a woman at the edge of a hidden area, then push or pull her into it;
- trick or lure a woman into a hidden area; or
- find a lull in activity, allowing an attack in a less hidden area.[73]

Forcible rapes usually occur either within private spaces or in the shadowy parts or periods of other spaces. Rapists use the cover of darkness or spaces that are seldom populated, or they attack after most people have gone home. Some offenders are casual acquaintances of the victim and use that recognition to trick her into entering private space, such as his own home, or hers. The *edges* between a dark or hidden portion of a public park or sidewalk are especially dangerous for women. Sometimes a rapist lurks in the shadows until a woman arrives home, then follows her inside or forces his way in. Once in private space or other hidden locations, a rapist has a better chance of controlling the situation for his sexual advantage. Some public park areas are concealed from public view, even in daylight. Semipublic and semiprivate space are publicly visible, but not all the time. Pedestrian movements change, leaving some spaces unwatched and allowing some time for a forcible rape to occur. These points explain why lighting and design are by no means trivial, impinging on the security of real people in daily life.

The rapist who attacks in the shadows of a public area must act quickly to avoid detection. The rapist who enters the victim's private space might have more time to carry out his attack. Experts in sexual attack methods find these differences extremely important for determining whether the offender can penetrate the victim.[74] A safer environment helps prevent forcible rape from being attempted; even an environment that is slightly safer gives victims a greater chance to escape and to avoid the worst rape outcomes.[75]

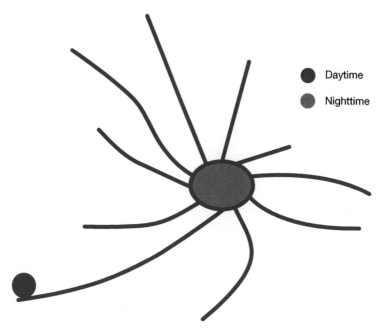

FIGURE 6G
Forcible Rape, Stockholm, Sweden, Night and Day
Source: Adapted from V. Ceccato (2014). The nature of rape places. *Journal of Environmental Psychology,*
40, 97–107.

Figure 6g maps the risk of forcible rape in Stockholm.[76] At night, the risk is greatest in the center of the city, where entertainment venues are located (Unit 6.4 relates nightlife to danger for women). However, women are also at risk during the day and at dusk along commuter train lines. Women are especially endangered when they get off the train at a ***desolate spot*** next to wooded areas, outside the visual range of other people. That gives assailants the opportunity to hide, attack, and escape.[77] Women are also endangered by poor lighting, few pedestrians, and alcohol sales nearby—all risks that are preventable with good design and management of public space. We should not be surprised that women express greater fear in environments with

> forests, recreational areas, and desolate transit stops. The first are perceived as opportunities for criminals to trap their victims, while the second may allow potential offenders to conceal themselves and act outside the visual range of others. . . . Fear-inducing factors in public environments include darkness, desolation, lack of opportunities for surveillance by the general public, lack of maintenance, and poor environmental quality.[78]

Business establishments with windows onto the street can increase street security. In contrast, establishments which block the view outwards impair security for pedestrians. You can see why good metropolitan spaces are important for society in general, but especially for women. Although this unit has focused on dangers when women go out on the street, those same streets bring danger to their doorsteps.

FLASHCARD LIST FOR UNIT 6.2

- Concealed space
- Crime Prevention Through Environmental Design (CPTED)
- Desolate spot
- Edges

- Manspreading
- Metro systems
- Natural surveillance
- Population density
- Rape-testing
- Repetitive pattern

- Safe cities movement
- Sight lines
- Street harassment
- Walking routes

DISCUSSION QUESTIONS

1. Pick two streets that you know well, one that is safe for women and one that is not. Say why.

2. Think of a bar or other recreation area. What are the risks for women and how could they be reduced without extra police?

Notes

1 Goffman, E. (2008 [1963]). *Behavior in public places*. New York: Simon and Schuster.

2 Dymén, C., & Ceccato, V. (2012). An international perspective of the gender dimension in planning for urban safety. In V. Ceccato (Ed.), *The urban fabric of crime and fear*, pp. 283–310. Amsterdam: Springer.

3 Logan, L. S. (2015). Street harassment: Current and promising avenues for researchers and activists. *Sociology Compass, 9*(3), 196–211.

4 Bastomski, S., & Smith, P. (2017). Gender, fear, and public places: How negative encounters with strangers harm women. *Sex Roles, 76*(1–2), 73–88.

5 Roman, C. G., & Chalfin, A. (2008). Fear of walking outdoors: A multilevel ecologic analysis of crime and disorder. *American Journal of Preventive Medicine, 34*(4), 306–312.

6 Valentine, G. (2014). *Social geographies: Space and society*. Abingdon, U.K.: Routledge.

7 Kearl, H. (2010). *Stop street harassment: Making public places safe and welcoming for women*. Santa Barbara, CA: ABC-CLIO.

8   Gardner, C. B. (1995). *Passing by: Gender and public harassment.* Berkeley, CA: University of California Press.

9   Valentine, G. (2007). Theorizing and researching intersectionality: A challenge for feminist geography. *Professional Geographer, 59*(1), 10–21.

10 Madan, M., & Nalla, M. K. (2016). Sexual harassment in public spaces: Examining gender differences in perceived seriousness and victimization. *International Criminal Justice Review, 26*(2), 80–97.

11 Robin West, quoted in: Bowman, C. G. (1993). Street harassment and the informal ghettoization of women. *Harvard Law Review, 106*(3), 517–580; p. 522.

12 Bowman, Street harassment and the informal ghettoization of women.

13 Shah, S. B. (2015). Open season: Street harassment as true threats. *University of Pennsylvania Journal of Law and Social Change, 18*(5), 377–401.

14 Carasik, M. (n.d.). Sexual harassment in the book of Ruth [online]. Bible Odyssey. www.bibleodyssey.org/en/people/related-articles/sexual-harassment-in-the-book-of-ruth (retrieved April 10, 2017).

15 Walkowitz, J. R. (2013). *City of dreadful delight: Narratives of sexual danger in late-Victorian London.* Chicago: University of Chicago Press.

16 Dubinsky, K. (1993). *Improper advances: Rape and heterosexual conflict in Ontario, 1880–1929.* Chicago: University of Chicago Press.

17 Craker vs. the Chicago and Northwestern Railroad Company, 36 Wisconsin, 657, 659 (1875); see also appeal at 679, p. 566.

18 Bowman, Street harassment and the informal ghettoization of women.

19 Vera-Gray, F. (2016). Men's stranger intrusions: Rethinking street harassment. *Women's Studies International Forum, 58* (September–October), 9–17.

20 Street, A. E., Gradus, J. L., Stafford, J., & Kelly, K. (2007). Gender differences in experiences of sexual harassment: Data from a male-dominated environment. *Journal of Consulting and Clinical Psychology, 75*(3), 464–474.

21 Ceccato, V. (2013). *Moving safely: Crime and perceived safety in Stockholm's subway stations.* Lanham: Lexington Books.

22 Fitzsimmons, E. G. (2014). A scourge is spreading. M.T.A.'s cure? Dude, close your legs [online]. *The New York Times,* December 20. www.nytimes.com/2014/12/21/nyregion/MTA-targets-manspreading-on-new-york-city-subways.html?_r=0ht (retrieved May 15, 2017). Hilkevitch, J. (2015) Courtesy goes a long way, new CTA campaign advises riders [online]. *Chicago Tribune,* May 27. www.chicagotribune.com/news/ct-cta-courtesy-campaign-met-0527-20150527-story-html (retrieved May 15, 2017).

23 Tuckel , P., Milczarski, W., & Benediktsson, M. (2016). *Etiquette of riders on New York City subways: An observational study conducted by students at Hunter College.* The City University of New York. http://silo-public.hunter.cuny.edu/798320a76b1c330347bb7155d717c86bdf278c0f/Behavior-of-New-York-City-Subway-Riders_v.8.pdf (retrieved May 15, 2017).

24 Clark, S. K., Jeglic, E. L., Calkins, C., & Tatar, J. R. (2016). More than a nuisance: The prevalence and consequences of frotteurism and exhibitionism. *Sexual Abuse, 28*(1), 3–19.

25 Gardner, N., Cui, J., & Coiacetto, E. (2017). Harassment on public transport and its impacts on women's travel behaviour. *Australian Planner, 54*(1), 8–15. Buckley, N. G. (2016). *Sexual harassment on public transit and the influence of perceptions of safety on travel behavior.* Doctoral dissertation, The University of Texas at Austin.

26   Thompson, D. M. (1994). The woman in the street: Reclaiming the public space from sexual harassment. *Yale Journal of Law and Feminism, 6*(2), 313–348; p. 321.

27   Shah, Open season: Street harassment as true threats.

28   Jaspard, M., & EVNEFF Team. (2001). Violence against women: The first French national survey. *Population et Sociétés (Bulletin Mensuel d'information de L'Institut National D'Etudes Demographiques), 364,* 1–4.

29   Sabbadini, L. L. (1998). *Molestie e violenze sessuali.* Rome: Istituto Nazionale di Statistica.

30   Heiskanen, M., & Piispa, M. (1998). *Faith, hope, battering: A survey of men's violence against women in Finland.* Helsinki: Statistics Finland.

31   Aronson, E. (2015). *Psst, schatje! Mapping and resisting street harassment in Amsterdam, online and beyond.* Doctoral dissertation, Utrecht University Budapest, Hungary.

32   Laniya, O. O. (2005). Street smut: Gender, media, and the legal power dynamics of street harassment, or "hey sexy" and other verbal ejaculations. *Columbia Journal of Gender and Law, 14*(1), 91–130.

33   Ilahi, N. (2009). Gendered contestations: An analysis of street harassment in Cairo and its implications for women's access to public spaces. *Surfacing: An Interdisciplinary Journal for Gender in the Global South, 2*(1), 56–69.

34   Meza-de-Luna, M. E., & García-Falconi, S. (2015). Adolescent street harassment in Querétaro, México. *Affilia, 30*(2), 158–169.

35   Natarajan, M. (2016). Rapid assessment of "eve teasing" (sexual harassment) of young women during the commute to college In India. *Crime Science, 5,* Article 6. https://doi.org/10.1186/s40163-016-0054-9. Akhtar, C. (2013). Eve teasing as a form of violence against women: A case study of District Srinagar, Kashmir. *International Journal of Sociology and Anthropology, 5*(5), 168–178. Bhattacharyya, R. (2016). Street violence against women in India: Mapping prevention strategies. *Asian Social Work and Policy Review, 10*(3), 311–325.

36   Horii, M., & Burgess, A. (2012). Constructing sexual risk: "Chikan", collapsing male authority and the emergence of women-only train carriages in Japan. *Health, Risk and Society, 14*(1), 41–55.

37   Parish, W. L., Das, A., & Laumann, E. O. (2006). Sexual harassment of women in urban China. *Archives of Sexual Behavior, 35*(4), 411–425.

38   Tandogan, O., & Ilhan, B. S. (2016). Fear of crime in public spaces: From the view of women living in cities. *Procedia Engineering, 161*(2), 2011–2018.

39   Skalli, L. H. (2014). Young women and social media against sexual harassment in North Africa. *The Journal of North African Studies, 19*(2), 244–258.

40   Wirth, L. (1938). Urbanism as a way of life. *American Journal of Sociology, 44*(1), 1–24; p. 12.

41   Caldwell, M. (2015). *A short history of rudeness: Manners, morals, and misbehavior in modern America.* New York: Picador.

42   Oxygen/Markle Pulse. (2000). Oxygen-Markle Pulse poll finds: Harassment of women on the street is rampant [online]. PRNewswire Association. www.thefreelibrary.com/Oxygen%2FMarkle+Pulse+Poll+Finds%3A+Harassment+of+Women+on+the+Street+Is. . .-a062870396 (retrieved April 13, 2017).

43   Wesselmann, E. D., & Kelly, J. R. (2010). Cat-calls and culpability: Investigating the frequency and functions of stranger harassment. *Sex Roles, 63*(7–8), 451–462; p. 458.

44 Benard, C. & Schlaffer, E. (1984). "The man in the street": Why he harasses. In A. M. Jaggar & P. S. Rothenberg (Eds.), *Feminist frameworks: Alternative theoretical accounts of the relations between women and men*, second edition, pp. 395–398. New York: McGraw-Hill.

45 Solymosi, R., Borrion, H., & Fujiyama, T. (2015). Crowd spatial patterns at bus stops: Security implications and effects of warning messages. In V. Ceccato & A. Newton (Eds.), *Safety and security in transit environments*, pp. 156–178. London: Palgrave Macmillan.

46 Clarke, R. V., Belanger, M., & Eastman, J. (1996). Where angels fear to tread: A test in the New York City subway of the robbery/density hypothesis. *Preventing Mass Transit Crime, 6*, 217–236.

47 Hanaoka, K. (2016). New insights on relationships between street crimes and ambient population: Use of hourly population data estimated from mobile phone users' locations. *Environment and Planning B: Planning and Design.* Published online October 10. https://doi.org/10.1177/0265813516672454.

48 Hanaoka, K. (2017). Locational and temporal characteristics of public indecency incidents in Kyoto City: A spatial analysis using the geographic information system. *The Journal of Cultural Sciences* (Ritsumeikan Bungaku) *649*, 197–205 [in Japanese]. www.ritsumei.ac.jp/acd/cg/lt/rb/649/649PDF/hanaoka.pdf (retrieved August 1, 2017).

49 Newton, A. D., Partridge, H., & Gill, A. (2014). Above and below: Measuring crime risk in and around underground mass transit systems. *Crime Science, 3*, Article 1. https://doi.org/10.1186/2193-7680-3-1.

50 Foran, C. (2013). How to design a city for women: A fascinating experiment in "gender mainstreaming." *Citylab*, September 16. www.citylab.com/transportation/2013/09/how-design-city-women/6739/ (retrieved April 7, 2017).

51 Cozens, P., & Love, T. (2015). A review and current status of crime prevention through environmental design (CPTED). *CPL Bibliography, 30*(4), 393–412.

52 Grönlund, B. (2012). Is Hammarby Sjöstad a model case? Crime prevention through environmental design in Stockholm, Sweden. In V. Ceccato (Ed.), *The urban fabric of crime and fear*, pp. 283–310. Amsterdam: Springer.

53 Dame, T., & Grant A. (2001). *Kelowna Planning for Safer Communities Workshop report.* Cowichan Valley Safer Futures Program, Canada. Virtual Knowledge Centre to End Violence Against Women and Girls, United Nations Entity for Gender Equality and the Empowerment of Women. www.endvawnow.org/en/articles/251-safe-public-spaces-for-women-and-girls.html (retrieved July 27, 2017).United Nations Human Settlement Program. (2007). *Enhancing urban safety and security.* London, Kenya: Earthscan, UN-HABITAT. United Nations Human Settlement Program. (2009). *Planning sustainable cities.* London, Kenya: Earthscan, UN-HABITAT.

54 Dame & Grant, *Kelowna Planning for Safer Communities Workshop report.*

55 Hart, T. C., & Miethe, T. D. (2015). Configural behavior settings of crime event locations: Toward an alternative conceptualization of criminogenic microenvironments. *Journal of Research in Crime and Delinquency, 52*(3), 373–402.

56 Kinney, J. B., Brantingham, P. L., Wuschke, K., Kirk, M. G., & Brantingham, P. J. (2008). Crime attractors, generators and detractors: Land use and urban crime opportunities. *Built Environment, 34*(1), 62–74.

57 Groff, E. R., & Lockwood, B. (2014). Criminogenic facilities and crime across street segments in Philadelphia: Uncovering evidence about the spatial extent of facility influence. *Journal of Research in Crime and Delinquency, 51*(3), 277–314.

58 Armitage, R. (2014). Crime prevention through environmental design. In G. Bruinsma & D. Weisburd (Eds.), *Encyclopedia of criminology and criminal justice*, pp. 720–731. New York: Springer.

59 Rengert, G. F., & Wasilchick, J. (2000). *Suburban burglary: A tale of two suburbs*. Springfield, IL: Charles C. Thomas.

60 Wiebe, D. J., Guo, W., Allison, P. D., Anderson, E., Richmond, T. S., & Branas, C. C. (2013). Fears of violence during morning travel to school. *Journal of Adolescent Health*, *53*(1), 54–61.

61 Adams, W., Herrmann, C., & Felson, M. (2015). Crime, transportation and malignant mixes. In V. Ceccato & A. Newton (Eds.), *Safety and security in transit environments: An interdisciplinary perspective*. Houndmills, U.K.: Palgrave Macmillan, pp. 181–195.

62 Sohn, D. W. (2016). Residential crimes and neighbourhood built environment: Assessing the effectiveness of crime prevention through environmental design (CPTED). *Cities*, *52*, 86–93.

63 Foster, S., Knuiman, M., Wood, L., & Giles-Corti, B. (2013). Suburban neighbourhood design: Associations with fear of crime versus perceived crime risk. *Journal of Environmental Psychology*, *36*, 112–117.

64 Van Dijk, J. (2007). *The world of crime: Breaking the silence on problems of security, justice and development across the world*. Thousand Oaks, CA: Sage.

65 Hood, C. (2004). *722 miles: The building of the subways and how they transformed New York*. Baltimore, MD: Johns Hopkins University Press.

66 Krieger, D. (2012). Why women-only transit options have caught on [online]. *Citylab*, February 8. www.citylab.com/transportation/2012/02/why-women-only-transit-options-have-caught/1171/ (retrieved August 1, 2017).

67 Graham-Harrison, E. (2015). Women-only carriages around the world: Do they work? [online]. *The Guardian*, August 26. www.theguardian.com/world/2015/aug/26/women-only-train-carriages-around-the-world-jeremy-corbyn (retrieved April 11, 2017).

68 Schultz, D., & Gilbert, S. (1996).Women and transit security: A new look at an old issue. *Proceedings of the Women's Travel Issues Second National Conference*, October 25–27, Baltimore, MD.

69 Smith, M. J., & Cornish, D. B. (2006). *Secure and tranquil travel: Preventing crime and disorder on public transport*. Abingdon, U.K.: Routledge. Smith, M. J., & Clarke, R. V. (2000). Crime and public transport. *Crime and Justice*, *27*, 169–233.

70 Schrag, Z. M. (2014). *The great society subway: A history of the Washington metro*. Baltimore, MD: Johns Hopkins University Press.

71 Irvin-Erickson, Y., & La Vigne, N. (2015). A spatio-temporal analysis of crime at Washington, DC Metro Rail: Stations' crime-generating and crime-attracting characteristics as transportation nodes and places. *Crime Science*, *4*(1), 1–13. La Vigne, N. G. (1997). *Visibility and vigilance: Metro's situational approach to preventing subway crime*. Washington, DC: National Institute of Justice.

72 Smith, M. (2017). Metro ridership drops 12 percent; $125 million revenue shortfall projected [online]. *WTOP*, February 21. https://wtop.com/tracking-metro-24-7/2017/02/metro-ridership-drops-12-percent-125-million-revenue-shortfall-projected/ (retrieved May 18, 2017).

73 Beauregard, E., Proulx, J., & Rossmo, D. K. (2005). Spatial patterns of sex offenders: Theoretical, empirical, and practical issues. *Aggression and Violent Behavior*, *10*(5), 579–603.

74 Hewitt, A., & Beauregard, E. (2014). Sexual crime and place: The impact of the environmental context on sexual assault outcomes. *Journal of Criminal Justice*, *42*(5), 375–383.

75   Leclerc, B., Chiu, Y. N., Cale, J., & Cook, A. (2016). Sexual violence against women through the lens of environmental criminology: Toward the accumulation of evidence-based knowledge and crime prevention. *European Journal on Criminal Policy and Research, 22*(4), 593–617.

76   Ceccato, V. (2014). The nature of rape places. *Journal of Environmental Psychology, 40,* 97–107.

77   Ceccato, V. (2012). Understanding the nature of outdoor rape. Paper presented at *Women, crime and criminal justice practice: Diversity, diversion, desistance and dignity,* Cambridge, U.K., 10–12 January.

78   Loukaitou-Sideris, A., & Eck, J. E. (2007). Crime prevention and active living. *American Journal of Health Promotion, 21*(4 suppl), 380–389; p. 382.

Unit 6.3 Risky Homes

Women will never feel safe in their homes until their risks and fears of burglary are considerably reduced. Fortunately, criminologists know quite a lot about burglary and its prevention and how to reduce *danger for women*. The issue of burglary is important for women for several reasons. As noted in Unit 6.1, the shadow of rape applies especially to burglary because a woman is very upset when an uninvited man *intrudes into her private space*.[1] Four factors help explain this fear:

- *Unplanned burglary-rapes*. Some burglars accidently discover a woman at home and forcibly rape her.[2]

- *Planned burglary-rapes*. Other burglars break into a home knowing a woman is there, intending to rape her from the outset.[3]

- *Burglar-rapist overlap*. at least one-fourth to one-half of sex offenders have committed burglary before or after their sex offenses.[4]

- *Burglary-rapes by non-strangers*. About 30 percent of acutely battered women had to deal with former or recent intimate partners breaking into their homes.[5] Women are especially vulnerable to assaults during periods when sexual relationships are breaking up.[6]

A poorly designed residential setting makes it easy for an offender to enter unseen and unheard by neighbors. As explained in Unit 6.2, a well-designed residential area makes an outsider enter through semipublic and semiprivate space, while avoiding hidden areas. The same principle that protects against strangers might afford some protection against *uninvited men known to the woman* in a residential setting. At least somebody might see him enter or leave, and he might be aware of that fact. None of these environmental protections guarantees the safety of women, but better designs make women considerably safer. Much of what we know about safe design was learned by interviewing burglars directly.[7] Other evidence comes from statistics showing very high **concentrations of residential burglary** in very vulnerable places.[8] Burglars focus on specific types of housing and street configurations. All of this tells us that high residential risk is avoidable.

Security Isn't Obvious

Many people adopt security measures that *seem* obvious but do not really work. Some of these efforts backfire, making people less secure than they were beforehand. Knowledge gathered by professional criminologists and designers helps translate security ideas into more successful outcomes.

As we learn what works and what fails, we also begin to understand more about offenders and how they think. Here are seven examples of "obvious" **security measures that backfire** in the real world because they neglect the **social factors** that affect burglary risk.

1. *Solid walls and security fences?* Surprisingly, solid barriers are not as secure as they look, and they tend to backfire. They enhance burglary by hiding the intruder after his entry.[9]

   Social factors: Intruders tend to be young males who are strong enough to climb over fences quickly. Police may not be and will not be able to see if the intruder has a weapon. See-through fences work much better because an offender can still be noticed by neighbors and police after climbing over.

2. *Lighting without thinking?* Most residential burglary occurs around midday, when lighting is irrelevant. Nonetheless, lighting does still help at night.

   Social factors: Daily activities, such as work and school, take people out of neighborhoods during daylight hours, attracting burglars. At night, motion lights are most likely to attract human attention and discourage illicit entry.[10]

3. *Gated communities?* Gated communities do not clearly or consistently produce more security.[11]

   Social factors: Some of the people living inside a gated community are themselves burglars.[12] Gated communities might not be that small,[13] and many of the people living within gated communities are strangers to one another.

4. *Seclusion?* Burglars like to enter homes on the edge of town, those on a large lot, or those that are far from the street.[14]

Social factors: Many middle-class people live in residences like these; they do not realize that burglars are very likely to be local middle-class youths traveling relatively short distances within suburban areas, including those on the outskirts of town.[15]

5. *Parking behind a building?* A car hidden behind a building is not safer. Cars and the women using them are safer when they park in front.[16]

    Social factors: Jane Jacobs taught us with her famous 1961 book, *Death and Life of Great American Cities*, to funnel as much activity as possible to the front of local homes.[17]

6. *Covered with trees?* Evergreen trees help conceal offending and make residential areas and parks more dangerous. Trees without low branches allow neighborhoods to be safer.[18]

    Social factors: Landscape architects need to become socially aware and criminologically informed. Otherwise the results of their work will interfere with social interaction and visibility, producing dangerous neighborhoods.

You can see that security is not a mechanical process and should not be an afterthought. Hiring expensive guards is not a viable solution for most neighborhoods, so it makes much more sense to protect women by designing safer environments in the first place.

Busier and Calmer Streets

One of the key decisions made by urban planners is where to locate residential buildings. Those located on busy streets have much more risk of crime victimization compared to houses and apartments located on slower and quieter streets. Recent research in Southern California compared homes on **calmer streets** to homes next to busy highways. The latter homes have

*   70 percent more aggravated assaults;

*   78 percent more motor vehicle thefts;

*   108 percent more burglaries;

*   127 percent more larcenies; and

*   three times as many robberies.[19]

Living near *busy streets* and commercial places is a serious disadvantage for families. Each length of arterial highway is six times riskier than an equivalent length of street that is located away from highways.[20] A review found 14 independent studies confirming that homes on streets with high levels of traffic have notably more crime than other homes.[21] These dramatic differences and strong confirmations are telling. Clearly, criminologists and designers should trade notes more often. By locating new residential areas away from the busiest streets, women will face fewer dangers.

Neighboring Houses

Figure 6h compares three designs for middle-class neighborhoods in terms of women's safety. Plan A prevents neighbors from seeing each other. Trees with low branches further block their view. Burglars can easily enter and leave unnoticed, and women are not very secure. Plan B uses trees with higher branches, allowing sight lines that make women safer. Plan C, a traditional middle-class neighborhood with houses lined on each side, is the most secure for women. Note the many sight lines among most houses, increasing a burglar's risk of being seen.

To review some of the evidence already cited, homes are most at risk when

- set back too far from the road or on large lots;

- hidden by dense shrubs, especially evergreens, near doors and windows;

- concealed by solid walls and privacy fences;

- located near major thoroughfares, alleys, or pedestrian paths;

- with windows or doors on sides, backs, or out of sight of other homes.[22]

We have shown in Parts 4 and 5 that the same principles can be followed to make people safer in different sorts of neighborhoods, rich and poor.[23] We have also learned that public housing can be constructed and managed to produce relatively moderate crime rates. A natural experiment compared aggravated assault risks for women living in public housing in two different cities. The first city had an extensive high-rise public housing complex containing numerous buildings and violating all the rules of safe design. The second city had a smaller complex with low-rise buildings that had fairly good sight lines. Women experienced considerably less violence in the second city, with suitable design, and were relatively safe within the public housing complex itself.[24]

We do not wish to give the impression that apartments are necessarily unsafe. It is possible to design apartment buildings in such a way that women living there can

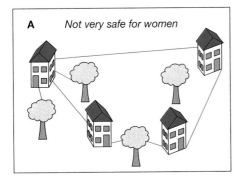
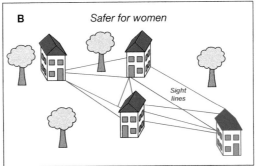
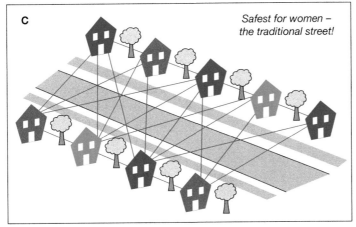

FIGURE 6H
Comparing Women's Safety for Three Middle-Class Neighborhoods

be quite secure. They can have entry doors and entry phones so outsiders cannot enter uninvited.[25] Apartment buildings designed with fewer apartments per main door have less crime than buildings packing in more apartments.[26] With better apartment planning, women face less danger of strangers entering unnoticed. Outdoor greenery can be trimmed and maintained so that women have fewer worries about men being able to conceal their uninvited entry.

These ***street designs*** remind us that we are not full masters of our own destiny. Each of us is affected by decisions that others have made. Consider this example: A building contains a poorly designed staircase with uneven and surprising steps, lacking a graspable handrail. Fortunately, building codes and designers are able to help prevent this scenario, reducing the risk of people falling down stairs by requiring safe staircases.[27]

Public health applications are much broader than this. In 2002, the Centers for Disease Control and Prevention started an effort among physicians and public health experts to study how a community's **built environment** affects health.[28] Many people cannot easily take a walk or bike ride because the design of their neighborhoods is so forbidding. Public health officials have paid much greater attention to walkable neighborhoods,[29] safer parks and greenspace,[30] and locating new residential buildings to minimize exposure to air pollution while also protecting children from dangerous traffic.[31] The medical world is increasingly aware that crime is linked to public health, and that both are linked to our built environment.[32]

How Open Is Good?

Unit 5.3 described extreme examples of exclusion, such as the gated communities that carved up London in the Victorian era. Street systems can go to the other extreme—opening each neighborhood to a chunk of the larger world. That happens for those living right next to a freeway exit or right beside a major boulevard. As we noted in Unit 6.2, researchers repeatedly find that big streets make for big crime risk.

A more secure neighborhood allows strangers to enter, but finds ways to slow down and soften their entry. Oscar Newman explained (Unit 6.1) how semipublic and semiprivate spaces provide a softer transition between public and private worlds. Residential areas can soften the entry of outsiders by narrowing and curving streets and establishing lower speed limits. These examples show how to find a middle ground between total exposure and total exclusion. In the best case, safe design is built into a neighborhood at the outset. Yet a city sometimes must remedy mistakes from the past.

Chicago, Illinois, is the **alley** capital of the United States. Almost all houses and apartment buildings have an extra street behind it—an alley that allows garbage trucks to enter and delivery and repair trucks to provide services. Most cars are parked in the alley, and most private garages are located there. Chicago's alleys date to 1838, and well over 90 percent of the city's homes have alleys behind them.[33] Alleys are very interesting from a burglar's viewpoint, for each one provides easy access to homes as well as a good chance of avoiding being seen. Alleys also make it easier to attack women as they go to and from their cars, or to follow them to their back doors.

Alleys are not exclusive to the United States. Liverpool is an older city in the United Kingdom consisting largely of row, or terraced, houses with alleys running behind them. To counteract the high burglary rate that resulted, the city spent several years implementing an intensive "**alley-gating**" program. They installed robust and lockable gates to block alleys and prevent burglars from entering, giving keys only to residents.

A total of 3,178 alley gates were installed, producing a 37 percent decline in burglary in the gated areas, with no displacement indicated.[34] The gates paid for themselves in a year. Others have designed out crime by slowing down entry into streets that previously had serious problems. These efforts have lowered burglary, drug dealing, and other crimes considerably.[35] Gates and street closings are very simple to explain. More complicated "secure by design" efforts apply many details to make housing safer. Over a five-year period, these designs reduced local burglary by 75 percent.[36]

We have introduced you to the literature on designing safer streets and houses. These designs can never remove entirely the dangers to women or the risks of modern life. Yet our crime statistics show that some homes and streets face much greater risk than others. To be sure, many designs are already in place and cannot be changed completely. However, the alley-gating example demonstrates that old urban areas can learn new tricks. Moreover, new housing can follow the lessons learned over the ages. Old areas should not be allowed to enter the path to decay that has proven so harmful to all, with extra harm to women.

Street Drinking

Danger in the streets creates problems, too, for nearby homes. Women who live in those homes face risks when they go out and also face risks at their doorsteps or even inside. The literature on fear and disorder repeatedly finds that women are quite apprehensive about men drinking in the street. This is likely to be even greater when there are groups of men. A study in Melbourne, Australia, found that street drinkers were predominately male and were involved in creating social disorder for others. Two-thirds of the 30 street drinkers interviewed had seen fellow street drinkers yell at people passing by, several admitting to abusing strangers themselves. The most common size of drinking group was five to ten youths.[37] Problems with *street drinking* have provoked the British government to ban street drinking in the entertainment zones of most British cities and to work out arrangements to reduce drinking problems with several dozen smaller communities.[38] It is difficult to measure how many street-harassing males are under the influence of alcohol and how many are not. However, there is evidence that male employees who drink heavily are more likely to harass females who work in the same units.[39] Alcohol consumption by male abusers is further documented in a study of Australian women. Of those aged 15 to 17, 39 percent reported abuse and aggression by someone who was drunk and 40 percent received unwanted sexual attention. Among women aged 18 to 24, almost two out of three reported being threatened by others who were drunk.[40] Clearly, verbal abuse and threatening behavior are a recurrent theme in the alcohol literature. We should not be surprised that so many women feel threatened by groups of males drinking in the street or the park.

We can see that poor design and mismanagement of public spaces serve to endanger women—*even after they have entered their own private spaces.* Poorly designed and mismanaged public space allows strangers to enter private space nearby and to endanger women in or near their homes. Improving these conditions would enhance security for women heading home, at home, and leaving home to go elsewhere.

FLASHCARD LIST FOR UNIT 6.3

- Alley
- Alley-gating
- Built environment
- Burglary-rapes, by non-strangers, planned, unplanned
- Burglary-rapist overlap
- Busy streets

- Concentrations of residential burglary
- Danger for women
- Intrusion into her private space
- Security measures that backfire
- Social factors

- Street designs
- Street drinking
- Streets, busy, calmer
- Uninvited men known to the woman

DISCUSSION QUESTIONS

1. What characteristics of your home and neighborhood make it safe or unsafe for burglaries?

2. Can you think of a place where alley-gating might be done?

Notes

1   Ferraro, K. F. (1996). Women's fear of victimization: Shadow of sexual assault? *Social Forces, 75*(2), 667–690.

2   Warr, M. (1988). Rape, burglary, and opportunity. *Journal of Quantitative Criminology, 4*(3), 275–288.

3   Pedneault, A., Beauregard, E., Harris, D. A., & Knight, R. A. (2015). Rationally irrational: The case of sexual burglary. *Sexual Abuse, 27*(4), 376–397.

4   Harris, D. A., Smallbone, S., Dennison, S., & Knight, R. A. (2009). Specialization and versatility in sexual offenders referred for civil commitment. *Journal of Criminal Justice, 37*(1), 37–44. Soothill, K., Francis, B., Sanderson, B., & Ackerley, E. (2000). Sex offenders: Specialists, generalists – or both? A 32-year criminological study. *The British Journal of Criminology, 40*(1), 56–67. Leclerc, B., Chiu, Y. N., Cale, J., & Cook, A. (2016). Sexual violence against women through the lens of environmental criminology: Toward the accumulation of evidence-based knowledge and crime prevention. *European Journal on Criminal Policy and Research, 22*(4), 593–617.

5   Mechanic, M. B., Weaver, T. L., & Resick, P. A. (2000). Intimate partner violence and stalking behavior: Exploration of patterns and correlates in a sample of acutely battered women. *Violence and Victims, 15*(1), 55–72.

6   DeKeseredy, W. S., Rogness, M., & Schwartz, M. D. (2004). Separation/divorce sexual assault: The current state of social scientific knowledge. *Aggression and Violent Behavior, 9*(6), 675–691.

7   Cromwell, P. F., & Olson, J. N. (2004). *Breaking and entering: Burglars on burglary.* Stamford, CT: Thomson/Wadsworth. Bernasco, W. (2013). Offenders on offending: Learning about crime from criminals. Abingdon, U.K.: Routledge. Decker, S. H. (2005). *Using offender interviews to inform police problem solving.* Problem-Oriented Guides for Police, Problem-Solving Tools Series, No. 3. Washington, DC: Office of Community Oriented Policing Services.

8   Tseloni, A., Wittebrood, K., Farrell, G., & Pease, K. (2004). Burglary victimization in England and Wales, the United States and the Netherlands a cross-national comparative test of routine activities and lifestyle theories. *British Journal of Criminology, 44*(1), 66–91.

9   Chula Vista Police Department. (2001). *The Chula Vista Residential Burglary Reduction Project.* Chula Vista, CA: Chula Vista Police Department.

10 Farrington, D. P., & Welsh, B. C. (2002). *Effects of improved street lighting on crime: A systematic review.* Home Office Research Series. London: Home Office.

11 Blandy, S., Lister, D., Atkinson, R., & Flint, J. (2003). *Gated communities: A systematic review of the research evidence.* CNR Paper 12. ESRC Centre for Neighbourhood Research.

12 Breetzke, G. D., & Cohn, E. G. (2013). Burglary in gated communities: An empirical analysis using routine activities theory. *International Criminal Justice Review, 23*(1), 56–74.

13 Breetzke, G. D., Landman, K., & Cohn, E. G. (2014). Is it safer behind the gates? Crime and gated communities in South Africa. *Journal of Housing and the Built Environment, 29*(1), 123–139.

14 Weisel, D. L. (2002). *Burglary of single-family houses.* Problem-Oriented Guides for Police Series, No. 18. Washington, DC: Office of Community Oriented Policing Services. Brantingham, P., & Brantingham, P. (1984). Burglary mobility and crime prevention planning. In R. Clarke & T. Hope (Eds.), *Coping with burglary,* pp. 77–95. Boston: Kluwer.

15 Bowers, K., & Johnson, S. D. (2015). Poetry in motion: The case of insider and outsider offenders. In M. Andresen, M., & G. Farrell (Eds.), *The criminal act,* pp. 115–130. London: Palgrave Macmillan.

16 Poyner, B. (2013). *Crime-free housing in the 21st century.* Abingdon, U.K.: Routledge.

17 Jacobs, J. (1961). *The death and life of great American cities.* New York: Vintage.

18 Coupe, T., & Blake, L. (2006). Daylight and darkness targeting strategies and the risks of being seen at residential burglaries. *Criminology, 44*(2), 431–464.

19 Kim, Y. A., & Hipp, J. R. (2017). Physical boundaries and city boundaries: Consequences for crime patterns on street segments? *Crime & Delinquency.* Published online January 23. https://doi.org/10.1177/0011128716687756.

20 Wuschke, K. E. (2016). Planning for crime: Exploring the connections between urban space, development and patterns of crime. Doctoral dissertation, Simon Fraser University.

21 Armitage, R., Monchuk, L., & Rogerson, M. (2011). It looks good, but what is it like to live there? Exploring the impact of innovative housing design on crime. *European Journal on Criminal Policy and Research, 17*(1), 29–54.

22 Armitage, R., & Joyce, C. (2016). *"Why my house?" Exploring the influence of residential housing design on burglar decision making.* Abingdon, U.K.: Routledge.

23 Rengert, G., & Wasilchick, J. (2000). *Suburban burglary: A tale of two suburbs,* 2nd edition. Springfield, IL.: Charles C. Thomas.

24 Holzman, H. R., Hyatt, R. A., & Dempster, J. M. (2001). Patterns of aggravated assault in public housing: Mapping the nexus of offense, place, gender, and race. *Violence Against Women, 7*(6), 662–684.

25 Poyner, B. (1994). Lessons from Lisson Green: An evaluation of walkway demolition on a British housing estate. In R. V. Clarke (Ed.), *Crime prevention studies*, Vol. 3, pp. 127–150. Monsey, NY: Criminal Justice Press.

26 Clarke, R. V., & Eck, J. E. (2005). *Crime analysis for problem solvers in 60 small steps.* Washington, DC: Center for Problem Oriented Policing.

27 Dusenberry, D. O., Simpson, H., & DelloRusso, S. J. (2009). Effect of handrail shape on graspability. *Applied Ergonomics, 40*(4), 657–669.

28 Dannenberg, A. L., Jackson, R. J., Frumkin, H., Schieber, R. A., Pratt, M., Kochtitzky, C., & Tilson, H. H. (2003). The impact of community design and land-use choices on public health: A scientific research agenda. *American Journal of Public Health, 93*(9), 1500–1508.

29 Frank, L. D., Sallis, J. F., Saelens, B. E., Leary, L., Cain, K., Conway, T. L., & Hess, P. M. (2010). The development of a walkability index: Application to the Neighborhood Quality of Life Study. *British Journal of Sports Medicine, 44*(13), 924–933.

30 Bogar, S., & Beyer, K. M. (2016). Green space, violence, and crime: A systematic review. *Trauma, Violence, & Abuse, 17*(2), 160–171.

31 Shekarrizfard, M., Faghih-Imani, A., Crouse, D. L., Goldberg, M., Ross, N., . . . & Hatzopoulou, M. (2016). Individual exposure to traffic related air pollution across land-use clusters. *Transportation Research Part D: Transport and Environment, 46*, 339–350.

32 Tuckel, P., & Milczarski, W. (2015). Walk Score™, perceived neighborhood walkability, and walking in the US. *American Journal of Health Behavior, 39*(2), 241–255.

33 Grossman, J. R., Keating, A. D., & Reiff, J. L. (Eds.). (n.d.). Alleys [online]. The electronic encyclopedia of Chicago. www.encyclopedia.chicagohistory.org/pages/38.html (retrieved May 9, 2017).

34 Bowers, K. J., Johnson, S. D., & Hirschfield, A. F. (2004). Closing off opportunities for crime: An evaluation of alley-gating. *European Journal on Criminal Policy and Research, 10*(4), 285–308.

35 Clarke, R. V. G. (2004). *Closing streets and alleys to reduce crime: Should you go down this road?* Problem-Oriented Guides for Police, Response Guides Series, No. 2. Washington, DC: Office of Community Oriented Policing Services.

36 Armitage, R., & Monchuk, L. (2011). Sustaining the crime reduction impact of designing out crime. Re-evaluating the Secured by Design scheme 10 years on. *Security Journal, 24*(4), 320–343.

37 Dwyer, R., Horyniak, D., Aitken, C., Higgs, P., & Dietze, P. (2007). *People who drink in public space in the Footscray CBD.* Melbourne: Burnet Institute.

38 Beckford, M. (2008). Drinking restricted in 613 public places in England and Wales. *The Telegraph* (London), August 19. www.telegraph.co.uk/news/uknews/2586413/Drinking-restricted-in-613-public-places-in-England-and-Wales.html (retrieved April 14, 2017). Newton, S. (2017, January 30). Local alcohol action areas will tackle alcohol related harms [online]. www.gov.uk/government/news/local-alcohol-action-areas-will-tackle-alcohol-related-harms (retrieved April 14, 2017).

39 Bacharach, S. B., Bamberger, P. A., & McKinney, V. M. (2007). Harassing under the influence: The prevalence of male heavy drinking, the embeddedness of permissive workplace drinking

norms, and the gender harassment of female coworkers. *Journal of Occupational Health Psychology, 12*(3), 232–250.

40   Taylor, J., & Carroll, T. (2001). Youth alcohol consumption: Experiences and expectations. In P. Williams (Ed.), *Alcohol, young persons and violence*, pp. 15–30. Research and Public Policy Series, Report 35. Canberra: Australian Institute of Criminology.

UNIT 6.4 Risky Nights

We have discussed how homes and streets are risky for women. We turn now to nighttime behaviors that are especially risky for women. As we discussed in the introduction to Part 6, nighttime entertainment changes patterns of danger. Safe locations by day can become danger zones by night. In addition, women are likely to enter **nighttime danger zones** for social reasons as darkness approaches. We focus here on relatively risky nighttime settings, taking alcohol consumption into account. We also discuss how situational prevention techniques can help mitigate the risks.

Feminism and the Temperance Movement

Saloons were different a century ago compared to the barrooms of today. Except in the Wild West[1] and on "skid row,"[2] American saloons at that time were mostly located in urban neighborhoods, allowing patrons to walk there and home. Saloons were often moderate in size, with patrons likely to recognize each other. Almost no women were present, but men of different ages might well drink together. The local saloon filled the role of an informal social club.[3] Yet many men drank far too much, producing a definite danger. This led to a historic organized effort by women to protect themselves and their families.

Many of the historic figures in the feminist movement were crusaders against saloons and liquor consumption. These included Susan B. Anthony, Amelia Bloomer, Jane Addams, Carrie Nation and Elizabeth Cady Stanton. **Feminist leaders** led groups of women to the doors of saloons, picketing, shouting, and forcing many of them to close.[4] Some of them went into the saloons and smashed the liquor bottles. This was called the **temperance movement**—the feminist effort to outlaw or contain alcohol sales. Given the historic male dominance of saloons and the surrounding streets, the link between feminism and liquor control was not accidental. During that era, "respectable" women did not drink alcohol in public.[5]

Perhaps angered by too many drunken husbands and risky streets, progressive and religious women formed the ***Woman's Christian Temperance Union*** (WCTU) in 1874. The WCTU not only advocated liquor control but also campaigned for a women's right to vote, setting up shelters for abused women and children, equal pay for equal work, founding of kindergartens to help working mothers, and stiffer penalties for sexual crimes against females—ideas that are well over a century old.[6]

The WCTU was instrumental in passing the Eighteenth Amendment to the United States Constitution in 1919, which prohibited the production, sale, and transport of intoxicating liquors. This was repealed in 1933. The period 1919 through 1933 was referred to as the ***Prohibition era*** in the United States. Despite the repeal of Prohibition, the United States and many other nations[7] continue to legislate many restrictions on when, where, and how liquor is sold.[8] Full prohibition is not necessary for alcohol policy to have an influence.[9] Indeed, ***closing hours***, ***barroom size***, and ***serving practices*** can have a definite impact on the security of women, as we shall see as Part 6 continues. However, many of these regulations are not enforced in practice, leaving women highly vulnerable to attack.

Female Drinking Patterns Today

Since Prohibition and women being granted the right to vote, the role of women has changed.[10] They are out of the home into the work force and into college in greater numbers. Their careers are less likely to be in teaching than in the past.[11] These changes have affected the safety of the home during the day[12] and put women on the streets not only during the day, but also at night, when they are now more likely to be coming home from work or school. We have noted the many incivilities that affect women; rude behavior is even more threatening to women at dusk or after dark.

Drinking patterns have also changed. Drink specials are offered to women to increase their presence in bars, increasing ***binge drinking*** and intoxication levels.[13] Women join men in drinking contests, notably producing higher blood alcohol levels.[14] In both the United States[15] and European nations,[16] drinking games have a major impact on the blood-alcohol levels of women and the men in their vicinity. A common practice is ***pre-loading*** (also called pre-gaming), where women and men begin to drink in private parties or on the way to major events and are already well on the road to intoxication even before they arrive.[17] The process is found not only in the United States, but also in Australia,[18] the United Kingdom,[19] Denmark,[20] and Switzerland.[21] Fraternities and sororities on American university campuses often play active roles in encouraging excess drinking.[22] Alcohol consumption also increases on special occasions (such as turning 21 years old), a ***rite of passage*** for women (as for men).[23]

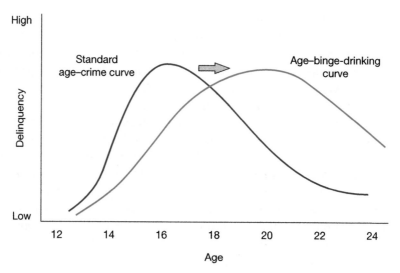

FIGURE 6I
Binge Drinking Has a Slightly Older Age Curve than Crime

As shown in Figure 6i, the age–binge-drinking curve peaks further to the right than the age–crime curve, closer to age 20 (light blue curve) rather than around age 16 or 17 (dark blue curve).[24] However, the age–binge-drinking curve (like all age–crime curves) is just a summary picture. Some youths start binging in early or mid-adolescence. Some people never grow out of it. The important point for this unit is that many of these bingers are women, and much of the binging occurs in settings where women are with men or at least near enough to be attacked. Binging assembles likely offenders with suitable targets for sexual aggression while also reducing the capability of possible guardians against such aggression.[25]

More generally, modern drinking patterns endanger women much more than was the case a century ago. Drinking today is almost as prevalent among women as among men.[26] It often occurs in

- private zones lacking any public regulation;[27]

- bars where excessive drinking is the norm;[28]

- very large venues with several hundred people and few controls;[29] and

- settings with youths together but older persons absent.[30]

While the drinker may appear normal and carry on conversations, they may experience ***blackouts***, leaving them with no memory later of being drunk or of any sexual behaviors involved.[31] The list above helps explain why young women are especially at risk of sexual attack in modern drinking contexts. Although women are also capable of violence or other aggression in barroom settings,[32] that fact does not keep us from recognizing that nightlife puts women at significant risk. Moreover, we find no evidence that binge drinking among students has been declining recently.[33]

Mapping Sexual Danger at Night

We already included one map of danger spots for forcible rape (for Stockholm; Figure 6g in Unit 6.2). It showed that daytime risks for women were walking from public transit, while nighttime risks were in the center of Stockholm, which included an entertainment area. An even stronger illustration of nighttime risk is mapped in Figure 6j. It shows that the location of barrooms in Anchorage, Alaska, closely relates to the concentration of rapes. This tells us that that society should pay much closer attention to alcohol policy and nightlife if it wishes to protect women.

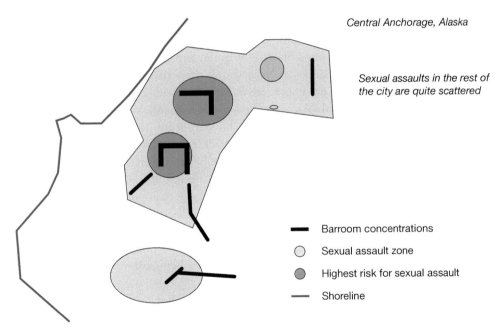

FIGURE 6J

Overlap between the Sexual Assault Zone and Barroom Locations, Anchorage, Alaska, 2000–2001

Source: Adapted from A. B. Rosay & R. H. Langworthy (2003). *Exploratory spatial analysis of sexual assault in Anchorage.* Anchorage: Justice Center, University of Alaska.

Women experience higher rates of injury for the same level of alcohol intake as men,[34] including exposure to risk of sexual harm.[35] Although not all intoxication is linked to barrooms, the alcohol–injury link is quite strong, confirmed by emergency room data from 16 nations.[36] The contribution of alcohol to crime is disproportionately high for violent crime, and highest for harassment crimes. In one British city, half of all harassment offenders were influenced by alcohol.[37] Evidence tells us that intimate partner violence is also related to alcohol excesses,[38] something the feminist movement told us a century ago. Modern society increasingly finds that urban nighttime entertainment districts become hosts for alcohol-related crimes, especially violence.[39] Researchers find a strong association between intoxication and aggression, including serious attacks, in and near entertainment venues.[40] The research leads to policy recommendations to reduce intoxication levels across bars in general and to focus attention on the worst barrooms.[41]

The Journey Home at Night

Many young women ride home from social events with men who are drunk or highly influenced by alcohol. This has been reported in Canada,[42] New Zealand,[43] the United Kingdom,[44] and the United States.[45] Women as passengers are risking not only accident but also sexual attack in cars with drunk male drivers. Often there are no other passengers, or the other passengers are dropped off and the woman is alone with a man who could be harmful. An estimated 3 million college students have been passengers in a car with an intoxicated driver.[46] A significant number of drunk drivers seek to evade law enforcement by driving on back roads,[47] which exposes a female passenger to extra risk of attack. College students who smoke marijuana are also likely to ride in cars afterwards with other smokers, who are also disinhibited.[48]

Well-known policy efforts encourage drinking groups to appoint a ***designated driver*** at the outset of the evening. Researchers find that some designated drivers drink alcohol anyway, so they might be subject to interference from drinking passengers. Moreover, the others in the group tend to drink more than they would have when driving themselves.[49] It is not clear that a designated driver policy makes women safer from sexual aggression.

A different program is known as the ***safe ride home***. For example, *Be On the Safe Side* (BOSS) is a ride-share program operated by the Student Services Department at the University of Wisconsin-Milwaukee. Student fees support the program, but it is free at the point of service. Students call for a ride and wait indoors until a van arrives. The program mainly operates at night, taking students to any destination within a 1.5-mile radius around campus, including bars and residence halls; it provides over 130,000 rides a year. An econometric evaluation of the program concluded that the program was associated with a 14 percent reduction in crime in the area.[50] A smaller safe-ride program at the University of Oregon provides nearly 15,000 rides a year but has not been evaluated. At the University of Arizona, there has been a safe ride program for 30 years, and an honors student recently designed a prototype app to help women summon a safe ride home.[51]

We hope that modern electronic methods will make these policies more universal and effective, and that they will also help determine whether the efforts reduce crime. The importance of the trip home from nightlife is reinforced by a study of Uber trips in New York City. Researchers learned that ride-sharing reduces forcible rape, especially in high-risk areas and times and in trips to outer boroughs of the city. They concluded that *a ride-sharing platform helps greatly to reduce sexual assaults*.[52] Although taxi drivers and other hired drivers might occasionally pick up victims or offenders,[53] information technology can be used to reduce passenger anonymity and enhance security. In addition, female drivers tend to enhance security for women passengers. The potential for ride-home services to reduce danger for women is further illustrated by a study of the Washington, DC, subway system, which extended its hours of service by three hours per week in 1999. That expansion was associated with a noteworthy reduction in drunk driving arrests.[54] However, public transit systems generate their own late-night risks, as noted in Unit 6.2.

Concentration of Bar-Related Aggression

Consistent with Figure 6i, numerous studies show that crime is highly concentrated in and around bars. Areas with high density of bars have more crime. Inside, victimization is also more likely at barrooms than at other locations. Women in bars who socialize with male strangers in a bar setting are especially likely to experience aggressive victimization, including verbal, physical, or sexual aggression.[55]

It became clear to Cincinnati researchers that public officials could cut barroom violence at least in half by focusing enforcement on a handful of bad bars.[56] In major cities, we can expect about one in seven bars to produce from 50 to 90 percent of bar-related criminal offenses. The evidence is overwhelming that barroom danger is preventable:

- Violent bars are often next to nonviolent bars, indicating that the neighborhood is not the cause of the problem.

- Low-income neighborhoods include many bars that are quite peaceful and orderly.

- Affluent neighborhoods include some bars that generate crime and disorder.

The Cincinnati study concluded that bars are microenvironments, partially insulated from external neighborhoods. Bar owners and managers can create and maintain peaceful settings without violence. A violent or nonviolent bar is the product of decisions made by bar owners and managers about everyday business operations.

How Bars Can Make Things Worse for Women

Many decisions and practices within a drinking venue directly impinge on the safety of women. As we've mentioned, women drink considerably more *while drinking in mostly male groups* and considerably less in mostly female drinking groups.[57] Women are also more likely to be harassed in male-dominated drinking locations,[58] especially in very large venues. Large cities in many modern nations have barrooms covering multiple floors with large numbers of patrons at once.[59] In Toronto, a study of 118 bars, each serving over 300 patrons, found widespread sexual activity, aggression, and sometimes violence across venues.[60] Some bars emphasize heavy drinking and draw high proportions of male patrons, building in environmental features that invite aggressive behaviors and disperse aggression into the surrounding area.[61] Large size, sprawling layout, discomfort, low level of cleanliness, high noise levels, crowding, and low levels of expected decorum—all of these features contribute to aggressive behavior.[62] Many such bars welcome enough young women to attract a plentitude of males, but leave these women outnumbered and endangered.

One study clearly illustrates that risky situations in barrooms vary greatly. Trained observers spent 444 hours observing patrons and bar personnel inside 25 licensed drinking establishments in Hoboken, New Jersey. Observations took place at two separate time periods, 7:30 pm to 10:30 pm and 11:00 pm to 2:00 am, on Thursday, Friday, and Saturday nights.[63] Researchers learned that aggression levels are dramatically higher in some circumstances compared to others. As Figure 6k indicates, when bouncers, doormen, or servers were themselves drinking, aggression multiplied by six to eight times compared to when they were not drinking. Patrons drinking in rounds were almost three times as likely to generate an aggressive situation. Periods of crowding and difficult movement generated about four times the risk of uncrowded periods, when movement is easy. The same study shows that aggression increased markedly in later hours when people were more under the influence of alcohol. During aggressive periods, the bars were at least four times more likely to be serving customers who were already intoxicated. Again, we see that danger is not uniform or automatic; it results from decisions and behaviors over which bar owners and managers have considerable control.

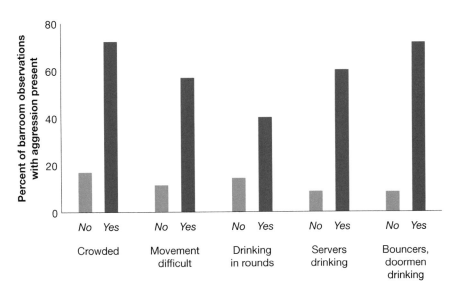

FIGURE 6K

Relationship between Barroom Aggression and Barroom Situational Factors, Hoboken, NJ, Observational Study

Source: Adapted from J. C. Roberts (2007). Barroom aggression in Hoboken, New Jersey. Don't blame the bouncers! *Journal of Drug Education*, 37(4), 429–445.

Enforcement of Existing Liquor Laws Can Make It Better

It does not suffice to pass laws to protect women from drunk men. The laws must be enforced. In many cases, open and systematic violation of those laws is the rule rather than the exception. A survey of a thousand local law enforcement agencies across the United States measured efforts to enforce laws against sales to intoxicated patrons at licensed alcohol establishments. More than half of local agencies admitted that sales to intoxicated persons were common. Only 20 percent of local agencies reported enforcement efforts to reduce sales to obviously intoxicated patrons over the past year. Fewer than one in ten agencies made such checks monthly. "Enforcement of laws prohibiting alcohol sales to obviously intoxicated patrons is an underutilized strategy to reduce alcohol-related problems, especially among local law enforcement agencies."[64]

When liquor laws are taken more seriously by law enforcement, women are the most likely beneficiaries. In a study of 50 California cities, those receiving state funding for underage drinking enforcement activities were able to reduce underage drinking.[65] Another study found that drinking and driving declined at colleges where governments restricted high-volume consumption and enforce their laws on beverage sales.[66]

To be sure, modern societies contain plentiful well-managed bars that avoid attracting aggressive people or enhancing aggression among those who arrive. Alcohol-related violence can be reduced by systematic approaches by police to reduce bar-hopping and free or discounted drinks for women.[67] Well-designed and managed bars have much lower levels of violence. Staff behavior has an important impact, especially if there are enough staff to serve people and to quiet down incidents. But staff serving people too much alcohol and a large amount at closing time sets the stage for aggression.

A remarkable randomized control study was carried out in Toronto, Canada, involving the **Safer Bars Programme**. The experimental intervention involved training 373 bar staff, owners, and managers on how to reduce environmental risks. The goal was to reduce severe and moderate aggression, including punching, kicking, shoving, and grappling. Trained researchers made 734 observations on Friday and Saturday nights, from midnight to 2.00 am in 18 bars with capacity for over 300 patrons. Even though the intervention was brief, it notably reduced aggression in these barrooms.[68] This reinforces our main point: Nightlife aggression is preventable and women can be safer.

The "Last Drink Survey"

Suppose you were the new police chief in a city of 200,000 people. With sufficient support from the mayor, you could make women safer. Your first task would be to figure out the worst bars in town and the worst liquor stores—the ones that sell to minors or have men hanging out in front. Camarillo, California, is a city of 65,000 people. Police asked those picked up for driving under the influence of alcohol where they had their last drink, and received 88 answers. Fifty-two of these 88 problems could be traced to just four local barrooms.[69] **Last drink surveys** were used to improve barrooms and reduce alcohol problems in several cities.[70] Many cities put in the newspaper the names of bars that created the worst problems for the community. Other cities targeted liquor law enforcement on their worst bars. Last drink surveys not only put pressure on bar owners and managers, but also force police and liquor authorities to face up to their own responsibilities under the law.

Potentially Aggressive Pedestrian Flows

Nightlife districts have outdoor problems too. Often these problems occur in busy bottlenecks or cluster points where drinkers wait and compete for services. Sometimes they are in line waiting for fast food or entry into another pub or club. Sometimes they are competing for taxis or pushing to get into public transit vehicles. Incidents are triggered when drinkers are arguing for services.[71] Many of these problems result from poor planning and management of services in entertainment districts. Changes in street layout, staggering barroom closing hours, removing congestion points, providing better public transit—these efforts have resulted in violence reduction in city entertainment districts.[72] We continue to find overwhelming evidence that nightlife crime can be reduced. However, there are also ways to make things much worse.

Switzerland's Grand Experiment

Cities with Little Crime, published in 1978, documents why Switzerland and its largest city (Zurich) have such low crime rates, with few Swiss youths involved in crime.[73] That situation has changed completely in the past 15 years. Switzerland has moved up from one of the lowest-crime nations in the developed world to having normal modern levels of crime, including violence. Swiss crime went way up while other modern nations' crime rates were going way down. What happened?

Since the year 2000, Switzerland has undergone a revolution in nightlife. A third of the Swiss population resides in metropolitan Zurich, where only a handful of pubs could open until 2:00 am in 1999. Zurich today has more than 600 pubs, bars, and restaurants that open all night. In the past, the last public transit left the center of town a half-hour before midnight. Today, public transit operates all night. In 2010, nine times as many passengers used Zurich public transport from midnight to 6:00 am on weekend nights as in 2002. That revolution in nightlife transformed the Swiss crime rates, including violent injuries, even though domestic violence rates did not go up at all.

> Interestingly, this increase is entirely attributable to violence in the streets. [. . .] [F]or young men and women, violence increased only in the streets, but not in other settings. Further, the increase was concentrated on late nighttime hours on Friday and Saturday evenings in major urban areas.[74]

This is a clear example that human decisions set the stage for crime-rate trends. Swiss legislators and administrators changed the nature of their society. Switzerland today is lively, but risky as well. Perhaps the Swiss will turn to some of the same alcohol control efforts that other nations consider.

Alcohol Prices and Taxes Can Make It Better

When enforced, alcohol policies have real impact on drinking and then on crime. Some policy changes get people to drink more and get in more trouble. Other policy changes reduce drinking and lessen the problems of crime and disorder.

Alcohol price is the most powerful policy instrument. Tax increases can greatly enhance the cost of packaged alcohol beverages or liquor by the drink. Analysis of over 100 studies confirmed that high taxes on alcohol reduce how much people drink.[75] Findings from the United States estimate:

- A 1 percent increase in the price of an ounce of pure alcohol would reduce the probability of intimate partner violence against women by 5.3 percent.[76]

- A 10 percent increase in the price of beer would reduce the number of college students involved in violence each year by 4 percent.[77]

Younger drinkers, including college students, are especially sensitive to alcohol prices.[78]

> The price students pay for alcohol is an important factor in their drinking. Low price and very easy access to alcohol are strong correlates of binge drinking. Underage drinking and binge drinking by female students is sensitive to the price of alcohol. Students who pay a higher price for alcohol are less likely to transition from abstainer to any alcohol use and to binge drinking, and this effect is equal across thresholds. These findings, in concert with research on price in other populations, suggest that raising the unit price of alcohol may reduce student consumption.[79]

The link between alcohol policy and crime has also been documented. Criminologists have established the link between local liquor sales establishments and local crime (Unit 5.7). Many public health researchers have documented the link between alcohol outlets and crime.[80] Alcohol hours of operation and days of sale have also been used to control the quantity people drink and resulting crime problems.[81] One Brazilian city closed its alcohol retail stores at 11:00 pm, resulting in a significant decrease in homicides as well as in assaults against women.[82] Another Brazilian city also gained reductions in violence after restricting alcohol sales.[83] An Australian city that restricted bar closing times saw a reduction in resulting incidents of almost one-third.[84] The other side of the coin is that studies indicate that cities that relaxed alcohol trading hours end up with more interpersonal violence.[85] There was sufficient evidence in ten studies to conclude that increasing hours of sale by two or more hours increases alcohol-related harms.[86] Late trading hours in Australia were associated with increased violence inside and around the barrooms.[87] In addition, a study of 55,000 Finnish respondents found that conveniently located liquor and beer stores clearly get people to drink more.[88]

Variety of Alcohol Restrictions

Modern societies have enacted quite a variety of policies to restrict and contain liquor consumption without imposing total prohibition. Important restrictions on liquor short of prohibition include restricting where liquor can be sold, both in packages and by the drink. Many states and nations limit alcohol content in beverages, and some impose very stiff excise taxes that increase the cost of alcoholic beverages, especially those that contain the highest alcohol content. These various restrictions have a very noteworthy impact on the quantities and the content of what people drink, where they drink, their perpetration of violence and their victimizations. Controlling the size, location, and concentration of liquor establishments is important for minimizing aggression, along with training and licensing servers. To protect women from aggression, a jurisdiction must be willing to close a bar for the weekend or, with repeat violations, to revoke their liquor licenses entirely. In many cases, bars can flagrantly violate liquor laws and endanger their own community with total impunity. Many incidents occur outside of the bar itself and are never statistically linked to the bar that helped intoxicate the offender or victim. Yet crime mapping techniques can associate bars with surrounding violence, and then pressure can be put on these bars to clean up their acts.

You can see that nighttime creates many risky situations for women and that alcohol contributes a lot to making these riskier. Luckily, there is much we know about controlling alcohol sales and serving alcohol that can reduce some of the risk.

FLASHCARD LIST FOR UNIT 6.4

- Barroom size
- Binge drinking
- Blackouts
- Closing hours
- Designated driver
- Drinking patterns (female)
- Feminist leaders

- Last drink surveys
- Nighttime danger zones
- Pre-loading
- Prohibition era
- Rite of passage
- Safe ride home
- Safer Bars Programme

- Serving practices
- Temperance movement
- Woman's Christian Temperance Union

DISCUSSION QUESTIONS

1. What advice would you give to Swiss authorities that might reverse their increasing problem with nightlife crime?

2. How do you think danger to women shifts from early to late evening, and how might their security be improved at different times and places?

Notes

1   Dixon, K. J. (2005). *Boomtown saloons: Archaeology and history in Virginia City*. Reno and Las Vegas: University of Nevada Press.

2   Stuart, F. (2016). *Down, out, and under arrest: Policing and everyday life in Skid Row*. Chicago: University of Chicago Press.

3   Kingsdale, J. M. (1973). The "poor man's club": Social functions of the urban working-class saloon. *American Quarterly, 25*(4), 472–489.

4   Kerr, K. A. (1985). *Organized for prohibition: A new history of the Anti-Saloon League*. New Haven, CT: Yale University Press.

5   Murdock, C. G. (2001). *Domesticating drink: Women, men, and alcohol in America, 1870–1940*. Baltimore, MD: John Hopkins University Press.

6   National Woman's Christian Temperance Union, (n.d.). Early history [online]. www.wctu.org/history.html (retrieved November 12, 2016).

7   Tyrrell, I. (2014). *Woman's world/woman's empire: The Woman's Christian Temperance Union in international perspective, 1880–1930*. Chapel Hill, NC: University of North Carolina Press.

8   Stockwell, T., & Chikritzhs, T. (2009). Do relaxed trading hours for bars and clubs mean more relaxed drinking? A review of international research on the impacts of changes to permitted hours of drinking. *Crime Prevention and Community Safety, 11*(3), 153–170.

9   Dwyer, R., Horyniak, D., Aitken, C., Higgs, P., & Dietze, P. (2007). *People who drink in public space in the Footscray CBD*. Melbourne: Burnet Institute.

10 Bianchi, S. M., Robinson, J. P., & Milke, M. A. (2006). *The changing rhythms of American family life*. New York: Russell Sage Foundation.

11 The National Bureau of Economic Research. (n.d.) Why do women outnumber men in college? [online]. www.nber.org/digest/jan07/w12139.html (retrieved May 16, 2017).

12 Cohen, L. E., & Felson, M. (1979). Social change and crime rate trends: A routine activity approach. *American Sociological Review, 44*(4), 588–608.

13 Thombs, D. L., Dodd, V., Porkorny, S. B., Omli, M. R., O'Mara, R., . . . & Werch, C. (2008). Drink specials and the intoxication levels of patrons exiting college bars. *American Journal of Health Behavior, 32*(4), 411–419.

14 Sönmez, S., Apostolopoulos, Y., Yu, C. H., Yang, S., Mattila, A., & Lucy, C. Y. (2006). Binge drinking and casual sex on spring break. *Annals of Tourism Research, 33*(4), 895–917.

15 Thombs et al., Drink specials and the intoxication levels of patrons exiting college bars.

16 Beccaria, F., & Sande, A. (2003). Drinking games and rite of life projects: A social comparison of the meaning and functions of young people's use of alcohol during the rite of passage to adulthood in Italy and Norway. *Young, 11*(2), 99–119.

17 Wells, S., Graham, K., & Purcell, J. (2009). Policy implications of the widespread practice of "pre-drinking" or "pre-gaming" before going to public drinking establishments: Are current prevention strategies backfiring? *Addiction, 104*(1), 4–9.

18 MacLean, S., & Callinan, S. (2013). "Fourteen dollars for one beer!" Pre-drinking is associated with high-risk drinking among Victorian young adults. *Australian and New Zealand Journal of Public Health, 37*(6), 579–585.

19 Foster, J. H., & Ferguson, C. (2014). Alcohol "pre-loading": A review of the literature. *Alcohol and Alcoholism, 49*(2), 213–226.

20 Measham, F., & Østergaard, J. (2009). The public face of binge drinking: British and Danish young women, recent trends in alcohol consumption and the European binge drinking debate. *Probation Journal, 56*(4), 415–434.

21 Labhart, F., Graham, K., Wells, S., & Kuntsche, E. (2013). Drinking before going to licensed premises: An event-level analysis of predrinking, alcohol consumption, and adverse outcomes. *Alcoholism: Clinical and Experimental Research, 37*(2), 284–291.

22 Nuwer, H. (2001). *Wrongs of passage: Fraternities, sororities, hazing, and binge drinking.* Bloomington, IN: Indiana University Press.

23 Lewis, M. A., Lindgren, K. P., Fossos, N., Neighbors, C., & Oster-Aaland, L. (2009). Examining the relationship between typical drinking behavior and 21st birthday drinking behavior among college students: Implications for event-specific prevention. *Addiction, 104*(5), 760–767.

24 Tucker, J. S., Ellickson, P. L., Orlando, M., Martino, S. C., & Klein, D. J. (2005). Substance use trajectories from early adolescence to emerging adulthood: A comparison of smoking, binge drinking, and marijuana use. *Journal of Drug Issues, 35*(2), 307–332.

25 Courtney, K. E., & Polich, J. (2009). Binge drinking in young adults: Data, definitions, and determinants. *Psychological Bulletin, 135*(1), 142–156.

26 Bewick, B. M., Mulhern, B., Barkham, M., Trusler, K., Hill, A. J., & Stiles, W. B. (2008). Changes in undergraduate student alcohol consumption as they progress through university. *BMC Public Health, 8*(163). https://doi.org/10.1186/1471-2458-8-163.

27 Clapp, J. D., Reed, M. B., Holmes, M. R., Lange, J. E., & Voas, R. B. (2006). Drunk in public, drunk in private: The relationship between college students, drinking environments and alcohol consumption. *The American Journal of Drug and Alcohol Abuse, 32*(2), 275–285.

28 Roberts, M. (2015). "A big night out": Young people's drinking, social practice and spatial experience in the "liminoid" zones of English night-time cities. *Urban Studies, 52*(3), 571–588.

29 Scott, M. S., & Dedel, K. (2006). *Assaults in and around bars,* 2nd edition. Washington, DC: Office of Community Oriented Policing Services.

30 Treno, A. J., Alaniz, M. L., & Gruenewald, P. J. (2000). The use of drinking places by gender, age and ethnic groups: An analysis of routine drinking activities. *Addiction, 95*(4), 537–551.

31 Wetherill, R. R., & Fromme, K. (2011). Acute alcohol effects on narrative recall and contextual memory: An examination of fragmentary blackouts. *Addictive Behaviors, 36*(8), 886–889.

32 Krienert, J. L., & Vandiver, D. M. (2009). Assaultive behavior in bars: A gendered comparison. *Violence and Victims, 24*(2), 232–247.

33   Hingson, R. W., Zha, W., & Weitzman, E. R. (2009). Magnitude of and trends in alcohol-related mortality and morbidity among US college students ages 18–24, 1998–2005. *Journal of Studies on Alcohol and Drugs*, Supplement, *16*, 12–20.

34   Stockwell, T., McLeod, R., Stevens, M., Phillips, M., Webb, M., & Jelinek, G. (2002). Alcohol consumption, setting, gender and activity as predictors of injury: A population-based case-control study. *Journal of Studies on Alcohol*, *63*(3), 372–379. Bellis, M. A., & Hughes, K. (2008). Comprehensive strategies to prevent alcohol-related violence. *IPC Review*, *2*, 137–168.

35   Nolen-Hoeksema, S. (2004). Gender differences in risk factors and consequences for alcohol use and problems. *Clinical Psychology Review*, *24*(8), 981–1010.

36   Macdonald, S., Cherpitel, C. J., DeSouza, A., Stockwell, T., Borges, G., & Giesbrecht, N. (2006). Variations of alcohol impairment in different types, causes and contexts of injuries: Results of emergency room studies from 16 countries. *Accident Analysis & Prevention*, *38*(6), 1107–1112.

37   Bromley, R. D., & Nelson, A. L. (2002). Alcohol-related crime and disorder across urban space and time: Evidence from a British city. *Geoforum*, *33*(2), 239–254.

38   Foran, H. M., & O'Leary, K. D. (2008). Alcohol and intimate partner violence: A meta-analytic review. *Clinical Psychology Review*, *28*(7), 1222–1234. Fals-Stewart, W., Leonard, K. E., & Birchler, G. R. (2005). The occurrence of male-to-female intimate partner violence on days of men's drinking: The moderating effects of antisocial personality disorder. *Journal of Consulting and Clinical Psychology*, *73*(2), 239–248.

39   Finney, A. (2004). *Violence in the night-time economy: Key findings from the research*. Research Findings 214. London: Home Office.

40   Hobbs, D., Hadfield, P., Lister, S., & Winlow, S. (2005). Violence and control in the night-time economy. *European Journal of Crime Criminal Law and Criminal Justice*, *13*(1), 89–102.

41   Graham, K., Osgood, D. W., Wells, S., & Stockwell, T. (2006). To what extent is intoxication associated with aggression in bars? A multilevel analysis. *Journal of Studies on Alcohol*, *67*(3), 382–390.

42   Adlaf, R., Mann, E., & Paglia, A. (2003). Drinking, cannabis use and driving among Ontario students. *Canadian Medical Association Journal*, *168*(5), 565–566.

43   Tin, S. T., Ameratunga, S., & Watson, P. (2008). Riding in a motor vehicle with a driver under the influence of alcohol and drinking patterns: Findings from a national survey of New Zealand youth. *Australasian Epidemiologist*, *15*(1), 18–20.

44   Calafat, A., Adrover-Roig, D., Blay, N., Juan, M., Bellis, M., . . . & Kokkevi, A. (2009). Which young people accept a lift from a drunk or drugged driver? *Accident Analysis and Prevention*, *41*(4), 703–709.

45   McCormick, L. K., & Ureda, J. (1995). Who's driving? College students' choices of transportation home after drinking. *Journal of Primary Prevention*, *16*(1), 103–115. Hingson, R., Heeren, T., Winter, M., & Wechsler, H. (2005). Magnitude of alcohol-related mortality and morbidity among US college students ages 18–24: Changes from 1998 to 2001. *Annual Review of Public Health*, *26*, 259–279.

46   Hingson et al., Magnitude of alcohol-related mortality and morbidity among US college students ages 18–24.

47   Sarkar, S., Andreas, M., & De Faria, F. (2005). Who uses safe ride programs: An examination of the dynamics of individuals who use a safe ride program instead of driving home while drunk. *The American Journal of Drug and Alcohol Abuse*, *31*(2), 305–325.

48   Whitehill, J. M., Rivara, F. P., & Moreno, M. A. (2014). Marijuana-using drivers, alcohol-using drivers, and their passengers: Prevalence and risk factors among underage college students. *JAMA Pediatrics*, *168*(7), 618–624.

49   Rivara, F. P., Relyea-Chew, A., Wang, J., Riley, S., Boisvert, D., & Gomez, T. (2007). Drinking behaviors in young adults: The potential role of designated driver and safe ride home programs. *Injury Prevention*, *13*(3), 168–172.

50   Weber, B. (2014). Can safe ride programs reduce urban crime? *Regional Science and Urban Economics*, *48*, 1–11.

51   Miller, D. B. (2015). *Creating a mobile application for the University's SafeRide Program*. Honors College Thesis, University of Arizona.

52   Park, J., Kim, J., Pang, M. S., & Lee, B. (2017). *Offender or guardian? An empirical analysis of ride-sharing and sexual assault*. KAIST College of Business Working Paper Series No. 2017-006. https://papers.ssrn.com/sol3/papers.cfm?abstract_id=2951138 (retrieved May 22, 2017).

53   Gambetta, D., & Hamill, H. (2005). *Streetwise: How taxi drivers establish customer's trustworthiness*. New York: Russell Sage Foundation.

54   Jackson, C. K., Owens, E. G. (2011). One for the road: Public transportation, alcohol consumption, and intoxicated driving. *Journal of Public Economics*, *95*(1–2), 106–121.

55   Parks, K. A. (2000). An event-based analysis of aggression women experience in bars. *Psychology of Addictive Behaviors*, *14*(2), 102–110.

56   Madensen, T. D., & Eck, J. E. (2008). Violence in bars: Exploring the impact of place manager decision-making. *Crime Prevention & Community Safety*, *10*(2), 111–125.

57   Graham, K., & Homel, R. (2012). *Raising the bar*. Abingdon, U.K.: Routledge. Lang, E., Stockwell, T., Rydon, P., & Gamble, C. (1992). *Drinking settings, alcohol related harm and support for prevention policies: Results of a survey of persons residing in the Perth Metropolitan area*. Perth: National Centre for Research into the Prevention of Drug Abuse.

58   Fox, J. G., & Sobol, J. J. (2000). Drinking patterns, social interaction, and barroom behavior: A routine activities approach. *Deviant Behavior*, *21*(5), 429–450.

59   Boivin, R., Geoffrion, S., Ouellet, F., & Felson, M. (2014). Nightly variation of disorder in a Canadian nightclub. *Journal of Substance Use*, *19*(1–2), 188–193.

60   Graham, K., Bernards, S., Osgood, D. W., & Wells, S. (2006). Bad nights or bad bars? Multi-level analysis of environmental predictors of aggression in late-night large-capacity bars and clubs. *Addiction*, *101*(11), 1569–1580.

61   Quigley, B. M., Leonard, K. E., & Collins, R. L. (2003). Characteristics of violent bars and bar patrons. *Journal of Studies on Alcohol*, *64*(6), 765–772.

62   Homel R., & Clark J. (1994). The prediction and prevention of violence in pubs and clubs. In R. V. Clarke (Ed.), *Crime prevention studies*, Vol. 3, pp. 1–46. Monsey, NY: Criminal Justice Press.

63   Roberts, J. C. (2007). Barroom aggression in Hoboken, New Jersey: Don't blame the bouncers! *Journal of Drug Education*, *37*(4), 429–445.

64   Lenk, K. M., Toomey, T. L., Nelson, T. F., Jones-Webb, R., & Erickson, D. J. (2014). State and local law enforcement agency efforts to prevent sales to obviously intoxicated patrons. *Journal of Community Health*, *39*(2), 339–348; p. 339.

65   Paschall, M. J., Grube, J. W., Thomas, S., Cannon, C., & Treffers, R. (2012). Relationships between local enforcement, alcohol availability, drinking norms, and adolescent alcohol use in 50 California cities. *Journal of Studies on Alcohol and Drugs, 73*(4), 657–665.

66   Wechsler, H., Lee, J. E., Nelson, T. F., & Lee, H. (2003). Drinking and driving among college students: The influence of alcohol-control policies. *American Journal of Preventive Medicine, 25*(3), 212–218.

67   Felson, M., Berends, R., Richardson, B., & Veno, A. (1997). Reducing pub hopping and related crime. In R. Homel (Ed.), *Policing for prevention: Reducing crime, public intoxication and* injury. Crime Prevention Studies, Vol. 7, pp. 115–132. Monsey, NY: Criminal Justice Press. Brennan, I., Moore, S. C., Byrne, E., & Murphy, S. (2011). Interventions for disorder and severe intoxication in and around licensed premises, 1989–2009. *Addiction, 106*(4), 706–713.

68   Graham, K., Jelley, J., & Purcell, J. (2005). Training bar staff in preventing and managing aggression in licensed premises. *Journal of Substance Use, 10*(1), 48–61.

69   Evalcorp Research and Consulting. (2009). *City of Camarillo and surrounding areas: Place of last drink report.* Camarillo: Ventura County Behavioral Health, Alcohol and Drug Programs Prevention Service. www.venturacountylimits.org/resource_documents/camarillo_city_pold_report_july08_dec09.pdf (retrieved May 13, 2017).

70   National Highway Traffic Safety Administration. (n.d.). A summary report of six demonstration projects to reduce alcohol-impaired driving among 21- to 34-year-old drivers. Washington, DC: U.S. Department of Transportation. https://ntl.bts.gov/lib/30000/30100/30164/810912.pdf (retrieved May 13, 2017).

71   Maguire, M., Brookman, F., & Robinson, A. (2017). Preventing violent crime. In N. Tilley & A. Sidebottom (Eds.), *Handbook of crime prevention and community safety,* 2nd edition, pp. 407–438. Abingdon, U.K.: Routledge.

72   Hopkins, M. (2004). Targeting hotspots of alcohol-related town centre violence: A Nottinghamshire case study. *Security Journal, 17*(4), 53–66.

73   Clinard, M. B. (1978). *Cities with little crime: The case of Switzerland.* Cambridge, U.K.: Cambridge University Press.

74   Killias, M., & Lanfranconi, B. (2012). The crime drop discourse – or the illusion of uniform continental trends: Switzerland as a contrasting case. In J. van Dijk, A. Tseloni, & G. Farrell (Eds.), *The international crime drop,* pp. 268–278. London: Palgrave Macmillan; p. 272.

75   Wagenaar, A. C., Salois, M. J., & Komro, K. A. (2009). Effects of beverage alcohol price and tax levels on drinking: A meta-analysis of 1003 estimates from 112 studies. *Addiction, 104*(2), 179–190.

76   Mar Su, H. T., Grabowski, J. G., Lesnick, T., & Li, G. (2002). Liquor license density and domestic violence in Baltimore County, Maryland. Paper presented at the *American Public Health Association Annual Meeting,* November 9–13, Philadelphia. Cunradi, C. B., Caetano, R., & Schafer, J. (2000). Alcohol-related problems, drug use, and male intimate partner violence severity among U.S. couples. *Alcoholism: Clinical and Experimental Research, 26*(4), 493–500. Kowitz, S. (2000). The price of alcohol, wife abuse, and husband abuse. *Southern Economic Journal, 67*(2), 279–303.

77   Grossman, M., & Markowitz, S. (1999). *Alcohol regulation and violence on college campuses.* NBER Working Paper No. 7129. Cambridge, MA: National Bureau of Economic Research.

78   Elder, R. W., Lawrence, B., Ferguson, A., Naimi, T. S., Brewer, R. D., . . . & Task Force on Community Preventive Services. (2010). The effectiveness of tax policy interventions for reducing

excessive alcohol consumption and related harms. *American Journal of Preventive Medicine, 38*(2), 217–229.

79   Wechsler, H., & Nelson, T. F. (2008). What we have learned from the Harvard School of Public Health College Alcohol Study: Focusing attention on college student alcohol consumption and the environmental conditions that promote it. *Journal of Studies on Alcohol and Drugs, 69*(4), 481–490; p. 485.

80   Gorman, D. M., Speer, P. W., Gruenewald, P. J., & Labouvie, E. W. (2001). Spatial dynamics of alcohol availability, neighborhood structure and violent crime. *Journal of Studies on Alcohol, 62*(5), 628–636.

81   Popova, S., Giesbrecht, N., Bekmuradov, D., & Patra, J. (2009). Hours and days of sale and density of alcohol outlets: Impacts on alcohol consumption and damage: A systematic review. *Alcohol and Alcoholism, 44*(5), 500–516.

82   Duailibi, S., Ponicki, W., Grube, J., Pinsky, I., Laranjeira, R., & Raw, M. (2007). The effect of restricting opening hours on alcohol-related violence. *American Journal of Public Health, 97*(12), 2276–2280.

83   Biderman, C., De Mello, J. M., & Schneider, A. (2010). Dry laws and homicides: Evidence from the São Paulo metropolitan area. *The Economic Journal, 120*(543), 157–182.

84   Wallin, E., Norström, T., & Andréasson, S. (2003). Alcohol prevention targeting licensed premises: A study of effects on violence. *Journal of Studies on Alcohol, 64*(2), 270–277.

85   Stockwell & Chikritzhs, Do relaxed trading hours for bars and clubs mean more relaxed drinking?

86   Hahn, R. A., Kuzara, J. L., Elder, R., Brewer, R., Chattopadhyay, S., . . . the Task Force on Community Preventive Services. (2010). Effectiveness of policies restricting hours of alcohol sales in preventing excessive alcohol consumption and related harms. *American Journal of Preventive Medicine, 39*(6), 590–604.

87   Chikritzhs, T., & Stockwell, T. (2002). The impact of later trading hours for Australian public houses (hotels) on levels of violence. *Journal of Studies on Alcohol, 63*(5), 591–599.

88   Halonen, J. I., Kivimäki, M., Virtanen, M., Pentti, J., Subramanian, . . . & Vahtera, J. (2013). Proximity of off-premise alcohol outlets and heavy alcohol consumption: A cohort study. *Drug and Alcohol Dependence, 132*(1), 295–300.

PERSPECTIVE ON PART 6

Part 6 has reviewed dangers to women and linked these dangers to crime theory and public policy options. We have shown that there are many distinct types of aversive experiences for women. These experiences fit within all four of the challenges noted in Part 1. Women are subject to rude encounters, often when leaving home. These encounters can lead to or relate to more serious incidents, including sexual attacks. Thus, the first two challenges to society—containing conflicts and constraining sexual abuses—both apply to the security of women. In addition, attacks on property create more fear among women than similar events do for men. Finally, although it is hard for both males and females to grow up securely, women have extra risks during that process, including a great variety of unwanted sexual experiences.

We have made many distinctions in Part 6. We distinguished feminism in terms of moral analysis, legal analysis, and practical policy analysis—focusing our work mainly on the latter. We noted that different forms of psychological harm emerge from different aversive experiences. We analyzed and documented why women often are more fearful of crime and disorder than men with similar exposures. We explained several feminist policy options, and we gave special attention to environmental designs that make women more secure.

A recurrent theme in Part 6 has been that harassment, aggression, and attacks against women are highly concentrated in specific places, times, and activities. We focused attention on the poor design and mismanagement of public places and activities. We showed how several policies can, often at little monetary expense, greatly enhance the security of women and reduce their fear and discomfort. We have also emphasized policy ideas that do not harm men and could easily enhance their security as well.

We have documented cases in which these solutions have been applied in real life with successful outcomes. Why, then, have these solutions not been instituted on a wider scale?

We offer two answers to that question. First, most Americans have a foot in both camps. On the one hand, we enjoy entertainment and social life, often involving alcohol and sexual flirtation. On the other hand, these same processes can generate aggression, frustration, and heartache. The good and bad sides of social life and night activities are too intertwined for easy extraction.

Second, the entertainment industry is one of the largest sectors of a modern society. The American Nightlife Association brags that its industry has $710 billion in food and drink sales and 590,000 bartenders.[1] A lot of money is made from people drinking, and even more money when they drink too much. The entertainment industry is not only a huge whole, but it also has outposts in thousands of towns and neighborhoods, creating ongoing relationships with customers and local politicians. Taking on the liquor industry is politically perilous at a local, state, or national level.

Major improvements in the security of women could occur in several ways. We begin with university campuses. First, universities in smaller cities could use their purchasing and political power to squeeze out the worst barrooms and pressure the others. That effort would not easily reach outside of town, but it would be a start. Second, universities could provide well-organized ride-home programs. Third, universities should play an active role in seeking enforcement of existing liquor laws and revoking licenses when barrooms have a pattern of noncompliance. Fourth, and most important, would be for universities to work to turn control of parties over to women, with alcohol permitted and non-drinking women controlling the flow of alcohol with their own security in mind.

Meanwhile, liquor policy needs to change at the state and national levels. This would be politically impossible unless a very active feminist movement took it as their central thrust. It would require tax increases to raise the price of packaged liquor and liquor by the glass. It would require ending large steins and pitcher service. Perhaps our most controversial suggestion is a return to age 18 drinking, happening in small and moderate-sized bars with strict rules limiting how much alcohol flows and how fast. No liquor policy is perfect, but some are better than others. By now, there is enough experience from around the world to know how to minimize danger to women.

Main Points of Part 6

- Women experience crime differently from men, generally having a worse subjective experience.

- The fear of sexual assault leads many women to have a more adverse reaction to intrusive behaviors and to public disorder.

- Public environments are often badly designed for security of men and women, but women are especially sensitive to disturbing environmental cues, including social and physical disorder.

- Careful environmental design has major effects in terms of making women safer while helping men as well.

- Women have seldom had much input into the designs that they have to live with.

- Badly designed environments create insecurity at home and when going to and from home.

- Alcohol policies impinge greatly on the security of women.

- Failure to enforce alcohol regulations is a common feature in modern societies, to the detriment of women but also having negative impact on men.

- Sexual assault rates are influenced by alcohol policy and by poor design and poor management of public places.

- Criminologists have contributed to these analyses and offered suggestions to help improve the security of women.

Note

1   American Nightlife Association. (n.d.). The official trade association of the nightlife industry [online]. www.nciaa.com/ (retrieved May 22, 2017).

PART 7

Crime Enhancers

Parts 5 and 6 showed how local processes in streets and neighborhoods can make risky places riskier. Part 7 continues the same theme, showing how additional social forces make crime worse. Unit 7.1 studies group processes enhancing crime, while Unit 7.2 explains cyber enhancements of crime levels. We can explain crime enhancers in the terms of Part 1, which presented the four challenges of society.

We began with society's need to contain disputes and their escalations. Part 7 helps explain that with greater group sizes, conflicts can become more dangerous and violence can become organized. We also explain how social media are used for aggressive purposes. Society's efforts to keep sexual urges within bounds are also more difficult in the face of group offending and new technologies, which can widen the span of sexual aggression. Protecting property is more difficult when groups steal or vandalize together, and even more problematical when they can attack and harm property via cyberspace. Children cannot grow up as safely when group influences enhance their early delinquency or when social media produce more virulent bullying and abuse. Part 7 illustrates how society provides increasing challenges for maintaining good relations and everyday security.

A recurrent theme in this textbook is that the good and bad in society are intertwined. Socializing with other youths is essential for growing up, yet this also provides the means for negative peer influences and group cooperation in crime. Social media and Internet access make the economy much more efficient but, at the same time, create new problems and crimes. Society today is in a period of invention. Offenders are inventing new ways to carry out crime; that requires the larger society to find new ways to counter those illegal efforts. We have spent much of our textbook discussing ways to reduce more traditional crime. New creativity will be required to contain crime as it takes new forms. We begin with an age-old process—group cooperation to commit crimes. After that we turn to the role of new cyber technology in crime.

QUESTIONS ADDRESSED IN PART 7

1. What are the varieties of cooperation for committing crime?

2. How can organizations commit or fall victim to crime?

3. How do people abuse their online access to harm others?

4. How does the Internet enhance crime access?

UNIT 7.1 Crime in Groups

For over a century, criminologists have noted that juvenile delinquency usually occurs in groups.[1] Part 4 was largely devoted to this very topic. Unit 4.3 explained peer influences generally, and Unit 4.4 discussed situational inducements occurring in peer groups. Unit 4.5 documented how time spent with peers, away from parents, enhances crime and delinquency. Clearly, youths socializing with one another plays a central role in delinquency. However, the group nature of crime changes greatly as people proceed through adolescence and into adulthood. This unit describes how, then it goes on to explain more organized forms of criminal cooperation.

Co-Offending and Criminal Assistance

The simplest crime is *lone offending*, in which one offender carries out the crime in the presence of no other offender. Yet we should not assume that an offender alone at the time of the offense is in fact acting with no assistance whatever. A lone offender can easily draw criminal assistance before or after the criminal act is committed. When another offender assists and attends the crime event, we call it *co-offending*. Other forms of assistance are also important.

Figure 7a depicts three circus tents representing the periods before, during, and after the crime. Assistance from others can occur during all three crime stages. Before the crime event, friends or acquaintances may know of the impending crime but not actually participate in it or lend any assistance at all. However, they might serve as an appreciative audience or egg on the offender[2] with no further assistance. If they offer planning or useful information for carrying out the offense, they become accomplices in the crime, even if they are not present when it happens. Legal terms such as *conspiracy* then become applicable.

If an offender goes along to the scene of the crime, that makes it a co-offense, since two or more persons commit the crime together, acting simultaneously. They

FIGURE 7A
Criminal Assistance during Three Stages of the Crime Process

may offer one another physical help, strength in numbers, or know-how, or they might serve as lookout or driver of a getaway car.

Do not assume that co-offending is proof of careful planning. Co-offenses are probably as likely to occur on the spur of the moment as lone offenses. Many group offenses are unplanned, with offenders seeing a suitable crime target and acting. It is possible that some friends or acquaintances see the crime unfold but do not consider themselves to be perpetrators. If apprehended, authorities might see it differently, especially if companions knew a crime was taking place.

After the first crime event has been completed, the offenders might gain further assistance from or participation by other offenders as they fence stolen goods, sell newly obtained drugs, or commit other follow-up crimes. A criminal act can be part of a sequence of illegal events, each crime feeding the next. This is true for a chain of illegal drug sales. Even a lone offender might well depend on others to assist in dispensing with stolen goods or contraband that needs a market. Others might also help hide an offender or conceal his offenses, or they might feign ignorance if questioned by police. A lone offender is not necessarily a lonely offender.

The Co-Offending Age Curve

Criminologists consistently find that co-offending is much higher during teenage years than during adult years. Co-offending also declines notably from early teens to later teens.

Based on police data, Figure 7b shows that at age 12, about 70 percent of crime participations involve co-offending (participations reflect multiple events for offenders). At age 15, the split between lone offender participations and co-offender participations is about half and half. From the early 20s on, about 20 percent of crime participations

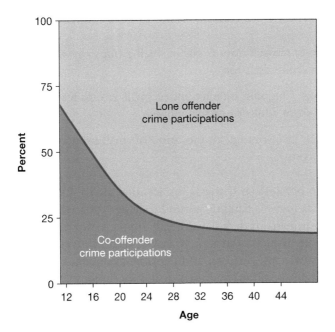

FIGURE 7B

Co-Offender and Lone-Offender Crime Participations by Age, British Columbia, Canada

Source: M. A. Andresen & M. Felson (2010). The impact of co-offending. *The British Journal of Criminology,* *50*(1), 66–81.

are co-offending and the other 80 percent are lone offending. However, police data might well underestimate co-offending. If one offender is arrested and the other escapes the scene, the first offender has good reasons not to turn in the second to police.

Nonetheless, co-offending patterns are well established in the criminological literature:

- Co-offending dominates at young ages.

- Co-offending usually occurs in groups of one, two, three, or four.

- These groups of co-offenders are not very stable.

- Co-offending declines by late adolescence.

- Lone offending takes over during adult years.

Even though adult offenders often cooperate before and after the crime events, they are usually alone during the event itself.

The teenage tendency to commit crimes in small groups occurs in three ways:

1. *Incidental.* Most teen activities occur in small groups anyway, so we should not be surprised that crime does too.

2. *Group dynamics.* Ongoing interactions of small groups leads to more dares, proof of autonomy from adults or of masculinity.

3. *Situational.* The size, timing, and location of small group activities puts teenagers near crime targets.

These three processes can better be understood after looking back to Part 4. If a group of five or six teens is hanging around together for a while, one of them might bring out some marijuana. If they have already smoked it together in the past, it could be incidental to the group's activities. If a new youth arrives, group dynamics push that youth to initiate marijuana use. If the group is hanging out near crime targets, a small subgroup might break off and then steal something.

Expansive Criminal Cooperation

Criminal cooperation is usually quite rudimentary and does not expand very much. However, on occasion it can expand dramatically, leading to full-blown organized crime. Figure 7c depicts the process by which this can happen. Reading from the bottom of the figure, sporadic co-offenders commit crimes in groups of two, three, or four—as discussed in the previous section.

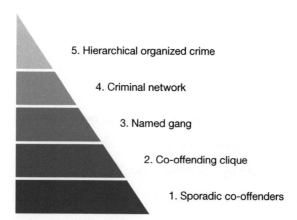

FIGURE 7C
Progression in Criminal Cooperation

Although co-offending groups are typically unstable, it is possible for that to change. Co-offending cliques can stabilize and begin to act as small gangs even though they have no gang name (layer 2 in Figure 7c). They might, however, be recognized in the local neighborhood and hang out together on the same corner or another location. Less often, youths join a named gang (layer 3), and still less often they form a criminal network (layer 4). The latter type is a form of organized crime, but it lacks a clear hierarchical structure and might retain an element of instability. Finally, in some cases, a hierarchical crime organization (layer 5) can form and gain longer-term regional hegemony. The next section discusses layer 3.

Juvenile Street Gangs, Rightly Understood

The image people have of gangs is much stronger than the reality. Not denying that *juvenile street gangs* do a lot of harm, they are nonetheless given more credit than they deserve for local crime. In gang areas, we can expect that:

- Most youths are not gang members, even though gangs are local.[3]

- Gang members do more than their share of crimes, but not most local crimes.[4]

- Gang members do more than their share of violence, but not all of it.[5]

- Gangs are not nearly as organized as their image suggests.

First of all, a good share of youths who hang out with gangs are not really members. Youths socialize across group lines, so non-gang and gang members often hang out together. A study of 452 middle school students who were *not* gang members found that more than a third had gang members as friends, while one in four hung out with gang members. Clearly some youths try to keep a *foot in each camp*, interacting with gang members without really joining in any formal sense. Some gang experts tell us that the process of joining a gang is gradual, even taking a period of years.[6] A similar process is noted for girls sidling up to gangs and perhaps eventually joining.[7] Some youths never clarify whether they are members or not.

In 1927, *Frederic Thrasher* published a famous study, *The Gang: A Study of 1,313 Gangs in Chicago*.[8] Thrasher distinguished gang affiliations as the "inner circle," "rank and file," and "fringe." This is consistent with our view that local youths try different ways to accommodate dangerous neighbors—a point we made in Unit 5.5.

The uneven nature of gang affiliation is confirmed in another classic gang study, by *Malcolm W. Klein*. He concluded that youths who enter the gang trajectory stay for varying periods of time and have unequal involvement in the life of the gang. Not all gang members are equal. *Peripheral members* circle the edges of the gang. Other

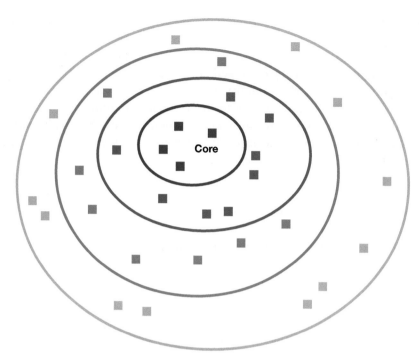

Figure 7d
Degrees of Membership in a Juvenile Street Gang

members are a bit more active. Relatively few are *core members*, ensnared in the center of the gang world.[9]

Klein sees the gang as a kind of "onion," with each outward skin farther and farther from the core. Figure 7d depicts a juvenile street gang with 32 members but only four core members, the others scattered in various degrees around the core.

The image of gangs as a lower-class subculture implies that gangs are long-lived and that membership is long term. Yet gang researchers have found these to be myths, repeatedly finding **high rates of gang attrition**. As Figure 7e indicates, only 60 percent of youth gang members in the United States remain in the gang after six months, and only about half are still members after a year. In five years, four out of five members have withdrawn, hardly fitting the subculture image.[10]

Figure 7f looks at the same issue from another perspective. Youths tend to join gangs in early adolescence, peaking at ages 13 and 14. **Gang-leaving ages** range from 15 through 17.[11] It appears that gang membership in the United States is most prevalent from ages 13 through 16. Very similar results are found in a study of gang participation in Montreal, Canada.[12] The ages of gang participation closely fit the general age–crime curve that applies to middle-class youths.

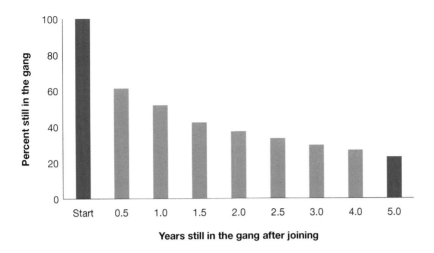

FIGURE 7E

Rapid Attrition in Gang Participation

Source: Data drawn from G. Sweeten, D. C. Pyrooz, & A. R. Piquero (2013). Disengaging from gangs and desistance from crime. *Justice Quarterly*, *30*(3), 469–500.

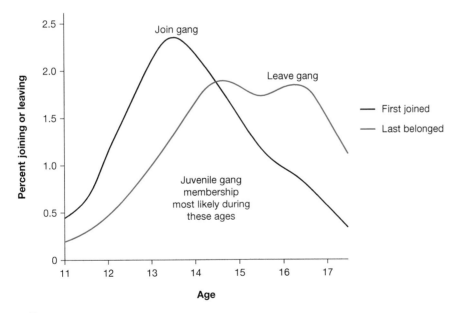

FIGURE 7F

Ages that Gang Members Join and Leave

Source: Adapted from D. C. Pyrooz & G. Sweeten (2015). Gang membership between ages 5 and 17 years in the United States. *Journal of Adolescent Health*, *56*(4), 414–419.

One reason for leaving juvenile gangs in later adolescence is that the hassle and danger of gang membership begins to outweigh any benefits.[13] Some leave after an overt experience with violence or violent loss of a family member or friend.[14] Others quit the gang as they enter new life-cycle stages: getting a good job, a partner, a spouse,[15] or becoming a parent.[16] These are the same patterns that criminologists observe for other delinquents who do not belong to gangs but, similarly, age out of illicit behavior.[17] This is also quite consistent with control theory, which tells us that conventional roles compete with and contain delinquent behavior.[18] Again we conclude that juvenile gangs do not fit the literal image of a deviant subculture.

Research indicates that gangs contribute to crime and delinquency indirectly through unstructured and unsupervised socializing with peers, exposing gang members to greater chances for breaking rules, including violent acts. Classic gang research by **James F. Short** shows us that juvenile street gangs are mostly informal in their activities. A recent review of the gang literature confirms that point:

> [G]ang members spend a great deal of time hanging out with peers, on street corners and porches, in cars and private homes, and at local parks and establishments. . . . "hanging on the street" was the most prevalent of 69 measured behaviors among the boys in gangs to which they were assigned (89.2% among the black gang boys; 95.5% among the white gang boys). Importantly, however, research findings suggest that gang members seldom are all together at the same time; instead, much of their time is spent hanging out in smaller cliques.[19]

That does not mean we should underestimate the damage that gangs deliver. These are prime ages of development and crime participation. Gangs enhance that participation and the violence levels involved. That harms the neighborhoods where gangs are found, other youths and adults who are victimized, and gang members themselves.

Gang membership is not a very good insurance policy. Members have especially high rates of violent crime victimization related to their risky activities.[20] Juvenile gangs promise security, without delivering it very well. They offer group identity, yet this service is also unlikely to persist for long. They do considerable damage to local communities, although they do not monopolize crime.

Even though gangs do not work out that well for members, new waves of youths reach the risky ages not yet having learned the lesson. New gangs spring up. Most gangs start out for defensive reasons. They offer protection from dangerous people by coming to the defense of any member who is attacked.[21] Although youths may also join delinquent groups for social reasons or to impress people, protection from danger is a recurrent reason teenagers give for joining.[22] Many (but not all) juvenile gangs are involved in enough violence to make their threats credible.[23] Yet their protective efforts can backfire; they end up antagonizing other gangs or police, producing more danger to themselves than they had intended.[24] Although gang members report higher levels of actual victimization than non–gang-involved youth, gang members have lower levels of *fear* of crime victimization. Membership reduces anxiety about future victimization. This seems irrational to an outsider, but it helps explain why youths join gangs and stay in, at least for a while.[25]

Juvenile gangs are more diverse than previously realized.[26] Gangs proliferate in the United States,[27] and in Europe,[28] and they are present in smaller cities and suburban locations.[29] Urban low-income subculture is not essential for juvenile gangs to exist. School surveys indicate that gang exposure is only marginally more common for lower-income youths than for those from middle-income households.[30] Big-city gangs are more likely to be violent and to commit overt crimes. In contrast, **small-city gangs** are more likely to stay off the police radar screen and out of the newspapers.[31] Such gangs are smaller in size and more tranquil,[32] but they still exist and are involved in crime.

Gang research also contradicts the widespread belief that drug sales are the central enterprise for juvenile gangs. As noted earlier, **drug gangs** and juvenile gangs are distinct.[33] To be sure, youth gang members are often *consumers* of illicit drugs.[34] Some of these members might also sell drugs, but are not required to share their profits from drug-selling or other illegal activity with other gang members.[35] The **profit-sharing test** is very important for it tells us whether the gang is a criminal organization or just a holding group, with subgroups carrying out their own crimes.

The Progression towards Organized Crime

Most juvenile gangs die out, as we have noted. However, some gangs continue and even progress towards organized crime. That is most likely to occur in very large cities with very long gang traditions. Such progression depends on an income source that allows adult gang members, illicitly, to earn a living.

Unfortunately, the term "gang" is used to mean too many things. Prison gangs are very different from drug gangs, which are in turn very different from juvenile street gangs. Racial images and gang images often intersect. Thus, organized drug criminals are referred to in terms of "organized crime" if they are white and "gangs" if they are nonwhite, even if the two groups of offenders do the same thing. We prefer to drop the term "gang" for adult offenders, and even drop the term "drug gang," thinking of this instead as "organized crime." Even that term has problems. Some organized crime is hierarchical, fitting the images shown in movies and on television. Other organized criminals interact mainly as networks of offenders who know one another and interact for criminal purposes, but do not have a clear hierarchy.

That is why we distinguish a **criminal network** from **hierarchical organized crime**. A criminal network includes people who do not all know one another or interact directly, but who systematically and repeatedly exchange illegal goods and services (layer 4 on Figure 7c). In contrast, hierarchical organized crime divides up territories, has leaders and bosses, and establishes stable control over illegal opportunities.

Figure 7g maps out a criminal network for producing and shipping out illegal marijuana. It has three central persons, who make more phone calls and know more of the others but might still have an informal approach. Not everybody in the network knows everybody else. Some are involved rarely and some more often. This diagram is based on a more elaborate network diagram. Some of those at the edges make additional calls for other purposes. For example, the person providing the hardware for growing marijuana will have suppliers who may not know (or only half know) that the items are being used for an illegal operation. The harvesting person will also need to buy tools and become involved with other suppliers. This network is not fully hierarchical even though it has three central players.

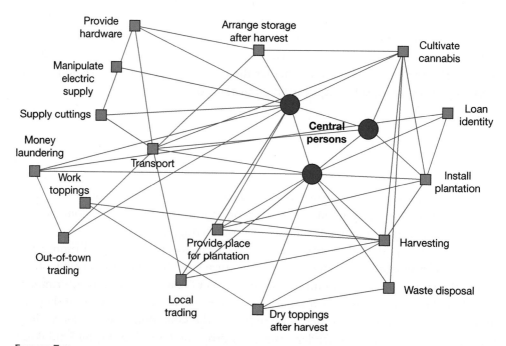

FIGURE 7G

Possible Depiction of a Cannabis Network

Source: Ideas simplified and adapted from P. A. Duijn & P. P. Klerks (2014). Social network analysis applied to criminal networks. Recent developments in Dutch law enforcement. In A. J. Masys (Ed.), *Networks and network analysis for defence and security*, pp. 121–159. New York: Springer.

Hierarchically Organized Crime

Hierarchically organized crime (the top layer of Figure 7c) is most likely to be found in places where governments are weak and subject to takeover or ongoing corruption. A good example is in southern Italy, including Sicily. Organized criminals often seek to corrupt the **public procurement** process—the purchases of public goods and services and construction of public buildings and roads. This is the process by which billions of government dollars are spent, and criminals devise methods to steal some of it. They are best able to do so where governments are weak and easily corrupted. The criminals' method is to corrupt the process by which government gives out contracts.

Suppose that a government appropriates 100 million dollars to construct a public building or road. To guarantee proper disbursement, the rules require sealed bids from competing contractors. Officials are supposed to take sealed bids, excluding known criminals from the bidding process, then award the contract to the lowest bidder. The crime organization seeks to win the bid illegally and corrupt the process by making sure that there is no credible competing bid so that their bid (which is above the market price) will win. Bribery is often used, but it is backed up by violence.

Construction is a complicated process that requires organized corruption if it is to be controlled. To win the bid, build the project, and receive an extra cut of the money, several stages of illegal activity are needed. The organized criminals need several cooperative persons in the right places, and they use corruption or intimidation to achieve this. Included are public officials at multiple levels, the managers of bidding and the building project, contractors, subcontractors, and various white-collar workers. In advance, organized crime groups divide up territories. They also corner the market on sand, stone, concrete, or other building supplies. To hide their criminal ownership, they set up front companies under different names, using corrupted public officials to certify these companies as legitimate. They have meetings to pick which subcontractors will be included and to make sure this happens, keeping other subcontractors out. They assign subcontractors and public officials the amounts of money to be kicked back to the crime organization and when it will be paid. Any noncompliance by government officials, subcontractors, or workers is controlled through murder, assault, arson, or threats.[36]

You can see that crime cooperation has a wide range. It begins with simple co-offending on a sporadic basis. Sometimes co-offenders form ongoing crime cliques, small gangs without a name. Sometimes a gang is named and lasts a while. Some gangs have longer duration. Some persist and grow into small organized crime networks. On rare occasions, hierarchical organized crime develops and can even corrupt and take over governmental functions. As crime groups become more active, they enhance and multiply the damage that crime does to the larger society.

FLASHCARD LIST FOR UNIT 7.1

- Conspiracy
- Co-offending
- Core (gang) members
- Criminal network
- Drug gangs
- Foot in each camp
- Gang-leaving ages

- Hierarchically organized crime
- High rates of gang attrition
- Juvenile street gangs
- Klein, Malcolm W.
- Lone offending

- Peripheral (gang) members
- Profit-sharing test
- Public procurement
- Short, James F.
- Small-city gangs
- Thrasher, Frederic

DISCUSSION QUESTIONS

1. If crime involves low self-control, how can offenders organize themselves?

2. Which crime collaborations make more sense as a casual network and which ones require more organization?

Notes

1 Breckenridge, S. P., & Abbott, E. (1912). Chicago housing problems. *American Journal of Sociology, 16*(3), 289–308.

2 Costello, B. J., & Hope, T. L. (2016). *Peer pressure, peer prevention: The role of friends in crime and conformity.* New York: Routledge.

3 Klein, M. W., & Maxson, C. L. (2010). *Street gang patterns and policies.* Oxford: Oxford University Press.

4 Tita, G., & Ridgeway, G. (2007). The impact of gang formation on local patterns of crime. *Journal of Research in Crime and Delinquency, 44*(2), 208–237.

5 Klein, M. W., Weerman, F. M., & Thornberry, T. P. (2006). Street gang violence in Europe. *European Journal of Criminology, 3*(4), 413–437.

6 Curry, G. D., Decker, S. H., & Egley, A. (2002). Gang involvement and delinquency in a middle school population. *Justice Quarterly, 19*(2), 275–292.

7 Miller, J. (2001). *One of the guys: Girls, gangs, and gender.* New York: Oxford University Press.

8 Thrasher, F. (1927). *The gang: A study of 1,313 gangs in Chicago.* Chicago: University of Chicago Press.

9 Klein, M. W. (1971). *Street gangs and street workers.* Englewood Cliffs, NJ: Prentice-Hall.

10 Sweeten, G., Pyrooz, D. C., & Piquero, A. R. (2013). Disengaging from gangs and desistance from crime. *Justice Quarterly, 30*(3), 469–500.

11 Pyrooz, D. C., & Sweeten, G. (2015). Gang membership between ages 5 and 17 years in the United States. *Journal of Adolescent Health, 56*(4), 414–419.

12 Lacourse, E., Nagin, D., Tremblay, R. E., Vitaro, F., & Claes, M. (2003). Developmental trajectories of boys' delinquent group membership and facilitation of violent behaviors during adolescence. *Development and Psychopathology*, *15*(1), 183–197.

13 Dong, B., Gibson, C. L., & Krohn, M. D. (2015). Gang membership in a developmental and life-course perspective. In S. Decker & D. C. Pyrooz (Eds.), *The handbook of gangs*, pp. 78–97. New York: Wiley.

14 Decker, S. H., and Lauritsen, J. (2002). Leaving the gang. In C. R. Huff (Ed.), *Gangs in America*, pp. 51–70. Thousand Oaks, CA: Sage.

15 Vigil, J. D. (1988). *Barrio gangs: Street life and identity in Southern California*. Austin, TX: University of Texas Press.

16 Moloney, M., MacKenzie, K., Hunt, G., and Joe-Laidler, K. (2009). The path and promise of fatherhood for gang members. *British Journal of Criminology*, *49*(3), 305–325.

17 Massoglia, M., & Uggen, C. (2010). Settling down and aging out: Toward an interactionist theory of desistance and the transition to adulthood. *American Journal of Sociology*, *116*(2), 543–582.

18 Cullen, F. T., & Agnew, R. (1998). *Criminological theory: Past to present*. Los Angeles: Roxbury Park.

19 Hughes, L. A., & Short, J. F. (2014). Partying, cruising, and hanging in the streets: Gangs, routine activities, and delinquency and violence in Chicago, 1959–1962. *Journal of Quantitative Criminology*, *30*(3), 415–451; pp. 417–418.

20 Taylor, T. J., Freng, A., Esbensen, F. A., & Peterson, D. (2008). Youth gang membership and serious violent victimization: The importance of lifestyles and routine activities. *Journal of Interpersonal Violence*, *23*(10), 1441–1464.

21 Felson, M. (2006). *Crime and nature*. Thousand Oaks, CA: Sage.

22 Baccaglini, W. F. (1993). *Project youth gang-drug prevention: A statewide research study*. Rensselaer, NY: New York State Division for Youth. Decker, S. H., & Van Winkle, B. (1996). *Life in the gang: Family, friends, and violence*. New York: Cambridge University Press.

23 Klein, *Street gangs and street workers*.

24 Hochhaus, C., & Sousa, F. (1987). Why children belong to gangs: A comparison of expectations and reality. *High School Journal*, *71*(2), 74–77.

25 Melde, C., Taylor, T. J., & Esbensen, F. A. (2009). "I got your back": An examination of the protective function of gang membership in adolescence. *Criminology*, *47*(2), 565–594.

26 Howell, J. C. (2015). *The history of street gangs in the United States: Their origins and transformations*. Lanham, MD: Lexington Books.

27 Curry, G. D. (2001). The proliferation of gangs in the United States. In M. Klein, H. J. Kerner, C. Maxson & E. Weitekamp (Eds.), *The Eurogang paradox: Street gangs and youth groups in the US and Europe*, pp. 79–92. Amsterdam: Springer.

28 Klein, M., Kerner, H. J., Maxson, C., & Weitekamp, E. (Eds.). (2000). *The Eurogang paradox: Street gangs and youth groups in the US and Europe*. New York: Springer.

29 Maxson, C. L. (1998). *Gang members on the move*. Juvenile Justice Bulletin. Washington, DC: Office of Juvenile Justice and Delinquency Prevention.

30 Howell, J. C., & Lynch, J. P. (2000). Youth gangs in schools. Juvenile Justice Bulletin. Washington, DC: Office of Juvenile Justice and Delinquency Prevention.

31 Glosser, A. M. (2016). Homies of the corn. In J. F. Donnermeyer (Ed.), *The Routledge international handbook of rural criminology*, pp. 85–92. Abingdon, U.K.: Routledge.

32   Howell, J. C., Egley, A., & Gleason, D. K. (2002). *Modern day youth gangs*. Juvenile Justice Bulletin. Washington, DC: Office of Juvenile Justice and Delinquency and Prevention.

33   Maxson, C. L. (1995). *Street gangs and drug sales in two suburban cities*. Rockville, MD: National Institute of Justice.

34   Fleisher, M. S. (2015). Gangs and drugs: Connections, divergence, and culture. In S. H. Decker & D. C. Pyrooz (Eds.), *The handbook of gangs*, pp. 193–207. New York: Wiley.

35   Decker, S. H., Katz, C. M., & Webb, V. J. (2008). Understanding the black box of gang organization: Implications for involvement in violent crime, drug sales, and violent victimization. *Crime and Delinquency, 54*(1), 153–172.

36   Savona, E. U. (2010). Infiltration of the public construction industry by Italian organised crime. In K. Bullock, R. V. G. Clarke & N. Tilley (Eds.), *Situational prevention of organised crimes*, pp. 130–150. London: Taylor & Francis.

UNIT 7.2 Crime via Cyberspace

The secret recipe for Coca-Cola reputedly includes caffeine citrate, caramel, cinnamon, citric acid, coca leaf extract, coriander, lemon, lime juice, neroli, nutmeg, orange, sugar, vanilla extract, and water. However, the details of their mixing are secret, and the company maintains strict security over that information, and does not admit to the ingredient list above.[1] On July 5, 2006, the FBI arrested three Coca-Cola employees for trying to sell the exact formula to Pepsi, their arch rival. Pepsi turned them in. A company surveillance camera had caught one of the Coca-Cola employees stuffing documents into bags. This is an example of stealing data without worrying about computers.[2] Today's forms of information theft tend to be digital. We show in this unit that the opportunities for crime are greatly enhanced by the digital world. This occurs in part because the crimes involving data are much easier to carry out. This in turn occurs because much of the value in modern society has been shifted into digital forms, becoming very attractive for theft and manipulation.

The Blurred Boundaries between People, Data, and Things

Crime targets fit into three general categories: people, data, and things. **Crimes targeting people** usually include assaults. **Crimes targeting things** usually include burglaries, thefts, or vandalism. Historically, most crimes targeted people and things, but **crimes targeting data** were probably less convenient. File cabinets full of data were too bulky to steal, although somebody could pilfer a crucial piece of paper. Traditional industrial spies stole product diagrams in paper form. Traditional military spies stole or copied forbidden paper files. Even going back to 1870, microdots were tiny photographs transmitted physically by carrier pigeon from one spy to another.[3]

This is completely different from the world we now know. Offenders today still target people and things, but it is now worthwhile to steal data—even in vast amounts.

Moreover, many forbidden modern "things" now take the form of data. Personal health data files once required physical stealth to view, but electronic trespassing takes over in the modern world.

The Transformation of Pornography

Models of sexual organs and portrayals of sexual acts have been discovered by archaeologists in prehistoric caves, continuing with the heavy sexual emphasis among the Greeks and Romans.[4] Modern technology has a major practical impact on the spread of sexual information, and it has played a part in the *transformation of pornography*.[5] New technologies greatly enhance the potential for sexual obsession and breaking sexual rules. Part of this occurs because sexual representations can now be translated into digital form and transmitted among many more people and at much greater distances. Pornographic pictures once had to be viewed physically or sold in plain brown wrappers, but now are digitized and can be transmitted electronically across the world.

Sex toys can already be constructed with at-home *3D printers* (devices that manufacture three-dimensional items from information files). Various websites advertise the sale of 3D printable files allowing users to print their own sex toys at home. One of their selling points is that buyers can avoid the embarrassment of purchasing sex toys at a store or having them mailed to their homes.

Another 3D print website promises ladies a custom dildo that perfectly fits her lady parts. Another offers males a 3D-printed model of a vagina, perfectly tailored to surround his penis. The websites offer instructions for manufacturing these sex toys using a personal 3D printer without leaving home or requiring a delivery service. None of these transmissions verify that users are of legal age or check the law in the jurisdiction to which information is sent. These opportunities to evade the law multiply as companies begin to sell software-guided virtual reality sexual devices. Still other vendors transmit hologram sex models to create remote sexual experiences. Inventors have designed and marketed remote sensory devices, and Amazon offers a remote vibrator allowing two people to sexually stimulate each other at a distance.

Although these technologies can be used legally, they also open the door for illegal applications. Even in jurisdictions permitting adult prostitution, underage solicitation is facilitated—both for face-to-face encounters and for online sexual communications. Virtual reality sex with children already exists,[6] enhancing the realm of *child pornography*.[7] Cybertechnology can also enable consensual sexual liaisons between adults and underage youths. One can envision technology being used for virtual prostitution, bestiality, sexual torture, and additional forbidden sexual activities. Cyberspace also enhances the opportunities to evade one's own spouse or partner with online sexual interaction with others.

Teledildonics is a term referring to technology for remote sex or remote mutual masturbation where tactile sensations are communicated over a data link between the participants.[8] Recent research and engineering progress enables interaction based on all five senses. Engineers have devised an electronic tongue that combines taste stimuli with thermal stimulation, creating the sensation of a real tongue.[9] Another device, the Teletongue, provides remote lollipops that allow two people to feel one another's oral vibrations and sounds.[10] Electronic tongues have also been combined with electronic noses[11] that transmit olfactory cues.[12] A "real-time bilateral kiss communication interface" works on cell phones.[13] All five senses feed into sexual sensation and can be digitized and transmitted in real time.[14] You can readily see that technology widens the span of sexual access, while making it easier to evade spatial barriers and social controls.

Technology also promises to transmit and recombine body parts as a virtual experience. Programs can thus alter a person's sexual attractiveness. The man who longs for a huge penis can achieve an electronic enhancement, as can the woman who is self-conscious about her breasts or waistline, thus editing and idealizing sexual intercourse. Although we may think of sexual experiences as occurring primarily within a relationship and being private, digital technology provides new opportunities for hackers, electronic voyeurism, and innovative forms of sexual–electronic intrusion into peoples' lives.

Box 7a describes three of the many new sex inventions approved at the United States Patent Office, all undermining the ability of social institutions to contain sexual behavior within traditional rules. Invention A is for a sex toy connected to a speech recognition module that can use the human voice to give control signals guiding sexual movements. We could imagine a user recording the voice of an underage child, or a woman he is stalking, or a fellow employee unwilling to have sex. The voice could be converted into sexual talk and then sexual action. Another invention (not included in Box 7a; U.S. patent 8729374 B2) can convert the words you choose into the singing voice of the singer you like. That would allow simulation of a musical-sexual experience with an underage celebrity singer, or for that matter with an unwitting local choirboy. Invention B in Box 7a allows two people who are forbidden sex partners to stimulate one another sexually from remote places, evading family controls and violating the rules of larger society. Invention C attaches micro vibrators to a garment worn by a second user. These devices do not know whether an underage youth is involved. You can see that the same technologies that offer many positive advantages to society also widen the potential for violating sexual rules.

Box 7A Three U.S. Inventions Providing a Window into the Future of Cybersex

A. *Speech controlled sex toy* (US Patent 20160300569 A1). A speech controlled sex toy receives verbal commands through an audio receiving device paired with the toy, converting the speech to control signals to adjust the operation or intensity of the motor within the sex toy. The sex toy has a speech recognition module to convert human voice to machine understandable control signals, and a microprocessor control module to communicate control signals to adjust the motion of the motor. If necessary, the temperature of the sex toy can be measured and adjusted according to verbal commands. The sex toy receives human voice from the user or user's partner.

B. *Method and device for interactive virtual control of sexual aids using digital computer networks* (US patent 6368268 B1). An interactive virtual sexual stimulation system has one or more user interfaces. Each user interface generally comprises a computer having an input device, video camera, and transmitter . . . with one or more sexual stimulation devices, which are also located at the user interface. In accordance with the preferred embodiment, a person at a first user interface controls the stimulation device(s) located at a second user interface. The first and second user interfaces may be connected, for instance, through a web site on the Internet. In another embodiment, a person at a user interface may interact with a prerecorded video feed.

C. *Garment with remote controlled vibration array* (US Patent 20150022328 A1). A communication system and method are provided for remotely reproducing a touch pattern or gesture as a vibrotactile output. At a touch screen, a first user device receives a touch pattern by a first user . . . and communicates the touch pattern data to a network. A tactile array of micro-vibratory devices is attached to a garment and worn by a second user. The touch pattern data is wirelessly received from the first user device via the network. Vibration of selected micro-vibratory devices of the tactile array is modulated in timing and intensity in response to the touch pattern data to reproduce the touch pattern.

Quoted and paraphrased from patent abstracts, accessed on Google by number.

Cyberstalking

The following is a very interesting account written from the viewpoint of a *cyberstalker*.

I could be called a "high tech" guy—I'm "into" technology, put my own computers together, and work in the computer industry. I take some pride about being informed about technology and friends often use me [as] a "tech" resource for questions. I'm not a trained private investigator, nor do I own a collection of "stalking" gadgets. Let's just assume that I am resourceful, learn fast, and know how to use most any technology just by picking it up and trying it. And one more thing: When I don't know something I'm really good at finding information on the internet.[15]

The stalker can find out where you live, names and relationships, friendships, where you went to school, your job skills, your email addresses and passwords, the kind of computer you use, your cell phone information, your preferences in restaurants, vacations, stores, clothing, music, movies, and cars. The stalker goes on to explain how he finds a trail to you. He notes that technology lets him know where you are and to "intercept information from you." He discusses stalking "to make you like me," "to hurt you," "to have a vicarious relationship with you," and "as a voyeur." Although stalking existed before the internet, new technologies increase the range of persons who have access to personal information and the depth of information they can obtain without tipping off the target.

Cyberbullying

Cyberbullying has received a lot of media attention and is often treated as a new form of delinquency. However, researchers find that cyberbullying and traditional bullying have almost identical age–crime curves—peaking around age 14 and declining quickly. Youths who commit cyberbullying also tend to bully other youths in person and vice versa. The two forms of bullying overlap substantially and are often predicted by the same factors,[16] including low self-control and lack of parental supervision.[17]

Although cyberbullying appears to be generated by similar motives and to have similar patterns to traditional bullying, the problem with the former is the sheer *quantity* of misbehavior. A Canadian study found that about half of middle school and high school students have been bullied online, and a third admitted to having bullied others online.[18] A study in the United States found that 54 percent of bullying incidents involved no electronics, while 31 percent combined bullying in person with bullying online. The remaining 15 percent were exclusively electronic. The combined personal and electronic bullying incidents were especially harmful to youths.[19] We suggest that electronic bullying is a new version of mistreating others, serving to widen and enhance the harm process. Researchers have found that the worst harm comes when there are multiple perpetrators and offline contact combines with cyberbullying.[20] Researchers have also learned that cyberbullying often comes after an earlier offline conflict.[21] Again we see that modern technology has widened the capacity for one person to harm another.

Cyberattacks on Business

It is very difficult to measure and verify how much cybercrime occurs. Figure 7h illustrates the problems encountered by RAND Corporation researchers when they tried to measure **cyberattacks** on U.S. firms. Many cyber events are never detected. Many of those detected are never disclosed to the public. Many of those are never recorded and the remainder, never prosecuted. However, these researchers offered their best estimates of the amount of cybercrime damage to business and industry over a decade (Figure 7i). The comparison shows us that while society faces many hazards, including natural disaster (Hurricane Katrina) and widespread insurance fraud, cybercrime is an important component of business losses, impacting in turn on society more generally.

We have shown that expanding information technologies enhance the human potential for rule-breaking.

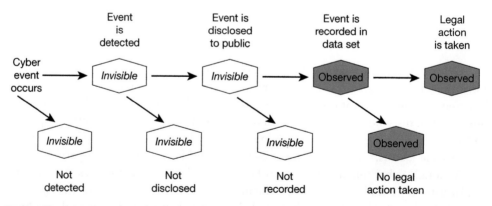

FIGURE 7H

Difficulties in Measuring Cybercrime Events

Source: Adapted from S. Romanosky (2016). Examining the costs and causes of cyber incidents. *Journal of Cybersecurity, 2*(2), 121–135.

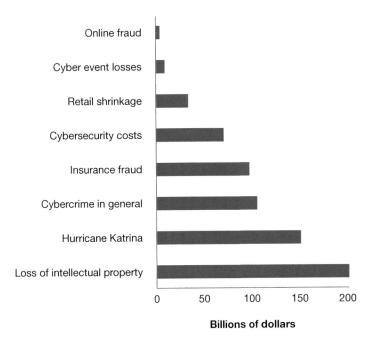

Billions of dollars

FIGURE 71
Cybercrime Losses in Perspective
Source: Adapted from S. Romanosky (2016). Examining the costs and causes of cyber incidents. *Journal of Cybersecurity, 2*(2), 121–135.

The Reach of Cybercrime

A recurrent theme in the study of cybercrime is its **reach**. It represents an extension of crime that has long taken place without the new technologies. There is also a growing understanding of ways that cybercrime is adding new dimensions to criminal behavior, including the **dark net**. The profiles of cyber offenders and victims have changed.[22] A leading scholar of cybercrime, **Peter Grabosky**, explained its role in the history and future of crime as follows:

Perhaps the most remarkable developments relating to crime in the digital age are its transnational implications, and the threats to personal privacy posed by new technologies. The speed of electronic transactions allows an offender to inflict loss or damage on the other side of the world, bringing new meaning to the term "remote control". In addition, digital technology facilitates surveillance, by public agencies and the private sector, to a degree that is quite revolutionary.

[. . .] By contrast, the variety and number of opportunities for cybercrime are proliferating. The exponential growth in connectivity of computing and communications creates parallel opportunities for prospective offenders, and parallel risks for prospective victims. As the internet becomes increasingly a medium of commerce, it will become increasingly a medium of fraud.[23]

Grabosky concluded that public officials will have no way to protect against cybercrime without substantial involvement of private information security specialists and individual users fending for themselves. We already see individuals and organizations developing and using cyber defenses and companies paying for full-time cybersecurity.

Box 7b categorizes several different reasons for the growth of cybercrime. First, cybercrime has wide reach and penetration. It reaches widely, across the globe, and deeply, into homes, businesses, and government agencies.[24] Second, cybercrime is convenient and easy to use, speedily and inexpensively allowing intrusions from almost anywhere to almost anywhere else.[25] The digital form of information makes it easier

---

Box 7B The Reasons Cybercrime Grows

1. Reach and penetration
   a. Global reach
   b. Into homes
   c. Into businesses
   d. Into government agencies

2. Convenience
   a. Easy to use
   b. Speedy
   c. Inexpensive
   d. Global availability
   e. Digital form of information

3. Security for offender
   a. Guaranteed anonymity
   b. Distance from the victim
   c. Opportunities for encrypting
   d. Difficult to investigate
   e. Underregulated by government
   f. Confused jurisdiction

to steal or use in some illicit fashion. Third, it provides the offender extra security, including anonymity and distance from victims to neutralize guilt about harming them.[26] Governments have trouble investigating encrypted information. Regulatory agreements and clear jurisdictions are also lacking. We should not be surprised that cybercrime and white-collar crime are increasingly intertwined.

The Transformation of White-Collar Crime

In 1939, **Edwin Sutherland** coined the term ***white-collar crime***. Sutherland was alerting criminologists to the fact that offending is not limited to lower-class people. The world has changed quite a bit since that time, as has our knowledge about crime. Most of the labor force at that time consisted of farmers and blue-collar workers— men working in factories, building buildings, and doing other manual labor at various levels of skill. Today, a majority of the labor force works in offices. That means that white-collar work is no longer for elites.

Moreover, it is not the case that white-collar crime is simply the rich and powerful stealing vast amounts of money. To be sure, high-profile cases such as the Enron scandal and the Bernie Madoff fraud case involved billions of dollars. However, in a study two decades ago of face-to-face white-collar fraud, typical cases involved a few thousand dollars.[27]

We prefer to redefine white-collar crime to reflect changes in the labor force. We also think that an auto repair shop that cheats its customers should not be excluded from the category simply because the people who cheat do not wear white shirts. That's why we call these offenses ***crimes of specialized access***. They are defined by the fact that the offender has special access to the victim. Included are crimes such as the following:

- A psychologist who talks a depressed patient into having sex with him as part of her therapy.

- An attorney who steals some of the funds held in escrow for a client.

- An auto mechanic who installs used parts but charges for new parts.

- A company that falsifies its financial statement, pretending to have a larger profit than in reality and thus pumping up its stock price.

- A drug company that falsifies research to make a medicine look effective.

- A restaurant that pretends to serve veal scaloppine but is really breading pork.

- A high school teacher who has a forbidden romance with a student.

- A boss who insists on sexual favors in return for hiring or promoting an employee.

- A store manager who sells company stock to another company.

- A warehouse employee who steals items for herself.

In all of these cases, somebody abuses their specialized position to take advantage of somebody else—a client, a customer, or an employee.

The modern information age enhances these crimes by enhancing specialized access. One employee might gain extra information about other employees, about clients, about the company, or about other organizations. A medical employee can access **_privileged files_** about a woman he knows and use it to stalk her or he can find out which patients are sexually vulnerable. A criminal justice employee can leak information about somebody she does not like. A manager can fiddle the delivery books to cover up a theft or loss. A bank employee can skim off small amounts and, under the radar screen, transfer that money to himself.

Next, consider how a world of computers sometimes makes white-collar crime worse. Information technology personnel now have access to a wide range of company activities and personal information of employees and clients. It is harder to lock information within a restricted room and to prevent an employee, former employee, or outsider from finding an illicit path to retrieve information. Moreover, the information system itself becomes an easy target for vandalism, extortion, and blackmail. Forbidden pictures can more easily be taken and dispersed. Industrial espionage is easier to carry out without having to use any paper. More skilled intruders can even hide their tracks and conceal both entry and exit.

We have shown that cybercrime helps enhance crimes that have already existed. Yet new technologies also produce crime opportunities on a scale never before imagined and harms never anticipated in the past. This makes it ever more difficult for society to meet its challenges. Disputes can be carried over into cyberbullying, and sexual activities can evade traditional controls. Property expropriation finds new avenues, and children have additional exposures to risk of being victimized or becoming offenders. New technologies can be used to deliver contraband or virtual experiences. Many of these possibilities are already taking shape, indicating that criminologists in the future will have their work cut out for them.

FLASHCARD LIST FOR UNIT 7.2

- 3D printers
- Child pornography
- Crimes of specialized access
- Crimes targeting data
- Crimes targeting people
- Crimes targeting things

- Cyberattacks
- Cyberbullying
- Cyberstalker
- Dark net
- Grabosky, Peter
- Privileged files
- Reach (of cybercrime)

- Sutherland, Edwin
- Teledildonics
- Transformation of pornography
- White-collar crime

DISCUSSION QUESTIONS

1. Think of an old crime that takes a new form on the internet. How do you think the new technology changes it?

2. Do you think law enforcement can keep up with cybercrime by developing new crime-fighting technology?

Notes

1 Poundstone, W. (1983). *Big secrets: The uncensored truth about all sorts of stuff you are never supposed to know.* New York: HarperCollins (William Morrow & Co).

2 Day, K. (2006). Accused in theft of Coke secrets. *Washington Post*, July 6.

3 O'Toole, G. J. (2014). *Honorable treachery: A history of US Intelligence, espionage, and covert action from the American revolution to the CIA.* New York: Grove-Atlantic.

4 Voss, B. L. (2008). Sexuality studies in archaeology. *Annual Review of Anthropology*, 37, 317–336.

5 Savona, E. U., & Mignone, M. (2004). The fox and the hunters: How IC technologies change the crime race. *European Journal on Criminal Policy and Research*, 10(1), 3–26.

6 Galbraith, P. W. (2011). Lolicon: The reality of "virtual child pornography" in Japan. *Image & Narrative*, 12(1), 83–119.

7 Maxim, D., Orlando, S., Skinner, K., & Broadhurst, R. (2016). *Online child exploitation material—trends and emerging issues: Research report of the Australian National University Cybercrime Observatory with the Office of the Children's eSafety Commissioner.* Canberra: Australian National University Cybercrime Observatory. https://papers.ssrn.com/sol3/papers.cfm?abstract_id=2861644 (retrieved June 3, 2017).

8 Wagner, M., & Broll, W. (2014). I wish you were here—not! The future of spatially separated sexual intercourse. *Proceedings of the 50th Anniversary Convention of the AISB.* http://doc.gold.ac.uk/aisb50/AISB50-S16/AISB50-S16-Wagner-paper (retrieved August 1, 2017). Liberati, N. (2017). Teledildonics and digital intimacy: A phenomenological analysis of sexual relations through new digital devices. *Glimpse*, 18, 103–110.

9 N. Ranasinghe, A. Cheok, R. Nakatsu, and E. Do. (2013). Stimulating the sensation of taste for immersive experiences, *Proceedings of the 2013 ACM international workshop on immersive media experiences ACM*, New York, 29–34.

10 Yukita, D., Assilmia, F., Anndhini, N., & Kaewsermwong, D. (2016). Teletongue: A lollipop device for remote oral interaction. In A. D. Cheok, K. Devlin, & D. Levy (Eds.), *Love and Sex with Robots: Second International Conference, LSR 2016*, pp. 40–49. Cham, Switzerland: Springer.

11 A. Legin, A. Rudnitskaya, Y. Vlasov, C. Natale, F. Davide and D'Amico. (1997). Tasting of beverages using an electronic tongue. *Sensors and Actuators B: Chemical, 44*(1–3), 291–296.

12 G. Ghinea, O.A. Ademoye. (2011). Olfaction-enhanced multimedia: perspectives and challenges. *Multimed Tools, 55*(3), 601–626.

13 Zhang, E. Y., Nishiguchi, S., Cheok, A. D., & Morisawa, Y. (2016). Kissenger: Development of a real-time internet kiss communication interface for mobile phones. In A. D. Cheok, K. Devlin, & D. Levy (Eds.), *Love and Sex with Robots: Second International Conference, LSR 2016*, pp. 115–127. Cham, Switzerland: Springer.

14 Casas, S., Portalés, C., Vidal-González, M., García-Pereira, I., & Fernández, M. (2016). Romot: A robotic 3D-movie theater allowing interaction and multimodal experiences. In A. D. Cheok, K. Devlin, & D. Levy (Eds.), *Love and Sex with Robots: Second International Conference, LSR 2016*, pp. 50–63. Cham, Switzerland: Springer.

15 Loveall, J. [Pseudonym]. (2005). Stalking by a "high tech" guy: A view from the other side [online]. Stalking Resource Center; p. 1. https://victimsofcrime.org/docs/src/stalked-by-a-high-tech-guy.pdf?sfvrsn=2 (retrieved June 5, 2017).

16 Kim, J., Song, H., & Jennings, W. G. (2016). A distinct form of deviance or a variation of bullying? Examining the developmental pathways and motives of cyberbullying compared with traditional bullying in South Korea. *Crime & Delinquency*, Published online October 25. https://doi.org/10.1177/0011128716675358.

17 Ybarra, M. L., & Mitchell, K. J. (2004a). Online aggressor/targets, aggressors, and targets: A comparison of associated youth characteristics. *Journal of Child Psychology and Psychiatry, 45*(7), 1308–1316. Ybarra, M. L., & Mitchell, K. J. (2004b). Youth engaging in online harassment: Associations with caregiver-child relationships, internet use, and personal characteristics. *Journal of Adolescence, 27*(3), 319–336.

18 Mishna, F., Saini, M., & Solomon, S. (2009). Ongoing and online: Children and youth's perceptions of cyberbullying. *Children and Youth Services Review, 31*(12), 1222–1228.

19 Mitchell, K. J., Jones, L. M., Turner, H. A., Shattuck, A., & Wolak, J. (2016). The role of technology in peer harassment: Does it amplify harm for youth? *Psychology of Violence, 6*(2), 193–204.

20 Mitchell, K. J., Ybarra, M. L., Jones, L. M., & Espelage, D. (2016). What features make online harassment incidents upsetting to youth? *Journal of School Violence, 15*(3), 279–301.

21 Jones, L. M., Mitchell, K. J., & Finkelhor, D. (2013). Online harassment in context: Trends from three youth internet safety surveys (2000, 2005, 2010). *Psychology of Violence, 3*(1), 53–69.

22 Llinares, F. M. (2015). That cyber routine, that cyber victimization: Profiling victims of cybercrime. In R. G. Smith, R. C. C. Cheung, & L. Y. C. Lau (Eds.), *Cybercrime risks and responses: Eastern and Western perspectives*, pp. 47–63. New York: Springer.

23 Grabosky, P. N. (2001). Virtual criminality: Old wine in new bottles? *Social & Legal Studies, 10*(2), 243–249; 243, 248.

24 Grabosky, P. (2004). The global dimension of cybercrime. *Global Crime, 6*(1), 146–157.

25 Savona, E. U. (Ed.). (2004). *Crime and technology: New frontiers for regulation, law enforcement and research.* New York: Springer.

26 Wall, D. S. (2007). Policing cybercrimes: Situating the public police in networks of security within cyberspace. *Police Practice and Research, 8*(2), 183–205.

27 Weisburd, D., & Waring, E. (2001). *White-collar crime and criminal careers.* Cambridge, U.K.: Cambridge University Press.

PERSPECTIVE ON PART 7

It is interesting that youths co-offend early but do so less and less as they get older. This is probably because they do not want to share the proceeds of crime with co-offenders. Nor do they want to risk the others getting them in trouble or turning them in to the police in return for easier treatment. As they age and tend to act as sole offenders, they are still willing to trade information about crime targets with other offenders, to exchange or sell contraband, or to consume drugs together. They are willing to fence stolen goods or trade illicit services. Through cooperation, offenders can enhance illegal activities and perhaps even widen their crime opportunities.

However, many offenders do not seem to get better with age. They develop addictions and bad habits. They become known as offenders and need to find a spot where nobody will recognize them. They cannot climb fences anymore, and their health goes down. Not all offenders get better with maturity. Nor can all offenders find a place in a crime network or organization providing illicit security. The tendency to age out of crime remains, just as it did in Quetelet's era.

The internet offers new opportunities and widens the span of offender participation. Offenders with programming skills can use new technologies to steal or carry out illicit trades of goods and services. Some use the dark net and learn to hide their activities from law enforcement. New crime niches allow both old and new offenders to find crime opportunities. Unskilled offenders also can benefit, purchasing from more skilled offenders some bogus credit cards or numbers. Interestingly, the dark net also provides many chances for one offender to cheat another: receiving money for illicit drugs that are never delivered or for pretending to fence stolen goods; or passing off counterfeit goods on other offenders.

Criminologists have long known that people trying to get something for nothing are the best targets for a fraudster. Those seeking to cheat are also the easiest victims for being cheated by someone else. Modern telecommunications create more and more contacts among people guided by lust, larceny, or a quest for intoxication. Although some online drug purchasers will be cheated, others will in fact receive deliveries, grow increasingly intoxicated or influenced by drugs, and experience growing health consequences.

Modern society is entering a very challenging historical period. Cyber communications push aside many of the barriers to breaking rules. In the meantime, robotics and artificial intelligence threaten to destroy many jobs at all skill levels and to leave people without employment. Even those employed might well be working part-time with nothing much to do the rest of the day or night. We are entering a period when traditional crimes are starved by the use of electronic money in place of cash, with old crimes replaced by new forms of cybercrime, new means of sexual stimulation, and new formulas for getting high.

Main Points of Part 7

- Most group crime occurs in groups of two, three, or four.

- Juvenile street gangs are highly volatile. Gangs come and go, and youths tend to leave the gang in six months or a year.

- Gangs have a few core members, but most members are peripheral.

- Adult offenders who organize in order to sell drugs or for other illegal activities often work in networks rather than gathering in a single place.

- More mature crime organizations rely on weak governments and their ability to corrupt local officials.

- Cybercrime often involves the ability to enhance traditional crimes.

- Modern technology also creates new crime opportunities.

- New inventions greatly enhance cybercrime potential, including violations of sexual rules.

- Cybercrime provides global reach, security for offenders, and easy use.

Wrapping Up

We began our textbook promising you a broad perspective on criminology. We have shown that the justice system is just one of the institutions that society employs as it seeks to contain human problems. We have also shown how crime fits within a wide range of aversive experiences, which in turn are related to ordinary behaviors. The very processes that make us human can lead both to good and bad outcomes. We cannot simply purge society of these human tendencies. Consider the following eight points:

1. We are social beings who spend time with other people.
   That same social tendency leads us into some harmful peer group activities.

2. We need to grow up, gain autonomy, and stand on our own two feet.
   That same quest for self-sufficiency feeds evasions from parental rules, some of which would keep us safe.

3. Sexual urges help propagate the species and keep partnerships together.
   Those same urges can lead to attacks on unwilling partners or to abandoning lovers and families for other sexual opportunities.

4. It is perfectly human to be cautious about strangers.
   The extreme form leads to xenophobia—hatred of strangers—including racial prejudice and discrimination against outsider groups.

5. Defending ourselves from attack is a natural tendency, without which we could not survive.
   The defensive instinct can get out of hand, leading to counterattacks, escalations, and gang formation.

6. Courage is a useful human trait, valuable in war and self-defense.
   Proving your courage can easily lead to risky behaviors, accidents, and even death.

7. Acquiring property is a natural process that helps people provide their material needs and prepare for a rainy day.
   This same tendency leads to thefts and trickery.

8. Parties release tension, and special occasions are a part of a normal society.
   Partying every day interrupts the normal workflow.

Society cannot and should not try to eradicate personal ties, autonomy from parents, sexual urges, caution about strangers, the defensive instinct, courage, acquisitiveness, or the need to release tension on special occasions. Rather, the challenge to society is to allow these human tendencies *in moderation*. That requires some subtlety among individuals and in social institutions so that these eight features of human life occur in reasonable forms.

It is not easy for society's institutions to teach exactly how to accomplish moderation. Parents are reluctant to tell their children to explore sex until they figure out just how much, when, and where, it will work. Communities are reluctant to permit loud parties. We do not have a simple guideline explaining for teenagers about when to be peaceful and when to fight back. You can understand why individuals and institutions go through a continuous trial-and-error process in seeking to draw lines. By a prolonged and complicated set of efforts, society seeks to contain human temptations and flaws, to prevent conflicts from escalating, and to avoid extreme violations of sexual rules. It safeguards property and helps youths grow up as best it can. These efforts involve individuals, households, neighbors, schools, private associations, civil justice, criminal justice, health organizations—all trying in their own ways to make society safe for those living within it, yet also allowing the young to spread their wings.

All these institutions fail to some extent. Yet all keep trying. They try to discourage maternal alcohol consumption, in hope of limiting prenatal damage to fetuses. They try to teach rules early in hope their children will be well-bred and well-behaved later. They instill social bonds in hope that misbehaviors will be contained. Society devises social checks and balances, hoping that individuals will influence one another to behave better together than they might do separately. Yet some forms of group life undermine these very controls, especially when youths assemble informally away from parents.

New temptations emerge at many stages of life, but are especially noted as adolescence progresses. These changes can draw individuals and small groups towards crime and provide insulation from control and supervision. Situational inducements are powerful, often helping youths to overcome self-controls and social bonds, and to outflank adult supervision. Neutralizations help people at various ages to suspend their own rules and deflect the intrusions of others. The same people who obey the commands of society in some circumstances evade those same commands in other settings.

Some begin with small evasions of substance-abuse rules, but end up with psychological or physical addictions with prolonged consequences.

These problems apply potentially to all people and all societies. However, some historical and geographical circumstances enhance the ongoing problems, making them worse. The grinding process of economic change leaves some local areas economically decimated and half-abandoned, making it difficult to prevent criminal takeovers, intimidation of residents, and unsafe childrearing. Creating neighborhood cohesion becomes nearly impossible in areas of concentrated disadvantage and unchecked decay. Even in safer areas, modern transportation makes it easier to evade neighbors and to shift illicit behavior outside the sphere of personal recognition or local control. That helps people with common illicit interests to find one another, trading sex or contraband. Covert crime, occurring indoors, allows middle-class people to commit crimes at home unseen by neighbors. Modern cybercrime widens covert crime options, providing new opportunities for offenders to find victims or for co-offending from afar.

Policing with traditional methods becomes increasingly difficult in the old parts of town, but that does not mean the rest of the region is secure. The dispersal of population yields far too much space for police to patrol and distances that make it nearly impossible for police to stop a crime in progress. On the positive side, crime mapping is increasingly precise, helping to focus police efforts in time and space. There is also a growing repertoire of tools for designing safer environments at the outset, or retrofitting old buildings and squares to make them safer for women—also for men.

On the other hand, danger emerges from the growth of a concentrated night economy, often in urban centers that had been abandoned or in small cities that become regional drinking centers. The dependence of many local economies on extremely active and concentrated nightlife produces benefits in jobs, profits, and tax collections. This same process invites local officials to ignore most laws about serving alcohol. The consequence is a convergence of intoxicated persons, some underage, some just over, and some older persons for whom alcohol is a central feature of life. Many are middle-class people who behave differently in the entertainment district than they would in their own residential zone.

We noted earlier that society is challenged to allow human tendencies in moderation, to prevent extreme misbehaviors. The justice system cannot be effective if it oversteps its own realistic potential. Its challenge is to *prevent extremes*. We do not view the legal system as a set of strict clear rules, all of which must be enforced as written. That view is totally impractical. The formal justice system

- can only act with full force against those crimes that are most extreme or most burdensome;

- can only exert a moderate influence to discourage behaviors falling short of these extremes;

- has no choice but to exert discretion at every level; and

- has no choice but to maintain order with minimal arrests.

And

- society must consider a wide range of options to avoid costly formal processes.

These points lead to two important consequences. First, procedural justice is essential for police and other justice officials to maintain credibility in larger society. Citizens must trust the police as they exert discretion, and police using informal methods must be able to explain their actions to citizens and gain compliance on the spot as often as possible. Moreover, alternatives to incarceration are essential options, given the costly arithmetic of the justice system. Substance abuses, drunk driving, and other issues are so voluminous and difficult to handle formally that alternative routes are needed.

The justice system burdens continue when the crime rate appears to drop. Calls for service and complaints respond to disorder, traffic issues, and ongoing problems that cannot be evaded, even in small cities, towns, or rural areas. That's why society depends so much on personal, social, and situational controls. Even for extreme offenses, criminal justice system resources must be used carefully, and require help from other control processes. The other institutions of society must play the dominant role in making society safe for its people. Among legal institutions, civil law—including the administrative rules and actions for controlling alcohol consumption—come to the fore. The criminal justice system is our backup system, the one we call upon when all else has failed. We need the criminal justice system, but we must not make it centerstage. Any society that does so misses the point. Any society depending on its criminal justice system to control crime has already lost the battle.

Our book has followed a framework. We first introduced the four recurring challenges to society, to control and contain disputes, sexual behaviors, property issues, and problems of growing up. We then explained the four key control processes: personal controls, social controls, situational controls, and formal controls. We showed how these control issues unfold from before birth to early childhood, to adolescence, to the time of the crime, to the period after a crime has taken place. We then showed how problems are exacerbated in neighborhoods, in social groups, and using modern technologies. We hope you put what you learned to work in your own lives, understanding how crime unfolds and finding chances to reduce it. We have offered you the tools you need and we hope you put them to use.

Index

Page numbers in *italics* refer to figures, tables and boxes